GEORGE JEFFREYS

PENTECOSTAL APOSTLE AND REVIVALIST

GEORGE JEFFREYS

PENTECOSTAL APOSTLE
AND REVIVALIST

WILLIAM K. KAY

CPT Press
Cleveland, Tennessee

George Jeffreys
Pentecostal Apostle and Revivalist

Published by CPT Press
900 Walker ST NE
Cleveland, TN 37311
USA
email: cptpress@pentecostaltheology.org
website: www.cptpress.com

Library of Congress Control Number: 2016956304

ISBN-10: 193593161X
ISBN-13: 9781935931614

Cover Photo: George Jeffreys at Royal Albert Hall, Courtesy Elim Pentecostal Church

To the memory of my friend Des Cartwright and the future of my grandchildren George, Olivia, Joel, and Ethan

CONTENTS

ACKNOWLEDGEMENTS

This book could not have been written without the help and support of many people. I received courteous and ready assistance from all those associated with the Elim Pentecostal Church including Maldwyn Jones and Phil Tompsett in the Desmond Cartwright Centre, John Glass the previous General Superintendent, Chris Cartwright the current General Superintendent, and Sally Gibbs the librarian. All gave unstintingly of their time and expertise and shared their recollections or made available documentation they held. On two occasions I stayed over at Regent's College and was given access to the archives and the bulging files of correspondence between Jeffreys and E.J. Phillips as well as the minutes of conferences and meetings, magazines, specialist books, and rarities like the unpublished history of Elim written by George Canty. Many of the photographs in this book are used by kind permission of the Elim Pentecostal Church.

My thanks also are due to Neil Hudson who thoughtfully read the text, John Boneham of the British Library who helped track down obscure documents, John Tonge, my brother Peter, and John Leese who read parts of the text and made valuable comments, Andrew Parfitt who proofread every chapter and provided reflective feedback as well, and my wife Anthea who not only read the entire text but who, over many hours, put up with my enthusiasms for the story of George Jeffreys and shared my astonishments as dusty documents revealed their secrets and as her own family memories of Elim were rekindled.

I'm grateful to Anne Dyer and Peter Cavanna of the Donald Gee Centre, Mattersey, for unearthing materials that were unobtainable anywhere else and to Colonel Don Underwood for providing insights drawn from his long memory. Nevertheless, whatever mistakes remain are mine alone.

INTRODUCTION

There is an apparent contradiction: on one side, Pentecostals estimate their numbers to be five hundred million adherents across the world; and, on the other side, there is little if any reference to Pentecostal activity in secular histories. One may read accounts of Britain in the 20th century written by eminent scholars and find occasional reference to churchgoing statistics or the role of the churches in supporting World War I or pacifism or the Archbishop of Canterbury's handling of the Abdication Crisis of 1936, but no one appears to have realised the extent of revivalism during the inter-war years even though it was reported in the national press. George Jeffreys hired the Royal Albert Hall annually from 1926 until 1939 to hold huge meetings where the sick were healed and hundreds were baptised in water. Oddly, secular historians – and surprisingly religious historians also – almost entirely overlook such events. Yet, revivalism gave a shot in the arm to ordinary Christianity which formed and sustained the daily attitudes of millions of British people. Revivalism took faith out of ancient church buildings and onto the streets and into hired halls and, for a while, challenged the lure of the entertainment industry and the slogans of political discourse.

Equally, there is a disjunction in Pentecostal studies between theology and history. While grand accounts have been written of Pentecostalism all over the world and while much work has been done on Pentecostalism in particular countries or settings, Pentecostal theology has danced to a different tune and sometimes been connected to history and sometimes quite disconnected. Pentecostal biography is a species of Pentecostal history and can illuminate understandings of the general course of events and the theology that interprets them. This book, then, attempts to fill a gap and innovate. It recounts Pentecostal history through the life of a single prominent British preacher, George Jeffreys, from his childhood until his death in 1962. It outlines Jeffreys' theology and shows how it spurred him into evangelistic campaigning, but it also shows how the political events of his day helped determine his end-time beliefs.

This book is offered as a full-scale Pentecostal biography that places its protagonist in the forefront of the narrative. It is intended to be comprehensive and to cover nearly everything he did. There is a case for abbreviating the story; but, in the interests of completeness, as much as possible has been chronicled. Several chapters are given the same structure: a short synopsis of political and economic circumstances, an account of Jeffreys' activities, and a concluding reflection. It should be possible for the reader to look at particular years in his life or places that he visited using the index or to enjoy the narrative as flows along. At the same time, it ought to be possible for secular historians to gain an idea of the extent and influence of Pentecostal revivalism, especially in the years between the end of World War I and the start of World War II.

Jeffreys was beloved by numerous people but also came to be treated with suspicion by others. Even long after his death there were those who defended his reputation with passion. The account that follows offers a rounded portrait of a man whose legacy remains alive within the many congregations he founded. More than 60 years have passed since his death and so the time has come for a dispassionate, and perhaps complex, assessment of his life and ministry. Comparisons with John Wesley are not out of place.

1

A WELSH VICTORIAN CHILDHOOD

George Jeffreys was born to a coalmining family in Maesteg, South Wales, after the Education Act of 1870 and before the Welsh revival of 1904–1905. His birth occurred 26 years after that of David Lloyd George, who was to become Britain's first Welsh Prime Minister, 30 years after the publication of Darwin's *Origin of Species* and a quarter of a century before the bloodshed of World War I. Like Lloyd George, Jeffreys was to become a national figure; and, arguably, the legacy of Jeffreys is greater than that of the libidinous Liberal leader. If an appropriate comparison with Jeffreys is to be drawn, it should be with John Wesley since both came from large families, strong Christian homes, and eventually demonstrated a mesmerising ability to preach to huge crowds all over the United Kingdom. Whereas Wesley lived before the British Empire had reached its full extent, Jeffreys grew up when the Empire seemed immoveable and capable of throwing its protective Protestant arms across still-unreached parts of the world.

According to his birth certificate George Jeffreys was born at home in 24 Metcalfe Street, Maesteg, on 28th February 1889. His father, Thomas, is recorded as being a collier and his mother was Keziah. By 1891, the family had moved to the slightly larger property of 8 Bangor Terrace and census returns for the year show George to be the youngest of seven children starting with Edward aged 18, then Stephen aged 14, and two other brothers and two sisters.

Little is known about Jeffreys' father although he must have been a believer and a chapel-goer and a hard-working man to support his growing family. He was five years older than his wife and had laboured in the mines for most of his life. The pay was not generous but sufficient and Desmond Cartwright, whose book *The Great Evangelists* (Marshall Pickering, 1986) is of enduring value, says the Jeffreys family 'were one of the many large, respectable but poor families living in the upper part of the Llynffi Valley'.[1] He also tells us that his father took the young George to see a 'well-known Swansea phrenologist' who produced an 'unusually favourable' prognosis.[2] Phrenology was within the range of Victorian sciences even if it was subsequently heavily discredited. Phrenology was concerned with the reading of the bumps and shape of the skull as a way of attempting to discern intellectual aptitudes and gifts. Presumably Thomas Jeffreys wanted to discover whether the young George was destined for a life beyond the coal mines and was prepared to make the journey to Swansea and then pay the consultation fee to satisfy his curiosity. What is interesting about this incident is that even at an early age George's character and gifts raised questions about the possibility of his having a distinguished career. Thomas showed his paternal concern for the boy by attempting to verify the impressions George was creating in the rest of the family.

A first-hand description of work in the mine details what the men endured daily:

> The machines are roaring and the air is black with coal dust ... At those times the place is like hell, or at any rate like my own mental picture of hell. Most of the things one imagines in hell are there – heat, noise, confusion, darkness, foul air, and, above all, unbearably cramped space. Everything except the fire, but there is no fire down there except the feeble beams of Davy lamps and electric torches which scarcely penetrate the clouds of coal dust ... You cannot see very far because the fog of coal dust throws back the beam of your lamp, but you can see on either side of you the line of half-naked kneeling men, one to every four or five yards, driving their shovels under the fallen coal and flinging it swiftly over their left shoulders ...

[1] Desmond Cartwright, *The Great Evangelists* (Basingstoke: Marshall Pickering, 1986), p. 14.
[2] Cartwright, *The Great Evangelists*, p. 24.

There is the heat – it varies, but in some mines it is suffocating – the coal dust that stuffs up your throat and nostrils and collects along your eyelids, and the unending rattle of the conveyor belt, which in that confined space is rather like the rattling of a machine gun. But the fillers look and work as though they were made of iron. They really do look like iron – hammered iron statues – under the smooth coat of coal dust which clings to them from head to foot. It's only when you see the miners down the mine and naked that you realise what splendid men they are … They are on the job for seven and a half hours, theoretically without a break, for there is no time 'off'.[3]

George Orwell's 1936 description in *The Road to Wigan Pier* was written when conditions down at the coalface were, if anything, marginally better than those experienced by the Jeffreys family because mechanisation removed some of the drudgery of the task. Yet coal dust, with or without machinery, led inevitably to lung diseases and the darkness to accidents with shovels or rock falls.[4] Under the ground the men bonded together because their lives depended upon each other's help in the event of disaster. They knew they were putting their lives in danger for the sake of the pay they received and they, unlike farmers, also sacrificed the pleasure of observing the changing seasons of the year. They descended to the pits before dawn, they worked in conditions without natural light, and they came up again to the surface after dark. The men only saw the sun on Saturday and Sunday afternoons. Working down there was, as Orwell says, like hell but it was the only work that most of them could take since, as we shall see, they left school at the ages of 11 and 12 and had no training for any other employment.

The bonding of men in the coal mines led to the powerful community relationships which were reflected in the most successful chapels and male voice choirs. It also led to the rituals of cleaning and bathing in the home. Without pithead baths, men needed to wash daily after their immersion in black coal dust and women were

[3] George Orwell, *The Road to Wigan Pier* (London: Victor Gollancz, 1936), Google Scholar edn, no page numbers.
[4] According to John Davies, *A History of Wales* (Harmondsworth: Penguin, 1990), p. 472, there were 1,117 deaths between 1880 and 1900 through mining accidents in Wales.

the providers of hot water in the small two-up-two-down terraced houses where families were crammed together. There is a description of the miner coming home and taking a bath in one of DH Lawrence's short stories.[5] Most of the cottages had large fire grates because one of the few perks of mining was in the provision of free coal; the heavy work of fetching water and washing the filthy clothes fell firmly on the women, as social historians have pointed out:

> Numerous social history museums in Wales boast a traditional Welsh kitchen complete with dressers, fireplaces, ovens, tin baths and lines groaning with washing ... The kitchen would draw attention to the fact that the women, particularly the miners' wives, often worked longer hours than male labourers and were also subject to dangerous working conditions ... Many social history museums have a tin bath on display as a central part of the kitchen scene ... It could be pointed out that in a household of three or four miners the women of the house would be constantly fetching, boiling and carrying water ... a midwife working in the Rhondda Valley in the 1920s estimated that most miscarriages and premature births were caused by carrying tubs of water to and from the bath.[6]

The life of the women was hard in other ways as well. Kezia ended up having 12 children of whom six predeceased her. George was three years younger than his sister Emily and was named after a brother who had died before him. The lists of names in the family home given by the 1891 and 1901 census returns suggest that two of George's siblings died while a further two were added, moving him from the youngest child to one in the middle of the family. More cataclysmic than the death of children was the death of his father, Thomas. He died at home in Picton Street on Tuesday, September 3rd, 1895 at the age of 47 'of chronic bronchitis and cardiac failure' almost certainly brought on by conditions in the pit.[7]

---

[5] 'The Miner at Home', in *Selected Stories* (Harmondsworth: Penguin Classics, repr., 2007), pp. 43-48.

[6] Kath Davies, 'Cleaning Up the Coal-face and Doing out the Kitchen: The Interpretation of Work and Workers in Wales', in Gaynor Kavanagh (ed.), *Making Histories in Museums* (London: Leicester University Press, 1996), pp. 105-15.

[7] Cartwright, *The Great Evangelists*, p. 14.

There was little or no financial assistance to the families when miners died; the owners of the mines washed their hands of responsibility. Industrial relations between workers and managers or workers and mine owners were fractious and precarious and always worsened after accidents or a spate of deaths.

George was bereaved of a father at the age of seven, old enough to feel the loss but too young to appreciate the full consequences of the tragedy. The only incident we have connecting the boy and his father concerns the visit to the phrenologist that must have occurred not long before Thomas died. We can speculate on the impact of the deaths of brothers and sisters on George and barely imagine what he felt when his father's life came to an end. Because the death certificate records 'chronic bronchitis', we must assume Thomas had been ill on and off for some time during the early 1890s and possibly absent from work. If the widow struggled for money, the family would also surely have been awakened to spiritual realities. We do not know if Thomas' body was laid out in the home; but, if he died there, we can assume the coffin was carried from the house to the cemetery. We can imagine George seeing the bitter tears of his mother, aware of the solemn chapel choir, the burial service intoned in Welsh and the empty place round the hearth.

The family was not left destitute because the older brothers started work in the pit at the age of 12. By the time Thomas died, the brothers Edward, Stephen, and James would have been old enough to draw wages.[8] George was particularly close to Stephen; but, in any case, all the older brothers would have been father figures to him and brought enough finance into the home to put food on the table.

Of George's mother we know a little more. She was the daughter of a Baptist minister and her brother was the director of Llynffi Ironworks.[9] This tells us two things: firstly, she was brought up as a Baptist and, second, that her father must have been a man of some

---

[8] According to http://www.wrexham.com/news/the-1904-1905-welsh-revival-43508.html, miners might expect to be paid three shillings per day though, because of private ownership of pits, pay was not uniform across the country. By some calculations three shillings equates to an average wage.

[9] Cartwright, *Evangelists*, p. 9.

education and substance. Baptist ministers were selected by their congregations and held office through the consent of their church members. A long-standing Baptist minister would have been a community figure as well as an effective public speaker. He may well have received education over and above that of the ordinary working man; and, indeed, because Kezia's brother became director of an iron works he also must have had a quick mind and probably extended education. If we are to look for natural explanations of the ministerial call of George and, indeed, of two of his other brothers who also became ministers, we might find them in the family history on their mother's side. There is evidence, too, that the death of a parent in childhood may deepen the child's sense of God's fatherly presence.[10]

Chapel Life and Beliefs

Anglicans in Wales, with their bishops and landed gentry, were historically seen to represent the establishment, the monarchy, the English, or the upper classes. On the other side of the equation a variety of Protestant preachers were active promoting popular Dissent (especially the kind of dissent that was found among the Puritans). The 'old Dissent' included Congregationalists and Baptists and later, in the Victorian era, Methodists by which time the whole expanded grouping came under the preferred title of 'Nonconformity'. The power of Welsh Nonconformity grew to the extent that even in the 1890s there was discussion about disestablishing Anglicanism in Wales. After many verbal battles and political manoeuvres, the Westminster government agreed that Anglicanism should be disestablished in 1912, and amid great rejoicing and in the year that was the 250th anniversary of the 'Great Ejection' (when 2,000 Puritan ministers unwillingly resigned their positions as Anglican clergy after the restoration of Charles II), the Bill received its third reading.[11] Properties and lands given to the church before 1662 were redistributed to Nonconformists and local authorities,

---

[10] W.K. Kay, 'Marital Happiness and Children's Attitude to Religion', *British Journal of Religious Education* 3 (1981), pp. 102-105.

[11] R. Tudor Jones, *Faith and the Crisis of a Nation: Wales 1890–1914* (Cardiff: University of Wales Press, 2004), p. 383.

and thereby provided them with significant income. Anglicans retained property and land given or bequeathed after 1662.

The Jeffreys family, while Thomas Jeffreys was alive, attended the old Dyffryn Chapel in Maesteg. It was one of a host of independent Welsh-speaking Congregational Chapels. In this case, it was formed in 1868 by William Watkins, an ex-coalminer, and would have been a strong and vibrant (if occasionally argumentative) community.[12] The Royal Commission of 1910 had investigated the churches and reported that the Independents 'are ... thoroughly evangelical and Protestant in doctrine and character'.[13]

The Welsh Independents belonged to the tradition of radical 17th century Christian separatism. By the end of the Victorian era, they comprised 1,124 congregations, 160,000 members, 145,000 Sunday school adherents, and 655 full-time pastors. As Densil Morgan has reported, their self-governing congregations retained the ideal that 'the kingdom of God was not begun by whole parishes but rather by the worthiest, were they never so few'[14] with the result that their members stood as a countercultural example of godly living against prevailing and fluctuating social trends. They were known for 'sometimes abrasive assertiveness' though as time went on, despite holding tenaciously to the principle of local church autonomy, they mellowed into a growing willingness to collaborate.[15] In 1872 the Union of Welsh Independents was formed and this gave rise to cooperative offshoots in the Union's Weaker Churches Fund in 1895, the Central Bookroom in 1907 and the Ministerial Assistance Fund in 1911.[16]

Although we do not know what these organisational changes looked like to the eyes of the young George Jeffreys, his quick brain must have seen the advantages of building supportive and collabo-

---

[12] http://www.genuki.org.uk/big/wal/GLA/Hanes16.html#Siloh (accessed 2 May 2014).

[13] Densil Morgan, *The Span of the Cross* (Cardiff, University of Wales Press, 1999), p. 19.

The commission began work in 1906 and was in session for nearly three years. The report – which is huge – was published in five foolscap volumes in 1910 by which time everyone was thoroughly exhausted.

[14] Morgan, *Cross*, p. 19.

[15] Morgan, *Cross*, p. 19.

[16] Morgan, *Cross*, p. 19.

rative structures for independent congregations. The congregation at Dyffryn was relatively new; and, again, Jeffreys would have been aware of the concept of church-planting as he reflected on all the efforts and activities that eventually led to the building of the chapel where his family worshipped.

Central to the activities of the chapel would have been preaching. The pulpit is prominent in the architecture of Welsh independent chapels and thriving congregations always had capable preachers. Welsh preaching among Nonconformists was known for its oratory; and, although the tradition began to wane at the end of the 19th century, it would still have been strong when Jeffreys was young.[17] Most of the preaching was expository in the sense that a text of Scripture was taken and explained in a detailed and logical way with contemporary or biblical illustrations to bring it alive before it was pressed home by a practical application to the lives of hearers.

Scholarly investigation of Welsh preaching and the whole culture of Welsh Nonconformity has concluded that in the 1890s 'public speaking in the Welsh language attained a polish and fluency that was quite exceptional' and that the congregations, like lively congregations today, would encourage the preacher by calling out during the sermon. What they wanted was the preacher to go into what in Welsh is known as *hwyl* or 'to speak in an inspired and influential manner' with the result that in responding to sermons 'weeping was quite a common reaction'. At other times, as when a sermon was preached to the Union of Welsh Independents in 1878, the entire congregation reacted by bursting into hymns of praise. As the century came to an end a new age of preaching was beginning to dawn, one that was more self-consciously 'clever' and less spiritually direct.[18]

The Dyffryn Chapel shared a minister with the Siloh chapel a couple of miles away and at some point, probably not long after Thomas' death, the family moved again and started to attend Siloh where the minister from 1901 to 1907 was Glasnant Jones, whose

---

[17] Tudur Jones, *Faith*, 'the death of a number of eminent preachers in the years between 1890 and 1900 indicated that an era was drawing to a close', p. 188.

[18] Tudur Jones, *Faith*, p. 117.

influence will be discussed later.[19] What we know of his preaching shows him to have been thoroughly evangelical in the sense that he wanted the gospel to be known and accepted by everyone – which is why he engaged in open-air preaching. Most Nonconformist chapels of the period would have had trust deeds that specified the precise beliefs that ought to be held by members, and becoming a member at a formal church meeting would have been in an important step for any individual. The chapels were not Calvinistic and so there would have been an acceptance of individual commitment to Christ – indeed, Christ and his cross would have been central to much of the preaching and worship. Conversely, because of the influence of Calvinism, there appears to have been a general sense among Independent chapels that salvation was initiated by God rather than being a human response to a divine offer of grace.

For the most part late 19th century Nonconformity in its preaching was willing to ignore Christ's Second Coming and God's final consummation of creation. These doctrines appear to have slipped below the horizon. It was important 'particularly during times of crisis when communities were rocked by disastrous accidents in the local works or collieries, or when terrible illness or disease ravaged communities, that preachers reminded their congregations of the need for the living to be prepared for death and the judgment that would follow, because this could come at any time'.[20]

One aspect of the chapels that is hardly found in British churches today is the Sunday school. The Sunday school movement in 19th century Britain was large and active though occasionally disorganised and amateurish. The Welsh Independents reported 162,621 Sunday school pupils in attendance with 15,818 teachers, and their numbers were by no means the highest in Wales. The Calvinistic Methodists could gather 193,699 pupils and 21,702 teachers.[21] Sunday school was a lively part of Welsh religious culture because it carried a residue of the esteem given to it when it was almost the only form of education available to large parts of the population.

---

[19] Cartwright, *Evangelists*, p. 15. See chapter 3.

[20] Email from Robert Pope, 3 May, 2014.

[21] Tudur Jones, *Faith*, p. 255. The figures are given to the Royal Commission on Disestablishment in 1906 and must have referred to pupils and teachers in 1905 or earlier. The figures in the 1890s would have been similar or higher.

In an attempt to upgrade and compete with the new day schools, Sunday schools were reorganised with syllabuses, competitive examinations, and prizes.

What happened next was completely the opposite of what was expected by the enthusiasts of Sunday school education. In their efforts to professionalise teaching, commentaries were provided on passages of Scripture or books of the Bible and these commentaries sold in great numbers. The Calvinistic Methodists sold 30,000 copies of a commentary on Hebrews in a few days; the Independents lagged behind with a commentary on Galatians that only managed to sell just over 7,000 copies. 'Taken as a whole, these commentaries reached a huge public and their influence was vast';[22] but, by 1902, the peak had been passed and the Sunday school was in serious decline. It appears that the syllabus' repetition of the least interesting or theologically valuable parts of the Old Testament turned young people away from their Bibles.

These commentaries, for all their erudition, essentially regurgitated German critical scholarship. In many instances they were so focused on the dating or provenance of biblical texts that the story of salvation was buried under a mound of scholarly detail. Although the introduction of critical methods was intended to implant a mature modern faith capable of withstanding scrutiny, the outcome was to lead teachers, young people, and the writers of commentaries into arcane debates about critical methods, the presumptions underlying these methods, evolutionary influences on the composition of the Pentateuch, and a host of other peripheral topics that were indigestible to the Sunday school scholars and ultimately damaging to their budding faith.[23]

Schooling

The Census forms completed by the Jeffreys family in 1891, 1901, and 1911 contain the information that they were bilingual in English and Welsh. This was an important capacity since monoglot Welsh were confined to unskilled work and the lower reaches of

---

[22] Tudur Jones, *Faith*, p. 257.
[23] Tudur Jones, *Faith*, p. 261.

society. There had been angry reactions to the provision of schools in the early part of the 19th century in Wales which forbade the use of Welsh, indeed tried to stamp it out, so as to make English the standard language. Many years later this policy was still remembered by Welsh nationalists; but, in the mid-19th century, multiculturalism was an unknown concept and a mastery of English was deemed to be the best way to improve the life chances of young people. So Welsh might have been spoken at home and in Chapel but education curricula were delivered in English, and English was the language of official communications. It was said that you would write a letter to your bank manager in English while you would speak to your grandmother in Welsh; and, indeed, when you prayed you were most likely to slip into your mother tongue.

The earliest sustained attempt to provide primary education in England and Wales stemmed from Napoleonic times. The National Society, which was funded by Anglicans, built a large number of primary schools all over England and Wales, many of which were attached to their local parish churches and supported by teachers trained in Anglican training colleges. There was a Nonconformist equivalent – the British Society – which had equally early origins. The Anglicans tended to be wealthier but both sets of schools provided a basic education that was also religious in the sense that school prayers were said, the Bible was taught, and clergy were welcomed on site. As the 19th century progressed and the numbers of children of school age increased, it became impossible to cater for them all through purely voluntary effort. The government, which had until then pursued a laissez-faire policy, began to make educational grants, particularly as it understood that the industrial revolution needed a skilled workforce.

The situation in Wales, which was more rural than much of England, required many small village schools. There was always a pull from the countryside because young children were expected to help in the fields at harvest time. Farm labourers thought their children could learn what was needed about farming from their fathers or mothers and 'book learning' seemed fancy and superfluous to many of them. There were heroic efforts made by philanthropic clergy to provide basic education as, for example, by Griffith Jones of Penboyr in Dyfed whose 'circulating schools' provided temporary education in barns or halls in an attempt to teach reading (in Welsh) and basic arithmetic. By 1847 11% of those under five attended school in Glamorganshire and 43% of those aged between five and ten.[24]

By 1870, when voluntary efforts to provide primary education for all children had obviously fallen short, the Liberal government of William Gladstone stepped in and agreed to 'fill in the gaps' with schools where voluntary provision was lacking. This resulted in the creation or strengthening of School Boards tasked with deciding where new schools should be built and how they should be maintained using a mixture of money from central government and local rates. The result of this parliamentary enactment was to create three basic categories of primary schools: Anglican, Nonconformist, and secular. The point of the legislation was to avoid duplicating provision with the consequence that, if there were sufficient National Schools in an area, the Board Schools did not compete with them. This was a worry to Nonconformists. They resented having to send their children to schools whose religious teaching was in the hands of Anglicans, and so the law went some way to allaying these objections by stipulating that religious instruction in all kinds of schools in receipt of public money should be non-denominational.

So, while every child from 1870 onwards received primary education, the education was given by unimaginatively trained teachers to large classes of children.[25] Sometimes the teaching followed a monitorial system whereby the teacher taught the monitors and the monitors taught the younger children and everybody was together in a single large hall. In other places the teachers took the children, usually in simple uniform and with boys and girls separated, in groups of 40 or more and routinely made them recite their multiplication tables, the kings and queens of England, the capes and bays around the British coastline, or, indeed, the Lord's Prayer. Education was conducted either in unison or to the sound of scratchy chalk on slates or quill pens on paper. Greater store was set on beautiful copperplate handwriting than on imaginative composition

---

[24] Gareth Elwyn Jones, *The Education of a Nation* (Cardiff: University of Wales Press, 1997), p. 37.

[25] One consequence of this was to reinforce the legislation forbidding child labour. If children were legally obliged to be in school, they were unavailable for work in factories and mines.

and there was no science of any kind. Disobedience was not tolerated and usually punished by a sharp stroke of a cane or strap
across the hand. Dickens in *Hard Times* gives us a grimly humorous
portrait of Mr Gradgrind, the headmaster of a mid-Victorian
school:

> Now, what I want is, facts. Teach these boys and girls nothing
> but facts. Facts alone are wanted in life. Plant nothing else, and
> root out everything else. You can only form the minds of rea-
> soning animals upon facts: nothing else will ever be of any ser-
> vice to them. This is the principle on which I bring up my own
> children, and this is the principle on which I bring up these chil-
> dren. Stick to the facts, Sir![26]

No doubt there were mild-mannered teachers within the system
who had the best interests of the children at heart but the tenor of
primary schools was against treating children sentimentally. After
all, if you sent children down coalmines at the age of 12, you were
hardly likely to view them as delicate and developing human beings.
The inspection regime of schools only served to reinforce the drills
of arithmetic and handwriting to ensure public money was spent in
raising a generation of clerks, factory workers, and shopkeepers.
The 'revised code' ensured 'payments by results': schools received
no grants if the pupils failed to satisfy the eagle-eyed scrutiny of
sometimes pompous and officious inspectors. Flora Thompson
(born in 1876) attended a National Society school and recalled
those days in her autobiography:

> Her Majesty's Inspector of schools came once a year on the date
> of which previous notice had been given. There was no singing
> or quarrelling on the way to school that morning. The children,
> in clean pinafores and well blackened boots, walked deep in
> thought; or, with open spelling or table books in hand, tried to
> make up in an hour for all their wasted yesterdays. So, after pray-
> ers, copybooks were given out and the children settled down for
> a long wait. A few of the more stolid, leaning forward with
> tongues slightly protruding would copy laboriously, 'lightly on
> the up strokes, heavy on the down' … at last came the sound of

---

[26] Charles Dickens, *Hard Times* (London: Bradbury & Evans, 1854), p. 1.

wheels crunching on gravel and two top hats and the top of the
whip appeared outside the upper panes of the large end window.

Her Majesty's Inspector was an elderly clergyman, a little man
with an immense paunch and tiny grey eyes like gimlets. He had
the reputation of being 'strict', but that was a mild way of describing his autocratic demeanour and scathing judgement. His
voice was an exasperated roar and his criticism was a blend of
outraged learning and sarcasm … He looked at the rows of children as if he hated them and at the mistress as if he despised her
…[27]

The ordered rows, the trembling children, the bullied teacher, and
the inspector with his top hat and horse-drawn carriage evoke the
hierarchies of Victorian Britain. George Jeffreys, we must assume,
attended a school – even if it was not an Anglican school – full of
orderly rows of obedient children. Almost certainly Jeffreys' school
was either run by the British Society (because Nonconformity was
strong in Maesteg) or by one of the Boards created by the 1870
Act.

It would be wrong to assume that all education in Victorian Britain was grim and miserable, and Flora Thompson is careful to contrast the general inspector with the more human and cheerful inspector of religion who appears to act like an enthusiastic Sunday
school teacher.

Another inspector, also a clergyman, came to examine the school
in Scripture. But that was a different matter. On those days the
Rector was present, and the mistress, in her best frock, had nothing to do beyond presiding at the harmonium for hymn singing.
Examination consisted of Scripture questions, put to a class as a
whole and answered by anyone who was able to shoot up a hand
to show they had the requisite knowledge; or portions of the
church catechism, repeated from memory in order round the
class; and of a written paper on some biblical subject. There was
little nervous tension on that day for 'Scripture Inspector'

---

[27] Flora Thompson, *Lark Rise to Candleford* (Oxford: Oxford University Press,
1939), p. 183. First published in 1939 and quoted here from Google scholar.

beamed upon and encouraged the children even to the extent of prompting those who were not word perfect.[28]

Reflection

Insofar as we can reconstruct the conditions of George Jeffreys' childhood, we find a Welsh boy born in Victorian Britain into a coal mining home, living in a small, cramped property. His father, down the pits, died at home when George was seven years of age. The emotional trauma of this bereavement may have deepened George's reliance on God but the event itself robbed him of the wise advice his father might have given in the later years of rapidly growing ministry. The older brothers, particularly Stephen, partially took over the role of the father and wage earner in the house and the family appears not to have wavered in its Christian faith. George's mother, the daughter of a Baptist minister, held firm.

Central to the life of this hard-working bilingual family was the independent Welsh-speaking chapel congregation. Here they would have attended on Sundays and probably also a midweek service and listened to the expository preaching of their minister, himself a man from the Welsh valleys. As a boy, George would have attended school nearby and been subjected to the unimaginative routines and disciplines of the primary education of the day. He must have shown early promise since his father would not otherwise have taken him to visit a phrenologist. Whatever basic education he received at school was supplemented by Sunday school which, in those days, was more serious and intellectually arduous than the simple re-telling of children's Bible stories.

We assume the key events of childhood helped shape the man George Jeffreys became. We may assume that the preaching he heard as a boy influenced his later style and assured him of the importance of the preached word. We may assume that the faith of his mother and his brothers and sisters after the death of their father put iron into his soul and strengthened him for battles ahead. We note that the limitations of his education – and the possible encounter with critical theology through the Sunday School move-

---

[28] Thompson, *Lark Rise*, pp. 185-86.

ment – would have inoculated him against the temptations of pursuing any kind of theological degree. However real his childhood faith was, the next few years brought him to the brink of Christian experiences beyond anything anyone in his valley had foreseen.

2

CAUGHT UP IN THE WELSH REVIVAL

The Elementary Education (School Attendance) Act of 1893 raised the school leaving age to 11 years. Modern readers, who are accustomed to compulsory schooling which lasts at least until the age of 16, will be shocked to read that it required an Act of Parliament to prevent children being taken out of school before the age of 11. Indeed, there were attempts in Wales and elsewhere to provide 'higher elementary schools' that took school leavers to the age of 14.[1] But the 1901 census return provides us with proof that George Jeffreys must have left school no later than the age of 12, and probably at 11.

We know from the 1901 Census held on 31 March that George Jeffreys was working underground in the coal mines as a 'door boy'.[2] It is possible that he had left school immediately after his 12th birthday in February of that year, but it is equally possible that he had left the year before once it was legal for him to do so. In either event, we know that his education did not extend beyond the primary level. There was not enough money in the family to pay for his education – rather the reverse, the family was short of money and needed every penny every child could earn. This must especially have been the case for Kezia Jeffreys after Stephen had married on

---

[1] G.E. Jones, *The Education of a Nation* (Cardiff: University of Wales Press, 1997), p. 43.

[2] The job of the door boy was to sit in the darkness of the pit and to open and close the doors within the mine to assist ventilation. The doors would be opened as the miners or underground railway wagons passed.

Boxing Day 1898 and left the house to set up his own home. George's salary would have been lower than Steven's but at least when the boy went down the pit he was contributing to the total income of Kezia's household.

There is evidence that she struggled to avoid sending George down the pit.[3] She had watched her husband's health and strength fade away and she could see, by looking at George, that he was less robust – or appeared to be – than the muscular figure of Stephen and the other older boys. George also suffered from some form of 'facial paralysis'.[4] There is no medical record of exactly what this complaint consisted of or how frequently George was affected by it. We do not know whether it was a nervous complaint or arose from an underlying physical cause. George's later account reports the complaint affected his speech and made his dreams of entering the ministry recede into the distance.

> I was first convinced of the Spirit's quickening power when, as a frail youth, I received the experience in my own body. My weak state began to manifest itself in facial paralysis, and I was heavily burdened, for I felt the creepiness of paralysis down one whole side. Being somewhat reticent I suffered in silence beyond measure, for I knew that unless a miracle was wrought in me, life was to be very short. When my mouth began to be affected, the one thing that distressed me greatly was the possibility of my not realising the one call and ambition of life, the Christian ministry.[5]

We do know from George's own testimony that he took up smoking at this time. In a day when smoking was common among all kinds of men and when the health threats of tobacco products were suppressed or unknown, we should not interpret smoking as indicative of anything apart from conformity to working-class male subculture. The chapels preached against drinking, but they were less outspoken against smoking since there were fewer biblical texts that could be directly applied to the practice. Often the most that

---

[3] Cartwright, *Evangelists*, p. 25.
[4] Cartwright, *Evangelists*, p. 25.
[5] G. Jeffreys, *Healing Rays* (London: Elim Publishing Company, 1932), p. 56. Given that Jeffreys refers to himself as a 'youth' and not as a child, I take this experience to have taken place when he was a teenager.

could be said against it was that it was a waste of money and therefore 'bad stewardship'.

Contemporary records appear to show that George's mother remarried in 1905.[6] He would have been 16 and a little before or at the same time he moved out of the family home to live with Stephen. We do not know whether George objected to his stepfather or if the move was simply because there was more room under Steven's roof and he could, perhaps, pay a little rent into Steven's household. That George and Stephen were close to each other is beyond doubt, and Steven's care for George was deeply brotherly and may have had a paternal quality to it.

Revival

Wales is known to be a country of hills and valleys. Typically, villages nestle on the floor of a valley along which a river runs. Each village, disconnected by steep hillsides from its neighbours, is a self-contained community served by chapels and with surrounding farmland grazing sheep. Towards the end of the 19th century when the industrial revolution gathered momentum, coal and iron were found underground and villages, sometimes new and sometimes old, clustered round the mineshafts and provided work for men who had previously been farm labourers. By 1871, when the railways were transforming the nation, over 15,000 miles of track had been laid.[7] Mobility increased and the villages were brought closer together by rail links while, along the south coast, seaports enabled international trade or the provision of coal for the British Navy. Any new revival in Wales would be shaped by its modernised infrastructure.

The heartland of Wales was noted for its nonconformist character, and this was borne out by the statistics showing the relative strength of various denominations. The figures do not show that

[6] There is a public record of Kezia Jeffreys marrying in the first quarter of 1905 in the Bridgend area. The record does not give the surname of the man she married and so makes it difficult to track her thereafter.

[7] P.J. Cain, 'Railways 1870–1914: The Maturity of the Private System', in M.J. Freeman and D.H. Aldcroft (eds.), *Transport in Victorian Britain* (Manchester: Manchester University Press, 1988), p. 92.

Anglicans and Roman Catholics were absent but rather that Anglicans were more closely associated with English-speaking landown-
ers while the nonconformists workers were more solidly Welsh and
Welsh-speaking even if they were theologically diverse.[8] There was
certainly a tradition in Calvinistic Methodism (dating to the revival
of 1859 and earlier) that saw all revival as a matter of divine initiative more than a matter of human effort: God, for reasons that
were usually beyond human comprehension, *gave* revival through
outpourings of grace. By this theological interpretation, human efforts to work up revival were reprehensible and dangerous – they
would lead to a counterfeit that might show the emotional trappings
of divine activity while lacking the pure gold of genuine faith.

The latent tension between what human beings could do to
bring revival and the invisible force of divine action on individuals
or communities helps to explain the perspectives of assorted partic-
ipants. No one wanted to engineer a 'revival' with advertising or
grandiose claims; but, equally, no one wanted to miss revival if God
was truly sending one. This might apply to the way individuals be-
haved. No one wanted to claim that God was speaking directly into
hearts and minds when such claims might only be informed by an
over-wrought imagination. This helps to explain why individuals
welcomed powerful and apparently irresistible emotions in religious
meetings: they wanted to be able to say 'this *must* have been an act
of God' and could not have been a matter of their own volition
because they never normally behaved in this way.

There were Arminian interpretations of revival that stressed the
effectiveness of human effort and dedication. Between the Calvinistic and Arminian views was a kind of meeting place whereby the
very thirst for revival was itself given by God and a sign of divine
action while, on the Arminian side, human effort was creditable
and, if made with tenacious faith, could elicit a divine reply. So in
the ordinary business of church life or outreach, Calvinists and
Arminians might comfortably cooperate.

Holiness itself can be defined variously. It may be seen as an ab-
stention from traditional worldly pursuits like attending the theatre,

---

[8] D.D. Morgan, *The Span of the Cross* (Cardiff: University of Wales Press,
1999), pp. 9, 23.

playing cards, drinking alcohol, and joining sporting events or it may emphasise social justice or overseas mission. In essence it may have an introverted dimension resulting in a desire to escape from the world into prayerful seclusion or an extraverted dimension resulting in a desire to challenge the church and change the world. Either way, because holiness is common to Calvinistic and Arminian theology, it unifies believers. Christian life styles are reasserted and worship reinvigorated.

The Keswick Convention held annually under canvas in the beautiful surroundings of the English Lake District from 1875 onwards was largely inspired by Anglican evangelicals. Yet it was an interdenominational gathering centred around the careful expository preaching of Scripture. Its preachers were respected and gave their sermons an intellectual structure rather than an emotional tone. They developed a notion of 'holiness by faith' parallel to 'salvation by faith' and they might include among their number both those who leaned to Calvinism and those who leaned to Arminianism. Moreover, as the 19th century drew to an end, there was a widely held desire for Christians to face the new challenges of the 20th century with fresh power bestowed by the Holy Spirit. In 1903 Welsh Christians organised a 'Welsh Keswick' situated in Llandrindod Wells.[9] Although this was never as influential as the English Keswick, its impact in Wales was considerable. In short, the beginnings of the Welsh revival 1904–1905 can be traced back to a diversity of preachers, agencies, and events.

There is evidence that the phrase 'baptism in the Spirit' was used quite extensively across the theological spectrum to refer to a powerful encounter with the Holy Spirit.[10] Beyond this, preachers did not go. There was no systematic and robust doctrine of charismatic gifts or Pentecostal phenomena in any of the circles of leading preachers. The best analysis of the work of the Holy Spirit in revival had been given much earlier by Jonathan Edwards in *The Distinguishing Marks of a Work of the Spirit of God* (1741) when he had described the phenomena accompanying the extraordinary awakening on the east coast of the United States. What was distinctive about

---

[9] http://www.keswickinwales.org.uk/history.
[10] Eifion Evans, *The Welsh Revival of 1904* (Bridgend: Bryntirion Press, 1987), pp. 53, 59, 65.

Edwards' acute analysis was his acceptance of a mixture of spiritual and carnal responses to the sweep of the revival. In other words, he was not prepared to reject the whole revival because of occasional exhibitionist excesses and nor was he prepared to state that only certain responses truly indicated the presence of the Holy Spirit. So when Welsh preachers spoke about baptism in the Holy Spirit, they referred to a spiritual encounter that was real and godly and powerful even if it was ill-defined. To the most fervent of them the Holy Spirit was the answer to theological liberalism which, through Sunday School material, was becoming known in Wales, and many sensed troubling social changes as the Victorian era crossed over the threshold into full-blown modernity.

While it is important not to overemphasise the role of Evan Roberts (1878–1951) in the Welsh revival, he is undoubtedly a key figure. The best overall record of the revival, and one that draws extensively on Welsh language sources, is still that given by R. Tudor Jones in *Faith And The Crisis of A Nation: Wales 1890–1914*. Jones shows how the revival occurred simultaneously in many parts of Wales through the ministry of many preachers functioning in an uncoordinated fashion. Yet it is Evan Roberts who epitomised the revival in the south of the country; and, once he disappeared from the scene, the revival subsided. We might argue that when Pentecostalism came into being about three years later it was a continuation of, and a reaction to, the revivalism exemplified by Roberts.

The birth of the revival, insofar as it had a localised birth, occurred on the western edge of Wales through the ministry of Seth Joshua (1858–1925), an evangelist with a roving commission. The picture was actually more complex than this because the person who invited Joshua was the minister of New Quay, Cardiganshire, Joseph Jenkins and his spiritual zeal had already stirred his congregation. In addition to what was starting to happen in west Wales, evangelistic meetings attended by thousands of people took place in Cardiff in October 1904 where the American evangelist, R.A. Torrey, was finishing a successful preaching tour. It was, however, Joshua's meetings that had most impact on Roberts. Joshua had been converted earlier through the Salvation Army and retained the rugged evangelistic zeal associated with the Army in its early days.[11] He held meetings in many parts of the UK and was an experienced campaigner. In January 1904 he became the official evangelist of the Forward Movement of the Calvinistic Methodists and was invited to preach at a church in Blaenannerch where the minister was anxious to bring his young people to a definite experience of conversion.[12]

About eight miles from Blaenannerch was the training school of the Calvinistic Methodists at Newcastle Emlyn. Among those accepted for training was Evan Roberts who had been brought up within a chapel-going family. On leaving school, he worked down the mines and then as a blacksmith. Roberts had a zealous and imaginative character (he occasionally wrote religious poetry) who had long sensed a vocation to full-time ministry. He was prepared to undergo training to become a minister, and had already read the Welsh version of A.A. Hodge's *Systematic Theology* and at least one Bible dictionary.[13] What was most arresting about him was the prolonged fervour of his praying and his capacity to receive visions. His biographer lists 20 such visions, 14 of which occurred in the 6 weeks between the middle of September and the end of October 1904.[14]

Roberts was sure that the visions received during his nightly prayers should be interpreted to mean that the burning sunlight of revival would shine upon Wales and that 100,000 people would be converted. Despite a heavy cold he walked with others from Newcastle Emlyn to Blaenannerch for the convention meeting. That morning he heard Seth Joshua pray for the 'bending' of the church in readiness for obedience to the will of God.[15] Roberts slumped forward over the chair in front, sweat pouring off his face, and

---

[11] Although Tudur Jones, *Faith*, p. 82 states clearly that Seth's brother, Frank, was converted through the Salvation Army, it is not clear whether the Army was also instrumental in Seth's conversion. I have assumed that it was. The family were originally Welsh Baptists.

[12] Tudur Jones, *Faith*, p. 288.

[13] Tudur Jones, *Faith*, p. 290.

[14] Tudur Jones, *Faith*, p. 291. See also John Harvey, 'The Agony in the Garden: Visions of the 1904 Revival', in D.W. Roberts (ed.), *Revival, Renewal and the Holy Spirit* (Carlisle: Paternoster, 2009), pp. 129-38.

[15] The words quoted are in English though Joshua may actually have prayed in Welsh.

cried out asking that God would indeed bend him: 'bend me, bend me, bend me'.[16] This heartfelt cry was the catalyst that led to his sense of being propelled into ministry. There was a pause of one month while Roberts returned to the college and engaged in weekend missions to the nearest chapels; but, on 31 October, he felt impelled to leave his college, board the train and return the 45 miles south west to his home chapel in Loughor to plead with the young people for their salvation. He did this after letters home had been written and with the blessing of the pastor at Blaenannerch.

While Seth Joshua was evidently a preacher and evangelist, Evan Roberts comes across as having a different kind of ministry. He was not, by normal standards, an expository or evangelistic preacher. He did not stand at the pulpit, open his Bible, explain Scripture for an hour and then make an appeal to his hearers to come to the front for prayer or counselling. His approach was unusual and unique. In some respects he functioned as the convener of meetings and in other respects as a man who stood before a congregation and paused for a 'word of knowledge' that he could apply. 'There is someone here harbouring unforgiveness who must repent immediately' or 'there is someone here who is blocking the work of the Holy Spirit'. These are the kind of statements that he made and he would wait in silence gazing at the congregation until someone broke. At other times, he would offer a short exhortation or would pray impromptu aloud. Often the congregation would respond by repeatedly singing hymns and sometimes the response would be in the form of the calling out of a verse of a hymn, usually in Welsh, that would initiate a bout of further singing. At the start of the revival he had composed a general fourfold plan that he followed when confronted with a new congregation but later this scheme seems to have receded into the background. His outline was:

1. If there is past sin or sins hitherto unconfessed, we cannot receive the Spirit. Therefore we must search and ask the Spirit to search.

---

[16] Brynmor Pierce Jones, *An Instrument of Revival: The Complete Life of Evan Roberts 1878–1951* (South Plainfield, NJ: Bridge Publishing, 1995), p. 24, gives a fuller account of what he felt and believed on this occasion based on an interview Roberts gave to a journalist some weeks later.

2. If there is anything doubtful in our lives, it *must* be removed – anything we are uncertain about its rightness or wrongness. That thing *must* be removed.

3. An entire giving up of ourselves to the Spirit. We *must speak* and *do* all he requires of us.

4. Public confession of Christ.[17]

Despite his youth and lack of training, he addressed the young people in his home chapel and broke through their consciences so that they responded to his call for faith and repentance. When this happened, other chapels in the area asked him to speak to them; and, bit by bit, he launched a campaign that gathered energy with nightly services. He was seen weeping in the pulpit, he was at a prayer meeting at 5.00 am in the morning at the pithead,[18] he was rebutted and mocked and there were times when his message to the young people was that Christians ought to be filled with joy rather than gloomy solemnity. People of all ages came to listen to him including miners in their best suits and women of all ages and classes. The four conditions for revival that he explained provoked scenes of great excitement; and, quite soon after the beginning of his growing campaign, two local sisters, Annie and Maggie Davies, would join him on the platform and lead the singing or offer solos that became part of the whole revival experience. The revival that started on 13 November in its first phase went on for at least six weeks during which Roberts visited the valleys of Aberdare, Rhondda Fawr, Rhondda Fach, Merthyr, and the Vale of Glamorgan 'delivering 93 addresses and everywhere he experienced the same thrilling atmosphere'.[19]

The excitement of the revival was fanned by the accounts in the biggest newspaper in south Wales, the *Western Mail*, whose reporter known only as Awstin, printed largely favourable accounts giving free publicity and a valuable record of typical meetings.[20] Later the

---

[17] Evans, *Welsh Revival*, p. 84.

[18] Tudor Jones, *Faith*, p. 297. Evans, *Welsh Revival*, p. 124.

[19] Tudor Jones, *Faith*, p. 298.

[20] Awstin was T. Awstin Davies (1857–1934), the son of a Pontypridd minister, who began as a mining correspondent for the *Western Mail* but later became a

London *Times* sent a reporter who also provided a description of what happened each evening. By Christmas Roberts was exhausted and surviving without much sleep because the meetings continued late into the night. Many of the meetings took place through the medium of Welsh which gave them a homely and intimate atmosphere and Roberts himself, because he did not preach in every meeting; and, indeed, often only made introductory remarks or interventions when he discerned individuals were ready for conversion, would sometimes leave the pulpit and walk up and down the aisles to address individuals, pray for them, and even, on occasion, walk out into the street to bring people into the meetings. There was a friendliness and personal touch in his approach while the congregations, drawing upon their shared experience of Sunday school and knowledge of the Bible, renewed the faith of their childhood and reformed their lives by rejecting habitual weekend fighting or drunkenness that wasted pay packets and impoverished families.[21]

The revival meetings led by Evan Roberts spread eastward across Wales and entered the Llynfi Valley where Maesteg was situated. We know from the totals given by Awstin that by December 31, 1904, 1,208 converts had been registered in the Maesteg area.[22] The conversion of miners known to Stephen Jeffreys made him uneasy.[23] His church commitments were consistent (he played in the flute band) but not held deeply enough to bring him into ministry. After hesitating upon the brink he made a decision for Christ on 20 November 1904 and his younger brother George made a decision on the same day. The preacher on that occasion was their own minister Glasnant Jones.[24] The two brothers had experienced classic and powerful evangelical conversion.

---

full-time journalist and eventually President of the National Eisteddfod Association (Jones, *Instrument*, p. 271).

[21] A reduction in the number of offences brought to magistrates' courts amply demonstrates this. Evans, *Welsh Revival*, p. 161, reports 'Convictions for drunkenness in Glamorgan fell from 10,528 in 1903 to 5,490 in 1906'.

[22] T. Davies (Awstin), *Religious Revival in Wales no. 2*, Western Mail, 31 Dec 1904 (www.revival-library.org).

[23] Cartwright, *Evangelists*, p. 18.

[24] See Edward Jeffreys, *Stephen Jeffreys: The Beloved Evangelist* (Luton: Redemption Tidings Bookroom, 1946), p. 3

The two brothers could hardly have avoided the raw excitement generated by the revival meetings and the effect made by these meetings on the daily lives of working men and women. Stephen, as we have said, saw and heard about the conversion of fellow miners and George, who may by this time have been working in a grocer's shop, would also have followed events in the newspapers even if no one else in the store was touched.[25] Miners, with their macho culture and profane language, would have been the hardest nuts for the revivalists to crack; but, when they made their commitments, their testimony carried weight in the tightly-packed industrial communities and then spread outwards as their upright lives benefited their wives and children. Stephen's son, Edward, was born in 1899 and he had three daughters as well. We must assume that, from the end of November onwards, the fire of the revival was felt intimately in the Jeffreys home, even among the children. Whether at this time or in his childhood, George was healed of his facial paralysis[26] and speech impediment. He recorded:

> We were kneeling in prayer one Sunday morning and were interceding on the subject of the services of that day. It was exactly nine o'clock when the power of God came upon me, and I received such an inflow of Divine life that I can only liken the experience to being charged with electricity. It seemed as if my head were connected to a *most powerful battery*. My whole body from head to foot was quickened by the Spirit of God, and I was healed (original italics).[27]

Criticism of the Revival

The revival continued almost unabated into the New Year. Roberts was only able to take a small amount of rest. There had been criticism of the two young women who accompanied him, sang in his meetings, helped direct them and offered public prayers. This was at a time when the ministry of women was almost unheard of (apart

---

[25] The 1911 census return gives George's employment as 'Grocer Assistant Coop Society'.

[26] Possibly caused by polio or infantile paralysis, which would be compatible with speech impairment.

[27] Jeffreys, *Healing Rays*, p. 57.

from in the Salvation Army) and when a man working closely with two young women might well be open to scurrilous gossip. This criticism, such as it was, came to nothing but it will have alerted Roberts to the opposition that might lie hidden beneath the excitement.

Similarly, there were employers who complained about the evening absences of their servant girls attending revival meetings. It was as if the girls were using their faith as an excuse to be gadding about late at night and then be too tired for their morning duties.[28] Yet the most damaging and lasting criticism of the revival was printed in the letter pages of the *Western Mail* on 31st January 1905. Peter Price (1864–1940), a Congregationalist minister, posted a lengthy letter to the newspaper complaining that they were really two revivals, one that was divinely sent and genuine and the other that was a 'false revival' made up of highly wrought emotionalism and theologically presumptuous claims by Roberts. Price did not pull his punches

> I have witnessed bursts of this real revival as far back as two years ago. I understand that there are several would-be originators of the revival; but I maintain that the human originator of the true revival cannot be named ...

> But there is another revival in South Wales – a sham revival, a mockery, a blasphemous travesty of the real thing. The chief figure in this mock revival is Evan Roberts, whose language is inconsistent with the character of anyone except that of a person endowed with the attributes of a divine being. Is Evan Roberts, then, a divine being, or is he not? ...

> I have heard people say, 'Evan Roberts is led by the Holy Spirit.' I say, 'no – quite the contrary: judging from his behaviour and talk, the Holy Spirit is led by Evan Roberts!'

> My honest conviction is this: that the best thing that could happen to the course of the true religious revival among us would be for Evan Roberts and his girl-companions withdraw to their respective homes, and there to examine themselves, and learn a

---

[28] Jones, *Instrument*, p. 248.

little more of the meaning of Christianity, if they have the capacity for this, instead of going about the country pretending to show the way of life to people many of whom know a thousand times more about it than they do.

Having distinguished between two revivals and accused Evan Roberts of lacking any outstanding spiritual knowledge, he went on to press his point:

But it is this mock revival – this exhibition – this froth – this vain trumpery – which visitors see and which newspapers report. And it is harmful to the true revival – very harmful ... Before Evan Roberts visited Dowlais, we had the holy fire burning brightly – at white heat; at my own church alone we could count our converts during the last five or six months by the hundreds. What happened when Evan Roberts visited the place? People came from all parts anxious to see the man, understand something of the movement and to get some of the fire to take home with them.

These damaging criticisms were aimed squarely at Roberts:

I will say that with much effort Evan Roberts, together with his co-operators (and, evidently, they understood one another thoroughly, and each knew his or her part well and where to come in), managed, by means of threats, complaints and incantations, which reminded me of the prophets on Baal, to create some of the false fire.

Price goes on to ask a series of questions including:

Why does he [Evan Roberts] wait until the meetings attain the climax of enthusiasm before he enters?

Why does he visit places where the fire has been burning at maximum strength for weeks and months? Would it not be more reasonable for him to go to places which the fire has not reached?

What spirit makes him bad-tempered when things don't come about exactly as he wishes?

Price signed himself ostentatiously 'BA Hons, Mental and Moral Sciences Tripos, Cambridge (late of Queen's College, Cambridge),

Minister of Bethania Congregational Church, Dowlais, South Wales'. The signature intentionally drew a sharp contrast between the uneducated Evan Roberts who had not even completed a term of his ministerial training and the academic status of Peter Price. At first glance the battle lines seem to have been drawn between revivalism and academic qualifications; but, in his letter, Price is careful to point to the evangelical success of his own church and so, though Price attracted considerable adverse comment in the letter pages of the newspaper; and, in general, scant respect from later historians, the main thrust of his comments was neither anti-Christian nor anti-evangelical. He just sounds dismally hypercritical – and he unquestionably disregarded the wider social benefit of the whole revival: drunkenness fell, industrial relations improved, ecumenical friendships between denominations sprang up, and families were reconciled. The editorial of the *Western Mail* on the day Price's letter was published did not believe there were two revivals; and, had Price read Jonathan Edwards, he would have understood revivals never exist in an entirely pure form.

We do not know the effect of such public disapproval on the Jeffreys brothers – presumably they read it and pondered what might happen if religious experience was stirred up and ran wild – but it is reasonable to ask whether George's later micro-management of Pentecostal meetings may have had its origins here. He may, too, have worried that academic study could lead to narrow and dismissive judgements, and this would have been why his approach to academic qualifications was always cautious. All that lay in the future. In 1905, the national success of both brothers was a long way distant. Roberts for his part, though he never responded to Price's letter, appears to have taken the censure to heart and at the end of February decreed a 'week of silence' for himself by cancelling engagements and withdrawing for prayer, study and rest.[29]

---

[29] 'The French observer, Professor Henri Blois, also saw the Peter Price controversy as a turning-point in the revival' (Evans, *Welsh Revival,* p. 135).

Theological Undercurrents

The revival continued at least until the autumn of 1905. Roberts moved northwards and held meetings in Liverpool before travelling westwards towards Bangor and Anglesey. Although it is important to note that there were numerous other meetings and numerous other preachers involved in the revival and that it by no means depended upon or revolved around Roberts, his life and ministry came to epitomise the whole extraordinary and marvellous episode in the life of Wales.

Roberts had already occasionally shown harsh reactions towards congregations or individuals whom he felt were resisting the Spirit; and this tendency, together with an odd unreliability over sticking to his appointments (he felt he should only go where he was prompted to go by the Holy Spirit and this led to a certain amount of hurried rescheduling), suggested that he was close to a breakdown.[30] Behind the scenes we now know that he was being pestered by letters from Jesse Penn-Lewis whose obsessive behaviour can only have helped to destabilise him. Penn-Lewis was a Keswick speaker and treated with respect in Christian circles. She adopted a strong theology of 'identification with Christ' that led to a holiness doctrine that appeared to preclude the possibility of error. At the same time, in a complicated way, she attempted to provide criteria by which to discern which promptings were given by the Holy Spirit and which were given by the devil. She wrote at least six letters to Evan Roberts probably starting in February 1905 trying to inveigle him into coming to live with her and her husband.[31] On the face of it, her concern was entirely for Roberts' well-being but her constant references to spiritual battle offered nothing of substance to help Roberts. During his 'week of silence' Roberts was trying to 'differentiate Thy voice from the cunning Evil One' and this kind of uncertainty dragged on for a long time afterwards.[32] To the students at Bala he said: '… the Spirit of God caused me to lose the joy, for a time that

---

[30] Evans, *Welsh Revival*, p. 122.
[31] William K. Kay, 'Why did the Welsh Revival Stop?', in D.F. Roberts (ed.), *Revival, Renewal and The Holy Spirit* (Milton Keynes: Paternoster, 2009), p. 180.
[32] T. Davies (Awstin), *Western Mail*, 3 Mar 1905.

I might come closer to men' which indicates that his retirement from the scene of revival did him no good but he went on

> God does exist; and the devil exists too. I had an experience of this one of these last months. The devil came to me – I knew not at first that it was he – and said – 'Thou art not worthy to be in this great work; it will be better for thee to give it up'.[33]

So, while the revival was continuing to stir the population and attract large crowds, one of the key leaders was himself struggling inwardly. Roberts felt himself in a huge spiritual battle even as he lacked any overall grasp of the scope and work of the Holy Spirit in the life of the Christian. A theology that placed the functioning of spiritual gifts in the wider context of the role of the Holy Spirit within the life of the church was entirely missing. Such a theology only began to be formulated in the late 1920s when Donald Gee constructed a coherent Pentecostal pneumatology and ecclesiology from a systematic examination of the New Testament. Roberts, without the benefits of a broadly based and robust Pentecostal theology, was floundering with religious experiences of unknown origin and swaying backwards and forwards between faith and doubt, trust in the Holy Spirit and fear of the devil.

Again, we can only speculate on the theological discussions that might have taken place between Stephen and George Jeffreys; but, in the case of George, we know that, by the start of the 1930s, he had formulated beliefs about the Holy Spirit and tested them practically in a way that gave him a stability in his ministry that Roberts lacked.

End of Revival

The revival continued in the first part of 1905 and Evan Roberts spent a week in the Maesteg area between the 14 and 21 February.[34] Given that the Jeffreys brothers lived in Maesteg, it is reasonable to assume they attended some or all of the meetings and were able to

---

[33] T. Davies (Awstin), 'Evan Roberts' at Bala College', http://www.welshrevival.org/misc/ bala/title.htm. The visit seems to have been in July 1905, see Jones, *Instrument*, p. 148.

[34] Tudor Jones, *Faith*, p. 314.

gain a first-hand view of the personality and influence of Roberts himself and to form an impression of his ministry; and, perhaps, to set it against Price's criticism which they would surely have read. Another crowd of 2,091 Maesteg converts was added bringing the eventual total for the area to a staggering 5,414.

By the time December 1905 was reached, the revival was beginning to subside. Various interpretations of its cessation are possible and it may be that, like fire, it had burnt up everything that could be burnt up and that everyone who might be converted had been converted. The churches were filled and trying to cope with the influx of new converts – some estimates put the figure for the whole revival at 100,000.[35] Wales itself was beginning to turn its attention to the 1906 General Election and many of the churches that had been caught up in the revival were now focused upon gains in political power for the Liberal Party and the benefits that might flow to Wales from the Liberal politician David Lloyd George.

Evan Roberts accepted the pressing and secretive invitation of Mrs Penn-Lewis to stay indefinitely in her comfortable house in Leicestershire. What Mr Penn-Lewis thought about this is not recorded but such insight we have into their marriage suggests that she was the dominant partner. Her influence on Roberts was considerable and in 1912 she published a book, *War on the Saints*, that was effectively a repudiation of the entire Welsh revival and all the spiritual experiences that went with it. If Roberts had any theological contribution to make to British Pentecostalism, it was quite lost and he never showed any inclination to join any of the Pentecostal denominations that came into existence over the next few years. Despite efforts by his family to extricate him, Roberts remained a guest in Leicestershire till around 1920 and lived largely as a recluse then and thereafter. He established no congregations and left behind only a fleeting memory and no solid legacy.

---

[35] Evans, *Welsh Revival*, p. 79.

3

STARTING MINISTRY

George Jeffreys was 15 years of age when he was converted in the autumn of 1904.

> He has told the story himself many times … he sat in the back seat of a Welsh Congregational Church in the Llynvi Valley, South Wales, and was gripped by the Rev. Glasant Jones's reference to Romans 10:13 'For whosoever shall call on the Name of the Lord shall be saved'. Through that simple but powerful quotation he found Christ as his Saviour – the only convert that night![1]

We only have a few glimpses of his life between the moment of conversion and his eventual emergence as an outstanding preacher. We know from his later autobiographical reflection that he had long dreamed of being a minister: 'the conviction that God had called him to the Christian ministry had been his since childhood'.[2] Whether the boy wanted to follow his grandfather's example or felt spurred on by his mother's encouragement or simply had an early intuition of vocation, we do not know.

Glasnant Jones wrote a pen portrait of George:

> At the open-air revival services I always found young Jeffreys at my side. I was privileged to give him his early religious tuition and a splendid scholar he was. Superior to other lads there was

---

[1] *The Pattern* 5.19 (Oct 1944), p. 5. The writer is Albert Edsor.
[2] E.C.W. Boulton, *George Jeffreys: A Ministry of the Miraculous* (London: Elim Publishing Office, 1928), p. 12.

character in his face: I knew he was a 'chosen vessel'. When I left Siloh, Maesteg in 1907 George Jeffreys was in business, and had he remained in that calling, I'm convinced he would have become a merchant Prince.[3]

This brief report tells us that between 1904 and 1907 George Jeffreys was working with his pastor preaching in the open air. By 1907 he would have been 18; and, presumably, on the way to becoming a good speaker in public while, in his spare time and when he was not earning a living, he would have been studying either the Bible or theological literature. His brother Stephen followed a similar pattern of life. Edward Jeffreys wrote, 'my father went on working as a miner for some years after his conversion, witnessing to the saving power of God down in the coal-pit, and on the corners of the streets, whilst God was quietly preparing him for a greater service'.[4] Indeed, 'after a hard day's work he would hurry to change for an open-air meeting somewhere in the neighbourhood … When the nights were dark and chill, prayer-meetings would be held at various places, and you could depend upon father being there!'[5] So it is evident that the two brothers, who were still living in the same house, were busy devoting all their spare time to activities organised by their local congregation. They were either outside preaching or indoors praying.

Wales itself was changing. There had been political battles over the Education Act of 1902, and these resurfaced in the local elections of 1904 through a widespread refusal to implement the law that had been passed in Westminster requiring children of Nonconformists to attend Anglican church schools. The dispute continued until December 1905 when the government backed down and this helped Liberals in Wales contribute to winning the general election of 1906. Welsh Nonconformists almost to a man voted Liberal and, when in power, were determined to remove Anglican privileges, which is why, many years later, the Anglican Church in Wales was disestablished.

---

[3] Boulton, *Jeffreys*, p. 11.
[4] Jeffreys, *Stephen Jeffreys*, p. 5.
[5] Jeffreys, *Stephen Jeffreys*, pp. 4, 5.

Wales found itself proudly represented by David Lloyd George, one of the leaders of the new Liberal government, who became President of the Board of Trade in 1905 and Chancellor of Exchequer in 1908. He was the first Welshman in 50 years to be a member of the Cabinet and he made much of his unprivileged origins. He portrayed himself as 'the son of the cottage' and his elevation was regarded as a sign of the new status of Wales itself.[6] We do not know what the Jeffreys brothers made of Lloyd George at this point in his career but if they followed the biblical injunction to pray for those in authority (1 Tim. 2.2), his name would have been called out within the prayers of their chapel and they might even have thought, 'If a Welsh politician can attain national importance, then why not a Welsh preacher?'

Sunderland

While the Jeffreys brothers were active in and around their local church and attempting to reignite the flame of revival, unexpected spiritual awakenings occurred in an industrial parish in the northeast of England. The vicar there was an exceptional individual – full of energy and curiosity – who had taken on a troublesome appointment. The previous incumbent had been an alcoholic and Alexander Boddy (1854–1930), a fine evangelical Anglican, drove himself to turn the situation around. He had learned about the dramatic scenes of spiritual outpouring during the Azusa Street revival in Los Angeles in 1906 and the Methodist preacher, T.B. Barratt (1862–1940), who, as a consequence of contact with the revival, had spoken in tongues in New York and then sailed home to Oslo. Here he had preached passionately and evangelistically on the restoration of spiritual gifts to the church. Boddy, who had already visited the Welsh revival and once stood on the same platform as Evan Roberts, took a boat across the North Sea to see Oslo for himself.[7] The scenes he witnessed were more extraordinary than those he had witnessed in the Welsh revival and he begged Barratt to visit his parish in Monkwearmouth, Sunderland.

---

[6] John Davies, *A History of Wales* (Harmondsworth: Penguin, 1993), p. 480.
[7] Quoted by Donald Gee, *Wind and Flame* (Croydon: Assemblies of God Publishing House, 1967), p. 20.

Intense preparatory prayer meetings were held in the vestry of the All Saints Parish Church before Barratt arrived to preach and teach. He landed early in September 1907 and stayed six weeks[8] and his ministry precipitated an outpouring of the Spirit accompanied by speaking in tongues and a realisation that the church in all its traditions and forms might be renewed. This spiritual event, coming as it did at the start of the 20th century, felt significant enough to point to the near return of Christ. And, though Boddy may not have known it at the time, there was a connection between the Welsh revival and the Azusa Street revival in Los Angeles.[9] So it became possible to see the outpouring of the Spirit as a continuation of the Welsh revival or a development of it that would re-energise and empower the church with charismatic gifts for a great end-time harvest of converts.

Boddy was unquestionably a leader, a man who took initiative and organised. He laid plans for a large Whitsun convention in Sunderland in 1908 and he launched a magazine, *Confidence*, to publicise the event while enabling Christians and scattered meetings all over the country to get in touch with each other. In the days before telephones and the internet, Boddy's magazine offered a forum and connection hub that built up a national and then an international list of congregations, preachers, and missionaries. It did more than this, though, because it gave sermons in written form and teachings on the new phenomena and provided a sense of rationality and balance to what might otherwise have become wild and ephemeral.

The Sunderland Conventions continued annually until the summer of 1914 and were only brought to an end by the outbreak of the Great War. All the major leaders of the British Pentecostal denominations that emerged at the start of the 20th century attended

---

[8] Gee, *Wind*, pp. 22, 23.

[9] Frank Bartleman had written asking for prayer for California and received a reply 'My dear brother in the faith: Many thanks for your kind letter. I am impressed of your sincerity and honesty of purpose. Congregate the people together who are willing to make a total surrender. May God bless you, is my earnest prayer. Yours in Christ, Evan Roberts'; see F. Bartleman, *Azusa Street* (Plainfield, NJ: Bridge Publishing, 1980), p. 15.

one or more of the conventions.[10] Consequently, Boddy's influence was considerable.

Miraculous signs

Stephen Jeffreys had taken on the pastorate of Island Place Mission, Llanelli, in 1914. On Sunday July 5, Stephen was preaching on the text "that I might know Him, and the power of His resurrection, and the fellowship of His suffering." Philippians 3:10.

Jeffreys said that he was conscious of a tremendous anointing and extra power and blessing as he was preaching, and he could see the people were riveted in his direction. On the wall behind him as he preached there appeared a remarkable picture. First it was blurred and indistinct but soon it became clear that it was the face of a lamb. After some time it changed to the appearance of Christ as the Man of Sorrows. The vision remained on the wall for around six hours where it was seen by hundreds of people. The building was finally locked at 2am the vision still there but by next morning it had disappeared.

The local newspapers reported the incident interviewing many who had seen the vision. The vision was thoroughly investigated and many accepted it as a sign from God. The vicar of Well, near Litchfield, Rev J.W.Adams, twice visited Llanelli in 1926 and then the following year. He questioned many eye witnesses and listed scores of people who could confirm the story. The most detailed account recorded is in *Confidence*, the magazine edited by Rev Alexander Boddy of Sunderland, which was printed in July 1916.

We remained in the chapel for a long time looking and scores of others who heard about it came to examine. Among them was a young sceptic, who declared, 'I have seen and now I believe.' He came in an infidel and went out a believer.

Stephen Jeffreys

Confidence Magazine, edited by Alexander Boddy, did a great deal to publicise the brothers Stephen and George Jeffreys in their early days. Stephen was George's older brother and a powerful evangelist but, unlike George, quite disorganised and unable to multi-task.

It was not long before the scattered Welsh congregations and meetings, still glowing in the aftermath of the revival, learnt about Sunderland and want to know more. Among the 'children of the revival' as they were called were members of the English Congregational Church in Waunllwyd about 45 miles from Maesteg. Slightly confusingly the minister here was Thomas Madog Jeffreys (no relation to George and Stephen) and his church received a visit in November 1907 from Moncur Niblock speaking about the Pentecostal outpouring across the world. Having travelled to Sunderland Niblock then returned on 22 December, 1907, and reported on what he had seen and heard. As a result, T.M. Jeffreys was baptised in the Spirit. About three months later four members of a group

---

[10] W.K. Kay, 'Sunderland's Legacy in New Denominations', *Journal of the European Pentecostal Theological Association* 28.2, (2008), pp. 183-99.

from Dowlais, seven miles away, visited Waunllwyd and were themselves baptised in the Spirit. One of the visitors was Price Davies who, in an itinerant ministry within Wales, travelled the 35 or so miles from Dowlais to Maesteg – something that was easily possible by train in those days because the railway network was then at its peak – and held meetings. At some point in 1910, in the old Dyffryn Chapel, the two Jeffreys brothers were baptised in the Spirit and spoke in tongues.[11]

Actually, the story is more complicated than this and merits further scrutiny.

Apostolic Connections

The story concerns the short-lived link between William Oliver Hutchinson (1864–1928) and George Jeffreys. For about two years Jeffreys was drawn towards the Hutchinson circle, but then, along with others, he decisively withdrew. The religious landscape after the outpouring of the Spirit and before the start of the Great War was unsettled and no one at the time knew whether the outpouring of the Spirit seen in Sunderland would become a renewal movement within the walls of existing denominations or break out and lead to the creation of fresh religious groupings. Nor did anybody know who the eventual leaders would be. Alexander Boddy was the most important British Pentecostal until 1914; but, to the more radical eye, Hutchinson appeared ready to become a leading national figure. He erected the first purpose-built Pentecostal building in Britain by opening Emmanuel Mission Hall in Bournemouth on 5 November 1908.[12] No less a person than the wealthy Cecil Polhill, evangelical Anglican to his core, spoke at the occasion. Less than

---

[11] This reconstruction of events follows Neil Hudson, 'A Schism and its Aftermath: An Historical Analysis of Denominational Discerption in the Elim Pentecostal Church, 1939–1940' (PhD, King's College, London, 1999). J. Robinson, *Pentecostal Origins: Early Pentecostalism in Ireland in the Context of the British Isles* (Carlisle: Paternoster, 2005), p. 94, points out that W.G. Hill had started Pentecostal meetings in Maesteg but George Jeffreys first spoke in tongues a few miles up the valley at the Duffryn chapel while Edward Jeffreys says that Stephen spoke in tongues first in Maesteg (Jeffreys, *Stephen Jeffreys*, p. 5).

[12] Kent White, *The Word of God Coming Again* (Bournemouth: AFC, 1919), p. 51.

two years later Hutchinson founded the magazine *Shower of Blessing* which may have had a readership of 10,000, a figure that would have challenged the predominance of *Confidence*.[13]

In the period between 1908 and about 1912 Hutchinson was an invited speaker at several international conventions and, from the coverage given to him by *Confidence*, it would appear that his preaching and doctrine were entirely acceptable to the majority of Pentecostal sympathisers. Hutchinson made an impact on the mini-revival in the Kilsyth area to which Boddy, in March 1908, had been an 'overwhelmed' visitor.[14] In 1909, T.B. Barratt preached at a Bournemouth convention. Hutchinson was a signatory to the London statement on baptism in the Spirit in 1909[15] and his travelling ministry enabled him to link up with proto-Pentecostal assemblies in south Wales that had vivid memories of the revival and still retained revivalistic features. Hutchinson had attended Sunderland in 1908 and was therefore among the very first wave of British Pentecostals. In 1910 he attended again but this time as an invited guest to share in the preaching on the topic of divine healing. Boddy thought his sermon 'wonderful'.[16]

Hutchinson's position began to fall apart after 1910. He began to believe that the 'spoken word' – by which he meant prophecies or interpretations of utterances in tongues – should be treated as if they were canonical Scripture and that any disobedience to such utterances should be treated as disobedience to God. Prophecies, in Hutchinson's opinion, should not be judged – thereby contradicting the specific New Testament injunction of 1 Cor. 14.29. Speaking two years later Hutchinson was to say, 'we passed through great testings on believing the "Spoken Word"'.[17] A year later Hutchinson

---

[13] Since *Confidence* peaked at about 6,000 copies per issue, I find the claim of 10,000 copies per issue for *Showers of Blessing* improbable. It is more credible to assume Hutchinson claimed a readership of 10,000, which would put his circulation at about 2,000 copies, a much less expensive print-run. The figure of 10,000 comes from James E. Worsfold, *The Origins of the Apostolic Church in Great Britain* (Wellington, New Zealand: Julian Literature Trust, 1991), p. 35.

[14] *Confidence* 1.1 (Apr 1908), p. 8.

[15] *Confidence* 2.12 (Dec 1909), p. 287.

[16] *Confidence* 3.6 (June 1910), p. 138.

[17] Malcolm Hathaway, 'The Role of William Oliver Hutchinson and the Apostolic Faith Church in the Formation of British Pentecostal Churches', *Journal of the European Pentecostal Theological Association* 16 (1996), pp. 40-57. Worsfold, *Origins*,

began to make a doctrine of the practice of 'pleading the blood'.[18] This practice entailed either speaking the word 'blood' rapidly and frequently or else in prayer calling the word out. The practice was equated with the Old Testament notion of sprinkling blood upon the altar to sanctify it. In the New Testament dispensation pleading the blood was seen as an ultimate defence mechanism to prevent any demonic interference in one's mind and heart. So, 'pleading the blood' produced a form of inviolability that, at the same time, guaranteed the free and pure operation of the Holy Spirit. The two practices, treating interpretation/prophecy as infallible and pleading the blood, reinforced each other since the second guaranteed the first. About two years later in 1912, Hutchinson was appointed as the 'first apostle' of his church in response to direction given by spiritual gifts.[19] Once installed into apostolic office, he was raised beyond criticism to a place where he was believed to be incapable of error.

Hutchinson's influence extended into South Wales. We know this because of reports within *Showers of Blessing* and because a group of Welsh churches were associated with him and accepted his leadership until they seceded in 1916.[20] There was an Apostolic Church in Swansea and other historians have indicated that George Jeffreys attended this on Sunday nights – the train service would again have made this an easy journey.[21] More arresting is a letter written by

---

p. 121, quotes Hutchinson's son-in-law, 'now to deal with the difference between the written and spoken word. Going straight to the root of the matter there is no difference at all, because if it is the Word of God – whether written or spoken – it cannot be anything else but God's Word and therefore in that sense the same, identically.'

[18] Benjamin Pugh, '"There is Power in the Blood": The Role of the Blood of Jesus in the Spirituality of Early British Pentecostalism', *Journal of the European Pentecostal Theological Association* 25 (2005), pp. 54-66.

[19] Worsfold, *Origins*, p. 121 says, 'Hutchinson even used the word "infallible" when it came to describing the nature of the ministry of the voice Gifts' (original capitalisation).

[20] A full account of the marathon meeting and the walk-out is given by Gordon Weeks, *Chapter Thirty Two – Part of: A History of the Apostolic Church 1900–2000* (Barnsley, Yorks: Prontaprint, 2003), p. 45.

[21] Hathaway, 'Hutchinson', p. 52 'George Jeffreys' first contact with Hutchinson was through James Brooke, pastor of the work at Belle Vue Chapel, Swansea'.

George Jeffreys to Hutchinson and published in *Showers of Blessing* in September 1910. It reads:

> Dear Pastor Hutchinson
>
> I really think that God would have me bear my testimony to the glorious work he has done in me. Hallelujah.
>
> Since I have been at Bournemouth 'all things are become new – old things have passed away'. Hallelujah. I have been saved, sanctified, baptised in the Holy Ghost with the scriptural sign of tongues, Mark xvi.17 and healed of sickness. This is the Lord's doing, and it is marvellous in our eyes. Glory to God: God has taken the cigarette from my lips, and put a hallelujah there instead. Hallelujah.
>
> I have the gift of tongues and interpretation; but the latter gift must still be developed.
>
> I cannot tell you all he has done for me, as no tongue can glorify God sufficiently. I feel free and happy; so very joyful and anxious to do something. Now comes my testing. I am going home to Wales, and it is but the beginning of a mighty battle. But 'Lion of the tribe of Judah' does not tell me to fight alone but he himself will do the worst part, and victory is always his. I thank you for your prayers. GJ.[22]

The letter indicates that Jeffreys had visited Bournemouth, presumably to attend the convention in 1910; that he had been baptised in the Spirit and spoken with tongues; and that he had been healed; that he had given up smoking cigarettes; and that he had a sense of having to return to Wales with a 'mighty battle' on his hands.[23] Yet the wording of the letter does not state specifically that Jeffreys was baptised in the Spirit in Bournemouth or healed in Bournemouth or sanctified in Bournemouth. The letter may simply outline to Hutchinson the spiritual credentials Jeffreys felt himself to possess in readiness for the 'mighty battle' he anticipated in Wales.

---

[22] Cartwright, *Evangelists*, quoted in full on p. 26.
[23] The letter also does not say he was baptised in water in Bournemouth, as it surely would have done if he had been.

There are several ways of squaring this letter with other evidence. We could assume that it contradicts the account Jeffreys himself gave of his baptism at the Dyffryn Chapel;[24] but, if we do this, we would also have to assume that the account given by Edward Jeffreys of his father's baptism in the Spirit somehow excluded George – which seems unlikely.[25] The two brothers lived under the same roof and if a preacher came to speak about the baptism Holy Spirit in Maesteg, one would assume that both brothers attended the meeting, as they did in the revival when they were converted.

It is much easier to assume that George did receive his baptism in the Spirit in Maesteg in 1910 and that his letter to Hutchinson has a different significance. It might be to suggest that some kind of commissioning or dedication occurred in Bournemouth and that George responded to this and intended to return to his native Wales with the idea of carrying forward the plans that had been given by Hutchinson or at Hutchinson's church. We know that Hutchinson later developed a doctrine of church government by apostles and prophets that turned upon the prophet giving commands and directions that believers were expected to obey. It was after a succession of prophetic or other utterances that Hutchinson was appointed as 'first apostle' in autumn 1912.[26] Such a method of appointing ministers would then have been in force when George Jeffreys was appointed as pastor to one of the congregations in Maesteg. As Hathaway put it, 'it seems likely that George Jeffreys' first ordination was to the pastoral charge of the Independent Apostolic Church, Emmanuel, Christ Church, Maesteg'.[27] Such an appointment is borne out by the Certificate of Ordination issued on 13 November 1912 'to regular work of the Christian ministry' discovered by Desmond Cartwright and reported in his MA dissertation.[28] An alternative and better explanation to this ordination is implied by Cartwright in his book on the two Jeffreys brothers: it is that George was set apart for ministry immediately prior to his going for ministerial and missionary training in Preston. In other words, his ordination was not

[24] *Elim Evangel* 10.34-35 (25 Dec 1929), p. 529.
[25] Jeffreys, *Stephen Jeffreys*, p. 5.
[26] Hathaway, 'Hutchinson', p. 45.
[27] Hathaway, 'Hutchinson', p. 53.
[28] Reported by James Robinson, *Origins*, p. 96.

intended to establish him in a fixed pastorate but to recognise his calling to full-time ministry of an indeterminate or missional kind.[29]

Later, when he had seen how Hutchinson had constructed a form of church government solely dependent upon spiritual gifts, Jeffreys wrote a powerful critique. His book, *Pentecostal Rays*, published in 1933 includes a chapter on prophecy and mentions by name 'the Apostolic Faith Church, with headquarters at Winton, Bournemouth' and 'the Apostolic Church, with headquarters at Penygroes, South Wales'.[30] In it he examined the verses on New Testament prophecy that were used by both these groups to justify their distinctive position. Jeffreys points out that there is no New Testament justification for 'enquiring of the Lord through prophets' or of 'setting' prophets within the New Testament Church. [31] His rejection of their position is logical and unemotional and, perhaps, explains the textual grounds upon which he and others in Elim came to ostracise the Hutchinson group or those once connected with it.

Hathaway, whose own grandfather was caught up with Hutchinson's movement, is of the opinion that in later life Jeffreys avoided all mention of any entanglement with Hutchinson as a way of protecting Elim's reputation.[32] There's no way of proving this but the biblical critique of the Apostolics in *Pentecostal Rays* would support this idea.

There is one other indirect piece of support that might be offered. E.C.W. Boulton wrote the first full biographical story of Jeffreys in a book published by Elim in 1928. Boulton's own account of the Pentecostal landscape before the formation of Elim is general and unspecific but makes a sharp contrast between the 'cold church ceremonialism' or 'dead traditionalism' of one set of churches and the other end of the spectrum in another set of churches that refused to 'recognise any and all human government' because it 'was regarded as opposed to the idea of guidance and

---

[29] Cartwright, *Evangelists*, p. 28.

[30] George Jeffreys, *Pentecostal Rays: The Baptism and Gifts of the Holy Spirit* (Clapham, London: Elim Publishing Company, 1933), pp. 172-73.

[31] See for instance D.P. Williams, *Prophecy in Practice or Prophetical Ministry in the Church* (Penygroes: Apostolic Church, 1931), p. 82.

[32] Hathaway, 'Hutchinson', pp. 53, 54.

government by the Holy Spirit'.[33] Boulton's account, to those who know about Jeffreys' connection with the Apostolics, rings true. Elim was going to place itself between the extremes of non-Pentecostal formalism and hyper-Pentecostal prophetic governance. But what also makes sense is that Boulton himself had been under Hutchinson's influence and one of the ministers who had been re-deployed through prophetic utterance and then left Hutchinson, re-joined, and finally left again.[34] He then came into Elim and, presumably, this would have enhanced Jeffreys' trust in him as an authorised biographer: they shared the same Apostolic past they were keen to forget.

Finding A Way Forward

When at the age of 40 in 1929, Jeffreys looked back on his life, he recalled the huge challenges he faced entering Pentecostal ministry.[35] He felt a call to ministry and equally clearly felt that by holding firmly to Pentecostal distinctives he was likely to be disqualified from ministering in any of the churches he knew. He also felt that, as the unmarried son of the family, he had a financial responsibility to his mother. The road appeared to be blocked. There were no proper Pentecostal churches for him to join once he ruled out the form of government embraced by the Apostolics. At the same time, he was aware of his lack of ministerial training especially since, in Wales, there was an expectation that ministers should first attend a training college – as Evan Roberts had briefly done. Given the absence of secondary education, ministers were conscious they need-ed something beyond primary school if they were to spend a life in the pulpit.

Relevant to his predicament was his water baptism by immersion in April 1911.[36] This is one of the dates known with certainty about this period of his life. To most Pentecostals and charismatics today,

---

[33] Boulton, *Jeffreys*, p. 7.

[34] Hathaway, 'Hutchinson', p. 53.

[35] *Elim Evangel* 10.34-35 (25 Dec 1929), p. 529.

[36] Hudson, *Schism*, p. 69. Letter from Cartwright to Hudson, 13 January 1997. Jeffreys was baptised by Pastor Price Davies 'on the side of the mountain at Yny-shir'.

as to most Christians in the Book of Acts, water baptism preceded baptism in the Holy Spirit. To both Jeffreys brothers the two events were in reverse order and about a year apart. Adult baptism by immersion implied allegiance to the tradition of the Baptist Church but this was not the one to which either Jeffreys belonged. So, by submitting to adult baptism, George Jeffreys was helping to cut himself off from the Independent Congregational Church where he had been converted and learnt so much. Without the necessary education, without a Pentecostal pulpit, and without access to the congregations of his childhood, he must have felt the obstacles blocking the way to full-time ministry were insurmountable.

In the period between his conversion in 1904 and his eventual launch into full-time ministry we note his steps along the way. At first he was active in his spare time either in open-air preaching alongside Glasnant Jones his minister or in prayer meetings. And then he found himself confronted by the new Pentecostal movement from 1907 onwards. At first both he and Stephen resisted this movement and spoke against it and only changed their minds after Edward Jeffreys, Stephen's son, spoke fluently in tongues and quoted scripture. It was the obvious charismatic endowment on the nine-year-old boy that persuaded both his father and his uncle George that Pentecostals were truly recipients of the Spirit. From this time onwards the two brothers shifted in a Pentecostal direction and, as we have seen, were baptised in the Spirit in 1910. Stephen appears not to have had any dealings with Hutchinson but George, younger and unmarried and perhaps freer to travel to meetings, thought for a while that this was where his future lay.

All this changed when George was accepted for Bible training in Preston.[37] In 1909 Cecil Polhill and Alexander Boddy had set up the Pentecostal Missionary Union (abbreviated PMU) with the intention of preparing men and women for work overseas, especially in India or China. Polhill, like Boddy, was an Anglican but had previ-

---

[37] 'A candidate schedule duly filled up and signed by George Jeffreys of Swansea with satisfactory recommendations was read and it was resolved that he be admitted on probation for training under Mr Myerscough at Preston and that the latter be notified and asked if he will kindly make the necessary arrangements for the reception of this candidate.' *PMU Minute Book* 1 (21 Sept 1912), p. 190, Minute 6.

ously been a member of the famous 'Cambridge Seven' who had gone out as missionaries across the world.[38] Polhill, who had worked on the borders of Tibet for many years before his wife died, had inherited money from his family estate and, travelling home to Britain via Los Angeles, had called in on the Azusa Street Revival, received a baptism in the Spirit, paid off the mortgage on the Azusa Street building, and then settled in Britain, remaining a widower who used his financial resources to further Pentecostalism in many discreet, generous, and gracious ways.[39]

He heard about George Jeffreys, probably through the leader of the Pentecostal work in Swansea. A note in *Confidence* for November 1912, p. 21, reports:

> George Jeffreys, who is well recommended by the leader and others of our Swansea centre, has been accepted for admission into our Missionary Training School at Preston, as a candidate for foreign service.

If the centre in question was Belle Vue Chapel, it must have been regarded as one of 'our' centres and acceptable to Boddy and Polhill as part of the network being fostered through the activities of the Sunderland conventions. The word 'centre' is interesting because it implies that Boddy did not see the Swansea gathering as a church because at this stage and, for the rest of his life, he never deviated from his view that the Pentecostal outpouring was intended to enhance existing congregations and denominations rather than to bring new ones into being. In any event, George Jeffreys applied to the PMU and was accepted for training in Preston, funded through the generosity of Polhill and put into the charge of

---

[38] He told readers about his missionary adventures in *Flames of Fire*, the journal he edited and published. For instance, in February 1913, he wrote about travels in the north-western part of the Yunnan province of China.

[39] John Usher, 'The Significance of Cecil H. Polhill for the Development of Early Pentecostalism', *Journal of the European Pentecostal Theological Association* 29.2 (2009), pp. 37-60. See also P.K. Kay (1995), *The Four-Fold Gospel in the Formation, Policy and Practice of the P.M.U.* (Unpublished MA Thesis, University of Gloucester). Kay (p. 64) lists Polhill's donations to the PMU between October 1909 and February 1926 and although the list is not exhaustive, the total amounts to £10,903, which is a very substantial sum of money and was roughly equal to the price of a central London house.

Thomas Myerscough (1858–1932), the fatherly figure who ran the Bible school.

The Men's Training Home operated in Preston from the summer of 1910; and, although this was seen as a temporary measure until better accommodation or arrangements could be made, it lasted for five years until a property in London was purchased. The Preston home was situated above Starkie's Wire Shop on Lancaster Road in the central part of the city.[40] By March 1911 there were some 25 students in attendance of whom three were expected to go out to a PMU mission field. The students received teaching on:

> [T]he Salvation set forth in the four Gospels; the Righteousness of God, the ruin of man by the Fall and by choice; the Great Provision set up for his deliverance, as seen in the Epistle to the Romans; the Glories of Christ and the eternal power and perfection of the Redemption and His High Priest Lord as set forth in the Epistle to the Hebrews. James, the two Epistles of Peter, and the Epistles of John, Jude, and to the Seven Churches, have received very careful consideration. Excursions have also been made into other portions of Scripture for special lessons on Sanctification, Healing, Church Officers and Governments, Gifts and the Ministry of the Holy Spirit, Dispensational Truth.[41]

Each Sunday students were sent out to preach at surrounding churches.[42] There is uncertainty about the planned length of the course – the earliest announcement envisaged two years while other indications give six months – and about the financial basis of study since students were expected to 'step out in faith' while being guaranteed board and lodging.[43] The course was formative in the sense that students were expected to gain practical experience in ministry and, according to one source, to get out of bed at 6 am each morning to pray.[44] The school's orientation and its training were distinc-

---

[40] I am grateful to Steve Jenkins for this information and other information about the Preston Training Home.

[41] *Confidence* 4.3 (Mar 1911), p. 68.

[42] I am grateful to Dr. Leigh Goodwin for providing information about the Training Home and George Jeffreys' time there.

[43] *Confidence* 2.6 (June 1909), p. 130.

[44] Presumably, the doctrine taught would have included the Pentecostal theology of 'The Baptism in the Holy Ghost with the Scriptural Signs' – a belief to be

tively Pentecostal and this must have meant that the 'dispensational truth' taught to students exploded the notion that spiritual gifts were confined solely to an earlier dispensation.

A photograph in *Confidence* shows six of the students.[45] Myerscough himself seems to have done most of the teaching. He was known for his scrupulous attention to the details of Scripture, levelheaded, trusted on all sides, thought to be originally from the Brethren[46] and perhaps Jewish and who had himself received Spirit-baptism at Sunderland in 1909. The students in Myerscough's care turned out to be an extremely distinguished group because they included not only George Jeffreys but also W.F.P. Burton (1886–1971), the founder of the Congo Evangelistic Mission. More important to Jeffreys' future, the students also included E.J. Phillips and Percy Corry who were later to serve with him in Elim.

In a valuable biographical sketch Donald Gee points out that the ministry of Myerscough was multiplied many over times through his students.[47] If one examines the sermons of George Jeffreys or of Willie Burton, one immediately sees a close attention to the biblical text, a logical approach to the meaning of the words on the page, and all this is contained within an overarching gospel-driven purpose. We know that Myerscough lectured on the priestly office of Jesus in the book of Hebrews, weaving together the Old and New Testaments. It is reasonable to suppose that at least some of Jeffreys' later expository power stems from the teaching he received in Preston even though, as it turned out, he was only there for about six weeks.[48]

---

held by all PMU missionary candidates (*Principles of the P.M.U.* – Section 6: 'Soundness of Faith').

[45] *Confidence* 6.10 (Oct 1913), p. 205.

[46] David Garrard, 'William F P Burton and the Birth of Congolese Pentecostalism', in Martin Lindhardt (ed.), *Pentecostalism in Africa* (Leiden: Brill, 2015), p. 78, cites a letter by John Carter stating Myerscough had come from the Plymouth Brethren, and Carter was a man keen on factual accuracy ... so perhaps the general view was correct. Others consider Myerscough to have had a Methodist background: see William Counsell, *Fire Beneath the Clock* (Nottingham: New Life Publishing, 2003), p. 21.

[47] Donald Gee, *These Men I Knew* (Nottingham: Assemblies of God Publishing House, 1980), p. 69.

[48] The site attended by George Jeffreys was in operation from 1910–1915. In 1913, Polhill opened another (unofficial) PMU Home at the same time under an

Jeffreys stayed a short time in Preston because he received an emergency call from his brother, Stephen. Behind the scenes there may have been slightly more to George's decision than that. Among early Pentecostals there was opposition to training on the grounds that the baptism in the Holy Spirit provided everything anybody needed to equip them for ministry. This might lead to an attitude that glorified ignorance or demeaned the human mind. Donald Gee, in writing about the early history of Pentecostalism, drew attention to opposition to even the simplest Bible training while pointing out that, oddly enough, Pentecostals accepted that missionaries would need preparation for spreading the gospel overseas.[49]

Beyond all this, again in the case of the training school at Preston, was another internal contradiction. The Pentecostal Missionary Union had been founded by two evangelical Anglicans who, nevertheless, had received a Pentecostal baptism and spoken with other tongues. Yet each of them remained Anglican and accepted the rightness of infant baptism. Both were too wise to resist adult baptism by immersion; and, indeed, the China Inland Mission, which Polhill knew well, had resolved internal tensions about variant modes of baptism or theologies of Holy Communion, by allowing individual missionaries to hold their own views. Nevertheless, Myerscough did not accept the validity of infant baptism while leading lights in the PMU did.[50] There is no evidence that tensions between Myerscough and Boddy and Polhill surfaced although recent correspondence has come to light showing that Burton, one of Jeffreys' fellow students, was strongly opposed to infant baptism and regarded it as a pernicious doctrine.[51] George Jeffreys by contrast, though he unquestionably believed in adult baptism by immersion, did not lose respect for the PMU.

Meanwhile, back in Wales, a small assembly in a colliery area at Cwmtwrch about 15 miles from Swansea decided to hold mission-

---

Anglican, Rev. H. Wallis, presumably because he wanted to encourage the Pentecostal movement to remain within the bounds of established denominations.

[49] Gee, *Wind and Flame*, p. 60.

[50] Myerscough had joined the council of the PMU in 1911. See Peter K. Kay, *The Four-Fold Gospel*, p. 67.

[51] David Garrard, 'Burton's Early Years of Ministry and Doctrine under the Auspices of the PMU', *Journal of the European Pentecostal Theological Association* 32.1 (2012), pp. 3-14. See also Garrard, 'William F.P. Burton', p. 77.

ary meetings over the period of the Christmas holiday. George, who had preached for the mission and knew its people, recommended that Stephen take the three-day preaching engagement. Stephen, still obliged to earn his living down the coal mine, accepted the invitation and, according to his son, told a friend of his, 'Well, Billy, if God blesses me this time, I shall never return to the coal-mine'.[52] Stephen saw the blessing of God on his preaching ministry as a sign that he could afford to leave the mining industry for good. His younger brother was finding a path into ministerial life and perhaps God would help him along the way too.

The three planned days of the mission stretched on for seven weeks and at some point early in 1913 Stephen, whose stock of sermons was limited, sent a desperate telegram to George asking for assistance. The story is told in Polhill's own journal, *Flames of Fire*, in February, 1913:[53]

> Mr Jeffreys was urged to come again and take a three days' mission, commencing Christmas Day. He went ... and the mission is still going on (as we go to Press). Mr. George Jeffreys, brother to Stephen, and a student at the Pentecostal Training School, Preston, Lancs, was urgently called to help Stephen, and has been with him since. The Missionaries have tried to get away, but all men throng them, they want to be saved, and there is none to tell them; they must stay. A look of solemn concern, of fear of the unseen, is on the faces of all. How they sing the hymns, too. The favourite is 'Send the light, the blessed Gospel light, let it shine from shore to shore.' ... Up to the present there must be 130 sinners saved, some whole families.

Polhill himself made the journey to south Wales and saw for himself all that was happening. He accepted that the demands of the classroom could not compete with the urgency of a living revival; and, although the PMU tried to persuade George to return to Preston, he never did.[54]

---

[52] Jeffreys, *Stephen Jeffreys*, p. 6.

[53] Polhill, *Flames of Fire* 10, p. 2.

[54] The minute for 14 May, 1913 reads, 'George Jeffreys having been absent from training at Preston for some weeks while conducting Mission in Wales and London, the Council thought it was very desirable for him to return to Preston

Further insight comes from the pages of *Confidence*.[55] The two brothers are described as engaged in 'an apostolic Welsh revival' and Stephen Jeffreys is compared to Evan Roberts. Hopes for a fresh revival fire are in the air though, this time, with Pentecostal phenomena: the two brothers pray for the sick and 'remarkable cases of healing are reported' (p. 28). George Jeffreys' letter is published:

Dear Pastor Boddy,

The work here is deepening, and numerous conversions are taking place daily, and many have received the Baptism of the Holy Ghost with the Signs following. Praise the Lord! Some miraculous cases of healing have also taken place, and it is a real Apostolic Revival … The dear Lord is once again drawing the multitudes after Him. We think of commencing at Llandrindod next week. Kindly receive our thanks for your earnest prayers on our behalf.

Yours in the Master's Service, GEO. JEFFREYS.

A photograph shows the two brothers with Stephen standing and placing a protective hand on the shoulder of George, who sits and looks young enough to be his son.

By the time a full haul of converts had been made and the new mission established sufficiently to appoint its own leadership, the two brothers took up an invitation to mid-Wales, not far from Llandrindod Wells, at Penybont where, in a long-standing Quaker area, they exchanged the industrial scenery of a mining district for the isolated countryside of Radnorshire.[56] Here, in an old Quaker meeting house, they began a new mission with a handful of people in attendance and the fresh challenge of creating new spiritual momentum. They shared the preaching, sometimes both preaching in the same meeting, and, at least on some days, holding afternoon and evening meetings.

---

for training under Mr Myerscough at an early date and it was resolved that Mr Polhill see G Jeffreys hereon' (original capitals).

[55] *Confidence* 6.2 (Feb 1913), pp. 27-29.

[56] *Confidence* 6.3 (Mar 1913), p. 49. A photograph on page 64 says the meetings took place near the village of Llandegly. The report also shows they preached in Penybont, with the implication that they preached in several nearby venues.

One afternoon, to their surprise, Alexander Boddy arrived unannounced. He had taken the train from Sunderland, booked into a local hotel and found his way to their services. He joined the brothers for lunch at a local farmhouse and soon came to know and like them – with a result that he invited them to speak at the Sunderland Convention later that year.

During the revival, the daughter of a local draper was miraculously healed and Boddy learnt about this and met her. The healing was so dramatic and so well attested in the neighbourhood that it seems to have been a turning point both for the campaign itself and the brothers. From this time onwards, their confidence in divine healing grew sufficiently for them to begin to make it a central part of their evangelistic outreach, which was how they saw their future ministry. There had been criticism of incipient Pentecostalism's tendency to look inward, to 'have a good time' and to avoid evangelism. The brothers turned outward from the beginning and understood the power of the Holy Spirit as committed to the great mass of humanity. Boddy continued,

> Brother Stephen and Brother George and I had a long heart-to-heart talk. They feel that the Lord needs evangelists in Pentecostal work to-day. There are many teachers and would-be teachers, but few evangelists. The Lord is giving an answer through this Revival to the criticism that the Pentecostal people are not interested in Evangelistic work, and only seek to have good times.[57]

Following the mid-Wales mission, George was invited to London and stayed from March 24 to May 16 at 'Maranatha', the missionary rest home run by Mrs Crisp. Based there, he held services in several city churches and halls – for instance the Welsh Wesleyan Church – and was well received without hitting the heights that were to come later in his life.[58]

---

[57] *Confidence* 6.3 (Mar 1913), p. 48.
[58] Cartwright, *Evangelists*, p. 35.

The Sunderland Convention, 1913, and Beyond

The Sunderland conventions appear to have had an entirely beneficial impact upon the George and Stephen.[59] They introduced the
two young men to a much wider circle of Christians than they were
accustomed to and helped them understand the role of the Pentecostal movement in relation to the rest of the church and, by extension, the rest of the world. By public affirmation, their preaching
and beliefs in healing and tongues were confirmed; and, in passing,
they learnt the importance of national publicity in the print media.
George spoke at successive evening meetings that were open to the
public. On the first evening the hall was 'crowded to the doors and
out into the street' and on the second evening, entitled 'Conditions
of an Apostolic Revival', he shared the platform with Smith Wigglesworth and took Isa. 52.1, 2 ('Awake, Awake; put on thy strength
O Zion') as his text.[60]

The 1913 convention also had a valuable consequence. Mrs
Penn-Lewis' book, *War on the Saints*, attacked the emotional and
Pentecostal elements in the Welsh Revival by connecting them to
deceiving spirits in the last days.[61] Mrs Penn-Lewis was firmly rebut-
ted in a dignified and rational manner, something both brothers ap-
preciated.[62] Given that her book was said to have been written 'with'
Evan Roberts, the Jeffreys brothers were leaving the hero of the
Welsh Revival behind and moving into a new theological landscape.

Perhaps the only unforeseen consequence of the conventions
was that John Leech, later a strong advocate of British-Israelism
and influential on Jeffreys, spoke at Sunderland; and, if the two men

---

[59] Although they were both invited, only George is mentioned as preaching at
the 1913 convention.

[60] *Confidence* 6.6 (June 1913), p. 114.

[61] *Confidence* 6.6 (June 1913), p. 111. The statement was issued by the International Advisory Council (Pentecostal).

[62] As much as possible, the brothers kept the lid on controversy. Boddy set an
example, 'There has been renewed opposition of late in England against the truth
and experience of the Pentecostal Baptism. The Editor of "Confidence" does
not feel that bitterness should be met by bitterness. He regrets the lack of generosity and chivalry in some of the things recently written' (*Confidence* 5.9 [Sept
1912], p. 202).

had not met before, George would have had heard him there. At the time Leech offered an innocuous sermon on Christology.[63]

George preached at nearby Silksworth after the convention ended and in this he was joined by Stephen.[64] The inclusion of George's name on the roster of speakers at the convention would have done more than bring him to public attention: he would have been seen as carrying the imprimatur of Boddy, a preacher who could be trusted and whose doctrine was in line with the developing tradition of British Pentecostalism. George himself would have heard convention discussions on the Second Coming, Pentecostal baptism, healing, and mission and would have extended his theological comprehension of the work of the Holy Spirit beyond Welsh nonconformity.

It is likely George read *Confidence*; and, for its part, the journal regularly reported the meetings he held – and this continued for at least four years.[65] Among the doctrines floating around the Pentecostal scene at the time was one concerning celibacy and the importance of abstaining from marriage in preparation for the Second Coming.[66] Although this doctrine never managed to gain a strong grip on Pentecostalism in Britain, it did provoke two sober and well-argued articles by Thomas Myerscough presenting the biblical bases of marriage and singleness.[67] George himself was never to marry and one might be forgiven for imagining that the debate forced him to weigh the arguments carefully. Singleness had the advantage of enabling unencumbered focus upon the work of God by saving the minister from the distractions of family life.

---

[63] He took a kenotic position, emphasising the self-emptying of Christ (Phil. 2.7).

[64] *Confidence* 6.12 (Dec 1913), p. 244.

[65] George drew attention to glossolalia (speaking in tongues) in the early church and quoted an article published in *Confidence* in May 1914 in his book *Pentecostal Rays* (London: Elim Publishing Company), pp. 162-70.

[66] 'Some false prophets are going about in our day from assembly to assembly (setting themselves up as teachers) secretly teaching and persuading married people to become eunuchs, or to adopt the eunuch life, with a great show of plausibility and holiness, teaching that eunuchs are holier than the married' (*Confidence* 6.7 [July 1913], p. 145).

[67] *Confidence* 6.7 (July 1913, p. 144 and 6.10 (Oct 1913), p. 203.

As the year 1914 arrived George is on the brink of his mature ministry. Stephen took a pastorate at Llanelly and his son speaks of his seven happy years there. In May, they held a convention where George preached and he wrote to *Confidence*:

> Greetings in JESUS precious Name! The first Pentecostal Convention at Llanelly came to a close on Sunday evening, after a ten days' glorious victory. Large numbers have been turned away from the hall every evening, unable to gain admission. Sinners of the deepest dye received cleansing through the precious Blood, and twenty-two received the Baptism into the Holy Ghost, speaking in new tongues. Praise the dear Lord! ...
>
> My Brother Stephen is at Cwmtwrch this week ... I am making arrangements for special Camp Meetings in Bangor, Ireland, during July and August.

One Sunday evening in July 1914, while Stephen was preaching, his son wrote,

> [A] very remarkable vision appeared on the wall during my father's address, which was reported in many of the leading newspapers ... a lady sitting near to my dear mother drew her attention to a Lamb's head which appeared on the wall at the back of my father.

And 'presently the vision changed in to the living face of Jesus Christ represented as "A Man of Sorrows"'. The vision remained on the wall for six hours and Stephen could only interpret it as

> [A] warning concerning the Great War ... it made a profound impression upon father's life and ministry, and he preached Christ as the only solution to all our problems with even greater power than ever before.[68]

On 28 June of that year, in the city of Sarajevo, within the Austro-Hungarian Empire, the Archduke Franz Ferdinand and his wife were visiting the more restless parts of their domain. A plot whose details are still obscure was hatched to assassinate the Archduke. His car took a wrong turning and was forced to roll backwards

---

[68] Jeffreys, *Stephen Jeffreys*, p. 11.

down the street (it had no reverse gear) and passed Gavrilo Princip who, armed with a pistol, fired two shots at close range and killed the Archduke and his wife.[69] These events within the Balkans were to trigger the First World War, lead to the deaths of 16 million people and deal a political and military blow that would ultimately result in the dissolution of the British Empire.

---

[69] I am following the account given by Max Hastings, *Catastrophe: Europe Goes to War in 1914* (London: Collins, 2013, Kindle edn, loc 501).

4

THE IRISH YEARS

Although George Jeffreys had shown himself to be a promising and effective preacher in Wales and a few places in England, it was in Ireland that he really made his mark. His ministry led to the formation of specifically Pentecostal churches. He grew from being an evangelistic preacher, and then an evangelistic preacher with a healing ministry, until he became a truly apostolic figure who left behind living and self-sustaining Spirit-filled congregations different from any of the other congregations that had previously existed in Ireland.

After his invitation to Ireland in 1913, Jeffreys sailed over to Belfast and stayed in the home of the Gillespie brothers and prepared to hold meetings in Monaghan, 65 miles to the southwest. Advertising leaflets were printed but then, at the last minute, the meetings were cancelled because the Methodists from whom he was hiring the hall discovered that Jeffreys held Pentecostal beliefs.[1] So nothing substantial came from the 1913 foray into Ireland although, with hindsight, a useful reconnaissance had taken place. Jeffreys had grown to know the Gillespie brothers better – and they remained steadfast supporters of him for the rest of their lives – and had seen Belfast with its shipyards and Georgian houses at first-hand as well as the more typical outlying market towns where he later preached. He would have found Ireland similar to Wales although with the important religious difference that the Roman Catholic Church in Ireland was far stronger than it was in Wales; and, in ad-

---

[1] Cartwright, *Evangelists*, p. 39.

dition, Ulster Protestants were politically attuned and politically conservative in a way that distinguished them from Welsh Noncon-formists who supported Lloyd George's Liberal party. More than this, Jeffreys would have found a sprinkling of tongues-speaking believers who had received their experience through attendance at Sunderland.

TENT PITCHED ON CHAPEL FIELDS.

Here we have a picture of the Tent taken one morning in the notable Chape
Fields, Belfast. Years before on this same spot David Rea, the well-know
Irish Evangelist, had preached to crowded congregations in his big tent. Th
Gospel that moved the masses under this great Evangelist saw them once agai

moved under the ministry of our leader. People streamed into the tent and cam
into contact with the Christ of the Foursquare Gospel. The Saviour, the Healer
the Baptiser, the Coming King, being presented to hungry crowds, many soul
were saved and bodies healed. Pastor William Henderson is seen standing o
the left and Frederick Farlow is on the platform on the right.

Early tent campaign in Chapel Fields, Belfast, during the 1914-18 war.

A young George Jeffreys preaches on the second coming of Christ. William
Henderson is seen standing on the left. At this stage in his life
Jeffreys wore a clerical collar.

We know that Jeffreys returned home to Wales and took part in a ten-day Pentecostal convention of 'glorious victory' at Lannelly. The convention had been evangelistic because his letter to *Confidence* contains a cameo of a 'notorious prizefighter' who had the 'tobacco demon destroyed in him'.[2] There were other healings on this occasion and the brother of Evan Roberts, Dan Roberts, was one of the preachers. It was still Jeffrey's desire to reignite the Welsh revival and this, perhaps, lay behind his desire to go to Ireland which had, in 1859, experienced a famous revival that had adjusted the religious landscape and strengthened Protestantism for several generations.[3]

Taking advantage of the steam ferry Jeffreys was able to cross backwards and forwards between Liverpool and Belfast.[4] During the first part of 1914 Jeffreys preached at the Emmanuel Baptist Church in Plymouth and saw the beginnings of revival there.[5] He then returned to Bangor, near Belfast, in Ireland to conduct a Full Gospel Convention in July and August with well-known speakers.[6] The terminology 'Full Gospel Convention' implies sensitivity to the Irish religious situation. The 'full' gospel might be another label for the Pentecostal gospel but was less provocative.[7] Photographs of the tent show it to be a white canvas marquee with a placard reading 'The Coming of the Lord Draweth Nigh' (Jas 5.8) outside. Jeffreys himself is prominent in the group wearing a winged collar and bow tie and next to visitors from London, New York, and Los Angeles.[8] People may have slept in tents near the marquee because Boulton makes reference to the 'Bangor Camp Meetings' but there is also a photograph of guests outside a substantial property to which 'friends were frequently invited'. Whereas Jeffreys had signed himself in *Confidence* in May 1914 as 'your little brother in Christ' he was now beginning to move to the centre of the action. He is not seek-

[2] *Confidence* 7.5 (May 1914), p. 92.

[3] J. Edwin Orr, *The Second Evangelical Awakening in Britain* (London: Marshall, Morgan & Scott, 1949).

[4] I am assuming this was the route he took. There was a ferry from Holyhead to Dublin but the train north to Belfast was not direct.

[5] Cartwright, *Evangelists*, p. 41. The 'spirit of revival' continued to the following year. See *Confidence* 8.4 (Apr 1915), p. 78.

[6] Cartwright, *Evangelists*, p 39.

[7] *Confidence* 7.6 (June 1914), p. 117.

[8] E.C.W. Boulton, *George Jeffreys: A Ministry of the Miraculous* (London: Elim Publishing House, 1928), facing p. 60.

ing to work for another denomination but is, mentally at least, starting to look as if he might found his own.

War was declared in August 1914 but daily life for ordinary people in England and Ireland carried on peacefully enough to start with. Britain's army was relatively small so that, once the war began in earnest, volunteers were welcome and the recruitment figures demonstrate that large numbers of young people quickly joined up in the confident expectation that the war would be 'finished by Christmas' and that the Kaiser would be taught a lesson for bullying poor little Belgium. Between August 1914 and February 1915 there were 50,000 volunteer recruits from Ireland as well – implying even where Irish nationalism was powerful, men still felt the justice of the Allied cause;[9] and, when the passenger liner, *Lusitania*, was torpedoed and sunk by a German U-boat off the west coast of Ireland and bodies washed ashore in May, Irish public opinion, like public opinion elsewhere in the world, was outraged. There were, it is true, financial inducements for joining up since, in places where unemployment was high, the Army provided consistent employment and promised to look after families in the event of casualties.

By the autumn of 1914 Jeffreys was in England again and reported in *Confidence* on his visit to a German camp with over 2,000 prisoners. He was accompanied by Booth-Clibborn and Dr Phair and was able to speak to the prisoners and to circulate gospels and tracts. 'We told them that we had nothing to do with the war, but to bring to them the gospel of Christ. After the meeting two came up to us and said: "we belong also to Christ".'[10] And then, at the end of the year, Jeffreys carried out 14 days of mission in Coulston, Croydon. The pastor reported to *Confidence* of 'days of great power and blessing' when 'souls were saved, backsliders reclaimed and many baptised in the Holy Ghost with Bible signs'. Jeffreys gave an unashamed proclamation of the evangelical message with accompanying visible phenomena. The pastor's report records the power of God knocking a man off his seat onto the floor.

---

[9] Keith Jeffrey, *Ireland and the Great War* (Cambridge: Cambridge University Press, 2000), pp. 7, 9, 17.

[10] *Confidence* 7.11 (Nov 1914), p. 205.

By December Jeffreys was back in Belfast. He spoke at a Christmas convention at the Elim assembly in Dover Street and then stayed on for the new year in 1915.

Formal Beginnings in Ireland

It was here in Monaghan on Thursday 7 January 1915 at a meeting convened in Knox's Temperance Hotel that the formal founding of the Elim Pentecostal Church may be dated. The minutes of the meeting and descriptions of it indicate how deliberately and seriously the seven people who gathered laid their plans to reach Ireland with the gospel.[11] This was not merely to be a convention or a series of services put together over a few weeks but a strategic long-term attempt to bring the full gospel to people – 'for the purpose of … reaching Ireland with the full Gospel on Pentecostal lines'.[12]

The group was to call itself the Elim Evangelistic Band and they concluded with the decision that:

> George Jeffreys, of South Wales, who was present with us, be invited to take up a permanent evangelistic work in Ireland and that a centre to be chosen by him for the purpose of establishing a church out of which evangelists would be sent into towns and villages, and that a tent be hired, for the purpose of holding a Gospel Mission during the month of July to commence the work in Ireland.[13]

The Irish believers had heard Jeffreys on several occasions and knew what he could do. They realised he would be an acceptable minister within Irish religious culture. He was sincere, logical, unemotional (and not English!) but also warm and determined and he could, like all Ulster's evangelical Protestants, say that he believed the Bible from cover to cover. If we are looking for the origin of Jeffreys' strategy in Ireland, it might lie with the circuit system set

---

[11] The seven were: George Jeffreys, Albert Kerr, George Allen, Fredrick Farlow, Robert and John Mercer, and William Henderson.

[12] Chris Cartwright, *Defining Moments: 100 years of the Elim Pentecostal Church* (Elim Pentecostal Church, 2014), p. 25.

[13] Cartwright, *Evangelists*, p. 43. Actually the name was first 'Evangelistic Band' then in the minutes of 8 July 1916 became 'Elim Evangelistic Band'.

up by John Wesley whereby Wesley himself broke new ground and then appointed local preachers to go out to sustain the freshly-formed groups of believers in villages and towns by operating out of a large central congregation. There is no reference to this system of church planting and itinerant ministry in the minutes of the first meeting held at the Knox Hotel, but the ideas sketched are compatible with the Wesleyan notion of a central church and orbits of co-ordinated evangelists. We know, in August 1915 when the mission had started, Jeffreys was conscious of walking in Wesley's footsteps. 'Monaghan is a place situated almost in the heart of Ireland', he wrote, 'where John Wesley was imprisoned for preaching the same Gospel which I am now privileged to proclaim'.[14]

There is another explanation of the origin of the strategy and this might be found in a vision one of the Christian ladies in touch with Jeffreys had received. He wrote in the *Elim Evangel* in 1920:

> At the time this vision was given she knew nothing of the plans proposed in Monaghan. The vision consisted of a large golden ring, out of which came a dazzling brightness brighter than the sun at midday, and out of the ring ran many other rings in all directions. She prayed to God for the interpretation, and it was given. 'The large ring is the first Elim assembly, and out of it shall come many other assemblies'.[15]

The January meeting looked ahead only as far as the summer of 1915. The tent campaign sounds as if it was to be a repeat of what had been achieved at Bangor the previous year, though this time further south in Monaghan. While summer evangelism was foreseen, this was to be backed up by the search for a permanent centre from which operations could be directed. R.A. Darragh and William Gillespie managed to find a building in Belfast, an old laundry in Hunter Street, that could serve as their base and so a three-year lease was taken out in the names of Jeffreys and Gillespie, with Jeffreys being named as the pastor.[16] The congregation was to be called Elim Christ Church and became the first Pentecostal assembly in Ireland – and Ireland at the time was a united country with-

---

[14] *Confidence* 8.8 (Aug 1915), p. 156.
[15] *Elim Evangel* 2.1 (1920), p. 6.
[16] Cartwright, *Evangelists*, p. 44.

out borders between north and south. Jeffreys was only 26 years old.

Jeffreys drew up a statement of faith for the church entitled *What We Believe* and made clear that the Elim movement was, in the words of the epistle of Jude, 'contending for the faith once delivered to the saints'. Jeffreys and his companions saw themselves as fighting against the fashionable dilutions of the gospel brought about by liberalism and modernism and knew that 'we can expect the onslaught of the enemy to be furious, in his seeking to counterfeit and produce extravagance, which we must be careful to avoid, by continuing steadfastly in God's precious word'.[17] This balance between a full-blooded Pentecostal message and an awareness of the dangers of wild emotionalism was to characterise the approach later taken by Jeffreys. Yes, they were to be committed to a Bible-based Pentecostal message; but, no, they were to avoid rabid emotional excess. They were also clear at the outset that they had no intention of luring people to join their movement from existing churches.[18] They saw themselves as an evangelistic agency rather than as a new denomination although, inevitably, as time went on a new denomination is what they became.

Hand in hand with their commitment to Pentecostalism was a belief that the gospel they preached was an answer to the problems of Ireland. In their Bangor camp-meeting they had sung, 'Ireland for Christ' because they believed the message of Jesus was the answer to all Ireland's woes – economic, political, or personal.[19] At a time when nationalism was volcanically bubbling under the surface and shortly before the uprising in Easter 1916, the men and women of Elim saw Christ as transcending all social and religious differences. For them, true hope lay not in politics but in the evangelical gospel.

There had been attempts to give home rule to Ireland since the end of the 19th century. The problem has been expressed as one of

---

[17] Cartwright, *Evangelists*, p. 44.

[18] Boulton, *Jeffreys*, p. 28. Cartwright, *Evangelists*, p. 44. In another sign of non-exclusivity the minutes of the Elim Evangelistic Band (7 Jan 1918) agree that full members of all churches can become members of Elim without leaving their own churches.

[19] Boulton, *Jeffreys*, p. 34.

'double minorities' in that Protestants were in a minority in the south and Catholics were in a minority in the north.[20] By and large political differences ran along religious lines although it would be simplistic to say that the underlying problems of Ireland were entirely religious. That analysis is conveniently advanced by those who are antireligious. Republicanism was a reaction against the British Crown; but, because Republicanism was strongly associated with Roman Catholicism, Protestantism was associated with Unionism. There was little secular republicanism in Ireland of the kind found in France and there is no inherent connection between Catholicism and Republicanism. The third Irish Home Rule Bill was finally given Royal assent in 1914 but shelved because of the outbreak of war. Consequently, the parties who wanted home rule felt thwarted even though the British, still an imperial power, were willing to consider an intermediate status for the Irish similar to that held by the dominions of Canada and Australia.[21] Beyond high-sounding political ideals, however, ran the realities of employment. The Belfast shipyards (where the Titanic was built) were manned by Protestant workers with the result that unemployment among Roman Catholics was high, and there was no comparable heavy industry in Dublin or the south. It was in these circumstances that Jeffreys and the Band hoped to change the hearts of Irishmen; they had, after all, seen peace break out in the Welsh coal mines as a consequence of the 1904–1905 revival and so their hopes were not completely unrealistic.

The Plan is Carried Out as the World Changes

Having made plans for a summer outreach at Monaghan in July 1915, Jeffreys was back in England in May of that year to continue his work in Plymouth.[22] He was there for six weeks and wrote that 'sinners of the deepest dye, Magadalens, drunkards, as well as professors of religion who had no possession, have come weeping their

---

[20] Orr, *Awakening*, p. 53, shows Roman Catholics amounted to 41% of the population in Northern Ireland.

[21] A.J.P. Taylor, *English History 1914–1945* (Harmondsworth: Penguin, 1975), p. 209 and *passim*.

[22] *Confidence* 8.5 (May 1915), p. 89.

way to Calvary'. More than successful evangelism he was able to report 'members are receiving the baptism into the Holy Ghost accompanied by Bible signs in the public meetings, without any laying-on of hands' and that 'in one meeting alone we counted over 20 who had received, and were speaking in new tongues for the first time'. These descriptions of revival meetings might have been reported by any of the great evangelists of the past apart from the reference to outbursts of speaking in tongues. What excited Jeffreys was the parallel with Acts 10.44 (which he cited in his report) when the apostle Peter had first preached to the Gentiles; they spoke in tongues without any preparation, teaching, or imposition of hands and this was taken as a sign by the Jerusalem church that mission to Gentiles should begin.

The report given by Jeffreys of the revivalistic meetings in Plymouth was backed up by the local pastor who added, 'Christians of all denominations are being brought into the blessing, baptised and "built it together for a habitation of God through the Spirit"', implying the Pentecostal revival was a force for Christian cohesion and sent for the renewal of the whole church.

At Whitsun, at the end of May, Jeffreys was at Caxton Hall, Westminster to speak at a London Pentecostal conference convened by the Anglican, Cecil Polhill. Alexander Boddy was also present and the dating of the event implies that it replaced the old Sunderland conventions which had now come to an end. Presumably the wealthy Polhill funded the hire of the hall, which is why the convening fell to him rather than to Boddy. By now the war was impinging on everyone's consciousness. Soldiers were being assembled in southeast London in readiness for a crossing to France and George took part in a mission to them, perhaps by speaking in a local church or at the camp itself. When George left for Monaghan, Stephen Jeffreys arrived to continue preaching to the soldiers. What no one knew at the time was that the Battle of the Somme was to begin on the first of July and result in death and disablement on an industrial scale.

George's commitment to Ireland was strong but not exclusive. Indeed, as the Irish outreach continued, there were times when George needed to return to preach in England to help fund what he was doing in Ireland. Against a background of war – the guns of the Somme could be heard on Hampstead Heath in London[23] – Jeffreys and his co-workers stuck to their plans. Urgency may have been added by the deteriorating military situation and the Herculean struggles of the British Empire, though it is doubtful whether anybody at the time quite realised how the history of Europe was now turning in a new direction. By pressing on to evangelise Ireland, the Jeffreys team was imposing its own vision on social reality. They could have given up their preaching, put on uniform and marched off to the trenches. Instead, they placed their ministerial calling higher than the call of king and country. Or, to put this in a way that W.F.P. Burton, a fellow graduate of the PMU mission school, put it to himself as he launched his mission into Congo in 1915: 'men were going to battle to give their lives for an earthly king so I must be prepared to sacrifice my life in the service of a heavenly king'.[24]

The tent was erected in Monaghan's town park and the outreach lasted a month and was successful from the beginning. The local paper, *The Northern Standard*, reported 'on each occasion there was good attendance'.[25] Jeffreys, in writing to *Confidence*, was able to say 'sinners have been trembling under conviction of sin' and a young man who had been stricken 'from his seat by the power of God and burned all his cigarettes the following day'.[26] The report made no reference to speaking with other tongues although 'people come from great distances, and a hunger for revival is such that people come from miles around, and the cry is everywhere, "come over and help us"'. If we draw any implications from this, they are that the meetings themselves were conducted along strictly evangelical lines and that the 1859 revival, a folk memory within the Protestant community, remained alive.

Jeffreys also reported, 'the young men who organised this campaign are on fire for God, and have received quite recently the outpouring of the Holy Ghost'. Such a report shows Jeffreys looked

---

[23] http://en.wikipedia.org/wiki/First_day_on_the_Somme.

[24] A paraphrase.

[25] Quoted by James Robinson, *Pentecostal Origins: Early Pentecostalism in Ireland and in the Context of the British Isles* (Carlisle: Paternoster, 2005), p. 130.

[26] *Confidence* 8.8 (Aug 1915), p. 156.

for a nucleus of enthusiasts within a locality to carry out the initial preparation and organisation. Later in the same report he said he planned to buy the 'Bangor tent' and go through 'the Irish districts' the following summer, an insight into Jeffreys' ability to think ahead strategically. The group who had prearranged the Monaghan outreach at the start of January met again in July and added two extra people to the Elim Band, Robert Ernest Darragh, who had been a student at Preston, and Margaret Montgomery Streight.[27] Jeffreys was beginning to assemble a team around him for carrying out pastoral work, evangelism, or other tasks connected with the busy campaigning schedule.

After the summer evangelism in Monaghan, Jefferys returned to England for a tent mission near Hereford. The report in *Confidence* states:

> The children of God have been strengthened and built up, and very many, precious souls saved – entire families in some cases – while dear ones have been baptised in the Holy Ghost and fire as they sat upon their seats in the meetings.[28]

The pattern here in response to Jeffreys' ministry is similar to what was seen earlier. There have been conversions and Spirit-baptisms. The report asks for prayer for 'many who are under deep conviction of sin' as well as converts who are 'going through severe persecution through coming to the mission' which indicates that the message of Spirit-baptism was unpopular and resisted, presumably by non-participating churches.

In the same issue, there is an account of mission at Westminster Central Hall with addresses given by John Leech as well as the two Jeffreys brothers while Cecil Polhill (again presumably paying for the hire of the hall) presided and spoke himself. A brief description is given of this sort of meeting in Donald Gee's portrait of Polhill who, while he admires the man, finds

> his continual repetition of 'Beloved friends' became a byword and a joke. Audiences that had come to hear Stephen Jeffreys

---

[27] Cartwright, *Evangelists*, p. 44.
[28] *Confidence* 8.10 (Oct 1915), p. 196.

squirmed with impatience as he inflicted on them his little homilies from the chair.[29]

During the first three weeks of October 1915 a united evangelistic rally was held in London and it is possible that this is the same set of meetings as was reported as being at Westminster Central Hall.[30] 'Mr Leech's preaching was clear, logical, and convincing' and 'a band of friends from Wales materially contributed to the brightness and power of the singing and prayer'. There was an 'enquiry room' for the men challenged by the preaching to confirm their commitment to Christ; and, poignantly, many of the hearers were servicemen who 'left almost immediately for the front'. After the initial enthusiasm for war, news of the casualty rate filtered back and filled the new recruits with foreboding. Where better place to face up to their mortality than in a religious meeting?

On Christmas Eve, 1915, Jeffreys was in Belfast when the minutes of the Evangelistic Band express thanks for the success of his ministry since taking over the 'Pastorate of Elim Christ Church' because 'many souls had been saved and accepted into membership'. The plans made at the start of the year were being fulfilled. 'Each one present at the meeting felt God had given them the desire of their hearts – the formation of a good centre for sending out Spirit-filled workers'. Moreover, the purchase of a large tent for £20 would enable summer evangelism. There is also a report of a 'missionary tour' in Galway, on the west coast of Ireland, which may have taken place in the late autumn of the year.

Expansion in 1916
By 1916 the war on mainland Europe had reached a bloody stalemate. So many thousands of young men had been killed that the British government was forced to introduce conscription with the result that able-bodied people within the correct age bracket were required by law to sign up for military service. A significant number of early Pentecostals had examined the Bible and come to believe that Christians should never kill; they were only excused from military service after having faced tribunals where their pacifist convictions were tested. Ordained clergymen were automatically exempt

---

[29] Gee, *These Men I Knew*, p. 75.
[30] *Confidence* 8.11 (Nov 1915), p. 214.

from military service and this is why Jeffreys' acceptance of the pastorate of the Elim Christ Church in Belfast the year before is significant (and there are occasional photographs of him wearing a clerical collar).[31] He was never expected to serve in the military although, in Ireland, where there were concentrations of the Republican population, pressure to join the army was less intense.

The Elim Mission Hall in Hunter Street, Belfast, was energetically active. By January 1916 there were two Sunday services and evening meetings on Tuesdays and Thursdays.[32] Robert Darragh, one of the first members of the Elim Evangelistic Band, organised and prepared a mission beginning on 9 January that year. The following month they planned to campaign in Ballymena, a prosperous mainly Presbyterian market town linked by rail with Belfast. The town had a long and distinguished religious history both Catholic, by association with Saint Patrick, and Protestant, by association with the 1859 revival. It was about three times larger than Monaghan and connected by minor roads and pathways with a scattering of farming villages within a few miles of the market square.

Jeffreys began his assault on Ballymena in February 1916, making use of the YMCA building. As with Monaghan, he was responding to the invitation of a group of people, in this case led by James and Angus Gault.[33] Initial meetings were promising enough to make an Easter campaign worthwhile. Jeffreys went for five weeks and saw 120 conversions as well as 23 'baptised with the Holy Ghost ... under the direct action of the blessed Spirit, without laying on of hands'.[34] Presbyterianism frowned upon emotionalism or extravagant behaviour; but, when men and women began speaking in tongues without any obvious physical contact with the evangelist, the vocalisations could be interpreted as being sent from heaven.

The number of converts was sufficient to allow the founding of a regular Pentecostal assembly although it is not clear precisely when this was formally instituted. Down in the south of Ireland, during Easter 1916, and while the five-week mission was in full

---

[31] E.g. in Boulton, *Jeffreys*, facing page 53.
[32] *Confidence* 9.1 (Jan 1916), p. 17.
[33] Robinson, *Pentecostal Origins*, p. 162.
[34] *Confidence* 11.7 (July-Sept 1918), p. 54.

flow, Republicanism in Ireland boiled over into militaristic violence. The central Post Office in Dublin was seized using smuggled arms and ammunition during an attempted political coup lasting six days. The Irish Republican flag was hoisted and a new republican government was proclaimed. The British quickly moved troops across the Irish Sea and the revolt was soon put down with a severity that was remembered bitterly. Leading perpetrators were executed by firing squad after brief military court hearings and the seeds of lasting resentment and hostility were sown, especially when the damaged city was then subject to military occupation.

One of those living in Dublin was John Leech (1857-1942), a distinguished barrister and a senior law officer, who had been devoting increasing amounts of time to preaching alongside Jeffreys. He and his wife were absent from Dublin at the time of the uprising because they were part of the Ballymena crusade. It was natural for the Elim contingent to believe Leech was being providentially protected. His house was not far from the shooting and shelling.

Jeffreys returned with the Evangelistic Band in June 1916. He must have found a friendly farmer with a field where he could pitch his 275-seat tent. He remained for five weeks preaching nightly to packed congregations; and, in a letter in *Confidence*,[35] he recalled kneeling down with Alexander Boddy and his wife at one of the Sunderland conventions and praying the Pentecostal blessing might reach Ballymena. The letter was written to show that this prayer had been heard. The context showed that Pentecostal preachers could rebut the criticism that they were primarily concerned with their own spiritual experiences and not with genuine evangelism. Jeffreys, along with Mrs Leech, had felt compelled by the Spirit to rise at 5 am to pray. During the evening one of the favourite hymns of the Camp was:

Ireland for Christ! the martial chorus
 Echo near and far,

With His banner floating o'er us,
 Bids us forth to war.

---

[35] *Confidence* 9.8 (Aug 1916), pp. 130-31.

Ancient land of saints and sages,
  Circled by the sea,

From the slavery of ages
  Rise to liberty.

There were echoes of the 1859 Revival, and these were confirmed by conversations with the 'old inhabitants' who could remember back that far. Unwittingly, perhaps, Jeffreys was tapping into the political anxieties of Irish Protestants since the words 'Ireland for Christ' surely implied that Ireland was not to be ruled by a Republican Dublin government swayed by Roman Catholicism.

Jeffreys returned to Ballymena on 31 December, 1916, and stayed for a week's convention.[36] 'The town hall was crowded to excess, and many turned away. Seven hundred were present on the Sunday evening meeting.'[37] The practice of a winter convention in a hall and summer meetings under canvas was paying dividends in the form of permanent congregations. There were beginning to be too many of these congregations for Jeffreys himself to look after single-handedly. He could not continue a hectic schedule of nightly meetings in one place after another without reliable pastors to nurture the congregations he was building up and leaving behind. And so the story of his years in Ireland is the story of the building of a team of loyal workers alongside the building of a set of congregations.

The Elim Evangelistic Band

The first meeting of the Elim Evangelistic Band took place, as we have said, on 7 January 1915. This was an informal occasion, and in it George Jeffreys is described as 'Evangelist Jeffreys' and the agreement was that a church should be established out of which evangelists could be sent to county towns and villages. The six men who made this decision had little or no money and so 'agreed that God promises to supply the temporal needs of every evangelist who would be called into the work, and that through prayer and

---

[36] *Confidence* 9.12 (Dec 1916), p. 196.
[37] *Confidence* 10.1 (Jan-Feb 1917), p. 10.

faith in his promises he would prove himself to each one Jehovah Jireh'.[38]

Here the faith principle is enunciated, a principle that was well known to missionary organisations ever since Hudson Taylor had set out for China with the same attitude in the 19th century. It comes from the Old Testament occasion when the name of God as the one who provides was given in Gen. 22.8. There was no big congregation or wealthy donor behind George Jeffreys when he committed himself to the evangelisation of Ireland.

The meetings of the Band followed at irregular intervals and the second, on 3 July 1915, noted,

> God had already answered our prayers and given a definite call to Mr RE Darragh and Miss Margaret Streight to work in connection with the band of evangelists which we had claimed by faith for the Pentecostal movement in Ireland.[39]

The language is aspirational in the sense that the band of evangelists had not existed but were 'claimed by faith', language that implies a determination to follow the biblical example of the heroes of Scripture. Darragh remained a loyal friend to Jeffreys until his death nearly 50 years later and Margaret Steight later married one of the other evangelists. She had already been rejected by the PMU for being too fanatical while Darragh had attended the training school at Preston.

The third meeting took place on 24 December, 1915, in Belfast and records the absolute delight of the group in the realisation of their plans and dreams. The congregation at Elim Christ Church in Belfast had been established and 'many souls had been saved and accepted membership, while lives and homes had been transformed'. In addition, the tent had been purchased for £20 to allow summer evangelism. At the fourth meeting, on 24 April, 1916, again in Belfast, there was reference to 'increasing blessing upon the general work of the evangelist especially in Ballymena' and 'a definite call by God had been given to Mr Henderson and Mr Frederick Farlow into the Evangelistic Band' so, little by little, the number of evangelists was increasing; and, although the minutes do not make

---

[38] Minutes the Evangelistic Band (7 Jan 1915).
[39] Minutes the Evangelistic Band (3 July 1915).

this explicit, the common life they lived and the common purse they shared were at the centre of their growing comradeship. They ate together and prayed together and, on occasions, shared the same dormitories.[40] Some structural differentiation begins to appear, however, with the agreement that John Leech KC and the Rev Thomas Hackett, the former an older and wealthier man in secular employment and the latter, also an older man, ordained within the Church of Ireland, should become 'advisory members of the Band Council'. Their appointment clearly gave Jeffreys, who was undoubtedly the leading light, the option of taking advice and sharing responsibility with a wider range of Christians than the young band represented.

At the fifth meeting, the band formally named itself as 'the Elim Evangelistic Band'; but, more significantly, Leech was elected as president of the Band and agreed that at future meetings members and Advisory members should be the only ones to be invited and that the invitations should be issued by the 'Superintendent', i.e. Jeffreys. In this way, an authority structure was being created, first by limiting membership and then by putting the frequency of meetings in the hands of an acknowledged Superintendent. What had begun as a kind of band of brothers and sisters working equally together has now some sense of hierarchy perhaps, one might speculate, as a consequence of Leech's legal mind being brought to bear.

At the sixth meeting on 4 January, 1917, in Ballymena, the minutes record that 'Mr John Leech, KC', is presiding and that three resolutions are carried, each of which requires a proposer and a seconder. The minutes of the previous meeting are accepted and a discussion of finances leads to a decision about collecting boxes being placed in the homes of 'Christians interested in the work' (rather than the public at large) for the purpose of 'applying the temporal needs of the workers'. The new basis of finance marks a slight shift away from the faith principle with which the group began. The group continues to tithe to foreign missions but now all the initial expenses of the evangelists should be paid. In this way a distinction is made between living costs and expenses. Finally, remaining monies after deducting expenses and tithes to foreign mis-

---

[40] Robinson, *Origins*, p. 192.

sions should be divided among members of the Band so, presumably, everybody received the same.

A year later, on 2 January, 1918, the Band met at the Town Hall in Ballymena and on this occasion the Superintendent, 'Pastor George Jeffreys', presided and again resolutions were passed, in this case unanimously, indicating that some show of hands or vote occurred. The finances were obviously stretched so that 'after considering the financial side of the work we agreed to discontinue the practice of having one common fund for all evangelists after this quarter ends' and, instead, all collecting boxes be kept separate and, it appears, the tithe taken out of these. Regular members of the Band, including the Superintendent were to receive all expenses for tents and halls, heating and lighting 'whether permanent or taken or taken for special missions'. So the costs of the operation were now impinging on the whole enterprise to the extent that rents and utility bills were a consideration. What is not clear is what happened to gifts given to individual members. In the past whatever one person received was placed in the common fund but this now appears to be discontinued, perhaps because there were obvious inequalities in the capacity of different members of the team to raise money. Additionally, one wonders, how Jeffreys' frequent travel costs back to the UK were paid. In any case once the money from the collection boxes had been used to pay the tithes and expenses, 'the remainder [was] to be divided by the Superintendent as the needs arise in the different parts'. This made the members of the team personally beholden to him even if, as, ex-Band members later recalled, Jeffreys was generous and fair.

Soon afterwards, on 7 January, 1918, a special meeting was held in central Dublin in John Leech's impressive home. The group expressed thankfulness for the 'many precious souls that have been saved' and then turned their attention to business. They agreed the necessity of allying for the purpose of 'uniting under one name the following branches viz Elim Evangelistic Band, Elim Assemblies and Elim Missions', the Alliance to be known as the Elim Pentecostal Alliance. Second, that the members of 'all churches who are born again and who stand for the Full Gospel can become members of the same without leaving their own churches'. This was a restatement of an earlier non-sectarian principle, probably to make Elim less threatening to existing Protestant denominations at a time when factionalism among Irish Protestants would have weakened their united political front. In addition it was agreed that a 'Council with plenary powers' should be formed and 'members of the Council should be chosen by the Superintendent, Pastor George Jeffreys' for the purpose of 'governing the work in all centres' and 'erecting and owning buildings that may be necessary for the work in the future'.

Here, again, the legal brain of Leech is surely discernible. All the different parts of Elim were brought into a single entity and the new Council's membership was going to be selected solely by Jeffreys – a device that placed enormous practical powers in one pair of hands, especially since the Council was intended to govern the work and own the buildings. There is a centralisation of power and ownership within this conception; and, undoubtedly, Jeffreys was the man whose faith, gifts, and energy were indispensable to the cause; his authority was now being legally recognised and established.

There was also a practical reason for the creation of the Council as a property-owning body. In November 1917 Jeffreys had been made the residuary legatee of Mrs Jane Rees.[41] She had heard Jeffreys preach in Hereford and got to know him and then died rather suddenly. The contents of her will revealed that she left her entire estate 'after payment of all debts and legacies' to Jeffreys so that he stood to receive approximately £5,000, a sum equal to approximately 40 times the average annual wage at the time. This eye-watering financial benefit would have settled many of the outstanding debts on buildings in Ireland and set the work on an even more favourable footing. Not surprisingly, perhaps, Mrs Rees' family contested the will so that, when the settlement was finally made in September 1925, only about £1,000 was forthcoming.[42] Had the money been left to a legally constituted entity like the Alliance Council, the payment would have been more difficult to challenge and perhaps easier for the family to understand. It is reasonable to assume Leech, after speaking with Jeffreys in December, foresaw the path down

---

[41] Cartwright, *Evangelists*, p. 46.

[42] Robinson, *Origins*, p. 156 gives the exact amount as £901 plus £150 in shares.

which Elim was moving and the prospect of other legacies and wished to forestall future legal dispute and delay.

The Band continued its work during 1918 although the minutes do not reflect either the end of the war or the changing social conditions in Ireland. The Band had to deal with a case of immorality after one member, T.J. Logan, had made a confession to two or three witnesses. Logan had actually confessed to Jeffreys in December 1917 but Jeffreys kept quiet though presumably received assurances that nothing like this would ever happen again. Yet in May 1919 Logan became involved with a different woman. The case was fraught with tension because Logan hit out at Jeffreys by accusing him of being 'a very bossy man and a hard man to work with'.[43] Leech was called in to preside over the disciplinary hearing and, after forensic questioning, exposed contradictions in Logan's story that led to his dismissal from the Band.

An important structural change occurred in 6 January, 1919, when it was agreed that the Elim Pentecostal Alliance Council should become the authority governing the Elim Evangelistic Band and that the Council should comprise Leech, Jeffreys, Hackett, Stephen Jeffreys, Henderson, and Darragh. In effect, the Band was now 'under' the Council and the vestiges of the system of government Jeffreys was to operate in his Elim heyday were now visible. He governed within and through a small close group of men whom he nominated. He was not in sole charge but he was in a position where he was unlikely to be strongly challenged within the group and where, indeed, he might expect emotional support and valuable advice.

The Band was at the heart of the dynamic expansion in Ireland. Its dedicated members were expected to attend all the conventions and some might carry out evangelism while others settled into pastoral ministry.[44] They worked hard, travelled often by train or bicycle, and acknowledged Jeffreys as their leader. Despite their disciplined lifestyle, Jeffreys was not short of potential recruits. He was choosy about whom he accepted and made a practice of listening to

---

[43] Robinson, *Origins*, p. 178.

[44] R. Mercer might be contrasted with R. Darragh in this respect. E. J. Phillips became the pastor of Milford near Armagh in 1920 (see Robinson, *Origins*, p. 175).

their preaching before taking them on. On one occasion he led them all down the aisle into a convention meeting and ensured that they served the congregation, and this was intended to be a symbolic act. They were an elite group, without uniform, but always, when they could afford it, smartly dressed. Joining the Band, indeed, was marked by a kind of ordination service.[45] A formal posed photograph taken in 1915 shows five of them and another, in 1920, shows how they had grown to 22.[46] Jeffreys himself underwent an ordination at the hands of Rev Moelfryn Morgan, of the Welsh Congregational Church, on 18 July 1917 in a huge canvas tabernacle as part of a revival campaign in Belfast.[47] Whether this implies that Jeffreys saw the Elim congregations as having a special affinity with Welsh congregationalism is unclear; there do not appear to have been any subsequent formal links with congregationalism but in the light of what happened in the late 1930s, it would be possible to argue that Jeffreys did not originally have a centralised ecclesiastical system in mind. In any event, the ceremony of ordination was obviously important to Jeffreys and those who were ordained were expected to be completely committed to ministry.

By December 1919, when Jeffreys was considering a return to England, the first edition of the *Elim Evangel* was published and the names of the band members are prominently displayed beneath the names of the Council.

Turning Towards England

The Great War came to a sudden end in November 1918 and troops were slowly decommissioned to return home. The Irish Guards, for instance, did not march through the streets of London until the Spring of 1919.[48] Yet the surviving troops with wounds to their bodies and their minds were gradually returning to take up their old jobs. Lloyd George, still prime minister, had promised a

---

[45] Robinson, *Origins*, p. 186.

[46] *Confidence* 124 (Jan-Mar 1921), p. 10.

[47] Boulton, *Jeffreys*, p. 40 describes the event and his words may imply that Stephen Jeffreys, who was in Belfast at the time, also took part in the service.

[48] Rudyard Kipling, *The Irish Guards in the Great War: The Second Batalion* (Staplehurst: Spellmount, 1997), p. 192. First published in 1923.

land 'fit for heroes',[49] and in most of Britain there were expectations of imminent financial uplift to the advantage of working people. Ireland was an exception. After the arrival of so many men with military experience, the country was teetering on the brink of an armed struggle, and this was fomented by the intransigence of partisan politicians. Leech was among those who took a strongly Protestant position. He no longer saw his professional future in Dublin and had moved north. In 1922, as the partition of Ireland loomed, he was given responsibility for the Commission that dealt with the boundary changes of electoral constituencies. His redrawing of the boundaries incensed Roman Catholics since it 'took a huge Nationalist majority to win a seat, thus eating up Nationalist votes' and protecting Protestant ascendancy.[50]

The so-called Irish War of Independence was fought between 1919 and 1921, with 1920 being known as 'The Year of Terror'.[51] On one side was the Irish Republican Army, a miscellaneous group of men determined to pursue Irish independence from England, and on the other British security forces including not only the armed police of the Royal Irish Constabulary but also auxiliary troops and temporary constables drafted in to support the Constabulary. Many of these were veterans of the 1914–1918 war, nicknamed 'black and tans' from the colour of their uniforms, who, because they were not well commanded, responded with excessive force to any challenge to British rule. Violence and reprisals, including the burning and sacking of towns – a substantial part of Cork was destroyed – and villages in the south of Ireland, occurred in the summer of 1920 and hardened attitudes on all sides making the normal rhythm of evangelism and church outreach impossible.

Jeffreys kept clear of political events although his preaching could at times deliver a political punch as when he urged Protestants not to surrender their historic rights. If he was beginning to consider a move across the Irish Sea to England, he proceeded cautiously. He returned to preach at conventions in Hull and

[49] Speech at Wolverhampton, 23 Nov 1918, quoted in *The Times* 25 (Nov 1918).
[50] Tim Pat Coogan, *Ireland in the Twentieth Century* (London: Arrow, 2003), p. 305.
[51] Coogan, *Ireland*, p. 82.

Wales and was given the opportunity of addressing meetings in places he had only infrequently visited before. But to transfer the whole operation to England was a large undertaking. By 1920 there were 15 Irish congregations and he had to ensure they were adequately housed and pastored. His regular funding came mainly from these congregations and it would take time to build up a similar base in England. Meanwhile the south of Ireland was progressively closed to him so that, although the original vision had been for the whole of Ireland, he now found himself far more welcome among the northern six counties where unionism was strong.

The roundup of news in the first edition of the *Elim Evangel* in December 1919 shows the progress made by the Irish centres. In Belfast 'the work of the Alliance is carried out in two different parts of the city, in the Elim Mission Hall in a poor district' and in the newer and more prestigious Elim Tabernacle in Melbourne Street. In Ballymena there is a resident pastor, Robert Mercer, where the assembly is 'a large one' whose 'blessing is spreading to several of the outlying districts'. There is reference to people receiving the fullness of the Spirit and visions during a prayer meeting. At Moneyslane there is also a large group of people but there is no full-time or permanent pastor to look after the congregation. In Portadown a Mr Fletcher is taking care of the congregation although 'there is still much opposition in the town'. In the seaside resort of Bangor there have been efforts to establish a congregation but 'the Devil seems to have opposed every inch of the way', although a Mission Hall has been opened and baptisms by immersion had taken place in the sea.[52] In Lisburn the congregation is small and there is no permanent worker but young men from the Elim Tabernacle, Belfast, keep it running. And there are missions at Eskyland, Cullybacky, and Milford.

So, having arrived to Belfast in 1913 for a reconnaissance; and, after committing himself to a visionary plan in January 1915, Jeffreys could look back with thankfulness and satisfaction on the planting of vibrant churches that would stand and thrive as, with the usual vicissitudes of nonconformist congregations, they have until the present day.

---

[52] Boulton, *Jeffreys*, photo opposite page 76.

The Crystal Palace, London

Twenty-first Anniversary Celebrations.
Crowds of 12,000 attended the meetings.

5

INVADING ENGLAND

The transition from Ireland to England and Wales was carefully made. The Belfast Tabernacle was the jewel in the Irish Crown and an extraordinary mark of the success that had followed five years of intense evangelistic activity. Could a similar centre be established in London? Beyond the Tabernacle, the Evangelistic Band showed a fervour and unity that made them 'a band of brothers' – even if there were women within the team. Wherever they went, the revival followed them and might lead to conversions in farmhouses or public places beyond the orbit of organised campaign meetings.

Jeffreys had, in any case, crossed over to England on numerous occasions even while his base was being established in Northern Ireland. His brother Stephen, meanwhile, was independently pastoring in Llanelly and causing a stir. Stephen had been introduced to his younger brother's success in Ireland and had been invited to preach in Belfast. Whether the brothers talked about jointly leading the Elim work is unknown. Probably not. Yet before making his bid for the major cities of England, George Jeffreys returned to campaign in his native Wales in 1920. E.C.W. Boulton, writing in 1928, is closest to these events and describes how the brothers combined in Dowlais and Merthyr Tydfil to hire and then buy the Ivor Street Independent Church which became the first Elim Tabernacle in

Wales.[1] Stephen Jeffreys became the first pastor by 'relinquishing the oversight of the Island Place Assembly, Llanelly, of which he had been the minister for some years'.[2] So the buying of buildings and the placing of congregations within these buildings was becoming part of George's mode of operation. The preaching in Wales brought memories of the revival. Large crowds attended and yet with the difference that, under the ministry of the Jeffreys brothers, divine healing and teaching on the baptism in the Spirit would have been prominent; and, with the sharp mind of George, supported by an underlying organisational structure: a year later a second building was bought.[3]

One of the events that would have fired the imagination of Stephen Jeffreys – and we can assume was meaningful to George also[4] – was the British capture of Jerusalem in 1917. In his biography of his father, Edward Jeffreys makes reference to the Balfour Declaration that followed the capture of the city and the beginning of a political process leading to the establishment of the state of Israel. Many Christians knew the text 'Jerusalem shall be trodden down of the Gentiles until the times of the Gentiles be fulfilled' (Lk. 21.24); and, according to Edward, his father understood v. 32 of the same chapter, 'this generation shall not pass away until all be fulfilled', to refer to the generation that had been alive when Jerusalem was placed in Jewish hands again.[5] So they believed they had witnessed a remarkably significant eschatological event that signalled they belonged to the last generation before the return of Christ. It has to be said that we do not find in the writings of George or in the *Elim Evangel* any concerted attempt to predict the date of the Second Advent of Christ; nevertheless, an added urgency was given to Pentecostal hearts and minds by events in the Middle East.[6]

---

[1] E.C.W. Boulton, *George Jeffreys: A Ministry of the Miraculous* (London: Elim Publishing House, 1928), p. 79. A photo of the building is given opposite page 92. The first building purchased was in Dowlais and the second in Merthyr Tydfil.

[2] Boulton, *Jeffreys*, p. 80.

[3] Boulton, *Jeffreys*, p. 82.

[4] He drew the same conclusions from these texts in a sermon in Westminster Central Hall in 1955 (cassette tape held in Donald Gee Centre).

[5] Jeffreys, *Stephen Jeffreys*, p. 24.

[6] As an exception to this statement, the article by T.E. Hackett 'Our Advent Hopes and AD 1923–1927', *Elim Evangel* 4.2 (Mar 1923), pp. 44-46, *does* fasten on the year 1923 as being predicted by the year-day theory that counted 2,520 years

George Jeffreys c. 1925

This is a copy of a postcard available to the Elim faithful. It shows Jeffreys,
probably in the 1920s, in a pose indicating he is ready to expound the bible.
Such photos could be purchased and sent through the post or framed
and put on a desk or mantlepiece to remind the owner to pray.

The Elim group was alive and spontaneously overflowing beyond the control of a single man. Two workers in the Channel Islands began to evangelise with the result that a report of their activities appeared in the *Elim Evangel* (March 1921, p. 47) and at the end
of September 1921 George Jeffreys and Robert Darragh went over

---

from significant dates in Old Testament history. An expectation of the rise of the
anti-Christ in the period 1923 until 1927 follows.

to hold a series of meetings on Guernsey and established a congregation.[7]

Although George Jeffreys had England in his sights, Elim in Ireland was booming to the extent that new halls were opening in 1920.[8] Among those who worked with George in Ireland was John Carter who was later to become an important figure within British Assemblies of God. Carter was a member of the Evangelistic Band and looked after the congregation in Lurgan to which he invited his brother, Howard, for eight days of meetings at some point early in 1921, and these were followed by Howard's preaching in Bangor.[9] The Carter brothers, therefore, knew Elim well and must have seen the power of George's preaching and the whole emerging cycle by which initially small meetings in tents became larger meetings in hired halls and eventually permanent congregations in Elim-owned buildings.

Even though George had preached for his old colleague E.C.W. Boulton in Hull and had spoken at the annual Kingsway conventions in London in 1921,[10] the first major effort in England made by George was at Leigh-on-Sea in Essex in the summer of 1921. The meetings (which may initially have had connections with the Apostolic Church) led to conversions and healings; and, when the water baptismal service was held in the Baptist church kindly lent for the purpose, nearly six hundred people gathered.[11] The newly pentecostalised congregation soon joined the Elim Alliance.

Two big Pentecostal pushes in London, one by Stephen Jeffreys at Horbury Chapel,[12] and the other by George near Clapham Common towards the end of 1921 illustrate the contrasting ministries of the brothers. Stephen's meetings in October 1921 were reported in *Confidence*, the *Elim Evangel*, *Flames of Fire* (Cecil Polhill's magazine) and the secular press.[13] Between 60 and 70 people committed their lives to Christ in a single evening of Stephen's campaign and testimonies of healing were included in the meetings. Stephen, indeed,

---

[7] *Elim Evangel* 2.5 (Dec 1921), p. 83.

[8] *Elim Evangel* 1.4 (Sept 1920), last page.

[9] *Elim Evangel* 2.2 (Mar 1921), p. 35.

[10] *Confidence* 13.2 (Apr-June, 1920), p. 24; (July-Sept 1920), p. 43.

[11] *Elim Evangel* 2.5 (Dec 1921), p. 84; Cartwright, *Evangelists*, p. 55.

[12] Now Kensington Temple.

[13] *Confidence* 127 (Oct-Dec 1921), pp. 53-55. *Elim Evangel* 2.5 (Dec 1921), p 74.

was known as a missionary of 'Pentecost with signs', implying not only propagation of speaking in tongues but also public miracles of healing.

Stephen was strongly Adventist.

> I expect the coming of Christ very shortly. The graves will open, the bones will form together in a new spiritual body, and will ascend into the air … Immediately among those who are left there will be fearful revolution and bloodshed. What Russia has gone through the whole world will experience.

This was a proclamation of the rapture followed by the rule of the Antichrist. 'I do not believe that either the Kaiser or Lenin is the anti-Christ. He will be of mean birth, very crafty, and full of guile, and will gain universal dominion over the world'.[14] Unsurprisingly such preaching created anti-Pentecostal reaction, especially among those whose expectations of the future drew from a different hermeneutical tradition. The Prophetical Society, an interdenominational association that gathered at Sion College, London, in its magazine, *Prophetic News and Israel's Messenger*, attacked Pentecostals:

> The movement is consecration gone off the rails … Most of the inspiration is emotional … its development … is a history of shame … Excesses of Pentecostalists open the door to immorality. They mistake hysterics for the baptism of the Holy Ghost.[15]

This caricature of Pentecostalism as being perpetually associated with wild behaviour is difficult to associate with the gentlemanly Cecil Polhill who, according to *Confidence*,[16] joined Stephen in praying for those who were ill during the Horbury Chapel meetings, and it does not accord with newspapers which took the trouble to send reporters to see at first-hand what was happening.

Overall, the secular press was less critical in many respects than anti-Pentecostal sections of the religious press. The *Yorkshire Post* (21 October, 1921), while acknowledging 'outbursts of religious fervour recalling the Evan Roberts revival scenes in Wales', reported on a young girl whose eyes were healed and a man on crutches

---

[14] Quotations taken from *Confidence* (Oct-Dec 1921), pp. 53, 54.
[15] Quotation taken from Cartwright, *Evangelists*, p. 49.
[16] *Confidence* 127 (Oct-Dec 1921), p. 53.

for more than 20 years who had walked home from the meetings without them. According to *Thomson's Weekly News* everything about the meeting 'first presented all the appearance of an ordinary chapel service, with Bible reading and hymns'. Once Stephen Jeffreys got up to speak, 'the proceedings quickly changed to the style of a red-hot Salvation Army meeting … Every now and again his melodious voice started a chorus'.[17]

George concentrated his efforts upon a disused, poorly maintained Methodist Chapel in Clapham which, late in 1921, he rented for twelve months with an option to buy at the end of the rental period.[18] The chapel was barely functioning and had land at the back that might be included in the sale. George engaged in detailed correspondence with the business-savvy E.J. Phillips over the best way of setting out the terms of the contract with the Methodists.[19] Park Crescent Church at first resisted Pentecostal ministry or, at any rate, the crowds failed to materialise until there was a breakthrough, probably brought about by a spate of local healings, which led to the enlivening of a growing congregation which, at the end of twelve months, gave an offering that was sufficiently large to justify the purchase of the building.[20] The chapel became the administrative centre of the Elim movement and offices were moved across from Belfast to Clapham.[21] So, while Stephen created a stir at Horbury, George took the decisive step of forming a congregation and in 1922 buying an administrative base from which future operations might be securely launched or, in Boulton's words, 'a centre of blessing from which lasting good has streamed to other needy districts'.[22]

---

[17] Quotation taken from *Confidence* 127 (Oct-Dec 1921), p. 54.

[18] Boulton, *Jeffreys*, p. 85. *Elim Evangel* 3.4 (Apr 1922), pp. 50-51; 3.6 (June 1922), pp. 83-84; 3.8 (Aug 1922), pp. 112-113; 4.2 (Feb 1923), pp. 23-26.

[19] E.J.P. Maldwyn Jones, *An Analysis of the Role of E.J. Phillips and an Assessment of his Leadership in the Establishment of the Elim Movement as a Coherent Christian Denomination* (MA, Bangor University, 2011), pp. 17, 18.

[20] Boulton, *Jeffreys*, p. 89.

[21] Cartwright, *Evangelists*, p. 55.

[22] Boulton, *Jeffreys*, p. 91.

Elim and Others

The fluid state of Pentecostalism in the early 1920s is illustrated by attempts to protect it from non-biblical doctrine while, at the same time, coordinating missionary activity. George Jeffreys was among eleven Pentecostal leaders who issued an advertising poster/broadsheet for a two-day conference of leaders at Sheffield in 1922.[23] The advertising called for 'more concerted action among the assemblies of Spirit-filled saints' and resulted in three resolutions. The first two concerned the setting up of a Provisional Council 'for the advice and assistance of the Assemblies in the United Kingdom and Ireland' and that this council should submit a plan for fellowship, business, and cooperation to the assemblies for their judgement. The third resolution is, in many respects, the most interesting because it agreed that:

> A solemn note warning should be sent to all assemblies concerned against the practice, not found in New Testament Scripture, of 'enquiring of the Lord' for guidance through gifts of tongues, interpretation or prophecy, a practice that has caused and is causing such havoc among the saints.

An important clue to the state of affairs and Pentecostal circles prior to the mid-1920s is revealed by this third resolution. There were obviously abuses of the gifts of the Holy Spirit and, indeed, possibly an oblique reference to the practice growing up or troubling 'apostolic' churches. The vocal gifts of the Spirit were being used

---

[23] It is true there had been earlier attempts to bring about some sort of organisation at Swanwick in 1920 and 1921. See David Allen, *Signs and Wonders: The Origins, Growth, Development and Significance of Assemblies of God in Great Britain and Ireland, 1900–1980* (PhD, London University, 1990), p. 102. There is reference in E.N. Bell's fourth letter (29 Mar 1922) to the Welsh Assemblies to a conference in Swanwick in 1922. 'We have just received notice from another bunch of good ministers, namely in England, who are planning to come together in what they call a Leaders Conference, and are to hold their meeting during the Swanwick Convention in April. The call for this meeting is issued by W. Burton, E.C. Boulton, A. Carter, J. Douglas, Geo. Jeffreys, T.H. Jewitt, G. Kingston, Thos. Myerscough, E.W. Moser, J. Tetchner, J. & L. Walshaw, E. Blackburn. Correspondence is to be addressed to Pastor E.C. Boulton, 2 May St. Hull, Yorks'. Given the dates and that Swanwick and Sheffield are only 35 miles apart, it seems likely that Bell is referring to the Sheffield conference of 1922 and not the earlier Swanwick conferences.

for guidance with the result that very subjective pseudo-divine directives could be given to individuals who were naive enough to ask for them. George Jeffreys, because of his earlier connection with William Hutchinson and his close observation of the Apostolic Church in Wales, knew all about these dangers.[24]

The 1922 conference was a disappointment to its organisers. Although a Provisional Council of nine men was elected by the 38 people present and although a constitution of 'the General Council of the Assemblies of God in Great Britain and Ireland' was produced and circulated to local assemblies (with a tear-off slip to be signed by those who accepted it), only ten in England and Scotland and one of the twenty in London felt they could sign.[25] The reasons for reluctance to identify with the General Council's Constitution are unclear: it may be that the suggestion that the General Council 'be empowered to exercise any needed discipline as required by Scripture over the recognised workers of the assemblies' smacked too much of an authoritarian central government.[26] Whatever the reason, George would have been able to gauge the generality of Pentecostal opinion outside the Elim sphere from this tepid response.

After the failure of the Sheffield 'unity conference', the Jeffreys brothers preached first in Grimsby, Lincolnshire, between January and March 1922 and then moved across the Humber estuary to preach in the port of Hull in May.[27] The brothers appear to have functioned in tandem as they did in Wales with Stephen making the initial impact and staying for longer and then George arriving to put his seal on the proceedings and transition the converts into their own building. This is not to say that Stephen's meetings were 'more

---

[24] The other dangers according to Donald Gee, lay in the direction of 'ultimate reconciliation' (a doctrine that assumed everyone would end up in heaven eventually) and Oneness Pentecostalism, which denied traditional and historical doctrines of the Trinity (Gee, *Wind and Flame*, p. 124).

[25] There were actually eleven leaders but the Welsh assemblies agreed to choose their two representatives from among themselves later. Footnote 15 above gives twelve but I cannot reconcile the figures.

[26] These paragraphs describing the Sheffield conference are taken from W.K. Kay, *A History of British Assemblies of God* (PhD, University of Nottingham, 1989), p. 73.

[27] *Elim Evangel* 3.1 (Jan 1922), p. 8; *Elim Evangel* 3.3 (Mar 1922), p. 43; *Elim Evangel* 3.4 (Apr 1922), pp. 51-54.

Pentecostal' than George's but those who knew the brothers and compared them were always astonished at the difference between them. In fact, it was suggested that they might be stepbrothers because they looked so different and their approaches were contrasting.[28] Stephen was broad shouldered, of medium height and came easily across as an ex-miner who preached with all the passion of a prophet but without the refinement that came so naturally to his brother. George was of slighter build and would have been at home in the drawing room of any great house. Whereas Stephen appears to have been extroverted, impulsive, and disorganised, George was introverted, organised, and most happy with a few friends. Both preached a full gospel though George slightly shifted his position on the significance of speaking with tongues. The original statement of faith held by the Elim Evangelistic Band put tongues as an evidence of baptism in the Holy Spirit, a position retained in the 1923 re-statement, but modified by 1934.[29]

By all accounts the two east coast campaigns were astonishingly successful in terms of the number of converts gathered, the varied and dramatic healings performed, the public impact on the community, and the subsequent establishment or enlargement of permanent congregations: 'ever since those memorable meetings of 1922 the writer has had the privilege and pleasure of ministering to the church which was formed as a result'.[30] The *Elim Evangel*, in a pattern that was to be repeated many times over the next 15 years, reported

> conversions, baptisms in the Holy Ghost, and special cases of healing. The outstanding service during the campaign was the service held at the 'Gaiety,' a large skating rink when about three thousand people listened intently to Pastor George Jeffreys for over one hour deliver in a scholarly, soul-inspiring style an address on The Second Coming of Christ.[31]

---

[28] Cartwright, *Evangelists*, pp. 51, 52.

[29] *Elim Evangel* 4.8 (Aug 1923), p. 169. Malcolm R. Hathaway, 'The Elim Pentecostal Church: Origins, Development, and Distinctives', in K. Warrington (ed), *Pentecostal Perspectives* (Carlisle: Paternoster, 1998), p. 36.

[30] Boulton, *Jeffreys*, p. 110.

[31] *Elim Evangel* 3.5 (May 1922), p.74.

After the exhausting demands of the first part of the year, the two brothers crossed over onto the Continent and took part in the annual Swiss Pentecostal Convention at Goldiwil. There was a baptismal service in the River Aare at Berne before the revivalists moved into Italy to visit Rome. They saw the 'great church buildings which were like prison houses, altars, statues, vestments and everything the carnal mind could devise to in order to obscure the light of the Gospel' and then moved on to the Appian Way where they imagined the Apostle Paul as a prisoner being encouraged by welcoming believers on his journey to stand before Caesar.[32] They descended to the catacombs and then saw the Vatican itself in all its splendour before travelling to Naples and viewing Mount Vesuvius. This kind of tourism was the privilege of the rich in the 1920s but the brothers had earned their holiday and by it acquired a taste for travel.

The year 1923 also saw continued preaching outside London. George Jeffreys held meetings in Letchworth and preached on Christ as God's gift to the world and the Spirit as God's gift to the church.[33] In August he held a convention in Cleethorpes on the east coast of England and then travelled up to Kilsyth, in Scotland, for 'a rich time of blessing' in what became a premier Pentecostal centre, though it remained denominationally independent for more than 50 years.

In September the brothers took ship to Stockholm where they saw the large trend-setting Pentecostal assembly pioneered by the ex-Baptist Lewi Pethrus. It was here, probably for the first time, that George Jeffreys came upon a form of Pentecostal organisation – or deliberate avoidance of organisation – that he was later to champion. Under the dominant influence of Pethrus the Swedish assemblies were fiercely independent of each other and shunned any connecting features that might have turned them into conventional denominations. The only entity was the local church with its satellite or daughter congregations and it was from the large mother church that mission work locally and overseas was directed. George was impressed by what he saw and wrote:

---

[32] Boulton, *Jeffreys*, p. 118.
[33] *Elim Evangel* 4.11 (Nov 1923), p. 230.

The local assemblies alone are organised. Love is the only tie holding the many assemblies together. This, combined with strict adherence to the plain Word of God, will EVER obviate the necessity for further organisation. From the commencement of the works, complete unity has prevailed. Sweden has been spared the intrusion of the various disciple-gathers and their shibboleths such as are found in other countries.[34]

From there the brothers travelled to Norway and met T.B. Barratt whose large congregation was known throughout the country. Moving on to Germany they stayed briefly in Berlin.

In the centre of the city we saw the statue of Martin Luther, the monk, who shook the world. One can easily imagine the thoughts that pass through our minds as we gazed upon the open Bible in the hands of the reformer. If Germany, with the other nations, had rejected the Poison of New Theology and higher criticism, they would have escaped the awful judgements that were now falling upon them.[35]

Jeffreys never accepted any criticism of the Bible, and this remained his position until the day of his death. He saw biblical criticism as the enemy of the Christian faith and believed the judgement of God fell upon nations which conceded the orthodoxy of the Reformation. Finally, after visiting Amsterdam and the home of the founders of Dutch Pentecostalism, he returned to England. There he completed a mission in Tamworth near Birmingham.

In March 1923, a young pastor from Edinburgh, Donald Gee, wrote to Elim to enquire about taking his church into the Alliance. Gee was to become the foremost Pentecostal historian of his day and a respected teacher whose ministry was eventually known all over the Pentecostal world. After conscientious objection during the Great War he had become the pastor of a small double-fronted building in Edinburgh.[36] The pressures on Gee built up partly because, until his arrival, the congregation had been accustomed to unrestrained self-expression and partly because soon after his arrival

---

[34] *Elim Evangel* 4.10 (Oct 1923), p. 214.
[35] *Elim Evangel* 4.11 (Nov 1923), p. 231.
[36] Donald Gee, *Bonnington Toll: The Story of a First Pastorate* (London: Victory Press 1943).

competing Pentecostals (including the Apostolics) began aggressive proselytization.[37] Gee had no salary to speak of and eventually devised a method for his remuneration that depended upon an offering box at the back of the church. It was a method designed to free him from controlling deacons but it had the effect of leaving him close to poverty which, when the wealthiest family of the assembly decided to emigrate to Australia, stole up on him and took him to the edge of a nervous breakdown.[38]

He had already preached in Ireland and contributed at least one article to the *Elim Evangel*.[39] So he wrote to Belfast asking about joining the growing Elim Alliance on the probable assumption that his financial difficulties would be relieved if he were part of a larger organisation. The correspondence between Gee and Elim has been preserved.[40] He was on the brink of committing himself to join but was held back from doing so by one of his trustees who objected to the handing over of their building to an outside body. And here is the nub. The buildings in Elim were held centrally and even those buildings which had not been erected as a result of the ministry of George Jeffreys were still expected to place themselves under the denomination's ultimate control. Even preachers as gifted as Gee were expected to submit to directions from the Elim Council, a circumstance that would have hamstrung Gee and hampered his later extensive travels. The incident gives an insight into the organisational requirements of Elim: presumably those who had been brought into their pastorates by Jeffreys and supplied with congregations and buildings through his ministry, had little or no objection. By contrast, men like Gee, who had come into the ministry along their own path and had taken independent congregations forward, found themselves being expected to surrender liberty in exchange for only a moderate level of financial security and pastoral support.

---

[37] R. Massey, *Another Springtime: Donald Gee, Pentecostal Pioneer* (Guildford: Highland, 1992), p. 40.

[38] Massey, *Springtime*, pp. 40-48.

[39] *Elim Evangel* 3.5 (May 1922), pp. 76-78.

[40] Massey, *Springtime*, pp. 41-48.

American Months and Deciding the Future

At the start of the year 1924, the organisational and relational shape of British Pentecostalism was undecided. By the end, and after statesman-like leadership, it was resolved. At the start of the year, George was focused upon campaigns in the light of the near return of Christ. The *Elim Evangel* carried a sermon George preached on the Second Coming from the text of Jas 5.1-8, a sermon that envisaged the rapture of the church and the tribulations visited on those left behind: 'unsaved will be left on the earth to pass through the fiery furnace of an indescribable time of trouble' and as a consequence 'the reins of government of the world will be thrown loosely upon the shoulders of ungodly men, and the dark forces of iniquity will break forth upon the maddening world'.[41] Jeffreys believed the 'revolutionary seed sown in days gone by will bring forth its harvest in blood' and that he could 'hear the clash of steel in the battles of the armies of the world'. It was a nightmarish picture full of foreboding.

Early in 1924, and quite unknown to Jeffreys, Nelson Parr, pastor of a Pentecostal congregation in Manchester, wrote a letter to fourteen Pentecostal leaders excluding any of those in Elim and asked them to meet to discuss the setting up of a group of churches organised on a basis that allowed local church autonomy to be retained; the meeting took place on 1 February.[42] The scheme had already been in operation in the United States since 1914 with the formation of the Assemblies of God. Each congregation was independent but subscribed to the same statement of faith. Each congregation sent one representative to an annual conference where decisions were made by voting and (in due course) elected councils could carry out collectively agreed policy on matters such as credentialing and missions.[43] The scheme was in direct contrast to the one already in existence in Elim since it invested authority in an elected body drawn from members of what became a ministerial confer-

---

[41] *Elim Evangel* 5.1 (Jan 1924), p. 6.

[42] Massey, in his PhD thesis, deduces 15 people were present at the initial meeting called by Parr (p. 88).

[43] In the early days, the word 'presbytery' was used instead of 'council'. So the General Conference was the 'General Presbytery', and so on.

ence. The leaders who met in Birmingham had, by the end of March, attracted 70 congregations which agreed to sign up to the proposals. The pastors or elders of these churches were invited to a meeting in London in May to finalise and refine the arrangements. The first morning of this conference was interrupted by a telegram from George Jeffreys asking why, in a discussion of unity among Pentecostal people in Britain, he had not been invited to attend.[44]

So Jeffreys, together with a delegation from Elim including E.J. Phillips, arrived on the second day. Despite enthusiasm for the creation of a big inclusive Pentecostal body, Howard Carter was cautious because nobody knew how well the newly created Assemblies of God would fare whereas Elim, having been in existence for nine years, was settled and stable.[45] Would the joining of the two bodies risk the future of both? At the point of impasse E.J. Phillips, presumably with George's approval, made the 'breath-taking proposal' that the Elim workers should become the evangelistic arm of Assemblies of God.[46] This would, presumably, have allowed Elim to retain its autonomy within the larger framework which would itself have become more varied and complex. Nevertheless, caution prevailed and the matter was left in abeyance until after the Elim Band had reviewed its progress at its own December meeting.

Returning to campaigning Jeffreys preached in Ulster and then in May revisited Leigh-on Sea. On 21 June of that year, in response to invitations, he and Stephen together with R.E. Darragh, E.C.W. Boulton and James McWhirter, embarked from Southampton upon the *Empress of Scotland* for a four-month tour of Canada and Cali-

---

[44] Massey, *Springtime*, p. 53 gives the text of a letter sent to the conference. The letter is a powerful plea for Pentecostal unity and was signed by Jeffreys, Phillips, and Boulton. It may have been communicated as a telegram, which would harmonise with the account given above.

[45] Indeed Howard Carter suggested that Elim should disband, a suggestion that reflects badly on Carter but was presumably made in the interests of creating a single united body. The reference to disbanding is given in a letter by E.J. Phillips to George Jeffreys (19 January 1925) and kept in the Cartwright archives at Regents Theological College.

[46] M.R. Hatthaway, 'The Elim Pentecostal Church', in K. Warrington, *Pentecostal Perspectives* (Carlisle: Paternoster, 1998), p 16. See Massey, *Springtime*, p. 54. An undated memoir entitled *Those Early Days* of a conversation between Howard and John Carter was placed in the Donald Gee archive at Mattersey uses the word 'breath-taking' of Phillips' proposal. The proposal appears to have been confirmed in a letter of the 8 May 1924.

fornia. They visited Montreal, Ottawa, Toronto, Winnipeg, Vancouver, Seattle, Fresno, and Los Angeles before returning home. A series of supplements to the *Elim Evangel* recounted the highlights of the trip and by implication proved the Jeffreys brothers were endowed with preaching gifts that would have made them successful anywhere in the world. They saw healings and Spirit baptisms and were able to return to Britain with a larger vision of future possibilities and a conviction that the outpouring of the Spirit was being enjoyed across the world. Among those they met was Aimee Semple McPherson whose Angelus Temple was already one of the great congregations on the western seaboard of the United States.

One of the unspoken purposes of the trip must have been to view the workings of Assemblies of God close-up and at first-hand. If Elim in the UK was to join with or become absorbed in British Assemblies of God, there would be no better way of seeing a living prototype of the future. Evidently, however, George did not like what he observed. While still in the USA, he wrote to E.J. Phillips from San Jose, California, on 25 August, 1924 saying:

> The further I go in this Pentecostal movement the more convinced I am that the democratic way of doing things is wrong. I am still persuaded that nothing will hinder me from going on with the Alliance as an independent work. Subject of course to the coming Band meeting. Don't have a single thing to do with them until we can meet to discuss the whole situation.[47]

And then, from the same place on 11 September, he wrote:

> Assemblies of God is not working here. I am still determined not to join them in Britain.

It is evident that Jeffreys rejected democratic conferences and voting procedures and that, even before Elim's December 1924 conference, his mind was made up: he did not want to join with Assemblies of God in Britain any more than, as it turned out, men like Howard Carter wanted to submit to Elim's system of organisation. At the December meeting Elim expressed a formal decision:

---

[47] Cartwright, *Evangelists*, p. 57.

We, having beforehand carefully examined the minutes and prayerfully considered the question of amalgamation with the Assemblies of God of Great Britain and Ireland, believe it to be the will of God that we work each on our own lines ...[48]

For the rest of the century Elim and Assemblies of God continued side by side, friendly but separate.

---

[48] Massey, *Springtime*, p. 56.

6

AMAZING PROGRESS

Having established a congregational bridgehead in London and office space, George Jeffreys was ready to evangelise consistently wherever he could on the British mainland. The war, though it had finished in 1918, dealt a lasting blow to the country. Thousands of young men had been slaughtered with the result that there was a noticeable imbalance of women in the population. Many were widowed and others would never marry. As many as 2.5 million men who survived the conflict were sufficiently disabled to receive a government pension.[1] There is evidence of a rise in spiritism in the post-war years as a consequence of the sense of loss felt by many families for their missing fathers, brothers, and sons.[2] Outwardly however, the churches remained central to British life. The Church of England mustered about 2.75 million, the Roman Catholics 2.5 million, and the Free Churches 2 million; and, although these figures are not strictly comparable, they indicate the rough proportions of each of the main Christian sectors within the population.[3] Most obviously among the educated, and less obviously among the ordinary people, belief in the great doctrines of Christianity weakened. The sight of Anglican clergy dressed in vestments blessing guns and armaments before battle was sickening to men and women who had

---

[1] John Stevenson, *British Society 1914–45* (Harmondsworth: Penguin, 1984), p. 267.

[2] W.R. Inge, *Lay Thoughts of a Dean* (London: Puttenham's Sons, 1926), p. 304.

[3] A.J.P. Taylor, *English History 1914–1945* (Harmondsworth: Penguin, 1970), p. 222.

once unquestioningly taken their spirituality and morality from the teachings of the church.

One of the consequences of this was that art, and particularly literature, took an antireligious turn. The classic poem of the 1920s, T.S. Eliot's *The Waste Land*, invoked fragmented consciousness, 'broken images', and self-questioning.[4] The leading cultural voices of the day, found in the Bloomsbury group, were all anti-Christian both in their lifestyles and their writings. Lytton Strachey in his written portraits of *Eminent Victorians* mocked the seriousness and achievements of 19th century heroes and heroines while Virginia Woolf, who later committed suicide, reported herself physically disgusted when she heard that Eliot had converted to Anglo-Catholic Christianity.[5] Other popular novelists like H.G. Wells, with his scientific background, deplored any form of conservatism. Only the music hall, which continued to entertain working people, recreated the normality of life before 1914. Here ordinary working people could sing along with the entertainers in a community solidarity that humorously or sentimentally celebrated the simple pleasures of life. The cinema, soon to be a potent cultural force, was still just about in the era of silent films and broadcasting by radio was in its infancy.[6]

It was into the London of the 'Roaring Twenties' that Jeffreys launched himself. The time was ripe for an assault on the capital. Its transport system was expanding and improving. Electric trams and petrol-engine buses, often originally decommissioned military vehicles, were pressed into service. Underground trains were modernised and equipped with automatic sliding doors and lines extended. Bus and train timetables were published with the result that the collections of scattered villages on the outskirts of the city proper were now absorbed into it. Busy stations like Piccadilly Circus were rebuilt with escalators and booking halls were enlarged. As the trains and buses extended their reach, so new suburbs opened up in outer London and daily commuting became a lifestyle.

---

[4] Thomas Stearns Eliot, *The Waste Land* (New York: Horace Liveright, 1922).
[5] Adrian Hastings, *A History of English Christianity 1920–1985* (London: Collins, 1986), p. 236.
[6] *The Jazz Singer* was not premiered in London until September 1928.

As part of the boom, salaries in many jobs doubled between 1920 and 1925 after the initial drops in 1921.[7] Electric light enabled evening meetings to go ahead and transport could allow congregations in one part of the city to travel to support meetings opening in another part. The effects of the Victorian Christian heritage and latent Christian morality were seen in the good-natured or excited crowds that were willing to attend campaign meetings. There was no crowd disturbance, heckling, graffiti, or public opposition. When Jeffreys held his meetings in London, he could display banners and advertisements without attracting any counter-cultural objection. Such objections as he did encounter were subtler, and came from liberal clergy rather than working people or national newspapers.

Added to the improvements in transport and personal income during the 1920s was also a willingness of many people to participate in uniformed organisations. Uniforms had been prevalent in the streets of the London during the war and were respected by the civilian population. To join an organisation and don a uniform at a time when individualism and unconventional behaviour were frowned on was to go with the social flow. As we shall see, Jeffreys set up the Elim Crusaders, a group of young people who assisted in the holding of the Crusades by giving out handbills or preparing buildings for evening meetings. There are photographs of them marching down the street carrying advertising placards and banners. By the time we reach the end of the 20th century, uniformed organisations in Britain were in decline, but in the 1920s they were in the ascendant.[8]

Medicine was making the slow transition from the primitive treatments available in the Victorian era to the astonishing possibilities of the 21st century. Operations under anaesthetic were feasible but antibiotics had not been discovered and many treatments were palliative rather than curative. Tuberculosis still blighted many lives and malnutrition in childhood resulted in rickets and other bone diseases. Children affected in this way could grow up wearing callipers on their legs or, if spines were affected, find themselves confined to large prams or spinal carriages. On top of this, smoking

---

[7] http://hansard.millbanksystems.com/written_answers/1925/jul/30/averag-e-weekly-wages (accessed 30 Apr 2014).

[8] Robert D. Putnam, *Bowling Alone* (London: Simon & Schuster, 2000).

was medically and socially acceptable with the result that the incidence of lung diseases and cancers was higher than today. But, when illness struck, access to hospitals was limited because about half of them were privately run, making them inaccessible to the poor.[9] In these circumstances it is understandable that a boldly proclaimed message of divine healing accompanied by genuine miracles was received with joy.

Early Tent Campaign c. 1930.

Tent meetings were the easiest way to reach large groups of people in the summer months and the cost of the tent was lower than the cost of hiring a building

The Back Office

The success of Jeffreys in Northern Ireland could not be repeated on mainland Britain without an efficient back office. In Ireland, towns and congregations were closer together and could be reached in an hour or two; but, as the work spread across England and Wales, it was impossible for Jeffreys to be present everywhere. There were buildings to be inspected, rented, and bought; meetings to be advertised; travel expenses for evangelists and soloists to be paid; and a magazine to be fed with a continual stream of reports.

---

[9] Taylor, *English History*, p. 230. These are the days before the National Health Service.

Elim was fortunate in having the services of E.J. Phillips, an administrator of extraordinary ability and energy with a capacity to handle financial and legal complications, doctrinal questions, to show tact, act with foresight, and cope with the endless demands Jeffreys made. Bryan Wilson in a well-regarded book on Elim, maintained that Jeffreys was out of touch with the back office and that, when later a split occurred leading to the departure of Jeffreys, the problem lay in the classic dichotomy between a charismatic leader and a plodding bureaucrat.[10] Such an account may appear to accord with Weber's sociological theory but is not sustained by the archival evidence.

There are really two parallel narratives in the development of Elim at this stage in its history. One is given in the fortnightly *Elim Evangel* which publicised coming campaigns or reported on the success of campaigns that had already been held. It contained numerous articles that throw light on the development of Elim from many angles. It is a public narrative. The other is given by the voluminous correspondence between George Jeffreys and E.J. Phillips in the years between about 1920 and 1940. This is a private narrative. They wrote to each other frequently, sometimes every day, and the correspondence was not one-sided. Although Jeffreys was the leader and Phillips carried out his policies, they would disagree on many topics and sometimes Phillips would persuade Jeffreys of a particular course of action; and, at other times, it was the other way round. What is evident from the correspondence is the heavy involvement of Jeffreys in the running of Elim. It would be quite incorrect to say that Jeffreys simply concentrated upon the preaching and left the office work to Phillips. Phillips asks Jeffreys for decisions; Jeffreys gives his decisions and Phillips may quibble with them but he carries them out to the letter. Sometimes Phillips suggests a line of action and Jeffreys cheerfully agrees or tells him to do what he thinks best. It is a true collaboration with Jeffreys as the final arbiter but Phillips is by no means the blinkered civil servant. Moreover, Jeffreys confides in Phillips, as when there is a discussion

---

[10] Bryan R. Wilson, *Sects and Society* (London: Heinemann, 1961), p. 52: 'Here was the crisis in which the charismatic leader finds his leadership can be sustained only if he permits it to be circumscribed by the legal instrument of the bureaucratic administrator'.

about Stephen Jeffreys. In handling his brother who, as we shall see, was almost impossible to organise, George lets Phillips know what he really thinks, being confident that Phillips will behave honourably and in the best interests of the movement.

Stephen Jeffreys

During 1925, after Assemblies of God was formed, George and Stephen worked together or, rather, they worked in a coordinated fashion. The coordination, so it seems, hinged on conversations between George and Stephen. Sometimes George would ask Stephen to go to preach somewhere; and, at other times, Stephen would accept an invitation and 'preach down a revival' which George would then finish up by arranging for the long-term future of the congregation that had been created.

Both evangelists appear to have funded themselves by taking offerings from the crowds they drew. Some of the money that came in was required to pay for the hire of halls, advertising, travel, and accommodation expenses; and, so far as we can tell, it was from this money that buildings were bought or mortgages serviced. In the early days, Elim would often attempt to buy buildings outright but if this was not possible a building would be partly bought and the balance of the money borrowed; and, once the congregation had been established in the building, its regular offerings could provide the income stream necessary to service the debt.

On June 18, 1925 a group was formed named the 'Full Gospel Forward Movement Council' with three members, E.C.W. Boulton, E.J. Phillips, and a businessman, Ludwig Naumann, who took on the task of managing Stephen Jeffreys and funding his ministry. The agreement stated:

> Pastor Stephen Jeffreys agrees to devote his full time to conducting the missions or other appointments arranged for him by the said Council, to preach the full gospel … For this he shall receive a salary of 5 pounds (£5) per week, in addition to being allowed all necessary travelling expenses and the occupation of the house free from rent, rates, or taxes…
>
> (4) in consideration of the above, all collections and offerings at all missions, together with all private gifts whatsoever to Pastor

Stephen Jeffreys or his wife are to be put to the funds of the Full Gospel Forward Movement Council.

All correspondence addressed to Pastor Jeffreys to be opened by the said Council.

(5) the agreement may be terminated by three calendar months' notice been given on any date by either party thereto ...[11]

The purpose of the agreement was to give Stephen the opportunity to direct all his energies to campaigning and to relieve him of any financial worries. He was a married man with a property in Merthyr Tydfil, Wales, and grown-up children. Some of the correspondence between George Jeffreys and E.J. Phillips concerns the handling of Stephen's family and the funding of the Full Gospel Forward Movement Council.

The Council could not tell Stephen where he should live or choose a house for him; and, in any case, Stephen's wife would not be dictated to about the location or style of her family home. George did not want to be seen as interfering with his sister-in-law's preferences and so would give his instructions to E.J. Phillips who then had to ensure all the financial transactions went ahead smoothly while keeping Stephen's family happy. The Council found itself responsible for Stephen's income tax, interest on the £650 borrowed for purchasing the new house and for arranging that £3-10s per week was available to Stephen's wife through the Merthyr Tydfil Post Office.[12] At the same time, the Council and, in effect Phillips who was expected to run it, had to make sure that Stephen's offerings were paid into the Council account. By the end of February £500 was offered for Stephen's house in Merthyr Tydfil but he wanted a house in London worth £850, a disparity George seriously questioned – though not to Stephen's face.[13] Eventually Stephen agreed to buy a house in Leigh-on-Sea (which should have been cheaper than London itself) and George, by July of that year, was keen to ensure that Stephen and his son Eddie moved from the place where they were then staying (Adderly Grove, in south Lon-

[11] Cartwright, *Evangelists*, p. 62.
[12] Letter from GJ to EJP (6 Jan 1925).
[13] Letter from GJ to EJP (30 Feb 1925).

don not far from the Clapham headquarters) to prevent the Council being responsible for funding two properties at once.[14] So George wrote to Phillips to make sure that Eddie Jeffreys, Stephen's son, moved out on the same day as his father although not wanting to be party to any pressure put on Eddie to move. A similar family complication arose earlier when Stephen's wife refused to go to the Post Office to draw out her allowance and sent her daughter to do so. The Post Office book had to be adjusted to the daughter's name and the task of making the adjustment fell on Phillips.

That all these matters were sorted out satisfactorily without upsetting Stephen or his family must speak well of Phillip's diplomatic skills as well as his business capacity. Behind the scenes George is writing to Phillips in July saying, 'again I want to emphasise through your Council the need of preventing Stephen lifting or putting out his envelopes among our people, seeing we have to contend with the debts we have, while he goes on scot-free'.[15] People gave by putting money in envelopes and they could do this either in the meetings or from home. The envelopes were then put into the offering bag when it was passed round; but, if Stephen gave out envelopes for the Forward Movement and George gave out envelopes for Elim itself, there might easily be confusion or the diversion of funds from one bank balance to another. George knew this and instructed Phillips to be sure to put a tithe (10%) of the Forward Movement funds into the Alliance account because 'it will be much easier getting some money out of Central Fund for Forward Movement should the need arise than vice versa!'[16]

When eventually Stephen did move house, it was thought that he would occasionally preach for the new Elim congregation at Leigh-on-Sea; but, with extraordinary evangelistic zeal and little understanding of local pastoral sensitivities, he was inclined to start another congregation at Southend, about four miles away.[17] He was a force of nature who simply *had* to evangelise wherever he went and perhaps underestimated his own extraordinary gifts by assuming

[14] Letter from GJ to EJP (8 July 1925).
[15] Letter from GJ to EJP (24 July 1925).
[16] Letter GJ to EJP (16 Jan 1925).
[17] Letter EJP to GJ (13 Mar 1925).

that other preachers could rouse and retain the congregations that he so easily drew.

A similar difficulty arose when an attempt was made to hold a mission in Forest Hill, London, while Stephen was preaching elsewhere in the city: '... attendance is very poor ... Mr Darragh and Miss Adams say they cannot carry on any more missions in London while Pastor S. Jeffreys is running a campaign, because everyone flocks to hear Pastor Jeffreys'.[18] Darragh and Adams were younger members of the Evangelistic Band who had come over from Belfast to join the evangelistic assault on London. They found themselves eclipsed by Stephen and attendance at Forest Hill was poor partly because public transport in London allowed enthusiastic converts to attend campaign meetings wherever the train or bus network stretched. Given a choice between hearing Darragh or Stephen Jeffreys, people opted for Jeffreys every time.

In his desire to mobilise the best preachers, George considered inviting Dr Price, an American, who was already a tried and tested Pentecostal preacher with the capacity to pray for the sick. After consulting Stephen on the matter, George wrote to Phillips reporting, 'he is not in favour of supporting Dr Price in his campaign. He says Dr Price does not preach separation, and that he advises his converts to go back to their churches whatever they belong to'.[19] In this respect Price acted like most interdenominational evangelists who gather support for their meetings from a multiplicity of churches and then send them back to the churches once the mission is over. The Elim plan was much more focused on growing the Elim Alliance and the doctrine of 'separation' entailed coming out of worldly churches (if one were a churchgoer) and being totally committed to the dedicated lifestyle by which Elim members expressed their holiness. George was unwilling to risk a breach with Stephen on this point despite seeing the attractions of a charismatic American spearheading further growth.

While correspondence was taking place behind the scenes, Stephen Jeffreys was launching out into a revival campaign in Barking in East London. The campaign began in Barking baths and was ex-

---

[18] Letter EJP to GJ (2 Feb 1925).
[19] Letter GJ to EJP (10 July 1925).

tended for four weeks. The divine healing services took place on Tuesday, Wednesday, and Thursday afternoons – an arrangement made by George in letters to Phillips.[20] The evening meetings were presumably shorter to allow people to catch the last buses and tube trains home. But, of the afternoons when Stephen prayed for the sick, the secular *Barking Advertiser* (24 Jan 1925) reported:

> Those who desired to be healed were afterwards invited to take the platform, and there was a great response to the invitation. Pastor Jeffreys dealt with a number of cases, anointing them with oil and praying with them. Most of them afterwards declared themselves healed, but several failed to respond.[21]

The newspaper sent its own reporter to interview people who had been healed to verify the accounts given from the campaign platform. It also reported that Jeffreys 'knew nothing about spiritualism or Christian Science. He only knew that Jesus did these things.' In the second week the campaign continued with increased momentum so that 'invalid chairs and crutches have been much in evidence, and the general appearance of the hall has been at times more like the out-patient department of a large hospital than an evangelical mission'.[22] This continued into a third week so that the *Stratford Express* (7 Feb, 1925) was able to say:

> scenes undoubtedly without parallel in the history of the town are being witnessed in connection with Pastor Jeffreys' revival campaign at the Baths Hall, Barking, practically every day. Rather than diminishing, the interest aroused at the commencement of the famous revivalist's visit is increasing, and people from all parts of London, as well as from the most distant parts of Essex, are attending the divine healing services.[23]

Rheumatoid arthritis, heart troubles, and even what appears to be shellshock – reported as 'shattered nerves owing to being torpe-

---

[20] GJ to EJP (5 Jan 1925).
[21] The quotations in this section were gathered by Stephen Jeffreys' son, Edward, and reprinted in his biography of his father (Jeffreys, *Stephen Jeffreys*, pp. 51-68).
[22] Jeffreys, *Stephen*, p. 53.
[23] Jeffreys, *Stephen*, p. 54.

doed during the war eight years ago'[24] – were healed. These meetings continued into a fourth week so that the *Barking Advertiser* was able to report that 'hundreds have stood in the assemblies and professed conversion … at each service people have sought admission long before the time of commencing'.[25]

When E.C.W Boulton looked back on the career of Stephen Jeffreys he was able to write, 'there is little doubt but that it was this intrepid and fiery preacher who at that time set that part of London ablaze with remarkable revival healing power and blessing'. As a consequence 'from this pioneer campaign the wave of revival spread from centre to centre, East Ham, Ilford and Canning Town in turn being caught in the wondrous flood-tide of heavenly outpouring'.[26] And in the portraits of Jeffreys' preaching those who heard him remember his intensity that was 'both provocative and contagious' with the result that 'under his ministry there could be no sitting on the fence of neutrality. He drew a very sharp line of demarcation. He knew nothing of equivocation or compromise.'[27]

Later Pentecostal historians could see those months in 1925 as providential. Not only did they occur before the unrest of the General Strike the following year but they took place at a time when the economy had improved the lives of many working people. In writing of the miraculous healings in the campaigns of Stephen and George, it is possible to fall into uncritical reportage. For this reason accounts of healing given by secular sources carry a special weight. They were not written by believers as edifying tales for the Elim flock but, rather, came from the pens of hard-bitten local reporters with no predisposition to look at the revival meetings through rose-tinted glasses. Consequently, secular reports contain a built-in critical perspective that gives credibility to the cumulative story of early Pentecostal success. Indeed, Edward's account of Stephen's meetings at an earlier point in his ministry when he preached in Swansea shows how the miracles occurred *in spite of* the sceptical attitudes of some attenders:

[24] Jeffreys, *Stephen*, p. 55.
[25] Jeffreys, *Stephen*, p. 56.
[26] Jeffreys, *Stephen*, p. 67.
[27] Jeffreys, *Stephen*, p. 67.

Great things were taking place, and a few ministers entered the marquee before the evening service to examine the chair upon which the people sat for prayer. They could see nothing wrong with it, but they thought that it might be wired up in a secret way with a battery underneath the platform, so they were determined to find out. We arrived a little earlier that night and caught the ministers right in the act of looking for wires underneath the platform. You can imagine how embarrassed they were after crawling out with their hands covered with dust. 'What on earth are you doing here?' I asked. 'Well, to tell you the truth, Mr Jeffreys, we really thought that the chair was in some way linked up with an electric battery, and we were determined to find out and expose the whole thing'. The chair, or rather its occupant, was certainly linked up with a mighty power, but it was from above, and not beneath![28]

Moving across London about 20 miles west, Stephen prepared to open a revival campaign in Hendon on the 22 February 1925.[29] The Alexander Hall had been disused and was cluttered with rubbish and debris. The windows were filthy and the floors and walls needed cleaning. A band of workers organised by Elim rolled up their sleeves and set to work to make the building suitable for the opening night. Stephen Jeffreys, speaking to his son, saw the condition of the modern church as parallel to that of the Temple of God in the time of Jesus. Moneychangers and merchants filled the courts and needed first to be evicted before Jesus might begin to teach. The mainline church of the 1920s, so far as Jeffreys was concerned, was producing dancing and card-players and only when these were ejected might the lame and the blind come in. And so the hall was cleaned and the sick were invited, and arrived in large numbers. The opening meeting was well attended and according to the *Hendon and Golders Green Gazette* 'attended by an atmosphere of devotion rather than ridicule'.[30]

---

[28] Jeffreys, *Stephen*, p. 49.
[29] *Elim Evangel* 6.6 (16 Mar 1925), pp. 67, 68
[30] Jeffreys, *Stephen*, p. 59.

Interestingly the Gazette also points out that

Pastor Jeffreys makes a great point of impressing upon his hearers the fact that they must not look to him, personally, for aid. He was unable to do anything, but he believed Jesus could.

The report went on to say that

A representative of the Gazette attended the pastors meetings on Tuesday afternoon, and witnessed many remarkable scenes … This earnest little minister was undoubtedly the instrument of some Higher Power.[31]

A further report from another newspaper, the *Hendon and Finchley Times*, highlighted the remarkable case of Mr Palmer who had been deaf and dumb for 40 years but who, after prayer, regained the power of speech and was able to speak to 'a representative' of the newspaper.[32]

Having preached in east and west London, a united central campaign combining the two brothers was planned. This was to be a big event, perhaps their biggest to date. 'Our readers will rejoice to know that the large Surrey Tabernacle has been taken for the purpose of a united campaign in the centre of London. Pastors Stephen and George Jeffreys, assisted by the band of Elim evangelists, will hold forth the foursquare gospel of salvation, healing, baptism of the Holy Ghost and the second Advent of Christ'[33] and, to assist the transport of the anticipated crowds, 'arrangements to be made with the railway companies whereby cheap tickets will be issued from all stations in England, Scotland and Wales' and from the ports of Belfast and Dublin as well as Jersey and Guernsey. This was intended to be an event that drew in people from all the newly founded assemblies to re-affirm their faith by enabling them to feel part of a large body of Pentecostal people. It was also, with Stephen's drive, an evangelistic and divine healing crusade.

E.J. Phillips made the arrangements with the railway and ferry companies and was thoughtful about the cost of staying in London for visitors. The *Elim Evangel* reported on 'the greatest Pentecostal

---

[31] Jeffreys, *Stephen*, p. 60.
[32] Jeffreys, *Stephen*, p. 61.
[33] *Elim Evangel* 6.6 (16 Mar 1925), p. 70

convention ever held in the British Isles' and provided photographs of the packed auditorium.[34] The building had a seating capacity of about 2,000 people and it was filled day after day.

> The large building became the scene of a continuous revival, and a theatre of activities. From all parts of the country people brought their suffering ones for a touch of divine life. Cancers, tumours, and all kinds of dreadful diseases lost their grip of many victims. The power of the Lord was present to heal.[35]

It was here that a card system was introduced because the number of people was so great; and, having travelled from such long distances, there was a need to make a queue to receive the laying on of hands to avoid disappointment. George is described in the *Elim Evangel* as the Convenor but Stephen bore the brunt of the physical labour of praying for the sick. The *Sunday Express*, a national newspaper, reported:

> Stirring scenes are being witnessed in the old Surrey Tabernacle, a derelict building standing behind Walworth Road where a religious revival has been conducted by Pastor Jeffreys ... The lame, the blind, deaf and dumb are flocking for treatment. At one meeting 2000 people were present, while crowds were turned away.[36]

The hiring of large halls cost a lot of money. It is an evidence of the faith of Jeffreys and Phillips that such plans were boldly made with the barest hesitation or diffidence. The stress of preaching to large numbers of people night after night is psychologically draining. Preachers will often lose weight over a prolonged campaign; and, even though they might have a store of sermons, the consistent demand for new insights from Scripture can, if the preacher does not have a sermon worked out for the coming day, cause panic. Stephen was able to demonstrate the true gifts of an evangelist by preaching an essentially similar message in arresting new ways. George was more of a teacher and regularly convened meetings where others preached which meant that he held sway over the tim-

---

[34] *Elim Evangel* 6.9 (1 May 1925), p. 97.
[35] Jeffreys, *Stephen*, p. 62.
[36] Jeffreys, *Stephen*, p. 64 and *Sunday Express*, 19 Apr 1925.

ing and sequence of events during a service without having constantly to discover fresh Biblical material to expound.

The flow of letters between George Jeffreys and Phillips triggered the organisational infrastructure of the crusades. The booking of venues was vital but difficult if one did not know how long the previous set of meetings would run. If a campaign was going particularly well, then the option to extend the campaign beckoned. Why turn away from thronging crowds in one place to start again with an almost empty hall in another? Stephen had contracted himself to be exclusively available through the Forward Movement to Elim; but, if he deviated from a preaching plan to fulfil promises that he had previously given, this was stressful to Phillips. Above and beyond the arrangements for starting and stopping campaign meetings were the regular deadlines to *Elim Evangel.* Copy for this had to be delivered to meet immovable deadlines, and these deadlines also covered advertising schedules. Without advertising, there was a danger that meetings would be sparsely attended. So the organisational drive was dictated to by calendar commitments, and calendar commitments, once published, could not be changed. In their different ways both George Jeffreys and E.J. Phillips were subject to stress: George was thinking ahead to future commitments or wondering how he was going to find a pastor or evangelist for a congregation that had recently come into existence and E.J. Phillips was tearing his hair out trying to keep pace with George's most recent demands or launching a new set of meetings with an inadequate preaching team at his disposal.

The relationship between the two brothers appeared to be harmonious. George was deferential to Stephen in whose home he had lived when he was much younger, and Stephen had been like a father to him. George made sure that Stephen was properly remunerated for all his preaching but it is also evident that George was keen to bring new congregations into Elim, congregations founded by the efforts of Stephen. This is not to say that George was exploiting Stephen because Stephen willingly preached when arrangements were made for him but it is to say that the long-term fruits of Stephen's ministry were harvested by George. Stephen was George's star preacher and could be guaranteed to make an impact wherever he was sent. George, whether deliberately or out of a sense of his founding importance to Elim, made sure his own contributions were not eclipsed in the pages of the *Elim Evangel* by Stephen's. A comparison between the reports of the Surrey Tabernacle meetings in Eddie Jeffreys' book about his father and the reports of the same meetings in the *Elim Evangel* are revealing. In the first, there is no mention of George. This is Stephen's ministry and glory. In the second, George is given equal billing with his brother even though he preached much less frequently.

In the correspondence with E.J. Phillips a different stance again is revealed. George Jeffreys wrote:

> Surrey Tabernacle: I'm convinced that the taking over of this for a mission will not help in our plan, at present. There might be a big splash and a load of expense and wastage of money, but little that will strengthen our position in London. I suggest that we take a risk of getting it for the Easter Convention only. Indeed, I am content to go ahead in our present Tabernacle for this convention. Let it be packed out! Extra people that will come to a larger hall will never meet the heavy expense that must be added if we go to another hall.[37]

George is thinking strategically about enhancing the Elim position in London and wants to ensure that lasting congregations are brought into existence. Earlier in the year he is writing to Phillips about maintaining the congregation at Forest Hill after a disappointing period of ministry with Darragh and Adams. Within a few days he was looking for the right person to consolidate the congregation at Plymouth. It is no surprise that he was turning his attention to the founding of a Bible College for a constant supply of suitably trained pastors and evangelists.

Stephen's ministry contained several repeated themes including criticism of the modernist theology that pervaded mainline churches. Articles in the *Elim Evangel* backed up this anti-modernistic thrust: 'it is to be feared that many of our academies produce more cynics than saints – more parrots than thinkers'.[38] In an editorial Phillips wrote:

---

[37] GJ to EJP (10 Feb 1925).
[38] D.J. Davies, 'The Bible and Modernism', *Elim Evangel*, 6.8 (15 Apr 1925), p. 85.

The terrible responsibility rests upon those who deliberately mis-interpret that which God is doing in these days and so succeed in hindering many bound and burdened ones from entering into that precious blood-bought heritage which the Atonement pro-vides for all who believe. How significant it is that all this is tak-ing place amongst these despised and much maligned Pentecos-tal people, who at the sacrifice of their religious reputation have been prepared to follow the Lord into that which is undoubtedly a present-day counterpart of Apostolic Christianity.[39]

And as far as Stephen was concerned his preaching of healing came directly from the cross of Christ. 'It's in the Atonement: healing for the body as well the soul'.[40]

Despite George's concerns the year unfolded well. Stephen was in Ashbourne, Derbyshire, for eight days in March or April.[41] The brothers were able to open a new hall at Barking together on 17 May, 1925, a ceremony that marked Stephen's preaching and George's organisational leadership.[42] In June of that year, George baptised 152 people at the Surrey Tabernacle,[43] on 14 August an-other 105, and on 4 December another 71.[44] In August there are reports of healings under Stephen at Forest Hill with photos and miracles,[45] showing that Stephen was being used to shore up the faltering work in that part of London so that by the middle of Au-gust reports of revival and healing were now being published. In July Stephen is reported as being on holiday in Leigh-on-Sea but used the time to go to preach in Pontypridd in Wales to fulfil a promise to an old friend. Given that he had signed an exclusive con-tract with Elim on 20 June, his preaching outside the Elim circle might look provocative but by November he is back in London at Notting Hill and Sydenham and making fresh progress there.[46] The

---

[39] *Elim Evangel* 6.8 (15 Apr 1925), p. 90.

[40] *Elim Evangel* 6.8 (15 Apr 1925), p. 91.

[41] *Elim Evangel* 6.7 (1 Apr 1925), p. 86.

[42] *Elim Evangel* 6.11 (1 June 1925), p. 124.

[43] *Elim Evangel* 6.12 (15 June 1925), p. 136.

[44] *Elim Evangel* 6.18 (15 Sept 1925), p. 215; *Elim Evangel*, 6.24 (15 Dec 1925), p. 278.

[45] *Elim Evangel* 6.15 (1 Aug 1925), p. 170.

[46] Cartwright, *Evangelists*, p. 63.

Evangel reported his preaching at Pontypridd but after December he is hardly mentioned and gradually drops out of view.[47]

In 1926 the two brothers went their separate ways under circumstances that have never been fully disclosed. Stephen's bungalow in Leigh-on-Sea cost £1,300, about twice what his house in Merthyr Tydfil sold for, and we know from correspondence with Phillips that George disliked what he saw as the extravagant price of housing in the London area.[48] Cartwright suggested the difficulties lay with Stephen's wife or with 'those who put ideas in Stephen's mind to prejudice him against his brother and caused him to suspect George of less than worthy motives'.[49] At a later point, Eddie Jeffreys set up his own evangelistic association and Stephen worked with him. So there may have been a family rivalry between George the successful younger brother and Stephen, supported by his wife and son, who felt they should gather their own congregations together in their own organisation. There is some evidence for this from a fracas in 1929 when Stephen's campaigning threatened to start new congregations in the Barking area where they would inevitably have drawn people away from the Elim congregations that had already been established nearby.[50] Or it may have been that Stephen disliked having to hand over the offerings taken at his meetings to George, even though these offerings contributed to Stephen's salary and ministry. There was a later discussion in Elim about whether personal gifts to a minister properly counted as income[51] and so the taking of 'love offerings' for the evangelist right at the end of a campaign (when the congregation was likely to be at its largest) may have been a source of contention. Boulton, in writing about the split said, 'neither Stephen Jeffreys nor the Headquarters Staff of Elim were in any way responsible'.[52] This precise wording exoner-

---

[47] *Elim Evangel* 6.20 (Oct 15 1925), p. 237. He did preach at the Surrey Tabernacle with R. Mercer on Boxing Day 1925 and there is mention of this as a news items in the *Elim Evangel* 7.1 (15 Jan 1926), p. 21. But he took on no preaching for Elim in 1926 and his campaigns, though they continued, received little coverage.

[48] Cartwright, *Evangelists*, p 62. Letter from GJ to EJP (8 July 1925).

[49] Cartwright, *Evangelists*, p. 63. In private conversation, he suggested to me that Stephen's wife was probably responsible for the break-up.

[50] Cartwright, *Evangelists*, p. 64.

[51] E.g. General Presbytery minutes (15 Sept 1938).

[52] Jeffreys, *Stephen*, p. 67.

ates Stephen and E.J. Phillips and leaves only George as the culprit. A more charitable conclusion offered by Cartwright suggests temperamental differences lay at the root of the brothers' falling out.[53]

By 1 March 1926, Stephen had transferred his loyalties and, under the chairmanship of Nelson Parr, started to campaign successfully in cooperation with Assemblies of God.[54]

Fresh Turns of Events

Although relationships with Assemblies of God were friendly, it is possible to detect a competitive streak in those early years. This may have been caused by Howard Carter, the elder brother of John Carter, a former member of Elim Evangelistic Band in Ireland. Like the Jeffreys brothers, the Carters gave their time and talents to British Pentecostalism. Neither was as gifted as either of the Jeffreys as a preacher. John was more of a teacher and administrator.[55] Howard was known for his faith and understanding of spiritual gifts. He was an assertive character with a high opinion of himself and later caused dissension in Assemblies of God; and, at the founding meeting in 1924 already referred to, he proposed 'disbanding' Elim as a condition for enabling all the Pentecostal churches in Britain to come together.[56] The others present disagreed with him but Carter's proposal obviously rankled with George.[57]

The Carter brothers helped to gather together the scattered independent Pentecostal congregations into Assemblies of God in the period after 1924 when its growth was exponential. This entailed signing up existing congregations rather than going out boldly to evangelise among the unconverted. The early minutes of Elim show evidence that ministers and congregations were being wel-

---

[53] Cartwright, *Evangelists*, p. 63.

[54] Alfred E. Missen, *The Sound of a Going* (Nottingham: Assemblies of God Publishing House, 1973), p. 20.

[55] Though as a young man he did hold competent evangelistic campaigns. See John Carter, *A Full Life* (Nottingham: Assemblies of God, 1979).

[56] Howard Carter brought about the resignation from Assemblies of God of Nelson Parr on false charges. Carter later apologised, but the damage had been done. Parr (1972) gives a brief account in his autobiography *Incredible* (Fleetwood, privately printed), p. 43.

[57] GJ to EJP 16 Jan 1925. EJP to GJ 19 Jan 1925.

comed into the Elim Alliance by a process not dissimilar to the one by which other congregations and ministers were being welcomed into the Assemblies of God. It is only slightly straining the language to say that the denominations were competing with each other to sign up assemblies as fast as they could.

The Town Hall in East Ham Filled for a Crusade, c. 1925

Jeffreys preached in many parts of London. The city itself had once been a collection of villages and towns which eventually connected in a continuous urban sprawl that became Greater London. East Ham had its own ornate town hall and the working class 'east enders' were known for their cockney resilience and their Jewish immigrants.

The Carter brothers were also keen to start training Pentecostal ministers. They were aware that, without an explicit and rational grounding in the distinctives of Pentecostal doctrine, the first generation of Pentecostal ministers might be the last. To transmit the newly formed tradition, a college was necessary and Howard Carter possessed the requisite faith to take responsibility for what became the Assemblies of God training school even though, until he handed it over, it remained his own private establishment and subject only to a relatively light degree of oversight by an Assemblies of God committee.[58] Whether this college was what provoked George

---

[58] The Hampstead Bible School had originally been set up by the PMU and largely funded by Cecil Polhill. When the PMU was merged with Assemblies of

to act, cannot precisely be said but the correspondence shows that George and E.J. Phillips were aware of what the Carters were doing and of its significance.[59] George told Phillips to make arrangements for the founding of an Elim college and their correspondence shows how the project rapidly progressed.[60]

At first a sympathiser promised to make a property available with a sufficient number of rooms to allow dormitory accommodation for males and females. Hardly had this plan been formed than a Redemptorist convent with 4½ acres was located and bought. E.J. Phillips, in addition to his duties as the editor of the *Evangel*, became the dean of the college, and early photographs show the pleasant wooded grounds in Clapham not far from the office headquarters and tabernacle. Here the printing press and the growing circulation of the *Evangel* were invaluable for recruiting students.

George Leads Forward

Even while the relationship with Stephen during the second part of 1925 was showing signs of tension George continued his ministry in Ireland and England. He was often called upon to baptise in water those candidates who had been converted during a revival campaign carried out by Stephen or by others, and he crossed and recrossed the Irish Sea to maintain links with his earliest converts. He was in Bangor in August 1925 and back in London at the Surrey Tabernacle later that month. He campaigned at Forest Hill in London in September[61] and both the *Daily Mail*, a national paper, and *The Dulwich and Peckham Echo*, a local paper, reported on the Forest Hill revival, and their reports were reprinted in the *Evangel*.[62] George was down on the south coast in Bournemouth for an anniversary service in the autumn and then back again in London to open a new hall (15 October). For most of the time he and Stephen carried out the revival campaigns but he was also able to enlist the help of other Welsh or Irish preachers like Gomer Jones or Robert Mercer who took the pulpit when required.

God, someone needed to take responsibility for the school, and Carter was asked to do this.

[59] EJP to GJ 14 Jan 1925, 19 Jan 1925.
[60] EJP to GJ 14 Jan 1925, 26 Jan 1925. GJ to EJP 16 Jan 1925.
[61] *Elim Evangel* 6.18 (15 Sept 1925), p 214.
[62] *Elim Evangel* 6.19 (1 Oct 1925), p. 219.

During all this time the *Evangel* continued carrying articles with a strongly Adventist emphasis. The multi-part series by C. Kingston in June 1925 provides a diagram of future events.[63] The return of Christ to rescue the church from the earth – usually called 'the rapture' – occurs just before the Antichrist seizes power and inflicts seven terrible years of tribulation. These will only be brought to an end when Christ returns 'with his saints' to defeat the Antichrist in battle and begin a glorious millennial reign. This is the dispensationalist interpretive scheme of the Scofield Reference Bible and the Irish cleric J.N. Darby. It is a scheme that has the psychological effect of making conversion urgent because *only* the converted – and in some readings only those who are full of the Holy Spirit – will be raptured and so escape the predations of the Antichrist.

For Kingston the beast of the book of Revelation who arises during the time of the Antichrist will be 'the civil head of the European Nations (or at least as many as were in the old Roman Empire) during the tribulation' and 'in a mist of this unrest it is probable that there will be a cry for the UNION OF THE CHURCHES' (original capitals) which will be Roman Catholic in doctrine – an implication that the papacy commands what is or will become 'an apostate church'.[64]

Jeffreys held the conviction that the return of Christ was near; and, although the precise eschatological scheme he favoured is not readily apparent, his willingness to accept Kingston's articles in the *Elim Evangel* is proof enough that he found the dispensationalist scheme credible. Stephen, looking out on the atheistic regime of Soviet Russia, discerned the outlines of the Antichrist's empire. So we must see the preaching of the two brothers as being catalysed by eschatological urgency. Teachings on the millennium[65] or discipleship[66] were part of this powerful expectation of future cataclysmic events. No wonder 'separation'[67] was taught or that healing testimonies were so frequently printed. They formed a standing rebuttal of

---

[63] *Elim Evangel* 6.12 (15 June 1925), p. 139.
[64] *Elim Evangel* 6.18 (15 Sept 1925), p. 205.
[65] *Elim Evangel* 6.25 (15 Dec 1925), p. 280.
[66] *Elim Evangel* 6.24 (1 Dec 1925), p. 271.
[67] *Elim Evangel* 6.24 (1 Dec 1925), p. 267.

modernist theology and the weakened church that was destined to fall into apostasy.

Throughout the year George continued to juggle many balls in the air at once. He mentions the issue of local government of churches (letter, 25 July 1925) and notes the consequence for one of the Irish churches that refused this form of government: under the central system congregations were the financial responsibility of the Alliance. When churches were placed in the local government category, they became more responsible for their own affairs and less of a worry to George.

By 1926 Stephen is fading into the background of Elim and greater expectation was piled upon George's shoulders. He was the only person who could command public attention to draw new crowds and plant new congregations. None of the other preachers had this electric ability and so the reporting within the *Evangel* gives its headlines to George's meetings and does all it can to ensure their success by advertising them in advance. He goes to Plymouth in January and plans to return in the summer and encourages Elim members to combine their summer holidays with visits to the campaign.

Plans were drawn up for an Easter Convention in London's Surrey Tabernacle as this had become a traditional event spread over the whole Easter weekend. In an era when paid holidays were unheard of and most families relied on public transport, Easter conventions did not have to compete with the attractions of foreign travel. And, as far as Elim church members were concerned, the big meetings gave everyone a chance to share the excitement of the celebratory gatherings in London. For George Jeffreys all this was the apex of a punishing schedule. In March he had held a successful campaign in Plymouth and witnessed over 1,500 people make commitments to Christ.[68] Then, quite unexpectedly, Aimee Semple McPherson had phoned the Elim offices and offered to preach for Elim. Delighted by this, the *Evangel* was able to advertise a revised Easter programme. Aimee Semple McPherson, the glamorous, controversial, famous Canadian evangelist would take two of the four

[68] *Elim Evangel* 7.5 (1 Mar 1926), p. 52.

days of the weekend and London's Royal Albert Hall had been booked as the venue. Plan to attend now!

Aimee Semple McPherson had already founded Angelus Temple in Los Angeles and George Jeffreys knew her from his visit in 1924. She attracted a regular congregation of over 5,000 and about 40 satellite congregations in the Los Angeles area. Hollywood stars like Marilyn Monroe and Charlie Chaplin had attended her meetings so that, if she were billed to preach in London, a huge crowd and the attention of the press could be guaranteed.[69] Her stopover in London was part of a trip to the Holy Land arranged by faithful supporters because, after three years of non-stop work, they recognised she showed signs of exhaustion. Nevertheless, she came first to the Surrey Tabernacle for four days in March and her messages were received with pleasure and astonishment. As one newspaper said:

> A whirlwind revival struck Walworth yesterday afternoon, when Mrs Aimee Semple McPherson mounted the pulpit of the Surrey Tabernacle and delivered a 15,000-word sermon under the hour – a veritable Niagara of eloquence during which she never once hesitated for a word. She spoke of her great ambition – to proclaim the name of Jesus to every creature in the world.[70]

She told her life story, as she often did, and George Jeffreys who had planned a Liverpool campaign, postponed it so as to 'assist' at the Surrey Tabernacle.[71] She was a thoroughly Pentecostal evangelist who prayed for the sick and spoke in tongues, and she brought with her the uncompromising vehemence of the cultural wars she felt herself to be fighting for America's soul. Evolution and all its implications were, to her mind, alien to the central founding narrative of the Pilgrim Fathers and godly America, and it is likely that her anti-modernistic attitudes rubbed off on Jeffreys and early Elim.

After her successful participation in the Easter events, she crossed over to Ireland and gave a boost to the Belfast Pentecostals before returning home to Los Angeles and the kind of welcome

---

[69] E.L. Blumhofer, *Aimee Semple McPherson: Everybody's Sister* (Grand Rapids, MI: Eerdmans, 2003), pp. 279, 280. See also M.A. Sutton, *Aimee Semple McPherson and the Resurrection of Christian America* (Cambridge, MA: Harvard, 2007), p. 88.

[70] *Elim Evangel* 7.6 (15 Mar 1926), p. 62.

[71] *Elim Evangel* 7.6 (15 Mar 1926), p. 63.

that popular royalty normally receives. And then, after plunging back into her duties at the Temple, she went swimming in the Pacific Ocean on 16 May 1926 and disappeared and was presumed drowned.[72] Her mother, a powerful figure in the background, sent a telegram to Jeffreys demanding that he fill the pulpit in Los Angeles and Jeffreys, uncertain what to do, shared the peremptory request with Elim and asked believers to pray.[73] While they were doing so, about six weeks after Aimee Semple disappeared, she was found in Mexico after escaping kidnappers. It is true that salacious accounts of her missing weeks circulated journalistic gossip columns; but, despite a hostile court case during which she was called to the witness box and subjected to searching interrogation, she never deviated from her story, was never convicted of wrong-doing, and remained as popular as ever.

Understanding the Time

By Easter 1926 Elim and George Jeffreys were riding high. Behind him, extraordinary as it may seem, the British Empire had reached its largest ever extent, a change partly brought about by the removal from Germany of its own colonies and the settlement terms of the Versailles Treaty.[74] For someone with British Israel leanings, the auguries must have appeared favourable. Moreover the Empire was changing its character by allowing a moderate degree of self-government within the Dominions at the same time as having such prestige within many of its geographical borders that only a token military or administrative presence was necessary for the rule of law.[75]

The hiring of the Royal Albert Hall was also itself symbolic. This hall had been built as a memorial to her husband by Queen Victoria and occupied a unique place within British public life. It was inevitably associated with British imperial supremacy in the 19th century and its fine architecture and excellent acoustics made it

---

[72] Sutton, *McPherson*, p. 92.
[73] *Elim Evangel* 7.12 (15 June 1926), p. 142.
[74] A. Roberts, *A History of the English-Speaking Peoples Since 1900* (London: Weidenfeld & Nicholson, 2006), p. 145.
[75] Roberts, *History*, p. 149.

suitable for musical or preaching events. It was the *Royal* Albert Hall which, to any believer in British Israelism, gave an added frisson. When the hall was hired for the 1926 Easter celebrations, Jeffreys could hardly have believed that he would continue to hire it right through until 1939. It became a fixed and central point in his year to be fitted in along with summer campaigns and Christmas conventions; and, indeed, he tried to ensure the programme always included a Breaking of Bread (or communion) service and water baptism as two of the ordinances he believed Christ had given to the church.

When Aimee Semple McPherson vanished so soon after her return to the United States and while the memory of her visit to England and Ireland was still fresh, George must have received a considerable psychological shock. How could such a treasured servant of the Lord suddenly die at the height of her powers – it appeared she had been swept out to sea while bathing? And when Jeffreys was invited to take over the Angelus Temple and preach weekly to its Pentecostal throng, this must have been an endorsement of his gifts at the highest level. He and no other Pentecostal preacher was deemed worthy to fill the McPherson pulpit. And then, when she reappeared with harrowing tales of her kidnap, how grateful he must have been that he had not dropped everything to rush out to Los Angeles but had carefully weighed the options and discerned the will of God. Her reappearance must have confirmed to him the rightness of his decision to remain looking after the work in England and Ireland. If he paid attention to the journalistic slurs on her character, this must have reinforced his realisation of the need to retain moral integrity in high-profile ministry. Easter 1926, therefore, showed to Jeffreys himself and the Elim inner circle that he had attained a pinnacle of eminence within the Pentecostal world well above that of any of his European peers.

7

'OUR HEARTS OVERFLOW WITH GRATITUDE'

The next years of George Jeffreys' life constitute a golden era. Between 1926 and 1933 he continued to preach yearly at the Royal Albert Hall, he travelled from the south coast of England up to Scotland and from Yorkshire to Ireland attracting huge crowds, often favourable secular newspaper reports, seeing extraordinary healings and being able to buy and fill buildings with new congregations. And he did all this against a turbulent economic and political background. In 1926 there was a general strike for nine days and in 1929 a stock market crash. In 1933 Hitler was elected as Chancellor of Germany. Yet none of these events interrupted the determined evangelism of Jeffreys and his Revival Party. As they had throughout the 1914–1918 war, Jeffreys and his preachers continued with their fervent and potent presentations of the gospel without letting national and international events deflect them from their task. In many ways, the threat of political or economic uncertainty only added to the persuasiveness of the message they proclaimed: these were the terrible last days and men and women must turn to Christ before it is too late.

Public Speaking

The 1920s were still within the era of great public oratory, most of it political. Lloyd George was a spellbinding speaker who would hold almost any audience in rapt attention and he made his name campaigning politically in South Wales and functioning much like a revivalist preacher. Winston Churchill, a colleague of Lloyd George and a one-time member of the Liberal party, was also known as a powerful speaker even if he lacked the spontaneity of Lloyd George and the mesmerising quality of his Welsh friend. Across the political spectrum in the 1930s Oswald Mosley, rallying the almost forgotten British Union of Fascists, was also an orator while, across the Channel in Germany, Hitler perfected the art of addressing gigantic rallies to become a poisonous demagogue.

George Jeffreys does not belong in the political realm but he does fit within the great preaching tradition which had heard the eloquence of Charles Spurgeon whose Metropolitan Tabernacle was in south London not too far from the Clapham Elim churches. Preachers and politicians in this era addressed their audiences without the assistance of electronic amplification. Their powerful voices were sufficient on their own; and, although microphones and loud speakers were introduced during the 1930s, Jeffreys began with his unaided voice. The sheer physical effort of speaking day after day to large crowds is often underestimated. Billy Graham in his autobiography reports about being drenched in perspiration and barely able to undress and crawl into bed after his crusade sermons; the adrenaline rush is followed by muscular fatigue.[1] So in the case of George Jeffreys, as well as Stephen, physical fitness and strength were required to maintain their gruelling schedules. Both brothers consciously relied upon the Holy Spirit as they prepared themselves to face the huge crowds that came to listen. George wrote:

All who conduct prolonged evangelistic campaigns will admit that a great deal of physical strength is necessary. This in many cases could never be found if it were not for the Divine strength that is given. The body, tired and weakened by constant labour, needs a special inflow of Divine life. Sometimes towards the end of a campaign I have been confronted by monster congregations, and if it were not for the frequent quickenings of the body I would have been helpless. Even the voice is charged and changed as a result of the body being quickened by the Spirit.[2]

Sheer exhaustion, or burnout, threatened the health of passionate preachers and amazingly throughout the 1920s and into early

---

[1] Billy Graham, *Just as I Am* (London: HarperCollins, 1998), p. 316.
[2] George Jeffreys, *Healing Rays* (London: Elim Publishing Co, 1932), p. 57.

1930s George was able to sustain his punishing schedule. He mitigated the strains of preaching by opting also to function as a convener of meetings, especially at conventions. By so doing he was able to guide and lead a large gathering – with his name appearing on the advertising placards – while passing the demands of preaching over to other speakers.

Stress levels rose at the opening of campaigning gospel meetings. George preached to unbelievers many times but always without knowing just how he would be received. Convention meetings were more predictable and might have the air of a homecoming, a re-gathering of the Elim family of believers. As a healing evangelist, George also had to find ways to bring a miraculous touch to the many sick people who flocked to hear him. At the beginning when the meetings were small, it was relatively easy for him to lay hands on everybody who wished to receive prayer. As the meetings grew ever larger, this became problematic. If he prayed for the sick in the evening meetings and if people were dramatically healed, this would lead to fresh outbreaks of singing and testimonies with the result that the event would be prolonged and public transport be unable to cope with the departing surge. No one wanted to miss the last bus home. So afternoon meetings with shorter sermons but a more elastic allocation of time for prayer ministry were better. Conventions were different kinds of events because the preaching was paramount and adapted to the needs of the region. The sermons for a convention in Belfast might well be different from those given in south London. The Irish Christians usually came from highly burnished religio-political upbringings while the cockneys from south Londoners were mostly unchurched.

Following on from the physical exertions of preaching were the complications of an itinerant lifestyle. The evangelist sleeps in many beds during the year; but, as he became established, George began to create a stable environment that was not dependent upon fluctuations in local hospitality. Once he had acquired a car, he could avoid the jostling crowds of long train journeys and, with a car, came the possibility of towing a caravan where he might enjoy privacy and familiar surroundings. The Revival Party made up of his driver, Albert Edsor, who was also his pianist, his song leader, Robert Darragh, and the organiser, James McWhirter, could all fit into the car and then move smoothly into action in every new location.

The Revival Party formed a protective barrier round Jeffreys but it also gave him spiritual and practical support. Towards the end of his life, he still owned the large American Chrysler he had bought in 1937 and he and the party might be seen motoring purposefully down the road, all dressed in dark suits, coats, and homburg hats, and looking like businessmen speeding to important appointments.[3]

There are few remarks made by Jeffreys himself on his preaching but in September 1926 he wrote:

> When God ordained me as a minister of the gospel … I promised him I would go forth to excite people to love the Master. By his grace thousands of people been swept into the kingdom. My emotions belong to my soul, and I'm sanctifying my emotions for the sake and purpose of the gospel. How can you sit quiet … When you feel the powers of another world filling you with divine life. You cannot help saying hallelujah![4]

If we take this comment precisely, it tells us three things: first, at some point in his early ministerial life, Jeffreys made a promise to God that he would 'excite people to love the Master'. This is an unexpected way of viewing Christian ministry. It envisages ministry as being absolutely centred on Christ and solely motivated by love for Christ. It is not about politics, church constitutions, or sin. Second, the work of the Holy Spirit is broad and vital. The reference to the powers of another world is taken from Heb. 6.5 and points to experience of the Holy Spirit as a foretaste of either a heavenly or a millennial future. The Spirit belongs to another age when mortal bodies will have been raised from the dead and all prophecy will have been fulfilled. Third, Jeffreys places his emotions within his soul and believes the process of sanctification involves direct modification of his feelings. This is one of the rare references to his inner life: it does not hint at mental conflict but at a continuing quest for control and holiness.

Other aspects of Elim doctrine are fundamentally Christocentric. The foursquare Gospel arranges the teaching of New Testa-

---

[3] An insight given to me by Harry Greenway's son (Apr 2015). There is a photograph of the car in A.W. Edsor, *'Set Your House in Order'* (Chichester, New Wine Press, 1989), p. 94.

[4] *Elim Evangel* 7.17 (Sept 1926), p. 195.

ment around four roles of Christ in relation to the believer, the church, and the world. Christ is saviour, healer, baptiser in the Spirit, and soon-coming King. Consequently the preaching ministry of Jeffreys was intended to exalt Christ while demonstrating the operation of the Spirit in the present age. He could function as a pure evangelist and speak about Christ as saviour or he could speak in a convention meeting to congregations about holiness or spiritual gifts.

There are no recordings of the young George Jeffreys preaching, although he made gramophone records of his sermons, but these are flat and lack the verve of live delivery; they were made in recording studios rather than during campaign meetings. There is a cassette recording of Jeffreys preaching in Westminster Central Hall in 1955 and this confirms his fluency, solemnity, and dramatic timing. Donald Gee said of him, 'he had a voice like music, with sufficient Welsh intonation to add an inimitable charm. His platform personality was at times magnetic. His face was appealing.'[5]

After Aimee Semple McPherson's Disappearance

The disappearance of Aimee Semple McPherson; and, six weeks later, her reappearance stumbling across the border from Mexico where she had been held captive, caused consternation behind the scenes in Elim.[6] Those journalists who were hostile to her ministry held that she had secretly enjoyed a love affair with one of her employees and that the entire story of the kidnap was fantasy. Those who knew her in Elim believed no such thing; and, even though she was put into the witness box and cross-questioned after her return, none of the charges thrown at her were in any way substantiated with the result that, whatever the gossips might have said, her reputation was intact. Her popularity never wavered, and those who supported her believed she was the victim of a hostile and probably diabolical prosecution.

---

[5] Gee, *These Men I Knew*, p. 49. The cassette recording is held in the Donald Gee Centre, Mattersey and an audio file is also available in the Desmond Cartwright Centre at Regents, Malvern.
[6] As letters between EJP and GJ show.

During August 1926 E.J. Phillips wrote to Jeffreys about the fall-out from the publicity over McPherson and wondered whether it would affect the morale of Elim believers when, at that stage in the proceedings, there were doubts about the truth of her story. In reply Jeffreys writes back wondering whether to go to Los Angeles to find out 'the facts of this strange business'. Yet, seven months later in February 1927, the charges against McPherson were dropped. The *Elim Evangel* reported:

> As the result of the preliminary hearing the case was sent for trial last month before the Superior Court. Before the case was heard, however, the Prosecutor withdrew the charges, as the chief witness was found to be absolutely unreliable, and it was evident that Mrs. McPherson's story would be proved to the hilt if the case proceeded further. The devil was defeated, and the gigantic plot failed![7]

The *Elim Evangel* went on to say 'we now rejoice with her in God's mighty deliverance' and then re-printed McPherson's own words:

> The story of my kidnapping still stands. Whether it was but a part of this diabolical plan to ruin this great religious movement, with its thousands of followers, we do not know, nor do we care. We concern ourselves with the Master's work … we shall continue by word, deed and thought to preach and live the Gospel of Jesus Christ.[8]

George had received an urgent telegram from McPherson's mother at the height of the crisis: he must fly over to Los Angeles immediately to take on the pastorate of the Angelus Temple.[9] He resisted this demand and must have been glad that he had held steadily to his course without disturbing the stability or momentum of the

---

[7] *Elim Evangel* 8.3 (Feb 1927), p. 41.

[8] *Elim Evangel* 8.3 (Feb 1927), p. 41.

[9] The telegram read (20 May 1926): JEFFREYS ELIM CLAPHAM LONDON SISTER MCPHERSON DROWNED WHILE SWIMMING TUESDAY SOUL GLORIFIED SISTER HAD ANNOUNCED YOUR CAMPAIGN WHOLE WORLD LOOKING TO ANGELUS TEMPLE FOURSQUARE EVANGELIST IMPERATIVE NEED YOU HERE IMMEDIATELY THIS CRISIS HOUR CABLE EARLIEST POSSIBLE DATE YOU CAN LEAVE MOTHER KENNEDY.

Elim work in the United Kingdom. On her return from Mexico McPherson resumed her ministry with various degrees of controversy until the end of her life in 1944. She remained a popular preacher, sprinkled (perhaps too much) with the stardust of celebrity, and able to leave behind a distinctive Pentecostal denomination that, after her son took over its leadership when she died, continues to the present day.[10]

A Letter from Wigglesworth

While all this was taking place, the Elim Bible College (Elim Woodlands) was beginning to find its feet.[11] There were not enough students to fill the property and the curriculum had yet to be written. The whole project of setting up a training institution was planned as it went along. Jeffreys himself had only attended Thomas Myerscough's Bible school for a month or two and valued its close attention to Biblical exegesis; but, apart from this, Jeffreys was suspicious of biblical scholarship and frequently denounced the errors of modernism and the devaluation of the biblical text by rationalist critique. The course at Woodlands was not validated by any external academic authority. As a result arrangements had an ad hoc air. There was not enough money in the system to pay lecturers.[12] In the summer of 1926 Smith Wigglesworth (1859–1947), the Bradford plumber who became a legendary healing evangelist, was invited to stay at Elim Woodlands. He must have been brought in as an inspirational speaker for the staff and students and, possibly, the Elim congregations in the Clapham area.

Wigglesworth was an interdenominational figure: bluff, unpredictable, uneducated, gracious, and with amazing charismatic gifts, especially for healing. Wigglesworth admired what Jeffreys was doing in Elim but was also aware of what Howard Carter was doing in connection with the newly-founded Assemblies of God. Wiggles-

---

[10] Sutton, *Aimee Semple McPherson*, pp. 152-54.

[11] The advertisement said, 'the college is situated in its own beautiful grounds of 4½ acres in Clapham Park, one of the healthiest and most select residential areas around London. It is within easy access of the revival centres, and but 20 minutes from the heart of this great City.'

[12] EJP to GJ, 3 Aug 1926.

worth penned a letter to Jeffreys saying that he had 'paid a long look' to 'Brother Carter school'.[13] And he saw 'what did not ought to be' in that 30 or more young people were all packed in 'like fish in a box'. Carter did not have enough space to teach properly but he did have a big vision because he 'showed me a map of England and said now they want us here and there and there'. Carter's students were in training to pioneer new assemblies in places where Pentecostalism was unknown.

In a flash of insight Wigglesworth joined Carter's plan with the extensive premises controlled by Jeffreys: he asked if Carter could become 'Principal at Elim Woodlands'. Without having any right to do so, he had already put the question to Carter. Wigglesworth reported 'his [Carter's] face just shone' and he said, 'That is just what I would be delighted to do'.[14] Yet nothing came of the initiative and we have no record of any reply that Jeffreys sent him. That Carter was willing to become Principal of the new Elim college shows how, in these early days, emerging denominational identities were balanced between an overriding evangelistic urgency and the friction of personalities. The private correspondence between Jeffreys and Phillips reveals that, of all other Pentecostal leaders at the time, Howard Carter was the man about whom they felt least warmly.[15]

Carter's plan involved sending partly trained young men to pastor or start congregations by faith and largely from scratch. Jeffreys' plan involved holding his own large campaigns, gathering converts, raising money from them, buying a building and then putting in an experienced preacher as their pastor. In the years until 1934, the Jeffreys method was unquestionably superior.

Campaigning Hard

By the start of 1926, the evangelistic assault on London had planted nine Elim congregations.[16] The time was ripe for campaigning in the major provincial cities. George had already spoken in Plymouth

---

[13] 5 June 1926. Held in the Donald Gee Centre, Mattersey, England.

[14] Wigglesworth spells shone as 'shun', following his pronunciation.

[15] See previous chapter.

[16] George Canty, *Unpublished Manuscript* (Typeset by Grenehurst Press, 1983), p. 96.

in 1915 when he was a young and unknown preacher. In 1924 Stephen had held a successful healing campaign in the city with a small group that had left the Baptists.[17] So George made the 250-mile journey from Clapham to the south-west of England.

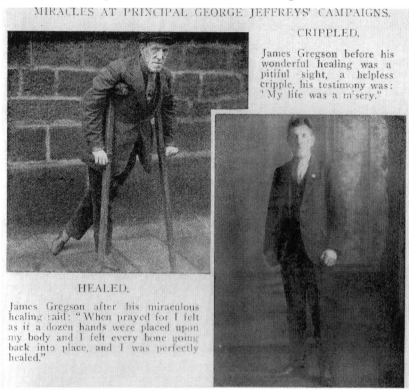

MIRACLES AT PRINCIPAL GEORGE JEFFREYS' CAMPAIGNS.

CRIPPLED.

James Gregson before his wonderful healing was a pitiful sight, a helpless cripple, his testimony was: 'My life was a misery.'

HEALED.

James Gregson after his miraculous healing said: "When prayed for I felt as if a dozen hands were placed upon my body and I felt every bone going back into place, and I was perfectly healed."

Before-and-after Photographs of a Man Who Had Been Crippled

The healing ministry of Jeffreys was evidenced by extraordinary miracles. Not only were industrial accidents more common than today but also soldiers returning from the war might bring home with them disabling injuries. At a time when prosthetic medicine was more primitive, the desire for healing was intense.

The campaign began in the Town Hall, Stonehouse, on 10 January 1926 and was 'uphill work' for a week. Attendance was mediocre but after a series of healings reported in the newspapers, the crowds began to congregate. The *Birmingham Sunday Mercury* gave a lengthy account:

---

[17] Canty, *Unpublished*, p. 96.

The culminating point was reached at a meeting held in Plymouth's historic Guild-hall ... The sick, halt, blind and lame flocked from over a wide area, charabancs even being run from Cornwall, to participate in the streams of healing power which are declared to flow from the pastor's hands.

Such wonderful things have been claimed that many ministers were included in the vast congregation and medical men were numbered among those who had been attracted there by curiosity.

The healing was not performed until the end of the service, which was characterised by great earnestness occasionally rising almost to the heights of typical Welsh revivalism. Pastor George Jeffreys is 'powerful in prayer', as he would be described in his native Wales, and his gospel addresses are charged very fully with that cascade-like eloquence and picturesque idiom which marked Evan Roberts and all his successors in religious revivalism.

Even sceptical policemen, whose duty it is to regulate the throng, have been swept off their feet by what they have seen and heard. One night two girls, one blind and the other dumb, enquired their way to the service of the officer nearby.

An hour or so later he was amazed when the couple returned to him, literally dancing for joy, the dumb girl speaking and the blind girl seeing.[18]

The crowd increased to 4,000. Eventually the Drill Hall, a huge, roofed structure used for army exercises, was hired and George 'preached to an acre of people' and saw 160 receive Christ at one meeting and the aggregate of converts climb to 1,500.[19] He had written to E.J. Phillips in January worried that, if he remained in Plymouth, he would derail the other bookings for the year. Phillips replied, 'you always leave your campaigns when the tide is rising, and I am afraid you are doing the same in Plymouth. If you stayed on and postponed Guernsey and Liverpool, it would be best for

---

[18] E.C.W. Boulton, *George Jeffreys: A Ministry of the Miraculous* (London: Elim Publishing House, 1928), p. 188. The quotation is from the *Birmingham Sunday Mercury* (31 Jan 1926).

[19] Canty, *Unpublished*, p. 97.

Plymouth.' So George stayed and three days later reported, 'I'm having the time of my life. Souls are continually flocking to Christ. Most startling and marvellous healings, while yesterday hundreds were turned away from the town hall an hour before starting time.'[20] The last meeting was held on the 14 February, 1926, making the campaign stretch over five weeks.

This campaign, now that George was out of the shadow of Stephen, was the first that seems to have brought about the realisation that whole cities could be stirred by the spiritual excitement of these huge meetings. They gave George the confidence to imagine large Elim congregations strategically placed within the main population centres of the British Isles. London was the most obvious target but London was, and remains, the largest, richest, most diverse, and most sophisticated and potentially sceptical city in Britain. George now asked that follow-up letters sent to the Plymouth converts should be headed 'Elim revival and healing campaigns' while ensuring that publicity identified his name with that of Elim. Until then publicity had tended to name the preacher and advertise revival meetings without underlining the Elim brand. It was George's intention to build up Elim and to prevent any confusion that might exist in the public mind about whether he or Stephen was its leader.[21]

Straight after the final meeting of the Plymouth Crusade, George boarded the ferry with Darragh and McWhirter and sailed to Guernsey where he held long-planned meetings.[22] There had already been Elim incursions to the Channel Islands through the preaching of members of the Evangelistic Band. Now George himself came to St Peter Port where, in the island's most spacious hall, 'upwards of 900' were present. On the final evening between 1,800 and 2,000 assembled, which must have amounted to a significant proportion of the island's population, and about 100 received Christ.[23] George was to return in 1934 and 1936 with the result that

---

[20] Cartwright, *Evangelists*, p. 75.

[21] Cartwright, *Evangelists*, p. 77. Letter 2 Feb 1926 GJ to EJP '... it was alright when Stephen worked with us, but now that he is in opposition I must do something to keep my name before the public. In fact self preservation demands it at the moment.'

[22] *Elim Evangel* 7.4 (15 Feb 1926), p. 43.

[23] *Elim Evangel* 7.7 (1 Apr 1926), p. 26.

there are several Elim congregations on the islands to the present day.

On 14 March Jeffreys was ready to begin preaching in Liverpool. There had already been postponements because of the extended campaign in Plymouth and the week in the Channel Islands. In addition Stephen Jeffreys, along with his son Edward, were campaigning in the Potteries and had also held, or were due to hold, meetings in Liverpool.[24] Once these complications were out of the way, George was ready to start his own push first in a local church and later in the boxing stadium in Lime Street and there are photographs of him ready to address a packed arena from within the boxing ring itself. It makes a dramatic picture to see Jeffreys standing on the canvas with a makeshift pulpit and a sea of faces all round him and advertising hoardings for garages and motor vehicles in the upper gantries. Despite its traditional Irish Catholic loyalty, Jeffreys made inroads into the city and saw 800 conversions during his first visit and, in July in tent meetings, hundreds more.[25] During the first visit he held a special service for children only and many of them received healing.[26]

The pace of these campaign meetings was relentless. One followed another in quick succession while, behind the scenes, frantic organisational activity was occupying Jeffreys' mind, as we shall see. After the successful Liverpool meetings, all the events associated with Aimee Semple McPherson described in the previous chapter took place: she came to the Surrey Tabernacle and then the great Albert Hall meetings were held and Elim people from all over the country converged on the capital for the celebratory gatherings.

Not content with these successes, Jeffreys planned a visit to the south coast. He encouraged Elim people to combine attendance at his Bournemouth campaign with their summer holidays.[27] He pitched a large tent with uncomfortable bench seating at the tram terminus in Bournemouth.

---

[24] http://www.liverpoolrevival.org.uk/biography.htm (accessed 3 Aug 2015).

[25] *Elim Evangel* 7.8 (15 Apr 1926), p. 93; 8.13 (1 Aug 1926), p. 156.

[26] Canty, *Unpublished*, p. 99. http://georgejeffreysandstephenjeffreys.blog-spot.co.uk/2011/09/george-jeffreys-crusades-in-liverpool.html (accessed 3 Aug 2015).

[27] *Elim Evangel* 7.10 (15 May 1926), advertisement.

Elim's offer to respectable Bournemouth residents of a long ride in a clattering tram to a flapping tent and seats as bad as a hair shirt, no great organ, no surpliced choir and no beauty, only to hear sermons, lacked something of the science of show business.[28]

Yet, the crowds started to stream in.

William Hutchinson, 18 years before, had opened Britain's first purpose-built Pentecostal church. It was here Hutchinson made his claims to apostolic status; and, although it is impossible to calculate how many of Bournemouth's citizens were aware of Hutchinson or his ministry, it is reasonable to suppose that echoes of the events of 1908 stimulated attendance at Jeffreys' meetings. He himself had visited Bournemouth as a young man and understood its potential.[29] Perhaps he wished to counteract the odd and damaging strain of Pentecostal teaching which was now emanating from Hutchinson or perhaps he knew Bournemouth was fertile ground for fresh Pentecostal planting. The 1,200-seater tent filled up.

After five weeks about 600 people had been converted. There had been many healings and several people had been baptised in the Spirit where they sat. Breaking of Bread services were held in the marquee (preparing new converts for settling into the regularities of church life) and still rare and expensive motorcars were to be seen parked outside. The *Bournemouth Times and Directory* described the interior of the tent as being decorated with flamboyant texts of Scripture and filled with lively songs of the Sankey and Alexander type together with airs that 'resembled Negro melodies' and others 'not unlike ragtime'. Jeffreys, the newspaper reported, 'possesses quite an original style of preaching. At the outset of his address he is conversational and communicates his thoughts in an easy, matter-of-fact way, making the audience feel perfectly at ease' and as he proceeds:

He makes a powerful appeal for faith in the Scriptures. At such a moment, in dramatic style, he lifts the Bible in both hands, and holding it tenaciously above his massive black curly hair, thunders with his deep musical voice, 'what saith the Scriptures?' The

---

[28] Canty, *Unpublished*, p. 99.
[29] Chapter 3.

audience is simply held spell-bound as he drives home, with a keen sense of logic, point after point in a rhetorical climax.

And afterwards the sick and suffering are invited to come forward to a large platform where they are ministered to while the congregation reverently sing. Healings of rheumatism, curvature of the spine, deafness, paralysis, and other ailments follow and 'Pastor Jeffreys believes we are on the verge of a great spiritual revival, which will precede the return of Christ'.[30]

At the start of September and after seven continuous weeks Jeffreys estimated a grand total of 1,500 conversions (although some of these must have remained attached to other churches) and the largest hall in the town was booked for the final rally.[31] Reports of the atmosphere and the astonishing healings were verified by secular journalists and confirmed by the headmaster of the local Grammar School.[32] Something like 3,000 people filled the Drill Hall and after the dust had settled and the tent been packed away 'not one but several churches resulted'.[33]

With what appears to be a systematic and strategic intention, Jeffreys headed to Carlisle, about 350 miles north of Bournemouth, situated on the northwestern border of England. It was a town touched by Methodism in the 18th century but George's visit followed the invitation of a small group of Pentecostals. The autumn weather was chilly and the outlook unpromising. The meetings took place in a succession of buildings. Jeffreys wrote to Phillips saying the Carlisle Hall '... is a kind of cellar underground without any windows and no way for air to get in, not a single ventilator and the roof nearly touching my head is held up by posts'.[34] Notwithstanding the unpleasant surroundings turnout swelled and followed the now familiar pattern. Preaching transferred to the Queen's Hall and then to the Drill Hall before pressure of numbers forced the hiring of the Military Riding School, a venue without benches or heating but large enough for 3,000 people and convenient as long as every-

---

[30] *Elim Evangel* 7.17 (1 Sept 1926), p. 194.
[31] Boulton, *Jeffreys*, p. 201.
[32] Boulton, *Jeffreys*, p. 205.
[33] Canty, *Unpublished*, p. 100.
[34] GJ to EJP, 26 Oct 1926.

one brought their own seating. By November a delighted Jeffreys reported:

> The whole town is a stir. I can see that Carlisle will probably eclipse Bournemouth. There are hundreds of young people captivated the like of which I have never seen before.[35]

He went on,

> The salvation of souls is marvellous in every meeting, I cannot keep count ... the cream of the city is now clamouring to get in ... The healings are more and greater than anywhere. Today the place was stirred by a young lad whose arm was in splints and broken. After he was prayed for, his mother took off the splints and the arm was perfect. I cannot possibly tell you how we have gripped the city.[36]

Every night and three afternoons each week thousands turned to Jeffreys. 'From far and near they came, bringing their halt, maimed, and blind to the healing services, while hundreds were drawn into the kingdom of God, making the total number of conversions about 1,200'.[37]

The General Strike

A bitter and mounting dispute between mineworkers and mine owners came to a head. It had simmered in the background during the first part of the 1920s but negotiations eventually foundered. 'It would be possible to say without exaggeration that the miners' leaders were the stupidest men in England', said Lord Birkenhead, 'if we had not frequent occasion to meet the owners'.[38] Both sides were intransigent, the miners toughened by their hard labour and the owners by greed for high profit. The government attempted to head off the action until, with Churchill as Chancellor of the Ex-

[35] GJ to EJP, 11 Nov 1926.
[36] H.C. Cartwright and D. Holdaway (eds.), *Defining Moments: 100 Years of the Elim Pentecostal Church*, (Elim Pentecostal Church, 2015), p. 42.
[37] Boulton, *Jeffreys*, p. 209.
[38] See https://en.wikiquote.org/wiki/F._E._Smith,_1st_Earl_of_Birkenhead (accessed 4 Aug 2015); a variation of the quotation is given in A.J.P. Taylor, *English History 1914–1945* (Harmondsworth: Penguin, 1985), p. 190.

chequer and after a debate in the House of Commons, it came to a point of decision: no fresh money to buy time for additional negotiation. The strike was called for 3 May 1926 and, although it centred on the mineworkers, spread out to other unions and so became general. The government had made contingency plans to continue the provision of transport and other basic services.[39] After nearly two weeks, the Trades Union Conference called the strike off; and, although the miners continued their resistance until their financial resources were exhausted, the emergency was over. It left a legacy of bitterness in the coal fields, and both the Jeffreys brothers must have been acutely aware of feelings within the mining community even if they themselves, at this stage in their lives, were largely detached from it.

There are no sustained references to the strike in the Elim literature of the period, simply a fleeting reference to the inconvenience caused to those who wished to attend campaign meetings while transport was paralysed.[40] There is no reflection on the role of the church in society, no outpouring of sympathy either for the miners or the government, no practical financial aid for the families of miners, and Elim churches never developed a tradition of social critique or attempted to found any humanitarian institutions. Given George's latent support for British Israel doctrine, it is likely that his own political leanings were conservative or certainly monarchist. Having said this, Nonconformity generally avoided political comment: this was left to a stream within Anglicanism represented most notably by William Temple and Christian Socialism.[41] In short, the charismatic gift of prophecy that Pentecostals believed to have been restored to the church was not a gift that was directed towards social inequality. Such a reading of the term 'prophetic' may belong to a different and more rationalistic theological tradition.

The Foursquare Gospel

The earliest Pentecostal churches – those connected with Parham or Seymour – had used the words 'apostolic faith' in their titles. Aimee

---

[39] Taylor, *History*, p. 312.
[40] Cartwright, *Evangelists*, p. 92.
[41] See Hastings, *A History of English Christianity*, p. 190 and passim.

Semple McPherson may have been the first person to use the term 'foursquare' in her title; and, if she was, she meant by it the same as Jeffreys. This was a gospel centred on Jesus as Saviour, Healer, Baptiser in the Spirit, and Soon-Coming king. It was distinct from the 'fivefold' gospel that preceded baptism in the Spirit by a definite experience of sanctification. The term 'fourfold' was precise and had the advantage of focusing specifically on the work and activity of Jesus – sanctification might appear redolent of human effort. This was not to say that Jeffreys disbelieved in sanctification but he was not prepared to highlight it; and, in this way, he moved his theological position close to that of Assemblies of God which also de-emphasised sanctification as a condition of Spirit-baptism. There was a further benefit to the term 'foursquare' as an allusion to the heavenly Jerusalem as a city 'built foursquare' (Rev. 21.16) and implying stability and biblical firmness.

During 1926 Jeffreys, after consultation with Phillips and other leaders, set up the Foursquare Gospel as an overarching organisation.[42] The Church of the Foursquare Gospel, sometimes known as 'Foursquareism' by its detractors, allowed Elim congregations that had been brought into being by George Jeffreys or the Evangelistic Band to be joined by other churches which had originated independently.

There was widespread uncertainty about the new arrangements and Jeffreys wrote:

> Yes! I quite see that we are misunderstood and will be *until* the constitution is in the hands of the people. I was blamed before for being an autocrat, now they blame me for making an honest attempt to join in with others not in Elim.[43]

Later that month he wrote from Plymouth, 'we hear down here that I have made a new sect, of which I am the pope and my aim is to smash the Assemblies of God'.[44] The gossips saw the new initiative as a ploy to divert the flow of independent congregations from As-

---

[42] E.J. Phillips worked on the Constitution with Pastor Pinch and had to decide, for instance, who should receive credentials and the minimum size of a congregation that would merit the granting of credentials (they decided on 50 people), EJP to GJ, 26 Jan 1926.

[43] GJ to EJP, 16 Jan 1926.

[44] GJ to EJP, 20 Jan 1926.

semblies of God into Elim, and it was certainly true Jeffreys wanted to attract congregations additional to the ones he had already founded. This led to a question from Phillips to Jeffreys 'which assemblies are to be Foursquare and which are both Elim and Foursquare?'[45] The looseness of the arrangement is also evident in remarks made by Jeffreys to Phillips about a good independent congregation that wished to join,

> Just write him[46] and explain the two constitutions and say that we would gladly consider his assembly being in Elim if he so desires, as well as being in Foursquare. Just say that all our centres are like this now.[47]

By July better explanations were offered in the *Elim Evangel*. There readers learned:

> The Foursquare Gospel Churches … those churches and ministers who have already perused the Constitution, will have been impressed by the gracious reconciliation of the *real spirit of liberty*, and *constitutional government*. As has already been pointed out, every encouragement is given to ministers to spread the glorious message along the lines of their personal vision. The only bonds in this new union of churches and ministers are the bonds of Christian love and fellowship.

> At a special inauguration meeting which was held in London during the Whitsuntide Rally, the churches which had made application were accepted …

> There is now an open door for a *common platform for all* who preach the full gospel. No church or assembly would be debarred from entering, providing of course its teaching and practice is in accordance with the Constitution of the Foursquare Gospel Churches.[48] (original italics)

---

[45] EJP to GJ, 25 Jan 1926.
[46] Henry Mogridge who had pastored the assembly in Lytham, Lancs, near the PMU training school.
[47] GJ to EJP, 24 Feb 1926.
[48] *Elim Evangel* 7.13 (1 July 1926), p. 151.

This organisational expansion was engineered in the midst of some of most astonishing evangelical campaigns ever held in the British Isles. Jeffreys, with Phillips' help, sustained demanding daily preaching while wrestling with the future composition of Pentecostalism. As his correspondence demonstrates, he had a capacity, probably not seen among preachers since John Wesley, to focus on small practicalities *and* matters of strategic principle.

Behind the Scenes

While campaigning was exceeding all expectations, Jeffreys was beset by an array of recurrent challenges. First, the question of money loomed large. Campaigns were financially unpredictable. Every combination of possibilities presented themselves. There might be thousands of people and generous offerings or, equally possibly, thousands of people and offerings insufficient to cover the hire of the venue; or, again, there might be small crowds and a welcome generous donor among them. The advantage of using the tent was that the cost was controllable and did not create many difficulties if the campaign needed to be extended. The disadvantage of the tent was that it could only be fully enjoyed in fine summer weather. The finances could be balanced by paying for one campaign from the proceeds of the campaign before – this might be the theory – but in practice income fluctuated too much to be reliable, with the result that Jeffreys found himself juggling money from one account to another. He might borrow money from one of the Belfast churches and then have to pay back or borrow money from the Publishing Office, which was now beginning to make a reasonable profit with the fortnightly sale of the *Elim Evangel*, but also have to pay that back, especially because Phillips kept the accounts closely and would not tolerate financial sloppiness.

And second, more pressing than money, was the matter of who would take over the campaign congregation once Jeffreys left. All the hard work would evaporate if a promising new congregation was put in the hands of an incompetent. Yet who could step into Jeffreys' shoes without disappointing new converts who had been brought up on the very best music and preaching that Elim could offer and with a flow of divine healing miracles on an almost daily basis?

The money was complicated. There were loans within the Elim system as well as personal loans to help cash flow. A Mrs. Owens was prepared to lend money to Elim and this, in its turn, enabled the Publishing Office to repay Belfast. Phillips made sure a promissory note was written to Mrs. Owens which Jeffreys had to sign. The surplus of the Plymouth offerings was then banked to the credit of the Ulster Bank.[49] Only Phillips and Jeffreys really knew what was going on here; and, amidst all this, there had to be some personal income going to Jeffreys which seems to have come from 'love offerings' taken by the evangelist for his own needs and expenses. This was a not uncommon pattern adopted by all kinds of evangelists but Jeffreys wryly commented, 'I got one love offering at the end of the first fortnight [from the campaign at Plymouth]. How to face asking for another I do not know.'[50] Jeffreys himself certainly had some money, and rightly so, given the enormous amount of work he put in, though whether what he earned was in any way related to the amount that had previously been agreed as Stephen's stipend is not known.

The complications arose because new accounts were opened for new projects. So there was a Clapham account that appears to be connected with the General Office and, perhaps, the costs of the staff working there. Even so, the people with the power to move the money around seem to have been Jeffreys and Phillips and they did so with commendable scrupulousness, Jeffreys found the financial strain wearing. At one point, when invited to preach in Belgium he wrote to Phillips 'I cannot promise to go. I must go on campaigns *where I can get finance to get myself out of a muddle*' (italics added).[51]

And it was not just the cost of campaigns that fell on Jeffreys. He was having to buy and erect buildings. Phillips wrote to him saying that extending the hall at Barking cost £130 and the new hall for Ilford would cost £634.[52] Jeffreys pleads, 'if there is any chance of the hall at Ilford going up, it wouldn't be necessary to enlarge Bark-

---

[49] GJ to EJP, 30 Jan 1926.
[50] GJ to EJP, 30 Jan 1926.
[51] GJ to EJP, 13 Feb 1926.
[52] EJP to GJ, 18 Feb 1926.

ing'.[53] And then, amidst all the building transactions, Phillips grumbles to Jeffreys that, after entrusting the buying of land to other people on one occasion, he found the dimensions were incorrect and the site was covered with rubbish. Phillips would only trust himself to do this job properly but complains to Jeffreys about the extra work this will entail.[54]

One of the greatest financial outlays threatening Jeffreys was the projected cost of buying the Surrey Tabernacle and the financing of this from the sale of land round Woodlands, which Mrs. Owens might not agree to. So Jeffreys wanted to backtrack on the offer for the Surrey Tabernacle and has *three sleepless nights* on the matter – a revealing detail about the way the weight of financial transactions burdened him.[55] Yet, even while Jeffreys was short of money, the worries sometimes went the other way. Phillips complained to Jeffreys of being short of cash and asks Jeffreys for help. 'We are on the rocks. I have about £40 in the bank and have to pay within a few days £215.'[56] Jeffreys does what he can:

> I borrowed four hundred pounds in Belfast to pay for the seats and architects and I expect a bill from the contractor to clear him off. I hoped to keep what I had in High St Branch Clapham to pay the bill when it comes but here is this tent business now. Well the only thing I can do at present is to let you have what will clear the tent and trust that enough money will come in from the surplus offerings of the assemblies to pay for the seats.[57]

In the same letter Jeffreys told Phillips, 'the last Liverpool campaign did not clear ... and I even had to pay out of my own private a/c all expenses'.[58] And then, a month later, Phillips takes a well-deserved holiday and Jeffreys writes to him 'so you are off to the Continent. How fortunate some people are! I hope I will find some responsible

[53] GJ to EJP, 18 Feb 1926
[54] EJP to GJ, 23 Feb 1926.
[55] GJ to EJP, 21 June 1926.
[56] EJP to EJ, 22 July 1926.
[57] GJ to EJP, 26/27 Aug 1926.
[58] GJ to EJP, 26/27 Aug 1926

person in charge so that I can communicate.'[59] After the switchback ride Phillips summarises his view:

> I can only see one way to work it, and that is to put all surplus offerings, after paying the running expenses, into the Building Fund. I have practically given them to understand this, but would like your confirmation. In fact I see it is the only right way with all assemblies, except where the initial expense of the campaign opening up the work has not been met.[60]

In the autumn Jeffreys complains, 'We will lose money in Carlisle. Very poor collection here.'[61] So these two campaigns in the north of England failed to break even and Jeffreys veers between expressing astonished delight at the response to his preaching and staring bleakly at all the runaway costs.

The deployment of ministers was also complicated. Sometimes a minister wanted to be in one place and Elim – usually Jeffreys or Phillips – wanted to deploy him elsewhere. Sometimes there was already a local pastor responsible for the original invitation to Jeffreys who, once the campaign was over and the congregation had been enlarged, was overwhelmed by the new responsibilities. On top of this, ministers local to an area might attempt to split the enlarged congregation by leading part of it into a new building or a new direction.

The hasty letters, often on scraps of paper and sometimes in pencil, are like dispatches from the battlefield:

> Let me know who I am [to] send to Plymouth. Just received a letter from JB Hamilton asking me for an opening again. A very pitiful letter. How foolish these fellows are.[62]

He continues saying he is 'simply worried over what is going to happen when we all leave'. And, despite one of the local pastors believing that he was the right man for the job, Jeffreys has little confidence that the young people who have been brought into the church will stay,

---

[59] GJ to EJP, 3 Aug 1926.
[60] EJP to GJ, 3 Aug 1926.
[61] GJ to EJP, 29 Oct 1926.
[62] GJ to EJP, 8 Sept 1926.

I can see now how Pastor Blackman[?][63] much as we love him cannot cope with the tremendous ingathering that is taking place here. The only bright spot in the whole business is that he has faith to believe he can. But just think of it. He will, if he takes on Springbourne have four churches and without a single worker who would appeal to the great company of young people.[64]

Jeffreys frets about the future: 'I can see signs of the work going to nothing'. This is a need of money as well as personnel and 'I do not think to suggest funding a good worker, because Pastor Blackman[?] really feels able to control the district'. The students from Elim Woodlands, who might have provided the necessary reinforcements, were not yet ready to step into the new pulpits. 'What am I to do?' cries Jeffreys, 'the situation is nearly crushing me'.[65]

There are also worries over a Mr. Nolan. By now Jeffreys is ready to hand over these difficulties to Phillips. 'I will leave this matter entirely in your hands as you are now in possession of all the facts'. But Jeffreys then adds, 'he is simply an ass that is all I got to say, and if he stays on, he will drive some of the best people out simply to have revenge on them'.[66] It is not clear what is afoot here but evidently Nolan was acting stupidly and money may have been at the root of the matter. 're his love offering if he does not hand it over to help clear the debt for renovations I feel like not offering him any place'.[67] It appears Nolan had taken a 'love offering' from meetings in September and kept the money himself rather paying for building work.

So Jeffreys tells Phillips to redeploy Nolan, 'just write him a line and say that you consider it best for him to come away and not to stay there under any conditions'. Nolan, it seems had organised a petition in his own favour but Jeffreys is unimpressed. 'These people who have signed the petition might sell him for tuppence any day. If we're going to allow workers to act like this, it is far better for them to work under a Committee of Elders'.[68]

---

63 Writing illegible.
64 GJ to EJP, 8 Sept 1926.
65 GJ to EJP, 8 Sept 1926.
66 The wording is clumsy and must have been written in a hurry.
67 GJ to EJP, 20 Sept 1926.
68 GJ to EJP, 20 Sept 1926.

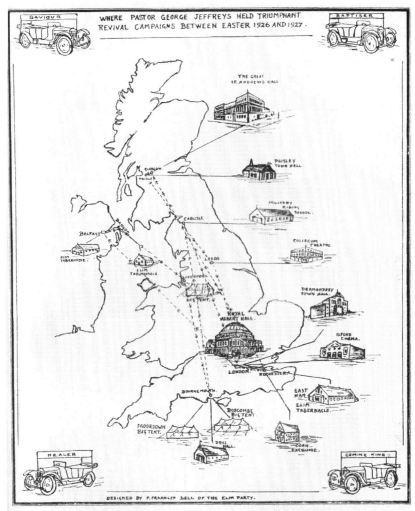

BETWEEN EASTER, 1926, and EASTER, 1927.

This sketch was designed by F. Franklyn Bell, one of Principal George Jeffreys' Campaign party in 1926. The revival wave swept through all kinds of buildings throughout the land.

One word about the car which carries the Principal and his co-workers to all parts of our beloved land with the Foursquare Gospel. This car is a wonderful testimony to the care of a loving Father over His children. Night after night demands were made for the Principal to preach to large and still larger congregations, and the glorious ministry of Jesus the Saviour and Healer meant that it was unusual for him to arrive home before midnight, till those who loved him grew anxious for his physical welfare. Twice money came in from the Lord's treasure house for the purchase of a car, but on each occasion pressing demands for means to carry on led to the sacrifice of this hope. At last a third child of God, a dear brother realising the necessity of a car for the campaign party, mentioned that it had been laid on his heart to make a gift towards God's work of a car or NOTHING! So the Lord's car arrived. Our Heavenly Father knew that a car was essential, and in His own perfect way He met the need.

Jeffreys' Travel Map

Up and down the country by car in 1926 and 1927 holding meetings,
buying buildings and establishing new congregations.

J.B. Hamilton seems to be copying Nolan because 'he carried on in exactly the same way as Nolan is now doing … For the time being you could suggest that he opens a mission in the district where he is at present and that we would recognise him'.[69] So the pastors wanted to run their own churches without being beholden to Elim and were prepared to lead their own missions drawing upon (presumably) Pentecostal people who had first been attracted through the big Jeffreys meetings. Elim sends its volunteers into the pulpits they will fit best. So Jeffreys writes in the same letter, 'Mr Davies would never suit Guernsey. Miss Allen, I think would.'

Behind the scenes Jeffreys' health occasionally falters. 'I have struggled to go to the services. Last night I spoke for about twenty-five minutes with both ears deaf.'[70] He was only 37 years old and fit enough to continue working despite physical setbacks of this kind. There was no one who could replace him at short notice and if he was advertised as the preacher then preach he must.

Reflection

It had been a year of lasting achievement. Phillips noted the places where new buildings had been opened in 1926. These were: Battersea, Bournemouth, Belfast (Ravenhill Road), Bermondsey, East Ham, Ilford, Hull, Plymouth, Liverpool, Rayleigh, and Bangor (Manselton).[71] The Bible School was starting to train suitable young pastors though it could not yet meet the demands of the new churches. When the final account for the year was compiled, the old stamping ground of Belfast was expanding while new London churches were being planted and the big campaigns had resulted in additional congregations with their own premises. Photographs of buildings were spread across the annual review printed in the *Elim Evangel*. The Foursquare Gospel was advancing; and, in his Christmas address to the movement, Jeffreys noted,

---

[69] GJ to EJP, 20 Sept 1926.
[70] GJ to EJP, 20 Sept 1926.
[71] *Elim Evangel* 7.23-24 (6 Dec 1926), p. 280. Battersea is missing from the photographs though listed in EJP to GJ, 4 Nov 1926.

The largest Pentecostal assemblies in the United Kingdom have been shepherded by Elim Pastors, Teachers and Evangelists … the Elim Crusaders (our young people) are becoming known everywhere. Their work – holding street meetings, visiting hospitals, workhouses, etc., distributing tracts from house to house – is being owned and blessed of God'. Well might he say, 'in looking back over the triumphs of 1926 our hearts overflow with gratitude to God'.[72]

---

[72] *Elim Evangel* 7.23-24 (6 Dec 1926), p. 277.

8

1927: A Telegram from the King

The United Kingdom of the 1920s and 1930s was a far cry from today. The school leaving age could be as low as 12 with the result that many young people started working in factories in their teens.[1] Standards of health were lower, partly because nutrition was less well understood. Life expectancy was short and perhaps as low as 65 for men. Smoking was still socially acceptable and its catastrophic effects on health appear to have been unknown. Antibiotics, although penicillin was discovered in the late 1920s, were not prescribed until the start of the Second World War. Tuberculosis was a killer and perhaps as many as 50% of those who contracted it died and those who survived were required to spend long months in a sanatorium isolated from friends and family.[2] And, if health was weaker, unemployment was higher. It ran at 12.5% in 1926, dropped to 9.7% after the General Strike, and then rose to 10.4% in 1929 at the time of the stock market crash and a year later was up to 16%. It was worst in the north-east of England where in 1930 it ran at 20% and in the shipbuilding sector was worse still – over a

---

[1] My mother-in-law (born 1915) went to work in a shirt factory in London at the age of 14.

[2] http://www.slideshare.net/JennaTackett/tuberculosis-in-the-1930s-80808-29; Whatever the purported benefits of the fresh air in the sanatoria, even under the best conditions, 50% of those who entered were dead within five years (1916) https://en.wikipedia.org/wiki/History_of_tuberculosis.

quarter of men were without work.[3] In areas of high unemployment, food was expensive, general levels of health deteriorated and life expectancy diminished. Beer and cigarettes remained the traditional consolations of the poor.

It is against this background that the success of Jeffreys' healing crusades must be seen, especially at a time when there was no National Health Service and where the poor were dependent upon voluntary hospitals of dubious quality.[4] The impression given by descriptions of healings in the crusades is that medical science was reduced to offering splints, callipers, braces, spinal supports, iron belts, body jackets, and other types of alleviation and that diagnosis lacked the precision most people in the West are accustomed to today.

The great cities of the land, like Birmingham, had developed slowly in an unplanned manner so that factories, shops, workshops, garages, and cheap housing might lie next to each other in a vast urban sprawl. There were no commercial districts or attempts to separate spewing factory chimneys from massed dwellings; and, where industry was set apart from housing, this was the housing of the rich. Only during the 1930s was suburbia with its neat houses, gardens, and leafy streets gradually built. Here an echo of the countryside could delight each middle-class household. For the poor, dampness, inadequate sanitation, dirt, and cold threatened to make life perpetually miserable.

> As you walk through the industrial towns you lose yourself in labyrinths of little brick houses blackened by smoke, festering in planless chaos round miry alleys and little cindered yards where there are stinking dust-bins and lines of grimy washing and half-ruinous w.c.s … Not a single one has hot water laid on.[5]

Elim opened its doors to everyone, and some of those healed emerged from slummy penury, but for the most part its members

---

[3] https://en.wikipedia.org/wiki/Jarrow_March.
[4] http://www.hospitalsdatabase.lshtm.ac.uk/the-voluntary-hospitals-in-history.php.
[5] Orwell, *Road to Wigan Pier*, ch. 4.

" That enormous building has surely never held a nobler office than giving shelter to thousands of God's people during the campaign. Gazing at the myriads of trembling lights and the masses of red and pink blooms which formed such a delightful setting for the Foursquare Gospel, whilst

PRINCIPAL GEORGE JEFFREYS AT FAMOUS ALEXANDRA PALACE.

is to us ever like an early morning blossom sparkling with the dew of heaven, our hearts were touched to the uttermost chord."—Mrs. Bernard Joe (Journalist and political correspondent).

appear to have been drawn from aspirational sections of the working population, not unlike the background from which the Jeffreys family itself came. Unemployment was the real fear because without work it was all too easy to lose self-respect and drop into the depressed underclass of the 'dole'. In one night in 1931 a census recorded over 1,800 men and about 170 women were sleeping on the streets of London or in shelters provided by charity.[6]

Revivals and Divine Healing

The years between 1927 and 1930 can be counted as the most productive of George Jeffreys' ministry. In 1927 he was constantly active and led at least nine major campaigns which were all successful. He had spent Christmas in Belfast preaching at the convention in the company of his old fellow student at the Preston Bible School, W.F.P. Burton, the Congo missionary. The Belfast visit was a standing arrangement and enabled Jeffreys to refresh the Irish roots of his ministry. And, from his correspondence, we learn the Belfast Elim believers were willing to loan substantial sums of money to support Elim's full gospel evangelism.[7]

Early in January, when he was meant to be on holiday, he decided to go to Rochester near the Kent coast, and hold a campaign there. We do not know what prompted this but it was often the invitation of a friend or acquaintance that took him from one place to another. He wrote in 1930:

> The work as we know it today is not the result of any carefully laid plan, neither has it materialised as a result of our copying any other work. By God's grace we have been carrying on from one step to another quite unconscious of the divine programme. While God was pleased to do the planning, we were privileged to do the praying.[8]

---

[6] George Orwell, *Down and Out in Paris and London* (Harmondsworth: Penguin, 1933), p. 219.

[7] See previous chapter.

[8] *Elim Evangel* 11.51-52 (25 Dec 1930), p. 801.

The days in Rochester attracted crowds and the *Evangel* reported 250 decisions for Christ and many healings.[9] The same edition shows how there were sufficient numbers of Elim churches in London for a regular Friday night gathering to take place at the Memorial Hall.[10] Jeffreys himself convened a meeting and opened with the topic of thanksgiving. There is an impression here that Elim churches were engaged in constant meetings night after night, a schedule that continued into the 1970s when Pentecostal churches could still be found expecting their people to come out on two or three evenings a week and twice on Sundays. In the 1920s, an era before nightly television, the bright and cheerful church fellowship was more attractive than staying indoors, especially if the home was cramped and small. Jeffreys himself continued to believe the end of the age was near and the *Evangel* in February 1927 carried an article detailing future divine judgements from whose escape the rapture of the church – its being lifted up to heavenly glory – was prominent.[11] But even the rapture would be followed by a strict judgement of the Christian's life and work so that beneath the singing and the joy of Pentecostal life was a biblical seriousness.

Leaving the south-east of England Jeffreys drove up to one of the main Scottish cities. Glasgow had always been divided between Roman Catholics and Protestants and was culturally linked to Ulster. For a man who had attracted huge crowds in Belfast, it was a natural destination. Like Ulster, Scotland was known for its solemn Calvinism and its strict Presbyterianism. No flippant or lightweight preacher would gain a hearing.

On January 23 1927, meetings began at the St Mungo Hall and the reception was distinctly chilly. On the first Saturday night reinforcements arrived by train. 'Eleven corridor carriages carrying seven hundred passengers left Carlisle station for Glasgow' and from this 650 'were Elim friends and converts from the newly-formed Church of the Foursquare Gospel, Carlisle'.[12]

---

[9] *Elim Evangel* 8.3 (1 Feb 1927), p. 39; see further *Elim Evangel* 8.4 (15 Feb 1927), p. 54.
[10] In Farringdon Street.
[11] *Elim Evangel* 8.3 (1 Feb 1927), pp. 44-46.
[12] *Elim Evangel* 8.5 (1 Mar 1927), p. 77.

On arrival at the Glasgow (central) station we noted the great crowds of people hurrying to the trains, trams and buses for the purpose of attending one of the great football matches for which Glasgow is so keen, but our train-load was hastening to St Mungo's Hall, to see our beloved Pastor and co-workers and to spend 'a day with God'.

What a sight! Pastor's car, skilfully piloted by our dear brother Fred Bell, moved slowly at the head of the procession, and with songs of Zion, the saints of God moved on through the busy Glasgow streets. The police were kind, helpful and so clever at handling the traffic and clearing the way for Elim. Eyes turned to see this great sight; crowds formed up to watch the procession; great interest was aroused as the march progressed.[13]

By 15 February the *Evangel* reported 150 people had professed salvation and that the 'signs and wonders' attending the meetings had broken down Scottish reserve.[14] Even the exacting standards of Scottish divines were met: Jeffreys' preaching style, passionate and logical, met with approval.[15] By 1st March a telegram reached Elim Headquarters in London:

REVIVAL FIRES BURNING IN GLASGOW CROWDS FLOCKING TO THE SERVICES HUNDREDS CONVERTED REMARKABLE HEALING TESTIMONIES BLIND EYES OPENED RUNNING WOUNDS DRIED UP PARALYSIS RUPTURE TUMOUR GROWTHS DISAPPEAR UNDER POWER OF GOD ALL KINDS OF DISEASES HEALED DAILY HALL SEATING TWO THOUSAND TAKEN TO CONTINUE REVIVAL[16]

A fortnight later the number of converts was said to total 750 and included those who had travelled from as far as Orkney. A list of healings took a full page in the *Evangel* and they included deafness, blindness, and a man wounded in the Great War.[17] Meanwhile,

[13] *Elim Evangel* 8.5 (1 Mar 1927), p. 77.
[14] *Elim Evangel* 8.4 (15 Feb 1927), p. 60.
[15] Canty, *Unpublished*, p. 110.
[16] *Elim Evangel* 8.5 (1 Mar 1927), p. 65.
[17] *Elim Evangel* 8.6 (15 Mar 1927), p. 84.

from the south, reports of special services and campaigning in Watford, Rochester, Hull, Ilford, and Liverpool were carried.[18] Arrangements for the Easter Monday meetings at the Royal Albert Hall were advertised as, after four weeks in Glasgow, Jeffreys prepared to move to Paisley, eleven miles west, and again huge crowds thronged the largest hall Elim could hire. The town hall is a huge classical building with steps leading up to the entrance, statues outside, and with pillars supporting the frontage.[19] A national paper, the *Daily Express* (24 March 1927), reported:

> Scenes in Glasgow and the surrounding towns during the past four weeks rival the most emotional incidents in Scottish history.
>
> Vast crowds, moved by the passionate pleading of Pastor Jeffreys, have risen in a body in reply to the evangelist's request to 'stand up for God'.
>
> Scores of people, blind, paralysed, deaf, suffering from all forms of 'incurable' maladies, have been brought to the meetings to join in prayer for healing.[20]

Eventually, at the final rally in St Andrew's Hall, Glasgow, more than 4,500 people packed the building. After a short respite, Jeffreys opened in Leeds.

Elim itself was thriving. The Bible College was advertising for students (at £1 per week) and the course covered, 'First and foremost is the study of the Scriptures. Other subjects include English and Original Languages, Church History, Homiletics' as well as practical training in the revival campaigns and local assemblies. A private tour 'through Palestine' to biblical sites was available for £75 and publicised in the *Evangel* at a cost too high for manual workers and showing that Elim was reaching into the middle class.[21] The meetings on Friday nights in London continued 'with a large company of the Lord's people'.[22] Elim was preparing for the future by training preachers and Christian workers and creating a culture cen-

---

18 *Elim Evangel* 8.6 (15 Mar 1927), p. 95.
19 *Elim Evangel* 8.7 (1 Apr 1927), p. 105.
20 *Elim Evangel* 8.8 (16 Mar 1927), p. 122.
21 *Elim Evangel* 8.7 (1 Apr 1927), p. 107.
22 *Elim Evangel* 8.7 (1 Apr 1927), p. 107.

tred round the music, busy lifestyle, and careful study of Scripture fostered by the *Evangel*. Outside the Elim circle darkness threatened and modernism, especially in the theology that rejected miracles, was 'a harbinger of the Antichrist'.[23]

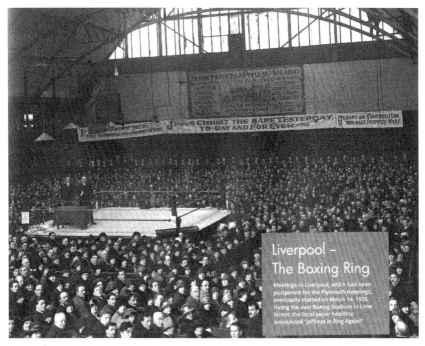

Jeffreys Preaching from a Boxing Ring – Liverpool, 1926

The banners behind carry texts declaring Jesus is the same yesterday, today, and forever and 'as many as touched him were made perfectly whole'. Elim hired any kind of large venue they could find for their crusades and usually filled them to capacity.

Jeffreys had preached in Leeds in 1913 and again in 1920.[24] The event held in March, 1927, eclipsed all that. It was a substantial city with, interestingly, a large Jewish population.[25] The 14-day mission resulted in 2,290 professed conversions and hundreds of healings of all kinds and were described by the pastor who had invited Jeffreys as 'the greatest feat of modern evangelism'.[26] The healings

---

[23] *Elim Evangel* 8.8 (16 Apr 1927), p. 115.
[24] Cartwright, *Evangelists*, p. 87.
[25] http://www.jewishgen.org/jcr-uk/Leeds.htm (accessed 3 Sept 2015).
[26] *Elim Evangel* 8.9 (2 May 1927), p. 129.

were liberally reported in the press, and the reportage was factual rather than dismissive. The *Yorkshire Post* which, despite its name, has a national reputation carried the subheadline 'INVALID GIRL'S CURE WHILE ATTENDING MEETING. Declares She was Free of Pain after being anointed at Leeds by Evangelist Pastor'.[27] 'Hymns were sung with fervour, and the scene throughout punctuated by deep-throated hallelujahs from different parts of the hall. At the close of the meeting those who had benefited shook hands with each other and the officials in a passion of gratitude' said the *Leeds Mercury*.[28] Among those healed was James Gregson who had been crippled for five years after an accident. He was to testify at the Royal Albert Hall a month later.

Royal Albert Hall

The Easter Monday celebration at the Royal Albert Hall in 1927 attracted huge crowds.[29] Organisation behind-the-scenes went smoothly: trains had been chartered, posters had been displayed, invitations had been sent, and the Elim people across the country had prepared for their annual visit to London. Although there was a splash of newspaper reportage with photos and headlines, the most vivid account is by Rom Landau, an observant and perceptive visitor, in a chapter of his book *God Is My Adventure*.[30] On arrival outside the building 'a jumble of taxis, bath chairs and even ambulances' filled the street outside where there were people on crutches 'men and women with deformed limbs or bandaged heads or eyes and mothers with sick children in their arms'.

Inside the long circular passages the congregation arrived carrying suitcases, sandwiches, chocolate, and oranges and 'the prevailing spirit was festive and good-natured' like a holiday outing of people with their picnic lunches. As the hall began to fill up so the organ began to play and 5,000 arrivals broke into the lilting song:

---

[27] *Elim Evangel* 8.9 (2 May 1927), p. 120.
[28] 6 Apr 1927. Quoted in *Elim Evangel* 8.9 (2 May 1927), p. 130.
[29] The cover photo shows one of Jeffreys' meetings in the Royal Albert Hall.
[30] Rom Landau, *God Is My Adventure: A Book on Modern Mystics, Masters, and Teachers* (London: Ivor Nicholson and Watson, 1935).

There never was a sweeter melody,
It's a melody of love.
In my heart there rings melody.
There rings a melody...

And by 10.30 am there was no empty seat. If middle-aged women predominated, the platform surrounds were filled with Foursquare Gospellers, boys in dark suits and girls in white dresses. Lilies, daffodils, and red azaleas framed the front of the platform where men were sitting, some with clerical collars and all of them in dark suits. By now the 10,000 people were singing

There will be music at the fountain
will you, will you meet me there?
Yes, I'll meet you at the fountain,
at the fountain, bright and fair...

And in response to the song leader

Faithful I'll be today,
glad day, glad day!

The crowd joyfully responded

And I will freely tell
why I should love Him so well,
for He is my all today.

The attention of the crowd was to be turned towards Jesus. As the people sat, 'the man whom 10,000 people from all over the British Isles had come to see and to listen to had mounted the platform quite unobserved'.[31] Wearing a dark suit and indistinguishable from the other men around him, there were no tricks to mark his entrance, no searchlight, no stage techniques. When he came to the microphone his voice was strong: 'it was a baritone, and full of the melody which we are accustomed to find in a Welsh voice'; and, as he began to pray, it was evident that he was no high priest but simply one of the people.[32] There was no altar of mystery, no vestments, no complex ceremony, no foreign language by which to disguise

---

[31] R. Landau, *God is My Adventure*, p. 153.
[32] R. Landau, *God is My Adventure*, p. 154.

religious ritual. He displayed none of the unctuousness of lesser preachers and his prayers 'were almost colloquial'.[33]

During the afternoon Elim dispatched a telegram to the king, George V, in Buckingham Palace:

> Thousands of loyal subjects who stand for the whole Bible gathered at Elim Foursquare Gospel demonstration in Royal Albert Hall send heartfelt greetings and loyal assurances and unite in prayer for God's blessing on your Majesty and the Royal household. Pastor George Jeffreys

According to the *Evangel*, 'never did a more heartfelt expression of devotion reach the throne of England'. That evening, a reply was received addressed to Pastor George Jeffreys, Royal Albert Hall, England, and reading:

> I am commanded to express the King's sincere thanks for your kind message of loyal greetings.

And it was signed 'Stamfordham', the King's private secretary.[34] When it was read out, the huge audience stood and spontaneously sang the national anthem. There had been a direct connection between Elim – between Jeffreys – and the king himself. Elim's voice was being heard in the highest reaches of the land and for men and women who saw the monarch as possessing more than symbolic power, this was a moment of religious significance and hope.

The morning meeting focused upon baptism by immersion in water. Jeffreys dismissed 'the pagan Catholic sprinkling of children' in his biblical address. 'There was in his words a natural persuasiveness ... The man who has identified himself with the spirit of the Gospels speaks as though from another level'[35] and

> many responded to his ringing voice and to the pleading of his hands ... At first one or two voices sounded in the general silence, and in the vast auditorium they were like the voices of children. ... More and more people – five, 10, 20, 50 – cried out

---

[33] R. Landau, *God is My Adventure*, p. 155.
[34] Boulton, *Jeffreys*, p. 244.
[35] Landau, *God is My Adventure*, p. 156.

that they wanted to be baptised. Jeffreys listened attentively to each one of them, and to each he exclaimed, 'God bless you'.[36]

The baptisms were to take place in the afternoon. In the meantime, the arena was being cleared in preparation for the healing service in the second part of the morning. Sick people made their way down to the stalls from all over the hall, assisted by relatives or nurses. There were some 400 or 500 waiting as Jeffreys came off the platform with one of his assistants carrying a little bottle of oil. Jeffreys approached one person after another, anointed their foreheads or merely put his hands on their heads, lent over them, and spoke a few words. Many were sitting or kneeling, giving themselves to the moment, and their hands were relaxed in their laps:

> Some of them had raised their heads and had opened their hands as though waiting for God's healing power to flow into them. Many remained in the same position after Jeffreys had laid hands on them, but some began to sway to and for for a while, and had to be helped by the attendant women. A few fell down on the floor as if in a dead faint, sometimes at the very moment Jeffreys touch them – sometimes after he left them.[37]

The organ played softly and the rest of the congregation was sitting quietly and some of them were crying. 'The playing of the organ had become so soft that the steps of Jeffreys and his helpers walking from row to row could be heard quite distinctly. Only when someone fell on the floor was there any commotion'.[38]

After lunch Jeffreys began by asking people to testify to their healings. 'Voice after voice cried back from different corners of the hall' and these included cripples, people who had been blinded in one or both eyes, people who had suffered tumours, growths or cancers, and others with tuberculosis.[39] Some of the people who had been healed had attended elsewhere or in previous years and they came down all the way to the front to tell their stories and some seemed to revel 'in horrors of previous sufferings'.[40] Those

---

36 Landau, *God is My Adventure*, p. 156.
37 Landau, *God is My Adventure*, p. 158.
38 Landau, *God is My Adventure*, p. 158
39 Landau, *God is My Adventure*, p. 159.
40 Landau, *God is My Adventure*, p. 160.

who spoke, according to Landau were 'workmen, artisans and small tradesmen', ordinary people belonging to the class that has always been strongly represented in Nonconformity, but 'it was difficult to doubt the honesty of their testimony'.[41] The point here is that the performance of miracles was the decisive argument against the debilitating effects of modernistic theology. That was the great statement being made by Pentecostal demonstrations to all who would listen.

When Jeffreys preached again, 'the whole of his afternoon discourse is devoted to a careful, critical and exhaustive examination of the present-day claims of the Gospel of Jesus Christ to miraculous power'.[42] This was partly to encourage the baptismal candidates in their potentially embarrassing public expression of faith, especially as journalists were present to watch and report. This was also for the benefit of the clergy on the platform whose denominations had floated away from the anchorage of traditional Protestantism. For ordinary Elim believers this is to build a rational defence against the scepticism of the pub and the workshop. Jeffreys had the ability to preach a 'big sermon' that took large and general themes and applies them to the spirit of the age. Emotionalism, the old accusation thrown at revivalism, is absent. Ostentatious emotional states were avoided and deep feelings were diverted through music and congregational singing. This was the Elim way.

Landau later talks to one of the pastors who says,

> Meetings like this are the greatest impulses in the life of these people. They are like an electric current that charges the batteries for months to come. When the batteries have run down a bit, another meeting will charge them. People simply live for months in the memory of these days. They are the greatest joys of their lives.[43]

That seems to make sense if people are to return to the dreary factories, the crowded streets of London, or the industrial heartlands of the Midlands. The meetings lift those who are immersed in the humdrum struggle for existence and enable them to find a meaning

[41] Landau, *God is My Adventure*, p. 159.
[42] *Elim Evangel* 8.8 (16 May 1927), p. 146.
[43] Landau, *God is My Adventure*, p. 163.

beyond the constant demands of work and putting food on the family table.

Interviewing Jeffreys, Landau found him 'painfully shy'.[44] He looked tired and with a trace of sadness. Asked about how he had come to know of the possibility of divine healing Jeffreys replied,

> 'Through personal experience. I was healed myself as a boy. The impression was terrific'.

> 'You mean the mental or the physical impression?'

> 'The physical impression. It was like an electric current that struck my head'. The words 'terrific' and 'current' and 'struck' were said with the emphasis that had been so convincing when Jeffreys spoke from the platform.

Asked whether he was conscious of what he was doing when he was laying hands on people he replied, 'It is the power of God that only works through me. I claim no powers of any sort. It is the Lord who manifests himself through me' and when asked whether the healing had anything to do with the mind of the sick people themselves, he replied,

> The one teacher I believe in is the Lord. I believe in the Gospels from cover to cover and all the fundamentals of the Christian faith. ... I accept the Bible in its entirety ... The sick must have faith, must pray, must hope that they will be healed. But it is not the effect of mind over matter that manifests itself in healing. It is solely and only the power of Christ over disease.[45]

Landau, who was sceptical about divine healing and looking for explanations covering many religions, appears to have been searching for a 'mind over matter' explanation. Jeffreys decisively rejects this hypothesis which, it has to be said, has not grown any more plausible with the passing years.

Landau changed the subject and asked whether Jeffreys believed in the second coming of Christ. 'I do with all my faith, and I see the signs of His second coming. I see them in the last war, in the unrest in the world, in crisis coming after crisis'.

---

[44] Landau, *God is My Adventure*, p. 165.
[45] Landau, *God is My Adventure*, p. 167.

Here Jeffreys reveals how he reads his own days. Without pinning his interpretation on one particular sign or any single scheme, he anticipates general political and economic unrest preparatory to the climactic moment of Christ's return.

The baptismal service made use of a large green canvas baptistery filled with hundreds of gallons of water and in which Jeffreys, with a few assistants, stood. The converts came down into the tank one at a time and Jeffreys put one hand on their backs and immersed them with the other while saying loudly, 'On the confession of thy faith I baptised you in the name of the Father and the Son and the Holy Ghost, Amen'. Some collapsed and others shut their eyes while many came out smiling. They were quickly provided with blankets or overcoats before being led away to the back of the building to be warmed and dried.

The evening service celebrated Holy Communion and the photographs show the stalls area now laid out with hundreds of trays containing little glasses of grape juice ready for distribution. When the service ended and as people were making their way home E.C.W. Boulton struck up a conversation with two police sergeants who had been detailed to keep an eye on proceedings. Asked how he liked the 'Elim Foursquare Gospel Demonstrations' one replied,

> Well, sir, I've just been talking to my pal here, and I'll say this, that of all the meetings I've been on duty at during my time in the force this has me beat. The singing of all those folk, the joy on their faces, the testimonies, and the message is something new in religious meetings; what is more, he's got the voice for the Albert Hall, and he can be heard all over the building. Believe me it's the goods!

If Boulton has reported the words he heard correctly – and there is no need to doubt his memory – we can picture the puzzled copper wondering what it all meant: all that singing, all those sick people swirling around in the midst of a good-tempered crowd. All those people crying 'Hallelujah'. Later, on his way out Boulton met one of the Royal Albert Hall attendants with boxes of unsold cigarettes in his arms. His daily stock was quite untouched, and so presumably he had made no money, but as he left he was singing.

The next morning the press delivered its verdict: VAST AUDIENCE MESMERISED, said the *Morning Post* (19 April 1927) and carried an account of the meetings and the 'miracle creed' of Pastor George Jeffreys calling out in a thundering voice 'How many people here today have been cured?' and receiving a response from several hundred raised hands. The reporter interviewed two of them, one who had been healed from an accident that had left him only able to walk with crutches and another from a childhood stammer. What is impressive here is reporting of miracles in the *secular* press. This is no in-house magazine for the faithful people of Elim but designed for circulation to the mass market. The reporter has done his job in describing what he saw and then following up by speaking personally with two witnesses who have experienced healing. There is no debunking or scepticism here, nor is the account second-hand. The witnesses were entirely credible to the reporter.[46]

Going South

Hardly had the baptistery and communion glasses been cleared away from the Royal Albert Hall than Jeffreys was setting off by car to Southampton, a major port on the south coast. He began preaching at the new Wesleyan Central Hall on 21 April. He was to continue for many months campaigning in these coastal towns and benefiting from the support given by one to another. When he opened in Southampton, only four people responded to the gospel in the first meeting; but, when 600 Elim converts and supporters arrived from Bournemouth, attention was grabbed, as it had been when the trainload of believers from Carlisle had descended on Glasgow earlier in the year. Whether this was a deliberate strategy on Jeffreys' part is unclear. By now he had preached in most of the United Kingdom and his name was known. Posters and notifications in local newspapers were likely to draw a crowd wherever he went. In those days it was common for the churches to use the 'small ads' pages of local newspapers to advertise the times of their services and Elim took advantage of this practice.

Like all seaports Southampton was not known for its morality or its piety but when Jeffreys arrived with his gospel message, he was

---

[46] Other press reports were similar: e.g. the *Westminster Gazette*, reported in the *Elim Evangel* 8.10 (16 May 1927), p. 149.

soon popular. A Miss Florence Munday who is described as having 'tuberculosis of the knee' and being at risk of amputation was brought to the meetings. On 4 May she arrived in an invalid carriage and was taken to the front of the hall. She heard Jeffreys preach on 'Christian disappointments' and many of her doubts were removed. The congregation sang 'All hail the power of Jesus' name' and she reported feeling the power of God coming upon her. Jeffreys was called over to her; and, when he came he asked, 'How long have you been lying in this old carriage?' she replied, '14 years. The trouble is my knee; it is a wasting disease.' Asked whether she believed that the Lord could heal she replied 'yes' and was told to return to the healing meeting the following afternoon. Jeffreys prayed for her and she stood and walked across the front of the hall. 'It was 4 pm and the congregation were ecstatic'.[47] The leg appeared to have grown during the night and the knee itself lost its wasted appearance. Miss Munday became the pastor of the Elim church in nearby Gosport until 1968 when she retired, and she died in 1980. Something like 800 conversions were recorded and a thriving congregation was established in Southampton that remains to this day.[48]

Meanwhile at Southampton one of the converts, James Gorman, took up pioneer evangelism and 'was instrumental in the opening of five Elim churches in the 1920s' before dying of tuberculosis in 1934.[49] This outcome spoke of genuine revival rather than organised campaigning and shows how the time for church planting was propitious. It also demonstrates that healing was by no means a certainty and that the men who drove their bodies into the ground on the assumption that miracles would always be granted *in extremis* were sadly mistaken. Jeffreys himself spoke of 'the natural law of healing in the use of natural curative means' and by this he seems to have meant that rest, diet, and the avoidance of infection were desirable. 'Sickness', he said, 'may and does arise from unhealthy conditions in which people live ... and from harmful conditions under which they are called to labour'.[50]

---

[47] Cartwright, *Evangelists*, p. 90.
[48] Canty, *Unpublished*, p. 111. *Elim Evangel* 8.11 (1 June 1927), p. 162.
[49] Cartwright and Holdaway, *Defining Moments Elim 100 Centenary*, p. 45.
[50] Jeffreys, *Healing Rays*, pp. 150, 157.

From the port of Southampton to the more refined side-by-side seaside towns of Brighton and Hove was a move of 70 miles. Brighton boasted a royal residence, the exotic Pavilion and Dome, built for George IV. Its architecture was Indian or Moorish in style and set in lush gardens. The campaign, which lasted 10 weeks, started in the Brighton Pavilion, moved across to the stately stone town hall in Hove with its traditional clock tower, and moved again to accommodate the swelling crowds to the Brighton Dome with its electrified candelabra, beaded ceiling lights, and great amphitheatre of terraced seating. At the end of the meetings sufficient money had been given or pledged to allow the acquisition of the old Nonconformist Glynn Vivian Hall in the centre of the town not far from the Dome that allowed the new converts to move into purpose-built premises as a flourishing Elim congregation.

A Baptist minister whose wife suffered from colonic cancer attended the first few meetings in a sceptical frame of mind. But this scepticism was overcome by the reverence and joy of the meetings; and, when he heard Jeffreys preach, the Baptist was delighted by the orthodox presentation of the gospel, the insistence upon new birth and, following this, the possibility of a divine healing as an integral part of the same gospel. The minister was won over initially by the demeanour and attitude of those who were conducting the meetings, and this again demonstrates the deliberately low-key approach taken by the Revival Party. Yes, they were joyful and fervent but they consciously avoided the caricatured excesses of revivalism. When the Baptist minister's wife was healed, he became utterly convinced of the truth of the Foursquare Gospel and wrote a glowing article in the *Elim Evangel*.[51]

The Brighton meetings grew impressively and managed to keep their momentum despite changing location. Any coastal town, unlike a city in the middle of the country, can only bring people in from three points of the compass; and, in addition, lateral movements by train tended to be inconvenient. The power of the meetings to hold the attention of a growing crowd in these circumstances is all the more extraordinary. There were certainly numerous

---

[51] *Elim Evangel* 8.12 (16 June 1927), p. 185. The wife's illness is not named but Cartwright assumes the disease was cancer.

healings and there must have been at least some general favour giv-
en to the Elim party by those who controlled the renting of the Pavilion and the Dome. Even the purchase of the Nonconformist
chapel in Brighton points to the acceptability of the gospel Jeffreys
preached and a recognition of its place within broadly evangelical
traditions.

While the Brighton revival was in full swing, Jeffreys went along
the coast to lay the foundation stone of the Elim tabernacle in
Bournemouth and there are pictures of him standing before a large
crowd and holding his Bible aloft.[52] The church planting strategy
was in full swing because the London churches were also acquiring
property. As many as 1,200 people were reported to have been converted in the Brighton revival; and, while this was happening, missionary thrusts to Congo were also being initiated. Public attention
was grabbed by a huge baptismal service in the public baths at
Brighton, with photos and attendant publicity.[53] If Jeffreys was trying to change the theological climate in Britain, a letter in the *Brighton and Hove Herald* on 25 June indicates he was having some success:

> Sir, – the remarkable revival healing mission recently held in
> Brighton and Hove calls for serious attention from all classes.
>
> In spite of the efforts of the churches to maintain the Christian
> faith, a wave of materialism, mainly promoted by Socialism is
> deeply affecting the age. Those who see evils in this decadence
> welcome help from any religious source.
>
> … the Pastor shewed strong spiritual perception when he dwelt
> on the power of the Gospel, for he said that Jesus came on the
> earth for something infinitely higher than social reform. 'The
> Communists say', he continued, 'it is not the Gospel we need,
> but better housing and environment'. But the speaker's point was
> that when the Gospel was received the environment would
> change …[54]

Such a letter is imbued with the natural conservatism of the retired
population and points to socialism as inimical to the Christian faith.

---

[52] *Elim Evangel* 8.12 (15 June 1927), p. 187.
[53] *Elim Evangel* 8.12 (1 Mar 1927), p. 187.
[54] *Elim Evangel* 8.15 (1 Aug 1927), p. 230.

This, at a time when the Bolshevik Revolution in Russia was still fresh in the minds of the British public, is a reminder of the political polarities of the 1920s.

From Brighton, Jeffreys went west 14 miles along the coast to Worthing. This was also a sedate town, popular among the retired, and a place to which Jeffreys would return two years later. This pattern of a short preliminary visit followed by a longer full-scale crusade had already been followed with spectacular results in Leeds. From Worthing Jeffreys moved 47 miles east to Hastings, another coastal town. He opened using his tent, presumably because no suitable buildings could be hired. The financial uncertainties of his campaigning are obscure at this point but when he summarised at the end of the year he wrote:

> We have passed through the troublous waters of financial difficulty, we have our testing times, we are called upon sometimes to stand with our backs against the wall, – but we stand together. In answer to the prayers of the Lord's people, deliverance comes.[55]

The tent was pitched in Ore Valley Farm and again turned out not to be big enough. 'Revival fires spreading at Hastings. Crowds flock to the big tent daily.'[56] The Elite Picture Theatre was hired; and, although it was three times larger than the tent, every available seat was occupied before the service and crowds stood outside. Jeffreys used some of the same arguments he had used before, 'atheists and agnostics, he said, had a right to demand these miraculous signs'.[57] As far as Jeffreys was concerned the Gospel *had* to be preached with miraculous signs following, for this was the biblical method. His was a double challenge: the mainline church should accept the Bible and start preaching a supernatural gospel and the atheists and agnostics, if they did see miracles, should abandon their disbelief and convert. Again, there remains an Elim congregation in Hastings to this day.

Finally, travelling back 80 miles to the west Jeffreys pitched his tent on Southsea Common until it was caught in a storm. He transferred to the 2,000 seater Guildhall in Portsmouth and in four

---

[55] *Elim Evangel* 8.23-24 (10 Dec 1927), p. 354.
[56] Boulton, *Jeffreys*, p. 252.
[57] From the local *Argus* (22 Aug 1927) and quoted by Boulton, *Jeffreys*, p. 257.

weeks saw 900 conversions.[58] A cinema was bought and converted to a church that prospered till 1939, when, as we shall see, difficulties arose.

Back to London

Everywhere he went that year men and women of all kinds responded to Jeffreys' impassioned, logical preaching. More than ever he believed the coming of Christ was drawing near; and, in an article published in the *Evangel*, one of the Elim heavyweights wrote about the Jewish people as a sign of the return of Christ. Taking the Jewish people as symbolic of the fig tree in the New Testament, when it puts forth its leaves and begins to bud again, Christians should expect the return of Jesus to be near. The sense of Jewish prominence in world affairs would later lead to the murderous anti-Semitism of Nazi Germany; here it was interpreted quite differently as revealing the preparation of human affairs for the fulfilment of biblical prophecy. 'It should be remembered', said the article, 'that today there are 19 Jews in the House of Lords'.[59]

Among those welcomed by Jeffreys and Elim pastors to preach in London in the autumn was Lewi Pethrus from Sweden who would later become a vocal supporter of Jeffreys in the arguments that troubled his later years.[60] Such arguments were in the future and few if any signs are visible at this stage of the turmoil that was to come. Unity seemed the order of the day and during October 1927 articles were written about the importance of the Foursquare Gospel Testimony as a way of linking together Pentecostal believers.[61] This is the big umbrella under which all kinds of Elim churches will sit.

The Bible College and the correspondence course were now running well. Jeffreys, who harboured suspicions about theological education, appears to have changed his mind. At any rate he writes lyrically about the Bible study course available to the Elim family. He wants to take his people on a journey from the beginning of

---

[58] *Elim Evangel* 8.20 (15 Oct 1927), p. 305.
[59] *Elim Evangel* 8.17 (1 Sept 1927), p. 260. Written by Charles Kingston.
[60] *Elim Evangel* 8.18 (15 Sept 1927), p. 281.
[61] *Elim Evangel* 8.19 (15 Sept 1927), p. 293.

time when the earth is without form and void through to the Garden of Eden and the unfolding years of Israel's history and the 'types and shadows' of the coming of Christ 'flashed upon the ever-moving scenery'.[62] It is an image of human history culminating in the return of Christ and Jeffreys has clearly decided that education is better than ignorance.

In the final weeks of the year he campaigns in north London and then in Wimbledon Theatre: 'the pits, stalls, boxes, gallery and dress circle were filled. The titled as well as the poor accepted a place in the cheapest of the 2,600 seats.'[63] About 500 converts are recorded in Hammersmith and a further 1,500 when the great Alexandra Palace is hired. Even John Wesley in his heyday never saw in a single year the scenes witnessed by Jeffreys in those 12 months. It is true that the population has grown since the 18th century, transport is easier, levels of education have risen, the Anglican church is less dominant; but, even when all these factors are taken into account, the energy and organisation, as well as the faith, demonstrated here by Jeffreys have not been seen in the British Isles ever before nor have they yet been equalled. Even Billy Graham, who preached to bigger crowds in the 1950s and 1960s, did not establish congregations or found a new denomination.

---

[62] *Elim Evangel* 8.21 (1 Nov 1927), p. 322.
[63] Canty, *Unpublished*, p. 113.

9

CAMPAIGNING BEYOND LONDON

Churchill had already written a book entitled *The World Crisis*[1] about the events of the First World War. It was the word 'crisis' that rang true with many readers of the signs of the times in the 1920s. The huge casualty list of the war together with the financial stagnation that followed it resulted in the oscillations of the 1920s. There was wealth and poverty, an era of jazz and surrealism, of Bertie Wooster's frivolity and of grim unemployment and financial re-trenchment as the British Empire paid the debt for its exertions on the barbed-wire fields of the front line. The war generated a new political and economic reality: it had bereaved families of their sons and women of their sweethearts, and led to fatalism and mental ill-ness.[2] The 1920s with its the General Strike and, in 1929, a stock-market crash justified alarmist language. From the desperation of working men and the confusion of intellectuals sprang opposing political ideologies that were expressed, during the 1930s, by communism and fascism, by red shirts and black.

No wonder, then, that Elim preachers felt the Second Coming was imminent. They only had to look in the daily newspapers to read about the 'distress of nations' (Lk. 21.25) and they set all this alongside the numbers of Jews returning to Israel, a return inter-preted as the fulfilment of prophecy.[3] They had learnt of the execu-

---

[1] Volume 1 published in 1923.

[2] Siegfried Sassoon is an example of an officer invalided home from the trenches with shell shock.

[3] *Elim Evangel* 11.42 (17 Oct 1930), pp. 665-66.

tion of the ancient royal house of Russia and seen atheism replace Christianity as the religion of its state and people. They were aware of – even if they dismissed – the claims of Darwinian evolution and knew about but resisted the conclusions of the Enlightenment critique of the Bible. Fundamentalism in the United States had confronted modernistic readings of the Bible head on, and Elim approved. Jeffreys in his preaching would attack modernistic theology and point to all the healings he had seen as evidence that he was right and modernists were wrong. As further evidence of the Elim position, the *Evangel* enjoyed publishing articles by Anglican or Methodist clergy who had been convinced by the Foursquare Gospel after attending Elim meetings. Some of the most ringing endorsements of Jeffreys came from such sources.[4]

Elim built up its own organisation and supported its own people, whether by meetings or Bible study materials or opportunities for Christian service. It did not have a grand vision for Christianity – unless it was that the whole church should embrace a supernatural gospel.[5] If they had a strategy for church and society in the UK, it was rooted in the hope of religious revival that repeated on a larger scale what Jeffreys had seen in his home town in 1904. The Revival Party was the living embodiment of this hope and at the zenith of their ministry Jeffreys went beyond healing evangelism and stirred whole cities.

Overall British church attendance declined in the 1920s and 1930s although the Roman Catholic community held steady.[6] Anglo Catholicism, which had the advantage of presenting itself as possessing a timeless doctrinal spine, was attractive to natural conservatives. The Church of England, having made an attempt to mediate during the miners' confrontation with their employers, adopted a reconciliatory social role and its brightest stars attempted to develop inclusive theologies that would benefit the poor.[7] William Temple, later to be Archbishop of Canterbury, was the outstanding intellec-

[4] E.g. *Elim Evangel* 10.11 (12 July 1929), p. 161.
[5] *Elim Evangel* 9.6 (15 Mar 1928), p. 81, 'The Foursquare Gospel represents the only real and possible Christian reunion'.
[6] David Thompson, *England in the Twentieth Century* (Harmondsworth: Penguin, 1985), p. 119. See also http://www.brin.ac.uk/figures/.
[7] Hastings, *A History of English Christianity*, p. 190.

tual of this approach and, while he held a firm personal faith, could not be described as evangelical.[8] For all the honour in which he was held by Elim the King, George V, could not be thought of as more than a middle-of-the-road Anglican even though he read his Bible daily.[9] It was possible to believe that the church was a 'force for good' without believing it should be a force for evangelism. But among the *avant-garde* of the day, Christianity was mocked and rejected.

This mockery might take the form of Lytton Strachey's satirical portraits of the heroes and heroines of Victorian rectitude.[10] Strachey was a member of the Bloomsbury group that had no time for religion and rejected conventional morality, especially monogamy and exclusive heterosexuality. Christianity was either despised or irrelevant and when the 1930s began to reveal the true nature of the choices facing Europeans, there was a swing to the political left and engaged writers and artists volunteered to serve with Spanish Republicans (almost all of whom were irreligious) against the Fascism of Franco that had connections with Catholicism. Little of this registered with the men and women of Elim because they were largely outside the circles where literary and artistic culture held sway. Indeed, it is arguable that for the intellectual elite in the 1920s, culture *replaced* religion – it was the preoccupation of their leisure time and the source of all their values.

The evangelistic preaching of George Jeffreys was compelling and, while it centred upon personal faith in Christ and miraculous healing, made reference to the urgency of the hour. In this he was not ranting or attempting to instil fear into the hearts of his listeners: if they were at all informed about the state of the world, they were likely to be fearful already. In *The Morbid Age*, Richard Overy describes the numerous organisations and associations that could find no answers to the challenges of their time.[11] There were those who placed their hope in the League of Nations as an international body that might prevent war. War itself was the cause of the crisis

---

[8] See *Oxford Dictionary of National Biography* entry on William Temple.

[9] See *Oxford Dictionary of National Biography* entry on George V.

[10] Lytton Strachey, *Eminent Victorians* (London: Chatto & Windus, 1918).

[11] Richard Overy, *The Morbid Age: Britain between the wars* (London: Allen Lane, 2009).

of civilisation and might be described as a human disease against which there appeared to be no remedy. The arrival of Freudian psychoanalysis began to filter through the consciousness of writers and thinkers, but psychoanalysis had nothing useful to say apart from underlining an assumption that violence was an inevitable part of the human condition. For Jeffreys and the Elim evangelists the darkness threatening civilisation lay with the sinfulness of human beings; the solution lay with the Foursquare Gospel, and only there.

Elim Leaders, 1928/1929

Back Row: F.B. Phillips, Wm Henderson, Margaret Streight, W.G. Hathaway
Middle Row: E.J. Phillips, G. Jeffreys, E.C.W. Boulton
Front Row: P.N. Corry, Joseph Smith

Continuing to Campaign

Jeffreys completed 1927 with persuasive preaching in a theatre among the sophisticates of Hammersmith, west London, before sailing to Belfast for his traditional Christmas convention. Belfast was 'the Jerusalem of the Elim work' and he was as faithful to it as it was to him. Crossing next to Glasgow Jeffreys chaired the 1928 New Year convention and found revival fires still burning. Returning to London he resumed campaigning by moving seven miles to the Baths Hall, Kings Cross, for six days a week and three afternoons as well as twice on Sundays to Finsbury Park and London's largest cinema, the Rink. Without showing signs of exhaustion he drew the London crowds who had never seen anything like this before[12] and then turning to the vast, glass Alexandra Palace (the 'Ally Pally' as cockneys affectionately knew it), he secured 1,200 converts. Most issues the *Elim Evangel* would carry big black-and-white photographs of imposing buildings and packed auditoria.

Transferring across London south of the Thames, Jeffreys began to campaign in Croydon. This had once been a village outside the capital. The campaign was announced for three weeks but Jeffreys sacrificed his week of rest and continued for a fourth. Attendance climbed rapidly and brought the headline 'Revival tidal wave at Croydon'.[13] The crowds streamed into the meetings and overflowed outside onto the streets where they sang hymns. Inside the hushed congregation was attentive:

> Revival scenes which have made indelible impressions upon thousands of hearts in the beautiful residential district of Croydon have been unprecedented and unparalleled in its history. The closing weeks of Principal George Jeffrey's Revival Campaign are beyond description. The crowded gatherings, afternoon and evening, the besieging crowds and long waiting queues, testify eloquently to the drawing power of the Revivalist's Foursquare Gospel Message. Visualise if possible the great congregations inside, hanging upon every word falling from the lips of the anointed preacher, whilst thronging crowds outside of the

---

12 Canty, *Unpublished*, p. 113.
13 *Elim Evangel* 9.7 (2 Apr 1928), p. 97.

closed doors sing, 'Jesus, blessed Jesus, Thou art mine,' and you have some faint idea of the scenes at Croydon.[14]

An extensive report written by a clergyman from another denomination summarised the sermons:

Throughout his deliverances from the platform, the Revivalist's messages were not calculated to provoke anything but that deep and serious attention which they always received, as the exposure of the natural man's condition and his urgent need of Christ, the striking and unexpected Gospel pictures drawn from Old Testament type-imagery, the vivid presentations of the Saviour's Passion in the Garden and on Calvary ...

And concluded with an account visualising the Second Coming:

[he] sketches the present drift of nations toward the last great struggle of this Dispensation, and the mental film of our Lord's imminent appearing to receive His people, began to grip the mind in anxious estimate of eternal alternatives.[15]

Over 1,600 converts were recorded and healings from numerous diseases including cancer were reported.[16] All this was done without any local organising committee or any prior collaboration with the local churches. The Croydon meetings resulted in the formation of congregations in Croydon itself as well as South Croydon, Thorton Heath, Wallington, and Woodside.[17] It is not always easy to reconstruct Jeffreys' precise itinerary because the reports of meetings in the *Evangel* did not necessarily follow the order of the meetings as they took place on the calendar. In addition, he would return to places where he had held successful campaigns to open buildings once they had been acquired or built. This also was reported, with photographs, in the *Evangel*. In general, the sequence in the *Evangel* was: advertisement, report, longer report with photos, report of opening of new building or second visit and then, perhaps, printed

---

[14] *Elim Evangel* 9.7 (2 Apr 1928), p. 97. This editorial comment is written by E.J. Phillips who, travelling the short distance down from Clapham, must have attended some of the meetings.

[15] *Elim Evangel* 9.7 (2 Apr 1928), p. 98.

[16] *Elim Evangel* 9.7 (2 Apr 1928), p. 99.

[17] Canty, *Unpublished*, p. 113.

testimony and photo of someone who had been healed. Jeffreys was constantly active at this time and was able to rely on McWhirter and Darragh, the former as an organiser as well as a preacher, and the latter as a song leader as well as an evangelist, to stand in for him or continue after him once he moved on. The Royal Albert Hall meetings at Easter were a regular fixture and the other meetings were distributed over the year as opportunities arose or commitments required.

Elim continued to grow throughout the year. A tabernacle was opened in Rochester and Jeffreys was in Reading for a fortnight's meetings and registered 300 decisions for Christ that resulted in the establishment of a 'living Foursquare Gospel Centre'. The wife of a Baptist minister healed in Bournemouth wrote an article about her healing – which showed that Baptists did indeed attend Jeffreys' meetings and that the healings lasted.[18] At the Easter 'never-to-be-forgotten scenes of revival' witnessed in the Royal Albert Hall it was claimed that Jeffreys 'immersed in water the greatest number of converts in one meeting since the day of Pentecost'.[19] There was a huge Elim Crusader Choir and the great organ was beautifully played. As a sidelight on these events the *Evangel* noted:

> The financial commitments connected with such gatherings as these would in themselves be sufficient to frighten a less lion-hearted leader than Principal George Jeffreys whilst the heavy burden of organisation involved might easily have dismayed less resolute hearts than those associated with him in his big forward moves.[20]

The implication here is that Jeffreys and his team might have been worn down by the tough financial commitments into which they repeatedly entered. The costs of hiring halls remained daunting and there was a sense in which the Elim movement lived from hand to mouth. Equally, the organisation of major events with the billboards, press advertising, discounted travel, choir rehearsals, hundreds of communion glasses, a mobile baptistery, baptismal gowns, stewards, and advice on accommodation demanded constant atten-

---

[18] *Elim Evangel* 9.8 (16 Apr 1928), p. 124.
[19] *Elim Evangel* 9.9 (1 May 1928), p. 129.
[20] *Elim Evangel* 9.9 (1 May 1928), p. 120.

tion to detail and planning. Jeffreys himself withstood the physical demands of baptising 1,000 people in water and the *Evangel* reported that all classes of people, high and low, rich and poor, learned and unlearned were present. The choir numbered 2,000 and attracted reports in the secular press including those from the *Daily Herald* (a Labour newspaper) and the *Daily Chronicle* (supporting the Liberal party). Among the preachers at Easter was John Leech who was given pride of place among Elim personnel even though he never became an Elim Minister. Jeffreys himself preached with his usual bravura and there were healings and photographs to follow.[21]

Elim continued to develop and the *Evangel*, while providing news reports, also offered a weekly 'family altar' that was a series of Bible studies for family prayers. It also carried children's puzzles and small advertisements for guesthouses, holiday homes, domestic servants, and so on and, in this way, created a holy circle in which members could be safe. In May 1928 the *Evangel* listed Elim Tabernacles by the seaside on the assumption that family holidays would also include a visit to the local assembly on Sunday. While these ordinary domestic events were part of Elim culture, sermons on the Second Coming of Christ were vigorously preached and written up as articles. Booth-Clibborn, a relative by marriage of the founder of the Salvation Army, warned about five coming calamities presaging a time of sorrows before the end of the age.[22] E.J. Phillips, connecting the Second Coming with the conversion of the Jews, looked forward to a time 'when Jewish hearts will welcome the Christ of God'[23] and a Professor Cooke, commending anointing with oil and prayer for healing, showed how miracles and expository preaching could comfortably co-exist.[24]

---

[21] *Elim Evangel* 9.9 (1 May 1928), p. 131.
[22] *Elim Evangel* 9.11 (1 June 1928), p. 161.
[23] *Elim Evangel* 9.11 (1 June 1928), p. 169.
[24] *Elim Evangel* 9.14 (1 June 1928), p. 219.

George Jeffreys

Jeffreys in a photo probably taken in the 1930s is seen in a visionary
pose looking steadfastly to the horizon.

Jeffreys, 'amid scenes of holy enthusiasm, opened the Elim Tabernacle in Carlisle' and was gladdened to find a growing congregation under a good local pastor.[25] Back on the south coast at the music pavilion in Eastbourne over 1,000 people testified to conversion
and over 100 to healing. This ratio of about 10 to 1 between conversions and healings occurs in other crusade statistics indicating

---

[25] *Elim Evangel* 9.10 (15 May 1928), p. 150.

that it may be a useful general guide to the underlying dynamics of the meetings.[26]

So, in addition to the breaking of new ground with Foursquare Gospel assaults on new cities (and the imagery of bombardment and barrage had been used from the start of the 1920s echoing the military language of the 1914-18 war), there was consolidation and diversification. There were revival and healing campaigns to be sure but also a residential Bible College, a correspondence course, a publishing office and printing works, an overseas missionary branch, Crusader activities for young people, and an attempt to start a magazine specifically for youth.[27]

When he looked back on 1928 Jeffreys found himself casting his mind forward in a lyrical expectation of a future family reunion.

The day of the second Advent of Christ is at hand, the children of God, now separated from their loved ones who have passed on before, are to be gathered home and awaiting expectantly for the call to their Father's house … What a homecoming! What a family gathering![28]

In a *resumé* of the year by one of the revival party there is reference to their whirlwind of activity and their confidence that God was saying to them, 'I have given you the land: possess it! … And so, we have taken it in his name, and every campaign held in the north and the south, and the four campaigns in the great city of London have been crowned with God-given success.' There is a note of awe as well as an insight into the changes in thousands of ordinary lives: 'homes have been turned into little heavens upon earth. Broken-down family altars have been built again. Long-standing debts have been paid, because men and women have become new creatures in Christ Jesus.'[29]

[26] E.g. *Elim Evangel* 10.26 (25 Oct 1929), p. 404 gives a ratio of 500+ conversions and 40 healings.

[27] The *Foursquare Revivalist* was incorporated with the *Evangel* in 1929, see *Elim Evangel* 10.5 (1 May 1929), p. 72.

[28] *Elim Evangel* 9.19 (1 Dec 1928), p. 289.

[29] *Elim Evangel* 9.19 (1 Dec 1928), p. 290.

1929

1929 saw the fall of financial markets and shocks run through the world economy leading to mass unemployment – the Great Depression, but it was a prodigious year for George Jeffreys. Essentially he continued campaigning in the United Kingdom but he also ensured the Elim organisation kept pace with increasing numbers of congregations. He began in Leicester with four days of meetings and established 'a witness of Foursquare Gospel truth in that city'.[30] He then 'disappeared from the public eye'[31] probably as a result of the death of his mother to attend to family affairs. And, if the pattern of other years was anything to go by, the start of January was set aside for rest following the exertions of the Christmas conventions.

Jeffreys may also have taken the opportunity of a break from preaching to focus on revising the rules and regulations governing Elim. There were at that time about 70 churches and the numbers climbed to about 170 by 1934. The basic rules in place since 1922 were revised several times and new rules came into operation early in 1929.[32] Because there were at least seven separate rulebooks, the constant drafting and revision must have required uninterrupted concentration and detailed discussion with E.J. Phillips and others. Each book of rules was marked 'private and confidential' and the system, because of the way it had evolved, entailed three forms of government: there was central government from Clapham for churches that had been founded entirely through the ministry of Jeffreys; there was personal government by a minister, and these will have been congregations brought into Elim by their minister and started independently; and there were congregations of miscellaneous origin under the government of deacons who were, presumably, elected directly by their members. The largest number of churches belonged to the first group. So, whether for personal reasons or by design, January was a quiet month for office work.

---

[30] *Elim Evangel* 10.33-34 (25 Dec 1929), p. 532. (These were double issues at Christmas).

[31] *Elim Evangel* 10.33-34 (25 Dec 1929), p. 532.

[32] Cartwright, *Evangelists*, p. 94.

After Leicester Jeffreys motored south to open an Elim Church in Southampton[33] before travelling up to Bradford, once a cotton town in northern England and, like many of the old mill districts, infused with varieties of Methodism that might quickly warm to Pentecostals. There was also another reason why Bradford might have been open to Pentecostalism: Smith Wigglesworth, whose unconventional healing ministry took him to many parts of the English-speaking world, had lived in Bradford and, at the Boland Street Mission, preached the message of miraculous healing for at least 20 years.[34] In his garden he had erected a flagpole and flag with the words from Exod. 15.26, 'I am the Lord that healeth thee', as a dramatic proclamation of his belief in the power of God to heal. Once Jeffreys started campaigning there was 'unbounded enthusiasm' and there were hundreds of conversions as well as miracles.[35]

The February edition of the *Evangel* contained an advertisement for a new book from the Elim Publishing Office. E.C.W. Boulton had written a biographical study of Jeffreys and his ministry. The tenor of the book is celebratory and conveys the atmosphere of the crusade meetings in those astonishing early days. There are reports of miracles, a slight overlap with pages in the *Evangel* itself, and there are plenty of valuable black-and-white photographs not found anywhere else. It was a book designed to justify Pentecostal 'signs following' evangelism and is appropriately subtitled 'a ministry of the miraculous'. Boulton might seem to be building Jeffreys up as a figurehead within Elim and putting him on a pedestal. There is no critical probing of Jeffreys' personality, doctrine, control, or financial management. There is little or no reference to the team surrounding Jeffreys: E.J. Phillips and the Clapham office are hardly mentioned because the spotlight is firmly on Jeffreys himself. Nevertheless Boulton does not foster a cult of personality. Rather, he conveys the enthusiasm and excitement of an eyewitness to extraordinary events.

The February edition of the *Evangel* also contained the report about a huge marble statue to be made of Mussolini, the fascist dic-

[33] *Elim Evangel* 10.33-34 (25 Dec 1929), p. 532.
[34] Desmond Cartwright, *The Real Wigglesworth* (Tonbridge: Sovereign World, 2000), pp. 45-46.
[35] *Elim Evangel* 10.1 (1 Jan 1929), p. 1.

tator. In March an article linked 'the act of Mussolini in making the Pope a temporal king' with Rev. 17.16. The biblical text was seen as predicting the spread of Roman Catholicism, with Rome as its centre, across the world followed by Ten Kings under Antichrist who would give their power to secure the Antichrist's deification. This is resisted by the papacy which attempts to gather all worship to itself whereupon the Ten Kings destroy Rome and the papal system completely including all its buildings across the world and appropriate 'the papacy's vast wealth unto Antichrist'.[36] This apocalyptic scenario saw a divine purpose in the rise of fascism without, at this stage, appreciating how deeply violence and inhumanity were buried in fascism's soul.

Jeffreys spoke at the Easter convention and ordained 18 candidates for ministry at a special service held in the Clapham Tabernacle.[37] Graduates of the Bible College were being prepared to staff the pulpits of the burgeoning Elim assemblies, another indication that eschatological beliefs did not prevent common sense planning for the future. It was always possible to believe fervently in the Second Coming without believing that it was quite imminent. This soon-but-not-yet mentality gave Elim preachers urgency while justifying attractive and high quality public events. Jeffreys himself never lost a conviction that the end of the age was near although, as we shall see, without being fully consistent.

The ordination of new Elim candidates was explained as 'but the Church's recognition of Christ's call, of which they had already given proof in their ministry'.[38] The ordination was not performed by a congregation or a church but came from an altogether higher authority and was only conducted when the candidates had already indicated by their preaching and ministry that they were truly servants of Christ. This high view of ordination avoided any trace of sacramentalism or congregationalism. It was quite in keeping with Jeffreys' perception that he himself and the whole of Elim were being raised up by God.

There were actually four separate Easter Conventions held in London and Jeffreys visited them all – in Islington, East Ham,

[36] *Elim Evangel* 10.3 (1 Mar 1929), p. 41.
[37] *Elim Evangel* 10.33-34 (25 Dec 1929), p. 532.
[38] *Elim Evangel* 10.5 (1 May 1929), p. 71.

Clapham, and Croydon.[39] Whit Monday meetings in a large canvas tent were conducted by Jeffreys in Brixton in preparation for a more prolonged campaign in south London. Behind these public events there were changes to the publication schedule of the *Elim Evangel*. As an article pointed out, the *Evangel* had first been published as a quarterly magazine. After a short time it became monthly and later on fortnightly.[40] In August 1928, when Jeffreys had insisted on the launch of the *Foursquare Revivalist* as a separate weekly paper, the *Evangel* dropped back to a monthly; but, in response to numerous requests, *Foursquare Revivalist* was discontinued as a separate paper and incorporated into the *Evangel* which was then which was scheduled to appear weekly. These events may speak of a private disagreement between Jeffreys and Phillips. It may be that Jeffreys was becoming impatient with Elim and preparing to spearhead a new revivalistic organisation supported by a new journal. If this is so, Jeffreys is even at this stage starting to chafe at the restrictions of the Elim organisational machine. Yet it may be that the work of producing a shorter weekly magazine as well as a longer monthly magazine was too exhausting for the publishing office or too expensive for Elim to sustain. It may also be that the revivalistic tendencies with their eschatological urgency were creating a tension with the homelier leanings of ordinary churchgoers unable to sustain the fervency of perpetual revivalism. Whatever the reasons, the result of the change was to create a more rounded *Evangel* that combined features of evangelism and nurture.

On 7 April Jeffreys opened a campaign by preaching to a small gathering in the town hall at Greenock, a Scottish city of 80,000 people on the Clyde, 25 miles from the centre of Glasgow. Heavy industry and heavy drinking shaped the lives of the working population. Fifty years previously the American evangelists D.L. Moody and R.A. Torrey had preached to large crowds in the area. But, as a writer who had seen these campaigns was to say, they could not compare with the Pentecostal meetings in 1929:

The divine healing aspect has been emphasised throughout ... In a town like Greenock, and at such a time, many things had to be

[39] *Elim Evangel* 10.5 (1 May 1929), p. 75.
[40] *Elim Evangel* 10.5 (1 May 1929), p. 72.

overcome. Mr Jeffreys set out alone; no church heralding his coming, and no church assisting his progress ... One other thing that struck me forcibly was, when Mr Jeffreys asked those who had received healing benefit from the mission to stand, there were hundreds who responded all over the hall area, and in the galleries.[41]

The whole area was affected and there were credible press reports of 900 conversions as well as the dramatic healing of a boy with polio.

Wonderful things can be related of the effects in the many homes which have been blessed by the acceptance of Jesus the saviour. Joy and gladness and real happiness now prevail, where discontent, misery and drink were dominant features before conversion.[42]

Occasionally the town hall was unavailable because of a prior booking so Jeffreys transferred to St Augustine's Church which, in 1930, was bought by Elim and became the permanent home of a new Elim congregation. The church has prospered and expanded and provided senior leaders for Elim over the years as well as several members of the local council including a Provost or Mayor.

After the long drive in their Chrysler to south London the Revival Party pitched their big canvas cathedral in Brixton in May and ran for three weeks. The brief Brixton campaign, situated as it was only a mile from the Elim base in Clapham, proved to be highly successful and the *South London Press* reported:

Principal Jeffreys' revival and healing campaign in Brixton is ended, but the magnetic Welshman's thunder will echo from that enclosed space behind the Town Hall for many a day ... The thousands who have packed the big tent every day for the past five weeks will tell you this ...

Long after the sceptics have ceased to decry the creed of the Elim Foursquare Gospel and the wave of religious fervour that swept South London, the grateful prayers of those who were

---

[41] *Elim Evangel* 10.6 (7 June 1929), p. 81.
[42] *Elim Evangel* 10.33-34 (25 Dec 1929), p. 532.

'saved' will still attend the memory of the inspired pastor whose deep voice swayed them – whose fluent phraseology it is a delight to hear – whose whole personality is as vital as living fire.[43]

What also delighted observers of the campaign was the outpouring of the Holy Spirit similar to that in Acts 10 when the household of Cornelius spoke in tongues while Peter was preaching to them and without any laying on of hands. According to McWhirter's review of the year, this is exactly what he observed. By contrast the Anglican Revd Kenneth Dodds, vicar of Christ Church, Richmond, was more general in his affirmation and wrote 'Praise God for the work of Elim campaigns'. At their conclusion, a large baptismal service was arranged in the grounds of the Bible College and over 600 people were immersed. Press photographs of these events were respectful and show a solemn outdoor event and 3,000 people covering the grassy slopes and terraces of the gardens.[44]

Turning south again Jeffreys opened a church building in Hove (29 June–3 July), a town adjacent to Brighton, before crossing the Irish Sea for a summer convention in Bangor, Ireland, and then returning to the Royal Dome in Brighton (5-7 Aug) and erecting the tent again in Worthing (21 July and throughout August). The south of England had the advantage of middle-class, middle income residents, some of whom had retired from London or continued commuting, while others were associated with the farming community. It was a world away from industrial Scotland and there was sufficient money in the pockets of the people to enable buildings to be bought. When he opened the Elim Tabernacle at Eastbourne Jeffreys made a short speech saying,

> It is just 12 months since I first started meetings on the pier. I started the campaign with just a few people, but we prayed on at the revival campaign, and at the end we were puzzling ourselves how to continue. It seemed as if every door was closed against us. And then we began to pray. Hundreds of people in East-

---

[43] *Elim Evangel* 10.33-34 (25 Dec 1929), p. 532.
[44] *Elim Evangel* 10.8 (21 June 1929); 10.9 (28 June 1929), p. 137.

bourne began to pray, and now we have a building (loud cries of 'Amen').[45]

The obstacles were not financial but from religious vested interests or secular apathy. Jeffreys himself attributed much of his success to the prayers of the enthused crowds rather than to his own oratorical gifts. He was up against the claims of spiritualism, too. Significant numbers of bereaved people had found a modicum of comfort in spiritualism because they believed they were able to contact their dead relatives through séances and mediums.[46] Pentecostalism was occasionally confused with spiritualism in the 1920s so the *Evangel* was pleased to note the conversion of a spiritualist[47] and to differentiate itself from spiritualism by speaking of 'divine healing' rather than 'faith healing', which was the preferred terminology of spiritualists. It is impossible to say exactly which part of the country was most prone to spiritualistic activity although it appears to have been a more middle-class predilection than a working class one. The cultured T.S. Eliot could speak in his poetry of Madame Blavatsky, a medium who was a minor sensation in fashionable circles.[48]

Although Elim avoided party political entanglements, the newly elected parliament assembling on 25 June provoked the *Evangel* to report that 'our prayers will ascend for the representatives of the British people. May the great responsibility of office bring every minister of the new government close to God for wisdom and guidance.'[49] There was regret expressed,

> such a man of God as Mr Rosslyn Mitchell (the ex-Labour MP for Paisley) is not taking his position among the new ministry, which undoubtedly would have been the case had he not resigned from political life prior to the election.[50]

---

[45] *Elim Evangel* 10.7 (14 June 1929), p. 98.
[46] W.R. Inge, *Lay Thoughts of a Dean* (London: Puttenham's Sons, 1926), p. 304.
[47] *Elim Evangel* 10.7 (25 Dec 1929), p 108.
[48] T.S. Eliot, 'A Cooking Egg', in *Poems* (New York: A.A. Knopf, 1920), pp. 8-9.
[49] *Elim Evangel* 10.8 (21 June 1929), p. 120.
[50] *Elim Evangel* 10.8 (21 June 1929), p. 120.

Exactly how Elim writers knew about the religious commitment of Mitchell is unknown since there was no obvious link between the Scottish Labour Party and Elim. The *Evangel* went on to say, 'The opening ceremony will be incomplete without the presence of our beloved King'. The King's illness removed him from public life for a while. Historians assess George's handling of the turbulent political affairs at the end of his reign largely favourably but for Elim he was simply 'our beloved king'.

Another person with whom Elim felt affinity was General Bramwell Booth who died that year. He had led the Salvation Army since the death of his father in 1912. The funeral service was held at the Royal Albert Hall on 23 June. Jeffreys attended and spoke of the 'indisputable evidence of high esteem in which the late General was held'.[51] Here was a role model for Jeffreys, someone who headed an organisation for many years, preached in many parts of the world, and died in office while continuing to be admired and liked by the people he led. This was a life Jeffreys could hope to emulate and a future to which he could aspire. Elim, a younger organisation than the Salvation Army, was growing fast and had reached a point of having sufficient numbers of churches to require a reconfiguration within the British Isles into five divisions each with its own headquarters. These were: London division (including Midlands) was actually in two sections because it was so large, the Northern division, the Southern division and an Irish division that also included Scotland.[52] We can assume these organisational refinements were made after intense discussion between Jeffreys and Phillips with some advice from other trusted figures. And it may be that the rulebooks that had been revised at the start of the year made provision for this kind of development.

South Coast meetings continued to bear fruit. From the very first day in Worthing people were converted or healed and Christians of long-standing found their spiritual lives revived.[53] The *Worthing Herald* reported on miracles[54] while the *Sussex Daily News*

---

[51] *Elim Evangel* 10.10 (5 July 1929), p. 152.
[52] *Elim Evangel* 10.15 (9 Aug 1929), p. 227.
[53] *Elim Evangel* 10.16 (16 Aug 1929), p. 243.
[54] *Elim Evangel* 10.16 (16 Aug 1929), p. 243.

spoke of 150 conversions.[55] The *Evangel* also carried a letter from
William Burton speaking of his troubles and triumphs in the Congo[56] while Elizabeth Sissons reminded readers of the Latter Rain
outpouring and the promise of the fullness of the Spirit for all
Christians.[57] Here was a positive reading of the end times and it
could be put alongside missionary labours at the ends of the earth.
Whether in England or Africa, the Spirit of God was equally powerful. This was the message Elim wanted to give and it was one that
could be made compatible with references to the return of the Jews
to Palestine[58] or the political strengthening of Jewish people in the
land to which they were emigrating. A tribute to Arthur Balfour and
reference to the fulfilment of biblical prophecy could go alongside
a statement about George V that 'many believed'[59] him to be a de-
scendant of King David – a statement that could only come from
British Israel sources since there was no historical evidence at all
that George had any connection either symbolic or genealogical
with Davidic monarchy. Nevertheless, through the mixture of ideas
circulating within the Elim, some clearly verifiable accounts of
families that had been reconciled and bodies that had been healed
and others obviously unverifiable and made up of suggestive corre-
lations between biblical prophecies and world events, a worldview
was created.

After Worthing, Jeffreys preached in Ipswich from 2-15 September and secured 250 converts.[60] Nothing in the year so far, though,
prepared him for what was to happen in Cardiff, where he opened
at the Cory Hall on the 22 September. An anonymous postcard had
reached Clapham with the words 'Cardiff needs Foursquare Gospel!' and Jeffreys, with his love for Wales, must have felt the rightness of the request. It was the largest city in Wales with a population of over 226,000. There was a mixture of industry and residential housing as well as a proud provincial history. Nonconformists
of all kinds had their churches and chapels here, and there were

[55] *Elim Evangel* 10.18 (30 Aug 1929), p. 275.
[56] *Elim Evangel* 10.15 (9 Aug 1929), p. 235.
[57] *Elim Evangel* 10.16 (16 Aug 1929), p. 245.
[58] *Elim Evangel* 10.19 (6 Sept 1929), p. 243.
[59] *Elim Evangel* 10.13 (26 Aug 1929), p. 294.
[60] *Elim Evangel* 10.22 (4 Oct 1929), p. 259.

strong rail links from Cardiff fanning northwards into the coal mining villages and valleys. As a young man Jeffreys had attended early Pentecostal meetings in South Wales; but, more to the point, he was a South Walian who spoke Welsh, sounded Welsh when he spoke English, and could speak from his heart to the hearts of those who heard him.

The hall was a large imposing building that appears to have housed the YMCA and the Wood Street Congregational Church.[61] It was originally a temperance hall and over the course of its life hosted a major conference for South Wales miners in 1915 as well as boxing events.[62] Lloyd George had held 'great political rallies' there and its acoustics were good.[63] Jeffreys was booked for three weeks but in the event stayed seven.[64] He was to speak every night as well as twice on Wednesdays and Thursday and twice on Sundays. He began with a handful of listeners and wrote to Phillips saying, 'it will take time …'.[65]

There was opposition to gospel preaching that emphasised the supernatural and the reality of contemporary healing.[66] Welsh Nonconformity had learned the lessons of modernism all too well and lost its evangelical power. Sunday school lessons introducing a watered-down version of 19th century German liberalism had done their work so that when Jeffreys insisted that Christianity was supernatural from first to last, he was challenging the shibboleths of many ministers. He was also seen as walking in the footsteps of Evan Roberts who, for the most part, was deemed a Welsh hero whatever his theology might have been. By the time Jeffreys had been preaching in Cardiff for three weeks, he had recorded an

[61] http://www.theguardian.com/cardiff/2010/oct/28/click-on-wales-cardiff-lost-buildings (accessed 31/10/15) and http://www.cardiffymcaha.co.uk/show-Gallery.asp?gid=5&imgID=48 (accessed 31/10/15).

[62] https://www.facebook.com/RememberOldCardiff/photos/a.2456030554-68091.76861.245602035468193/485304928164568/; http://discovery.nationalar-chives.gov.uk/details/rd/e057fba9-8d8a-4c41-af52-b401c6207178 (accessed 31 Oct 15).

[63] http://www.clickonwales.org/2010/10/no-longer-unloved-but-often-still-without-a-purpose/ (accessed 31 Ocotber 15).

[64] *Elim Evangel* 10.19 (6 Sept 1929): advertised for Sept 22 till Oct 13 every night as well as twice on Wednesdays and Thursday and twice on Sundays.

[65] Cartwright and Holdaway, *Defining Moments Elim 100 Centenary*, p. 46.

[66] *Elim Evangel* 10.26 (25 Oct 1929), p. 404.

astonishing 500 converts.[67] The meetings began to match the atmosphere of the Welsh revival itself. Converts or attenders might remember the tales told of the revival by their parents or grandparents. There would be testimonies to healings, snatches of prayer in Welsh, possibly quotations from the Welsh Bible, and all this spoke deep into the consciousness of men and women who had been brought up with at least a nominal Christian faith. The conversions, when they occurred, were not from atheism or another religion to Christianity but from nominal Christianity to a meaningful personal faith. When healings occurred, as they definitely did, the smart aleck sceptics were confounded. Jeffreys knew what Christianity meant to his fellow countryman and he understood how conversions could influence whole families and change the atmosphere around the fireside or meal table. He knew what happened when miners who spent too much of their money on beer began to abstain and put their earnings into the hands of their wives for the benefit of their children. Everybody started smiling apart from the publicans whose sales fell through the floor. And, whereas most of the arid contention between Welsh chapels had been over the doctrines of predestination and free will, a supernatural gospel that brought healing in its wake transcended all these arguments and made them seem irrelevant.

Jeffreys telegrammed Clapham with these words, which were then published in the *Evangel*,

NEARLY ONE THOUSAND HAVE PROFESSED SALVATION. PRINCIPAL GEORGE JEEFREYS AND PARTY ARE SIMPLY CARRIED ON BY THE LIVING STREAM OF REVIVAL FERVOUR. HEALINGS OF AN EXTRAORDINARY CHARACTER ARE TAKING PLACE. THE CORY HALL IS FAR TOO SMALL TO ACCOMMODATE THE CROWDS. IT HAD TO BE FILLED AND EMPTIED THREE TIMES IN ONE AFTERNOON.[68]

The extension of the crusade meant that the Cory Hall was not always available and so the crowds were moved to Splott Road Bap-

---

[67] And over 40 had been healed, thus maintaining the 10:1 ratio, *Elim Evangel* 10.26 (25 Oct 1929), p. 404.

[68] *Elim Evangel* 10.27 (1 Nov 1929), p. 418.

tist Church and then finally the largest church in Wales, Wood Street Congregational Church, in the centre of the city.[69] Even this was too small to provide seating for everyone. Descriptions earlier spoke of hundreds being 'turned away from Cory Hall which is packed out long before the meetings are due to begin'. And it was when 'numbers of sick people' were 'unable to gain admission after travelling long distances', Jeffreys knew he had to continue the campaign, and this led to tears of gratitude among those asking him to stay. We can say that the preaching of the Gospel was not harsh and condemnatory but, on the contrary, warm, clear, and bringing the promise of new spiritual life and health. The healings were outstanding including a woman who endured 18 months in a spinal carriage before being healed in the meetings and walking unassisted thereafter. A lady blinded by a cataract was cured. One journalist wrote 'as a rule, pressmen are inclined to be cynical … but I am bound to confess – and it is the experience of other newspaper men who have attended the services – that I have been deeply impressed'.[70] On another occasion, speaking of the emptiness of many other churches, the *Western Mail* gave the pithy diagnosis, 'Christian churches failed because they brought the world into Christianity instead of taking Christianity into the world'.[71] And we have a good idea of what Jeffreys preached because a book of his sermons entitled *The Miraculous Foursquare Gospel: Supernatural* published in 1930 centred around Christ as Saviour, Baptiser in the Spirit, Healer, and Coming King but a final chapter on divine healing with questions and answers reveals a thoughtful side to Jeffreys' ministry and a recognition of the benefits of medical help.[72]

By the time the crusade had finished it was estimated by the *News and Westminster Gazette* that a total of 150,000 'from all parts of South Wales and the West of England' had attended the services.[73] If this number is anything like accurate, the rolling impact of the seven weeks of meetings must have been enormous.[74] A total of

[69] Cartwright, *Evangelists*, p. 97.

[70] *Elim Evangel* 10.28 (8 Nov 1929), p. 433.

[71] *Elim Evangel* 10.26 (25 Oct 1929), p. 404.

[72] George Jeffreys, *The Miraculous Foursquare Gospel: Supernatural* (London: Elim Publishing Company, 1930).

[73] *Elim Evangel* 10.29 (15 Nov 1929), p. 470.

[74] *Elim Evangel* 10.29 (15 Nov 1929), p. 404.

3,000 people had been converted and a congregation of 1,000 had been collected for a new church that for a few years remained in the Cory Hall, which was hired at considerable cost, before it bought a piece of ground, built the City Temple and opened on 24 March 1934.[75] The congregation thrives to the present day as the largest Elim church in Wales.[76]

In response to further pleadings Jeffreys, with barely a pause, moved westward 41 miles and began campaigning in Swansea on 11 November. From the first few days there was 'a spirit of revival'.[77] Despite the atrocious weather a month later the *Evangel* was able to write:

> Crowded Meetings: unbounded enthusiasm: The Foursquare Revival is sweeping on through Swansea. The Central Hall during the week is packed to overflowing, and the Grand Theatre crowded from top to bottom and multitudes turned away unable to gain admission. Over six hundred souls have been saved and tremendous conviction is resting on people everywhere; *indeed the fear of God is resting upon the district* [italics added]. What a soul-stirring sight to see these hungry crowds listening attentively to the Word of God which at times is like a great hammer coming upon hardened hearts and at others like a sharpened sword penetrating the innermost parts of the soul, wounding sinners everywhere. We shall never forget the great sight in the Grand Theatre – the platform, boxes, circle, ground floor, and gallery packed, everyone spellbound under the influence of the mighty, captivating word that proceeds from the heart and lips of the Principal.

This insight into the meetings matches the photographs of attentive faces in the vast campaign congregations but what is highlighted here is the effect of the preaching on the whole town. Even those who did not attend, felt the effects.

The great influence of Principal George Jeffreys' Revival Campaign *upon the town and district in general can never be fully estimated*

[75] *Elim Evangel* 10.29 (15 Nov 1929), p. 471. *Elim Evangel* 10.32 (6 Dec 1929), p. 501 gives a figure of 800.
[76] Cartwright, *Evangelists*, p. 98.
[77] *Elim Evangel* 10.31 (29 Nov 1929), p. 487.

[italics added]. One of the most effective things that took place at one of the services was the singing of 'Jesus, Lover of my soul,' to the tune Aberystwyth, the huge congregation standing as a token of sympathy with the dependents of the brave men who lost their lives at a near-by mine. All classes are attending the revival services. Large numbers of ministers and the hundreds of young men are striking features in this spiritual awakening.[78]

Altogether it was estimated that 5,000 conversions had taken place when the numbers from both Cardiff and Swansea were added together. The size of the Elim congregations established in the two cities would have amounted to about 1,600 people, perhaps fewer, with the result that the other converts would have swelled numbers in other denominational groups. There was an apostolic congregation in Swansea that Jeffreys, as a young man, had attended and it is probable that there were similar apostolic gatherings in valley towns or in Cardiff with the result that some benefit for non-Elim Pentecostals would have been felt but there were also plenty of evangelical Christians in the area even if they belonged to denominations that did not normally accept divine healing. When the numbers of converts from the 1904 Welsh revival are examined, it becomes apparent that the largest beneficiary of the ministry of Evan Roberts and others was the Anglican Church, partly because it was the best organised and most widely distributed.[79] It is possible that the two Jeffreys crusades in Cardiff and Swansea swelled the numbers of Anglican congregations as well.

Jeffreys had long wished to reignite the Welsh revival and it is poignant that his one-time mentor, Glasnant Jones, now an old man, beside whom he stood during those early open-air meetings in Maesteg, attended one of the Swansea meetings.[80] Jones must have been proud of his *protégé*. Yet any attempt to replicate the Welsh revival was likely to fail simply because the ministries of Roberts and Jeffreys were so different. Roberts was not an expository preacher and he went from chapel to chapel holding long and

---

[78] *Elim Evangel* 10.33 (13 Dec 1929), p. 514.

[79] R.L. Brown, *The Welsh Evangelicals* (Cardiff Tongwynlais: Tair Eglwys Press, 1986), p. 155.

[80] C. Cartwright, *et al.*, *Defining Moments*, p. 46.

slightly disorganised meetings that were intended to bring backslid-
den Christians to repentance through urgent exhortations. Jeffreys
was more disciplined. He started the meetings at an advertised time,
allowed for a certain amount of singing but not so much as to fill
up the time allocated for preaching. The preaching was the most
prepared part of the service with a text and appeal at the end for
unbelievers or those who were looking for healing. In this, too, Jeffreys was different from Roberts because Roberts had no expectation of healing and nor did he make time for laying hands on the
sick. Similarly, Jeffreys welcomed people who spoke in tongues in
his meetings even if there was no expectation that tongues speaking
would be followed by interpretation or any other charismatic gifts
apart from healing. Indeed at least one comment on Jeffreys pointed out that, although the cynics had attributed his success to excitement and emotion, he could be criticised the other way since he
ruled out excitement and discouraged all outward and visible signs
of emotion.[81]

It seems unlikely that had Jeffreys stayed in South Wales any kind
of religious move similar to the Welsh revival would have restarted.
Apart from anything else the Welsh revival of 1904 depended upon
the ministry of other preachers than Evan Roberts; and, once the
revival was over, there were few if any free-standing congregations
left behind with converts – and none that were robustly Pentecostal.
This was quite different from the policy Jeffreys pursued in the
sense that he planned to leave congregations behind and made
strenuous efforts to buy buildings and put in pastors and build up
Elim. Whatever the lingering temptation to remain, Jeffreys, after
consulting with Phillips, decided to uphold his commitment to the
Christmas conventions in Belfast and so left Wales in time to do so.

Although the year 1929 was one of outstanding evangelistic and
Pentecostal triumph, Jeffreys had to contend with two painful matters. The first concerned his brother Stephen who had been campaigning in south London in a way that appeared to threaten the
solidity of the Elim churches that had already been established. In
October 1929 George wrote to the assemblies of East Ham, Ilford,

---

[81] *Elim Evangel* 10.29 (15 Nov 1929), p. 470.

Canning Town, and Barking warning them that Stephen was likely to cause dissension:

> Pastor Stephen by coming into your midst has broken a solemn vow … He has also made charges of a serious nature against myself personally, and also against the Elim work … I have had to meet these accusations in nearly every place I have ministered throughout the country.

> It is his avowed intention to open up churches close to our own, and such actions must inevitably result in splitting up Elim churches, which I know you will deeply deplore.

> Little did I think when I booked the Baths Hall, Barking in 1924 [*sic*] and engaged my brother, Pastor Stephen, as the evangelist to run the Elim campaign, that I should be called upon in 1929 to refute such misrepresentations of our work.[82]

As Cartwright has pointed out, Stephen was without malice and may well have seen an undifferentiated Pentecostalism as a perfectly reasonable outcome for the outpouring of the Spirit that he and his brother were enjoying. Yet it is the wounded note that 'charges of a serious nature' were made against George that stands out. It is not clear what these charges were but the most likely one is that George was seen as acting in a high-handed and dictatorial manner since this charge appears to have been made previously by Stephen, or by his son Edward, and arose from the desire that George had, once he split with Stephen, to establish himself as the only leader of Elim. He already met congregations that, having been started by Stephen or at least boosted by Stephen's healing ministry, presumed that Stephen was the real leader of Elim.

The second challenge came from a source outside Pentecostalism.[83] Here the Particular Baptists were concerned about the preaching of the Foursquare Gospel since they saw it as aligned with warnings in Scripture against devilish deceiving of the elect in the last days. This was an easier attack to defend since the Peculiar Baptists were a small sect that belonged to the hinterland of nonconformist Evangelicalism. They were a split-off from the main

---

[82] Cartwright, *Evangelists*, p. 64.
[83] *Elim Evangel* 10.33 (13 Dec 1929), p. 515.

body of the Baptists in Britain. The accusation that the Foursquare Gospel was unbiblical was one that all the senior leaders within Elim could rebut with indignant honesty. They were as biblical as they knew how to be and they felt that their interpretation of the gospel and presentation of the gospel was far closer to the original life of the early church than anything else that was to be seen in contemporary Britain. This branch of the Baptists shunned miracles even though the pages the New Testament were full of them; the reasons for propagating non-miraculous Christianity belong to the Reformation itself: the Protestant reformers, to distinguish themselves from Roman Catholics who attributed confirmatory miracles to the relics of the saints, took their rational stand on the word of God alone.

It was left to Percy Parker to rebut the Baptists.

> We are charged with rejecting salvation by free and sovereign Grace! We are content to leave this typical misstatement to the judgement of anyone who knows our work. Salvation by free and sovereign grace is the great foundation truth upon which the Elim Foursquare Gospel Alliance stands.

The confidence Elim had in its contention with the Particular Baptists is measured by the willingness of the Alliance to print the correspondence in the *Evangel*.

10

CRITICISM, CRUSADES, AND THE CRYSTAL PALACE

J.B. Priestley, a journalist, novelist, and broadcaster, published *English Journey* in 1933. He travelled by public transport all over the country and brought his sharp eye and reflective mind to bear on what he saw. He arrived by bus in Birmingham after passing gaudy pubs and bowling greens and recalling the Nonconformist heritage of what had become Britain's second city. This was where electroplating, gas lighting, and the steam engine were brought to commercial perfection and where liberalism in politics, as exemplified by the Chamberlain family (who made a fortune manufacturing metal screws), stood against the landed aristocracy. The old trade guilds of the middle ages had not controlled the growth of the city with the result that the industrial revolution, which was 'largely nonconformist', had thrived there: it was a place of 'big profits and narrow views'.[1] Its streets were lined by shops and small factories in a 'dirty muddle' so that, when Priestley escaped by taking a depressing tram ride to the top of a hill, he looked down on 'the vast smoky hollow of the city, with innumerable tall chimneys thrusting out of the murk'.[2] A dingy meanness pervaded, so he thought, which the inhabitants of Birmingham tried to forget in their pubs and cinemas or, on Sundays, their chapels.

---

[1] J.B. Priestley, *English Journey* (London: Heron Books, 1933), p. 78.
[2] Priestley, *English Journey*, p. 87.

Attending one of these, Priestley found the familiar rituals of his childhood. The hymns accompanied by an organist playing 'the same old stuff in the same old way', the deacons in their frock coats, gold-rimmed spectacles, and tremendous respectability and the sermon that took a tiny and apparently meaningless text and found 'an astonishing number of deeply significant meanings in it'.[3] And the congregation itself, serious and restrained, was middle-aged or elderly ('I doubt if there were half-a-dozen men under thirty-five in the chapel') and led by a dignified minister.[4]

Jeffreys in Switzerland, c. 1935

The meetings in the summer about 1935 in Lausanne, Switzerland, showed that Jeffreys still made an impact even when his sermons were interpreted.

This was the city to which Jeffreys would come in 1930 and where he would preach a momentous campaign considered the zenith of his ministry. But the year began in the afterglow of the Swansea revival. There were still descriptions and assessments of the meetings in South Wales in the first of the year's issues of the *Evangel*. All told, about 1,000 people in Swansea had become Christians; there were photos of the massed gatherings, reports of the

---

[3] Priestley, *English Journey*, p. 108.
[4] Priestley, *English Journey*, p. 107.

singing of hymns in English and Welsh, and sideways swipes at those, like the Anglican Dean Inge, who denied the possibility of sudden conversions.[5] In its wake the revival brought renewed vocations to full-time ministry. Jeffreys ordained a cohort of young men in the Welsh Tabernacle and was pleased to find that at least half had 'passed out from the ranks of the Elim Crusader movement'.[6] Whatever high expectations there might be about the Second Coming of Christ, long-term planning was on the agenda.

Turning his attention to Scotland, Jeffreys travelled up to Glasgow to consolidate the work there. The Glasgow City Temple became his headquarters in the north.

> The problem which almost invariably arises after such a campaign [with 1,500 converts] arose in Glasgow. A building to carry on the work could not be found. Therefore we were forced to improvise with rented halls which made the establishing of the work exceedingly difficult. Under these circumstances the adherents of the Foursquare Gospel had a severe test of loyalty imposed upon them. After three years it is with much satisfaction and delight that we recognise the fulfilment of our Lord's promise in the parable, that the good seed sown on good ground would be fruitful. Most sincerely we regard the faithful followers of the Elim Foursquare movement in Glasgow as worthy of this beautiful building for a meeting house [and here a photo was added showing a large and impressive traditional church building].[7]

As soon as he arrived Jeffreys plunged into his customary meetings and immediately the revival fires re-ignited. The *Evangel* reported 'revival scenes are again witnessed in Scotland in the City Temple' and went on to say, 'Elim's Scottish headquarters has become the centre of revival activity. Souls are being saved, bodies healed miraculously, saints baptised with the Holy Ghost, and there is great joy among the people.'[8] A week later the Temple was 'packed to ca-

---

[5] *Elim Evangel* 11.2 (10 Jan 1930), p 19.
[6] *Elim Evangel* 11.2 (10 Jan 1930), p 20.
[7] *Elim Evangel* 11.3 (17 Jan 1930), p. 33.
[8] *Elim Evangel* 11.4 (24 Jan 1930), p. 52.

204 George Jeffreys

pacity' and people from all over Scotland were 'being saved in every meeting'.[9]

What makes these meetings more remarkable was that Jeffreys undertook them after a malicious newspaper report was published in *John Bull* on the 18 January. *John Bull*, with a claimed circulation of two million,[10] was the brainchild of Horatio Bottomley (1860–1933) a self-publicist of enormous proportions who was full of financial schemes, jingoistic patriotism, and populist remedies for every social ill. Bottomley was voted into Parliament during his period of celebrity but, a few years before his magazine attacked Jeffreys, was convicted of financial fraud and sentenced to seven years of penal servitude.[11] What we know of Bottomley is that he was a reckless and persuasive financier whose personal morality included a string of mistresses, high living, and irreligion. As a young man he had worked for the premier Victorian spokesman for atheism, Charles Bradlaugh, and his uncle, who helped to raise him, was a 'radical agitator and the founder of secularism'.[12] Whether Bottomley was directly involved in the attack is impossible to say but the style of journalism and the anti-Christian impetus are all his.

The attack must have shaken Elim. It alleged the movement was set up to rob the gullible of their savings. The 'gang of pseudo religious apostles of faith-healing' were involved in the 'spiritual and financial exploitation of the suffering and the maimed' who used 'tongues and interpretation' as an 'infallible fortune-maker'.[13] The Jeffreys family along with Darragh and McWhirter were named and photos of them were splashed across the offending page. Believers were said to be worked 'stage by stage' into a 'frenzy' as 'choruses are sung at breakneck speed, some of them thirty or forty times'. The article opened by referring to a forthcoming debate in Parliament over the requirement for organisations collecting money from the public to be accountable to the Charity Commission and ended

---

[9] *Elim Evangel* 11.5 (31 Jan 1930), p. 70.

[10] https://livesrunning.wordpress.com/2014/01/10/horatio-bottomley-the-first-patriot/ (accessed 11 Dec 2015).

[11] Bottomley was released from prison in July 1927.

[12] Horatio Bottomley, *Oxford Dictionary of National Biography* (online).

[13] *John Bull* (18 Jan 1930), p. 9. The article is unsigned and headlined 'Frenzied Victims of Hypnotic Pastors'.

by saying 'it is obviously time the Jeffreys and their gang were broken up'.

Although George was in Glasgow, *John Bull* was on sale there and advertised on placards outside the church where Jeffreys was preaching. On a Tuesday evening in the City Temple a member of the congregation caused a disturbance and demanded that Jeffreys provide a public answer to the printed criticisms. George rose to the occasion and handled the matter coolly. He declared that if any people thought him guilty, they had a remedy. They could press charges with the public prosecutor – which in the event nobody did.

Behind the scenes there was consternation in Elim as different views were expressed about how to handle the matter. Phillips thought they could show *John Bull* had infringed copyright by using photographs of George without permission. Leech wanted to go to law because, in his expert view, the allegations were clearly libellous. What complicated the framing of a reply was that several other groups, including Assemblies of God, were mentioned in the article as if they were all part of the Elim Alliance. Jeffreys did not want to reply in a way that implied he was innocent while the other groups might be guilty. The meeting between Elim's solicitor and *John Bull's* solicitor made little progress, presumably because *John Bull* was battle-hardened to litigation and had won and lost a number of cases. After a flurry of correspondence Jeffreys and Phillips sorted out a response. George wrote a disclaimer that Phillips revised once he had consulted Elim's solicitor.[14] The text of the disclaimer was published in the *Elim Evangel* on 21 February 1930, although, surprisingly, was not signed by Jeffreys himself but by ten other senior people in Elim. This must have given the impression that they were running to his defence which was, of course, the case but not exactly in the way implied by the text. They were supporting him while defending themselves.

The denial of wrongdoing was absolute and made all the more convincing by the assertion that as individuals and as an organisation they absolutely repudiated malpractice: 'if you are correct' they implied, 'we would be the first to agree with you'. They went on to write:

---

14 See Cartwright, *Evangelists*, pp. 100-102.

Principal George Jeffreys and the Elim Foursquare Gospel Alliance absolutely deny each and every one of the charges made against them in the *John Bull* article. Such methods and practices have never been known in the organisation and would not be tolerated in any one of its churches or missions.[15]

And they continued by making no apology 'for the scriptural supernatural manifestations … such have characterised revivals of religion right down the ages'. As for their finances, these were 'controlled by the committees of the respective departments and not by any one person'. The accounts were 'audited by an independent firm of Chartered Accountants and submitted to the appropriate Government Departments'.

All this settled the matter without lasting damage. True, a woman who had intended to make a large donation withheld it.[16] Conversely, the attack may have done good by reminding Elim that its financial system should be a model of rectitude. Phillips, from the start, had been scrupulous in all his dealings, and some of the friction between him and Jeffreys through the 1920s had arisen over the need for exactness with who owed what to whom. Phillips not only counted every penny but also made sure every law was kept. The report that finance was 'controlled by the committees of the respective departments' must surely be correct if all the signatories said so and yet it is true that the impression to be gained by reading the correspondence between Jeffreys and his head office was that he made many decisions without consulting others. This initiative and decisiveness are not surprising given the pioneering and unpredictable nature of campaigning in dozens of hired halls all over the country. Jeffreys *had* to decide whether to stay in one town or another or whether to move from a packed small hall to a more expensive large hall, and these decisions could only be made in the heated flow of events. And these decisions must have been largely his alone, even though they had financial implications. What the evidence shows, however, is that at this point in his ministry Jeffreys could not be said to have gained excessively or secretly from all his exhausting campaigning, and nor could the rest of the Revival Party.

[15] *Elim Evangel* 11.8 (21 Feb 1930), p. 121.
[16] Cartwright, *Evangelists*, p. 102.

Every human life is lived out at a multiplicity of levels. We go out to earn a living, come home to a family or friends and behind this mixture of personal and professional events we are aware of the great march of public affairs. For Jeffreys and those in Elim, there was a further dimension to existence because they fully expected the actualisation of biblical prophecies. They believed they could detect the hand of God in contemporary historical and political events. Admittedly, these events were open to contradictory and contested interpretations that, if they were fused together, might all be true at once. An editorial article in the *Evangel* stated:

> Since the Great War, interpreters of the two chief schools of prophetic interpretation known as the Historicist and the Futurist have adopted a tone of less mutual asperity and more respect toward one another's views. It is now recognised that if the great prophecies respecting Antichrist, especially in the Books of Daniel and the Revelation, require a fulfilment which in important aspects is still future (as averred by Futurists), it is also necessary to recognise their partial fulfilment in the great apostate movements already recorded by history (as affirmed by Historicists). In other words, the Church of Rome, Islam, and Atheism (the last-named being the common fruit of the two former) have all contributed to historical and preparatory fulfilments of Antichrist's last great march against Christ.[17]

Two weeks later the *Evangel* pondered biblical prophecy again and wondered whether St Paul's statement about the 'man of sin' (2 Thess. 2.3, 4) implied the rebuilding of the Temple which had been destroyed in AD 70.[18] All this might be put alongside a complicated exposition of 'the rapture' that had long been central to the Pentecostal beliefs about the end times.[19] Pentecostals, along with many dispensational fundamentalists, believed that Christ would return to rescue his church from the increasingly desperate conditions on earth, that he would snatch them away, or rapture them, to glory so that if they were alive at the time they would never have to pass through the pains of death to reach heaven. This Adventist convic-

---

[17] *Elim Evangel* 11.3 (17 Jan 1930), p. 40.
[18] *Elim Evangel* 11.6 (7 Feb 1930), p. 86.
[19] *Elim Evangel* 11.4 (24 Jan 1930), p. 51.

tion gave them confidence in their own invulnerability while at the same time causing them to expect a spiritual and moral deterioration of all that passed on earth. The church's back was up against the wall and she must keep the faith and save the lost despite the enormous pressure to do otherwise. Later Pentecostals and charismatics rejected this strain of theological pessimism and replaced it by a type of triumphalism that anticipated the inexorable advance of the kingdom of God across every nation. Exactly what Jeffreys himself felt and thought at this stage is not clear although he can hardly have been a pessimist and he was certainly not paralysed by fear of the future, as his exploits in Birmingham show.

Jeffreys in Front of the Swiss Reformers c. 1935

To Jeffreys' right with a Bible in the air is Robert Darragh, his song leader, and to his left also holding up a Bible is Albert Edsor, his chauffeur and pianist. The message is unmistakeable: these are men of the Bible in the line of the great Protestant preachers of Reformation.

Birmingham

Birmingham's evangelical Christians were shocked when the city's Anglican Bishop, E.W. Barnes, published *Should Such A Faith Offend?*, a book denying many of the 'fundamental Christian doctrines such as the Virgin Birth and the physical resurrection of Christ'.[20] Modernist broadchurchmen, of whom the bishop was a leading light, attempted to raise the profile of the churches by marching through the city led by the Salvation Army band. Cartwright reports drily, 'the effort was not a success'.[21]

Jeffreys was exactly the man to confront the Bishop's approach head-on. Campaigning began in Ebenezer Congregational church, Steelhouse Lane, close to the city centre on the afternoon of 26 March 1930. As before, there were only a few people at the first meeting; and, in a letter to Phillips on 27 March, Jeffreys reported, 'my meetings opened yesterday with a real backwash from the meetings in Dudley'. Here his nephew Edward Jeffreys had preached ten days previously with great success. Attenders of Edward's meetings came now to George's meetings and 'it was a real uproar' when George invited people out for healing. 'Although the ground floor of the church only was full yet they rushed out like wild Indians' and the reason for this was that

> in Eddie's meetings he prays with a certain number *one* by *one* on a *chair*. When they found that I invited them all out, it came as a surprise. One man said at the end 'this man is a better preacher but the other performs more than he does'.

Within a day or two George's evening meeting was nearly full and the afternoon meeting that focused upon divine healing was 'splendid'.[22]

Five days later the large Congregational church was packed and the number of converts growing. People were rushing to the meetings and queuing before they started. Rising to the occasion, Jeffreys agreed to hire the 2,000 seater Town Hall for four days. This was typical of his willingness to seize the moment without being

---

[20] Cartwright, *Evangelists*, p. 103.
[21] Cartwright, *Evangelists*, p. 103.
[22] The letter is quoted in Cartwright, *Evangelists*, p. 104.

reckless: he booked the expensive and prestigious Town Hall for a short period; and, had the place been only half full, he would have reverted to a smaller building. In the event he had to transfer to somewhere bigger – the Town Hall quickly packed out – and announced that they would transfer to the 8,000-seater ice rink. By 2 May the *Evangel* reported:

THE LARGEST SKATING RINK IN EUROPE WITH ACCOMMODATION FOR EIGHT THOUSAND PEOPLE, OFFERING EVERY POSSIBLE FACILITY, PRIVATE MOTOR CAR PARK, RESTAURANT, ETC. ON WEEK-DAYS, THE SERVICES ARE BEING CONTINUED INDEFINITELY IN THE CONGREGATIONAL CHURCH, AND OTHER HALLS ARE BEING ACQUIRED. MIRACLES OF HEALING ARE BEING WITNESSED IN EVERY SERVICE, AND THE NUMBER OF CONVERSIONS IS WELL OVER FOUR THOUSAND.[23]

The extraordinary campaign was welcomed by the general population but opposed by significant churches. Clergy warned their congregations against the 'new sect' and a religious 'counter-attraction was put on by a leading Nonconformist to occupy Christian interest'.[24] We may assume that Bishop Barnes was also opposed to the message of Jeffreys because he had staked his entire reputation on reinterpreting Christianity so as to align it with the natural sciences. Miracles were impossible within such a conception of Christianity.[25] On the other side low churchmen, perhaps wrapping their robes of respectability tightly around themselves, shuddered at the out-and-out supernaturalism of Jeffreys. But as hundreds received evangelical conversion and hundreds more were healed, ministers found themselves 'confronted by their own members reporting on how they had found Christ and were delivered from their sicknesses'.[26] Slowly the clergy of the city, instead of condemning the meetings without first having attended them, took the sensible step of coming to see and hear for themselves. What

[23] *Elim Evangel* 11.18 (2 May 1930), p. 277.
[24] Canty, *Unpublished*, p. 118.
[25] See the *Oxford Dictionary of National Biography* entry on 'Bishop Barnes'.
[26] Canty, *Unpublished*, p. 119.

they found was a preacher at the apex of his powers, both dignified and forceful, and without the gross emotionalism of which he had been accused.

The secular press spoke of enthusiasm but not of fanaticism. A proper comparison with George Jeffreys' meetings would be with the great political gatherings of the age rather than with the staid liturgies of the church; by this comparison Jeffreys was more ordered and more joyful. According to the *Birmingham Gazette* (5 May):

> At a service of healing held during the afternoon, several hundreds were prayed over and anointed with oil, as the vast assembly sang with intense religious fervour. Many times the singing was interrupted by a vast cheer from the audience as one or other of the sufferers testified to having felt the touch of healing.

> It was estimated that at least 5,000 people attended a second service held in the evening, and when the Principal asked how many of them had been healed during the Birmingham campaign sixty-one testified to having obtained relief from limb disorders, twenty-one from cancer and tumours, nearly a score from deafness, and over a dozen from sight trouble. An appeal for testimony from all who had been healed of any complaint resulted in a roar of 'hallelujahs,' and hands too numerous to count were waved among the crowd.[27]

The *Evangel* could not resist a note of triumphalism: 'the Principal's message at one time crushes with irresistible force hollow cant and empty profession, at another revels in rapturing heights of Christian attainment'.[28] Jeffreys was at his best in arguing, as he had for a long time, that Christianity was supernatural from first to last – an argument elaborated in *The Miraculous Foursquare Gospel* which he published that year.[29] The *Evangel* continued, 'people are miraculously healed of all kinds of physical ailments – insomnia, diabetes, rheumatoid arthritis, abscesses, asthma, neuritis, deafness, goitre, and gastric ulcers'. And if congregations wanted proof they could see a man discarding a built-up boot as his shortened leg grew. 'A lad

---

[27] *Elim Evangel* 11.20 (16 May 1930), p. 310.

[28] *Elim Evangel* 11.16 (18 Apr 1930), p. 249.

[29] G. Jeffreys, *The Miraculous Foursquare Gospel* (vol. 2; Clapham: Elim Publishing Company, 1930).

healed of a paralysed arm waved it before the wondering crowd'.[30] Beyond the signs and wonders 'whole families together have been converted' and even, so the *Evangel* claimed, atheistic rationalists found their objections overturned.[31]

The momentum of the revival was apparently unstoppable. Eventually the Bingley Hall was hired from 28 May until 9 June. Two meetings a day were held, one at 3:00 pm and the other at 7:30 pm. It was the first purpose-built exhibition hall in Britain and it could hold 15,000 people. It was hardly the most comfortable location but no heating was needed because the summer had come and ventilation could be arranged simply by leaving the doors open. The crusade filled the space on 26 separate occasions and 'the final service began half an hour early since they could not fit anyone else in'.[32] Jeffreys was accustomed to asking those who wished to accept Christ to raise their hands but across 'thousands of square yards of seats' could hardly keep track of new believers.[33] It is thought some 6,000 people responded during this final phase of the two-and-a-half month campaign; and, when the total number of converts was added together, the figure reached over 10,000. Before he left the city Jeffreys baptised 1,100 and when, at the final Bingley Hall meeting he announced he would open Elim churches in the city, the crowd spontaneously rose to their feet in applause and cheering and over 3,000 people turned out for the opening of the Graham Street Church, the mother church of two others.[34] By any measure, this was an astonishing evangelistic effort and, in its planting of three new and still thriving congregations, has never been seen in the British Isles before or since.

A Southern Push

While still engaged in the Birmingham Crusade, Jeffreys took the Royal Albert Hall for the fifth year in succession and preached there on Easter Monday and broke all records 'in numbers, fervour and

---

[30] *Elim Evangel* 11.16 (18 Apr 1930), p. 249.
[31] *Elim Evangel* 11.16 (18 Apr 1930), p. 249.
[32] Cartwright and Holdaway, *Defining Moments Elim 100 Centenary*, p. 48.
[33] Canty, *Unpublished*, p. 119.
[34] Canty, *Unpublished*, p. 120.

power'.[35] 'Queues of enthusiastic Foursquare Gospellers lined up for hours ... they packed the historic hall from floor to roof'.[36] When the meetings were in full swing, people were asked to indicate where they came from and it turned out the gatherings had a wide international dimension. England, Scotland, Ireland, Australia, Canada, India, New Zealand, Africa, the USA, France, Armenia, Sweden, Java, Denmark, Switzerland, China, Japan, Spain, Portugal, Germany, and Russia were all represented.[37]

Jeffreys appears to have coped without any obvious sign of stress with the huge expectations his meetings generated. Reflecting on the year he simply wrote:

> As a result of your prayers I have been called to preach to the largest gatherings that have ever come under the sound of the combined message of Salvation, Healing, the Baptism in the Holy Spirit, and our Coming King, in the history of our beloved land, while the largest auditoriums in the country have rung with praises to God.[38]

There were reports in the *Daily Mail, Daily Express, Daily Herald*, and the *Daily Mirror* for 22 April 1930. All these were national newspapers and their headlines spoke of 'Kneeling crowds blessed amid "Hallelujahs" and flowers' or 'Amazing Faith Cure Claims'. Even the more sedate *Daily Telegraph* noted, '200 baptised in Albert Hall services of healing'.[39]

John Bull's attack appears not to have poisoned the rest of the press corps. After his preaching exertions in Birmingham and the extra effort at Easter, Jeffreys took a short break in Switzerland before returning to the Wandsworth area of London.[40] Here he undertook a further successful crusade. The *Evangel* reported:

> The spacious tent – situated right in the heart of one of London's great centres of population and on one of the main thor-

---

[35] *Elim Evangel* 11.51-52 (25 Dec 1930), p. 804.
[36] *Elim Evangel* 11.19 (9 May 1930), p. 289.
[37] *Elim Evangel* 11.22 (30 May 1930), p. 348.
[38] *Elim Evangel* 11.51-52 (25 Dec 1930), p. 802.
[39] *Elim Evangel* 11.19 (9 May 1930), p. 292.
[40] Cartwright, *Evangelists*, p. 106.

oughfares – is being besieged each night by a great crowd of eager and expectant people.[41]

There appears to have been a conscious strategy here as a report went on to pray, 'God grant that a chain of churches be established around London'. At the end of the year the *Evangel* could say that 'three more centres were opened, making a total of Foursquare Gospel centres in London alone twenty-seven in number'.[42] Jeffreys and others had learned that by campaigning in places a short distance apart, the congregations from one event could help another. Beyond this they wanted big urban centres to be served by multiple Elim ministries.

The focus of the *Evangel* and of Jeffreys himself, who could certainly influence the editorial direction of the magazine, was not solely inward or devotional but out towards world events read through the lens of biblical prophecy. There was a report in February stating, 'we do not, however, view the intervention of the Pope in the Russian crisis as helpful to the situation, nor the association there with the condemnation of the persecution by our own Archbishop of Canterbury'.[43] Parliamentary matters did not escape their attention. 'How grateful we are to know that the Blasphemy Bill has been withdrawn from Parliament … It was a Bill opening the way for Russia's blasphemous denial of God to be repeated in our own land'.[44] A list of contemporary dangers included population growth, immorality including rising murder and burglary rates, food shortages, science devoted to enormous bombs and machine guns, and gas attacks by aircraft.[45] Sometimes Elim itself gave the impression of being under attack – 'the mud of misrepresentation has been thrown at the movement – stones of scurrilous slander and shafts of unreasonable ridicule'[46] and Cartwright provides examples of Nonconformist writers who directed their scorn at Jeffreys himself. The secular press could add to these provocations by mixing up members of the Jeffreys family: the *Daily Mail* reported 'three peo-

[41] *Elim Evangel* 11.33 (15 Aug 1930), p. 521.
[42] *Elim Evangel* 11.51-52 (25 Dec 1930), p. 804.
[43] *Elim Evangel* 11.9 (28 Feb 1930), p. 136.
[44] *Elim Evangel* 11.12 (21 Mar 1930), p. 186.
[45] *Elim Evangel* 11.14 (4 Apr 1930), p. 209.
[46] *Elim Evangel* 11.19 (9 May 1930), p. 289.

ple go mad after "faith meeting" confusing Stephen with George while the *Daily Express, Daily Herald,* and *Sketch* reported (quite wrongly) that Edward Jeffreys had removed splints from a man undergoing treatment but carrying a picture of George. A press cuttings agency gathered these and enabled George to complain and receive a printed apology from each newspaper.[47]

Underlying this commentary was an expectation of the return of Christ prior to global tribulation. Christabel Pankhurst, famous as a suffragette, had come to embrace evangelical Christianity and now preached the Second Coming with the same vehemence that had marked her political campaigning; the implication for Elim readers was that political agitation, however just its objectives, could not meet the challenges of the day. The *Evangel* picked this up[48] while continuing to offer sporadic commentary on Palestine, 'all the East, both Far and Near, is in ferment'.[49] Government policy, without the benefit of subsequent Keynesian analysis,[50] put fiscal orthodoxy above human need with the consequence that 'unemployment is tragically increasing. Nearly two million people in the British Isles are now out of work' and 'the people of God are amongst those severely hit by the industrial situation'. Their best advice was to continue to seek the kingdom of God and then 'all other needful things shall be added'.[51] Later writers considered the British politicians holding office in the 1930s to be mediocrities quite unfitted for alleviating poverty at home or challenging fascism abroad.[52] 'We have done nothing. There is nothing we can do', said Montagu Norman, director of the Bank of England.[53] Understandably Elim writers felt themselves unqualified to offer political or economic solutions and so – wisely as it turned out – avoided diverting their energy and money into causes that have since vanished. After all, many of the

---

[47] Cartwright, *Evangelists*, pp. 107, 108.

[48] *Elim Evangel* 11.28 (11 July 1930), p. 436.

[49] *Elim Evangel* 11.28 (11 July 1930), p. 436.

[50] John Maynard Keynes the economist argued that government spending of money raised through taxation could provide employment and stimulate a stagnant economy.

[51] *Elim Evangel* 11.33 (15 Aug 1930), p. 525. The reference here is to Mt. 6.33.

[52] E.g. A.N. Wilson, *After the Victorians: The World our Parents Knew* (New York: Farrar, Straus and Giroux, Kindle edn, 2005), loc 6985.

[53] Quoted by A.J.P. Taylor, *English History 1914–1945* (Harmondsworth: Penguin, 1975), p. 361.

converts of the Welsh Revival had been quickly swept up with political enthusiasm for Lloyd George in the 1906 General Election that brought a Liberal government to power – the chapels had often been recruiting stations for the Liberal vote; the result was that the religious commitment of the converts declined as their political commitment grew and spiritual vitality ebbed away.[54] 'The spiritual excitement of 1904–1905 had secular implications also. Revivalistic passion was a factor in the struggle against the Education Act of 1902'.[55]

The crusade meetings at Wandsworth took place during the summer in Elim's big tent.[56] In what was becoming a normal practice, Jeffreys left behind a leading evangelist to continue the meetings. James McWhirter and R.E. Darragh remained while he went a few miles on to campaign in the Empire Theatre at Kingston-upon-Thames and made 1,000 converts.[57] By prolonging the cycle of meetings in this way, it was possible to build up a larger nucleus from which an Elim congregation could be permanently established. The campaign ended with a large communion service and 'the vast concourse of people which crowded together to hear the closing message and to sing the praises of God were visibly moved'.[58] It was estimated that over 500 conversions had taken place as well as miraculous healings of all kinds.[59] After Kingston, Jeffreys began campaigning in Elim and reverted to the tent and saw 500 further conversion decisions.[60] The big event of the autumn was, however, the hiring of the Crystal Palace in London on 13 September for two meetings.

The Crystal Palace had originally been erected in Hyde Park for the Great Exhibition of 1851 when a range of products and artefacts associated with the British Empire had been on display. It was a vast glass building erected on a metal frame and was unusual for

[54] The Nonconformists wanted the disestablishment of the Anglican church more than anything else. See R. Tudur Jones, *Faith and the Crisis of a Nation, Wales 1890–1914* (Cardiff: University of Wales Press, 2004), pp. 381-84.
[55] John Davies, *A History of Wales* (Harmondsworth: Penguin, 1993), p. 507.
[56] *Elim Evangel* 11.36 (5 Sept 1930), p. 563.
[57] Canty, *Unpublished*, p. 120.
[58] *Elim Evangel* 11.36 (5 Sept 1930), p. 563.
[59] *Elim Evangel* 11.36 (5 Sept 1930), p. 563.
[60] Canty, *Unpublished*, p. 120.

the time because, being completely transparent, it needed very little in the way of extra lighting; and, at a time when electricity was unknown, visitors found it a marvel of imagination and engineering. The original building was over 500 metres long; and, once the Great Exhibition closed, the entire structure, with significant modifications, was re-erected in a residential area south east of London and then supplied with two railway stations that allowed visitors to stream in. Although the building was expensive to maintain, it could be hired for large events of many kinds.

Jeffreys hired it and 'the vast palace rang with the praises of colossal congregations, and monster crowds were held under the spell of the Foursquare gospel message'.[61] Photographs appeared in the *Evangel* showing the distinctive rounded glass roof and immaculate gardens and fountains.[62] Boulton, in his distinctive way, conveyed his impressions,

> Everything conveyed THE IMPRESSION OF IMMENSITY! Those almost interminable rows of chairs – the huge transparent transept walls, towering upward towards the dome of the skies – the rustle of those thousands of glory-coloured song sheets, like the sound of softly fluttering wings or the whisper of countless aspen leaves borne upon the breeze – the thunderous outpouring of song, sometimes rising in one mighty and magnificent crescendo of harmonic sound, crashing out its conquering volume of vocal melody, anon to subside into the stillness of a great hush of heart as that vast congregation was led in earnest articulate prayer to the very throne of the Eternal.[63]

Not one to trim his words, Jeffreys preached on what he called the four great miracles of the Christian faith: regeneration, physical healing, baptism in the Holy Ghost, and the miracle of translation (the second coming and the general resurrection of the dead). 'I maintain', he proclaimed, 'that to believe in the Second Advent of Christ, and all that it entails, means believing in a tremendous demonstration with supernatural effects'. Our bodies 'at the Second

---

[61] *Elim Evangel* 11.39 (26 Sept 1930), p. 609.
[62] *Elim Evangel* 11.35 (29 Aug 1930), p. 545.
[63] *Elim Evangel*, 11.40 (3 Oct 1930), p. 625.

Advent' will 'be fashioned like unto the glorious body of Christ. The second coming of Christ is to be the closing act in the great dispensation of the Holy Ghost.'[64]

By October Jeffreys was in Kensington near Notting Hill Gate at the Congregational church there (which he bought from the Congregational Union)[65] in what became one of the most important centres of Elim activity in London and later one of London's megachurches. Later that month he opened at the Globe Theatre, Acton, to the west.[66]

Northern Push

At the end of the month the revival party set up in the historic Halifax Place Chapel, one time a hub of Nottingham's Methodism.[67] The beautiful and spacious building became a permanent centre for Elim and the scene of 'old-time revival'. Here Jeffreys was able to build upon the legacy of Wesley in an area long evangelised by Methodists and home to many families with solid Methodist pedigrees. The *Evangel* reported that 'over 70 have already decided for Christ, and the power of God is present to heal as in the early days of the Wesleys'. It is the nature of revival to bring churches to life again and here weary but faithful Methodism found itself transformed into a Pentecostal form, and that form then attracted others. An elderly lay preacher described the scene:

> As I turned out of Picher Gate, I caught the sound of singing, and when, a few minutes later, I looked upon that vast sea of faces, many memories stirred within me. I had not seen the building since it was closed as a Methodist Church, and left desolate as a hopeless proposition. There must have been at least 1,600 people in the church. As far as I could see, there were not six of them that I knew. The bulk of the congregation seemed

---

[64] *Elim Evangel* 11.40 (3 Oct 1930), p. 636.
[65] Canty, *Unpublished*, p. 121.
[66] *Elim Evangel* 11.42 (17 Oct 1930), p. 665.
[67] *Elim Evangel* 11.46 (14 Nov 1930), p. 729.

to me to be men and women who were connected with no church. Evidently they were moved by some great impulse.[68]

In a rare burst of interdenominational excitement, a writer in the *Evangel* proclaimed, 'denominational walls are falling flat, and members of various churches are uniting together on the one common platform of revivalism'.[69] Elim had resisted narrow sectarianism since its earliest days in Ireland and these latest hopes were for a broad coalition of revived and revivalistic churches, working together, forgetting their differences and keen to preach in the power of the Spirit. Perhaps such hopes were a flash in the pan – the passing hopes of an individual pastor – but that they could be expressed shows that *some* Pentecostals glimpsed an ecumenism of the Spirit.

McWhirter, a member of the Revival Party, writing about the Nottingham revival recalled that Lloyd George once said, 'John Wesley did more for England than all the politicians of that time'.

Testimony like this from one of our greatest statesman thrusts out of court the sophistry that legislation is the only remedy for our national ills. It argues eloquently and convincingly that the solution of our government problems lies in religious revival.[70]

The direct comparison and parallel between Britain at the time of Wesley and Britain at the time of Jeffreys stimulated McWhirter to see the Jeffreys' revivals as similar to Wesley's. The job of revivals was to convert the land and, when they had done this, legislative and other reforms would quickly follow and transform public morals and private prosperity.

The year ended with a hope that in 1931 'the living waters of the Spirit's last great appeal to dying men in this dispensation' would continue to flow.[71] The closing of the age seemed at hand. The *Evangel* found time to note how General Chiang Kai-shek, the president of the Nationalist Government of China, had been received into the Christian church. Yet, ironically, the General was later defeated, Mao Zedong with his atheistic Communism was victorious,

---

[68] *Elim Evangel* 12.1 (2 Jan 1931), p. 9.
[69] *Elim Evangel* 11.49 (5 Dec 1930), p. 769. The statement is unsigned.
[70] *Elim Evangel* 11.49 (5 Dec 1930), p. 769.
[71] *Elim Evangel* 11.51-52 (25 Dec 1930), p. 804.

and Christianity in China found itself forced underground for 50 years. Far away in England, there was to be a further irony: an accidental fire destroyed the Crystal Palace in 1936 and the blaze could be seen in eight counties.

11

Jeffreys' Evangelical and Pentecostal Theology

Introduction

Although Jeffreys wrote in the *Elim Evangel* regularly and his sermons were often reproduced there, his main theological output for the first part of his life is to be found in four books. The first of these, published in 1929, was entitled *The Miraculous Foursquare Gospel: Doctrinal* and running to only 80 pages is organised round the principle of the foursquare Gospel. It is a series of Bible studies with explanatory words linking the various texts that form the basis of the presentation. The final chapter comprises a series of questions and answers on the topic of salvation and it emphasises that only faith in Christ is sufficient for salvation and that no religious ceremonies and rituals will be adequate. The subject matter of this book is largely repeated at greater length in the second volume.

Jeffreys never gives us a systematic theology rooted in innumerable books and hours in the library but rather a theology that has been developed by early and intense study of Scripture and then formalised using four cardinal roles of Christ as an organising principle. It is a theology centred on Christ and presumes and defends the authority and validity of Scripture. It is vain to look here for a philosophical prologue or a set of deductions derived from the latest biblical scholars. It is a theology (despite Pentecostal additions) that is drawn from the revivalistic tradition which included Charles Finney, D.L. Moody, R.A. Torrey and Welsh evangelicalism and, further back, John Wesley. And, because it is preached, there is a di-

rectness and simplicity about the language which is only occasionally varied by poetic imagery or reference to contemporary events.
One has to imagine the sermons being delivered before large
crowds after introductory singing and before evangelistic appeals or
prayer for the sick.

The Miraculous Foursquare Gospel: Supernatural (1930)

This book contains six chapters, the first five of which seem to
have been originally preached. The epigraph of chapter one is 'Delivered by the Principal before 10,000 people at the Royal Albert
Hall, London, Easter, 1927'; and, although there is no indication
where the other chapters were first heard, they lay out the Foursquare Gospel familiar to Elim people and crusade crowds. The
first chapter asserts that the gospel is miraculous, and the others
work through the four basic doctrines that comprised the foursquare configuration. Jesus is saviour, healer, baptizer, and coming
king. The final chapter changes the format as 'I have dealt with
questions on the subject of healing that are continually being asked
by people everywhere'.[1] Here short and varied questions are followed by short and varied answers supported by quotations from
Scripture.

   Jeffreys was always keen to assert the supernatural and miraculous nature of Christianity, presumably because his youthful experiences of Christianity in Wales warned him against un-revived religion. He was always in some way a 'child of the revival' and perhaps, bearing in mind the damage done to Welsh Nonconformity by
Sunday school teaching that neglected the Bible in favour of a watered-down version of 19th century German scholarship, his stance
was entirely understandable. It was baptism in the Spirit that revolu-
tionised his hopes and took him out of the coalmine and into the
biggest halls in the country. His own life was an astonishing journey
from obscurity to celebrity and he wanted others to read the Bible
as a living book, as he did.

---

[1] George Jeffreys, *The Miraculous Foursquare Gospel: Supernatural* (Clapham,
London: Elim Publishing Company, 1930), II, p. 81.

He began by referring to the fourfold roles of Jesus and then dealt with church membership. 'It matters little whether you are an Anglican, a Presbyterian, Congregationalist, Methodist, Baptist, Brethren or Salvationist, – if you are born again you belong to the same church as myself'.[2] He saw all believers as belonging to 'the city of the living God, the heavenly Jerusalem'[3] (Heb. 12.22) and in this respect revivalism was a unifying ecumenical force. Christianity itself was miraculous from beginning to end: the Gospel, the virgin birth, the life of Christ, the miracles of the cross, the resurrection, ascension, the outpouring of Spirit, and the promise of the Second Coming were all supernatural events:

> Let me emphasise here that the Christian who denies the miraculous, denies Christianity: the Christian who rejects the supernatural, rejects the religion he professes to embrace.[4]

And so piling one event on another he affirmed that if supernatural evidences were available in the 'dispensation of the Father' (i.e. the Old Testament) and in the 'dispensation of the Son' (i.e. the New Testament) 'what reason is there to suppose that miracles were to cease during the dispensation of the Holy Ghost?'[5] 'Most Christians', he declared, 'agree that the present dispensation commenced on the Day of Pentecost' but if that is so, 'then they must agree that it started with a miraculous display of power'[6]; and, if it also ends with a miraculous display with the return of Christ, who is to argue that there should be no miracles now?

In speaking of Jesus as Saviour, Jeffreys begins by reference to the declaration of John the Baptist pointing to Jesus as the 'Lamb of God'. This allows Jeffreys to trace the theme of substitutionary atonement from Abel in Genesis through to the Passover and Israel's exodus from Egypt to Christ himself. Blood is shed for one person, Abel, and then for each household at the Exodus and finally for the world. The exposition follows the narrative of Scripture but also takes in verses from Isaiah and the epistle to the Romans. This

---

[2] Jeffreys, *Foursquare Gospel*, p. 2.
[3] Jeffreys, *Foursquare Gospel*, p. 2.
[4] Jeffreys, *Foursquare Gospel*, pp. 8, 9.
[5] Jeffreys, *Foursquare Gospel*, p. 20.
[6] Jeffreys, *Foursquare Gospel*, p. 20.

is not a detailed exposition appealing to a few precise texts but draws from the breadth of the Bible 'following the ever-widening stream of redemption'.[7] It ends by anticipating the 'atoning blood as the theme of the heavenly choir in the book of Revelation'.[8] This is not teaching on the atonement slanted one way towards Calvinism or the other way to Arminianism, nor is it centred upon the sins of the present age. Rather it builds a cumulative case from repeated instances of substitution and the shedding of blood and culminates in the death of Jesus who is nothing less than a sacrifice for the sins of the world.

In speaking of Jesus as Healer, Jeffreys begins by reference to the comprehensive and powerful healing ministry of Jesus himself. He takes as a context of his argument, 'two states of bliss found in the Scriptures: one at the beginning the Bible and the other at the end':[9] in Eden and in heaven there is no 'sin, sickness or disease'.[10] We are currently living in the era between these two states of bliss and are surrounded by diseases of many kinds that bring havoc in the human family. The cause of sickness is to be found in sin when Adam as the head of human race opened the door to 'corrupting disease that has since overwhelmed the world'.[11] The ultimate source of diseases is Satan who smites Job or the woman satanically bound for 18 years and freed by Jesus in Lk. 13.16. Jesus is anointed with the Holy Spirit to heal all who are oppressed by the devil (Acts 10.38). So Christ is the remedy for sickness who can uplift the oppressed by healing the sick today in the same way that he still 'destroys sin'. 'There's not a single verse in the whole Scripture to show that he has, in this age, ceased to heal the sick'.[12]

There is, even in 1930, a recognition that the preaching of healing throws up distraught questions since not everybody who receives prayer is healed. In a series of questions and answers Jeffreys shows his flexibility and pastoral insight. He prefers the term 'divine healing' to 'faith healing' and acknowledges that faith healing does

[7] Jeffreys, *Foursquare Gospel*, p. 36.
[8] Jeffreys, *Foursquare Gospel*, p. 36.
[9] Jeffreys, *Foursquare Gospel*, p. 40.
[10] Jeffreys, *Foursquare Gospel*, p. 40.
[11] Jeffreys, *Foursquare Gospel*, p. 42.
[12] Jeffreys, *Foursquare Gospel*, p. 48.

exist. He believes it is God's will to heal the sick today and that any reasons given for people not being healed as, for instance, that the iniquity of the fathers is visited on their children, misreads the text of Exod. 20.5, 6. Nor is Paul's 'thorn in the flesh' relevant since this was given particularly to Paul 'lest he become exalted' after receiving many revelations; and Paul prayed three times for healing indicating that he thought it 'most natural for him to be delivered'.[13] Nor, again, can disease be routinely attributed to the sins of believers since Job was a righteous man. As for the epistle of James there is a query about its intended recipients, the 12 tribes of Israel, but Jeffreys points out that this cannot be a consideration since other epistles written to specific recipients are deemed applicable to all Christians. Miraculous gifts were not withdrawn at the close of the apostolic age because 'the Christian religion is essentially a religion of faith that produces signs'.[14] Some people, it is true, do not receive healing because they are not prepared to comply with the conditions laid down in Scripture, e.g. listening to God and doing what is right in his sight. The nine spiritual gifts outlined in 1 Corinthians 12 operate today and the distinction between the healing and miracles is that healing suggests a gradual recovery while miracles are instantaneous.[15] But healing should not be confused with immunity from death.

In speaking of Jesus as Baptiser in the Spirit, Jeffreys makes an unusual distinction between the Spirit of Christ and the Holy Spirit. His argument is that the Spirit of Christ is given to all who are regenerate and that the disciples and even a number of people in the Old Testament (like Abel) were regenerate as a result of the work of the Spirit of Christ. They cannot have received the Holy Spirit at that point since the outpouring of the Holy Spirit only occurred on the Day of Pentecost. It is in Jn 7.37-39 that Jeffreys finds one of the foundational statements supporting his view: the Holy Spirit is not given at this point because Jesus is not yet glorified. It is unthinkable to suppose the disciples went out performing miracles before the crucifixion or saw Christ after his resurrection and worshipped him while being in an unregenerate state. The only explana-

---

[13] Jeffreys, *Foursquare Gospel*, p. 87.

[14] Jeffreys, *Foursquare Gospel*, p. 93.

[15] Jeffreys, *Foursquare Gospel*, p. 97.

tion is that regeneration is possible through the operation of the Spirit of Christ. The sinner may receive eternal life and be regenerated by the Spirit of Christ – like the woman of Samaria who could receive a well of living water that would keep her soul in perpetual satisfaction; by contrast the great gift to the regenerate believer is the Holy Spirit who flows like 'rivers of water' from the inner being.

The distinction Jeffreys draws between the Spirit of Christ and the Holy Spirit is not one that has recommended itself to other Pentecostals or biblical scholars. There is some evidence that Jeffreys took the distinction from Thomas Myerscough who is likely to have taught it at the Bible school in Preston.[16] It was designed to enable Pentecostals to explain the common experiences they shared with evangelicals while continuing to safeguard their distinctive experience of Spirit baptism. It predates or is contemporary with the dispute initiated in the USA by William Durham of Chicago over whether sanctification is a distinct stage following regeneration and prior to baptism in the Spirit or whether Christians should expect to be sanctified as part and parcel of the initial process of regeneration. It also does not address the doctrine associated with many Pentecostal denominations about the 'initial evidence' of speaking with tongues as a marker and proof that Spirit-baptism has taken place.

In speaking of Jesus as the Coming King, the manner of Christ's coming is given in Acts 1.11 with the words, 'this same Jesus, which is taken up from you into heaven, shall also come in like manner as ye have seen him go'.[17] When Jesus returns, the dead in Christ shall rise first, living Christians shall be changed, and the rapture will occur and the unconverted will find themselves in a world that has no true Christian in it.[18] The removal of the 'salt of the earth' will leave the reins of government with the ungodly. 'The revolutionary seed sown in days gone by will bring forth its harvest in blood. I hear the clash of steel in the battles of the armies of the world' so that the Great Tribulation will indeed have arrived.[19] And the signs of the return of Christ are given in Jas 5.1-8 with the lust for wealth, la-

[16] *Elim Evangel* 5.6 (June 1924), p. 135.
[17] Jeffreys quoted from the Authorised Version of the Bible.
[18] Jeffreys, *Foursquare Gospel*, p. 73.
[19] Jeffreys, *Foursquare Gospel*, p. 73.

bour and industrial unrest, immorality, flimsy promises of peace, fierce persecution of the just, and an outpouring of the Holy Spirit. All of these were recurring themes in Jeffreys' evangelistic preaching and he never seems to have lost his conviction about the imminent return of Christ, the pre-tribulation rapture, or the unmistakable warning signs continually implied by contemporary events.

Healing Rays (1932)

In this 200-page book Jeffreys states his doctrine of healing most completely with essentially the same argument but with greater detail and more supportive scriptural material. He also provides a lengthy account of healings in church history showing how miracles have continued since the time of Christ. The book is completed with photographs of a few of his largest meetings and a longer series of questions and answers. The tone is closer to the lecture hall than the pulpit.

The title comes from Mal. 4.2

> Unto you that fear my name shall the Sun of Righteousness arise with healing in his wings (or rays, Moffat's translation).

He comments:

> Healing rays! Yes, they radiate from our Lord and Saviour Jesus Christ, the glorious Sun of Righteousness. We have been conscious of them as we have ministered in His Name, and have come under their vivifying, health-giving and invigorating properties. The warmth of the spiritual calorific ray has driven away the coldness of unbelief, and the transforming effect of the actinic has resulted in changed lives and homes. The light that comes from Christ not only illuminates and beautifies the soul, it gives health and vigour to the mortal body.[20]

The front cover carries an imprint of the sun with its rays shining out. This almost mystical account again centres on the person of Jesus Christ. There is not a focus on logic-chopping or faith but instead upon Christ himself as the bringer of warmth and healing.

---

[20] Jeffreys, *Healing Rays*, p. xiv.

This may be what differentiates Jeffreys from other healing evangelists in the 20th century – his Christological focus rather than his
polemical thrust. By the same token what differentiates Jeffreys
from biblical scholars writing about healing is that he spent most of
his adult life preaching about healing and praying for countless
people in big public venues.

By way of introduction he considers natural healing in the physical world and is careful to point out how the bodies of human beings and animals have a natural propensity to recover from injury
and illness. 'It is a huge mistake on the part of many devout believers in the truth of divine healing to ignore natural healing'.[21] Unlike
a number of other Pentecostal preachers at the beginning of the
20th century, Jeffreys is quite willing to endorse natural methods of
healing, including medical methods, and sees no shame in doing so,
and in this respect, he is not an extremist or a sectarian.[22] Beyond
the natural physical realm he understands the supernatural realm
but hardly elaborates on this. He also distinguishes between 'higher'
and 'lower' critics. The former do not accept 'anything that cannot
be explained within the range of reason' and here he has in mind
the post-Enlightenment academic biblical critics.[23] The latter accept
the Bible in its entirety while inconsistently eliminating parts of it:
'He starts off by declaring his absolute faith in a present-day miraculous Bible with all its commands and its promises, and then argues
that miracles are not for the present'.[24]

Jeffreys believed in a literal historical Adam and a literal historical
fall. Much hinges on the parallel between Adam and Christ. What
Adam loses, Christ restores. Christ came into the world to put away
sin through his atoning death and to destroy the works of the devil
instigated at the fall so that eventually the whole creation is to be
completely delivered from the bondage to corruption to which it is
now subjected.[25] Although death comes about as a result of sin and
God can grant immunity from death – and will do so when Christ

---

[21] Jeffreys, *Healing Rays*, p. 6.
[22] J.N. Parr of Assemblies of God in Britain was negative about medical
treatments. J.N. Parr, *Divine Healing* (Springfield: Gospel Publishing House, 1955),
e.g. pp. 38, 61.
[23] Jeffreys, *Healing Rays*, p. 8.
[24] Jeffreys, *Healing Rays*, p. 8.
[25] Jeffreys, *Healing Rays*, pp. 22, 23.

returns to both humans and animals – some of the benefits of Christ's atonement will have to wait for a future dispensation before they are finally conferred.

For clarity Jeffreys provides a chart (shown below) explaining his thought: the original condition of human beings had no sin, no death, no bondage in the animal kingdom, no death, no curse, and no bodily sickness.[26] The loss of all these benefits was a result of the first Adam's disobedience and confirmed by our present experience. The last Adam's obedience brings deliverance from sin and provides bodily healing now but the destruction of death, the deliverance of animals, the removal of the curse, and immortality are placed in the final column and will have to wait for a future era.

Original conditions and results of First Adam's disobedience described in the Word of God	The Cross of Christ		Present and ultimate benefits of Last Adam's obedience definitely promised in the Word of God
Original condition	**Present condition confirmed by experience**	**Present benefits confirmed by experience**	**Future benefits**
No sin	Sin	Deliverance from sin	
No death	Death		Death destroyed
No bondage in the animal kingdom	Bondage in the animal kingdom	-	Animals delivered
No curse on the earth	Curse resting on the earth	-	Curse removed
		-	Immortality
No mortality	Mortality	-	
No bodily sickness	Bodily sickness	Bodily healing	

Having placed the atonement at the centre of his understanding of healing, Jeffreys addresses the sources of sickness and disease and makes 'scriptural affirmations – logical deductions'.[27] He argues that sickness can be inflicted by Satan on saints and sinners alike and that saints and sinners alike can be afflicted with sickness by a direct act of God in the interests of justice.[28] He then deals with

---

[26] Jeffreys, *Healing Rays*, p. 33.
[27] Jeffreys, *Healing Rays*, p. 37.
[28] Jeffreys, *Healing Rays*, p. 42.

'the marvellous mortal body' and provides examples from the journals of John Wesley and George Fox of healing or strengthening provided in answer to prayer[29] and gives the testimony of Evan Roberts who was strengthened 'when the power of God came upon him'[30] and enabled him to walk eight miles despite having been ill for four days previously. Jeffreys also gives personal testimony to his own healing when he was young:

> We were kneeling in prayer one Sunday morning and were interceding on the subject of the services of that day. It was exactly 9 o'clock when the power of God came upon me, and I received such an inflow of my life that I can only liken the experience to being charged with electricity. It seemed as if my head were connected to *a most powerful electric battery*. My whole body from head to foot was quickened by the Spirit of God, and I was healed.[31]

He went on to explain how more recently in the midst of his extensive campaigning his own body was 'tired and weakened by constant labour' and needed 'a special inflow of divine life'.[32] After speaking of the help he believed he received from God from his youth and later during his ministry, he provides three chapters laying out a dispensational scheme that he has long accepted.[33] He divided the Bible into three dispensations with the Old Testament being the 'dispensation of the Father' and he is able to find many examples of healing here. In the 'dispensation of the Son' there are numerous healings through the ministry of Jesus.

This leads to the 'dispensation of the Holy Ghost' and here again many examples of healing taken from the book of Acts are provided, although with minimal explanation or exposition. Here he refers to the charismatic gifts in 1 Corinthians 12 and the ministries placed in the church through apostles, prophets, teachers, and others. Ecclesiological discussion is absent. He defers his explanation of the distinction between the healing gifts exercised by a pastor in

---

[29] Jeffreys, *Healing Rays*, p. 53.
[30] Jeffreys, *Healing Rays*, p. 55.
[31] Jeffreys, *Healing Rays*, p. 57.
[32] Jeffreys, *Healing Rays*, p. 57.
[33] The scheme is found in Joachim of Fiore in the 12th century.

the local church and the healing gifts he himself exercised in large meetings until the end of *Pentecostal Rays* (see below).

Although there is no explicit attempt to connect the chart showing the benefits of the atonement with the dispensations of the Father, the Son, and the Holy Spirit, the two theological schemes or classificatory systems are not incompatible. But one would have expected Jeffreys to have argued that the healings which took place in the Old Testament, the dispensation of the Father, might look forward to Christ's atonement just as healings in the dispensation of the Holy Spirit might look backward to it.

The next section of the book gives examples of healings after the closure of the canon of Scripture and here he acknowledges his indebtedness to Dr. A.J. Gordon of Boston who had collected a lengthy roll call of healing references from Justin Martyr, Irenaeus, Tertullian, Origen, Clement, the Waldenses, the Moravians, Zinzendorf, the Huguenots, Martin Luther, and others. The point of this chapter is surely to rebut those 'lower critics' who argue that healings died out once the canon of Scripture had been completed. It was said healings were only necessary in the first years of the church to establish it but that, once the canon had been closed, there was no further need for confirmatory miraculousness.[34] It is not clear when Jeffreys had met these arguments but they may have circulated within the independent Welsh congregations during his teenage years.

In a further chapter Jeffreys quotes at length from books about the Scottish covenanters but also draws on Wesley who, in his *Notes on the New Testament*, remarks,

> the single conspicuous gift which Christ committed to his apostles remained in the church long after the miraculous gifts. Indeed, it seems to have been designed to remain always, and St James directs the elders, who were the most if not the only gifted men, to administer it.[35]

This refers to healing in James 5.

---

[34] Benjamin B. Warfield, *Counterfeit Miracles* (Edinburgh: Banner of Truth, 1918, 1972).

[35] Jeffreys, *Healing Rays*, p. 126.

J.N. Darby and various missionaries are also cited as well as A.B. Simpson, the founder of the Christian Missionary Alliance, who wrote *The Gospel of Healing*. Andrew Murray, the South African, is mentioned as well as Samuel Chadwick, the British Methodist. These writers are drawn from many traditions within Christianity and substantiate Pentecostal convictions about healing miracles as a continuing stream within the church across the world and down the ages. After a set of questions and answers similar to those given before, Jeffreys ends with a lengthy sequence of testimonies from 'miracles in our day', all of which derive from his own ministry. These are collected from crusades in the United Kingdom and names and dates and other details are given.[36] In other words, they are, or were then, open to verification. In most cases those who have been healed speak in their own words but sometimes a relative (e.g. the mother of a child) is quoted. Cumulatively this block of testimonies constitutes evidence for the validity of contemporary healing in evangelism and the church and has the purpose among other things of contradicting modernism.

Pentecostal Rays (1933)

This is Jeffreys' longest book and least like a set of printed sermons. We know from correspondence between him and Phillips that he read widely before completing it.[37] Although there is some duplication with his earlier publications much of what is written is new and relevant to modern Pentecostals. He begins by setting out the narrative of the day of Pentecost described in Acts 2 and draws attention to the purpose of the Jewish feasts that underlay the crucifixion and the day of Pentecost itself. Pentecost, also called the 'Feast of Weeks', required the priest to wave loaves, fruits of the harvest, before God; this typified the 'harvest of souls' the outpouring of the Spirit is intended to effect. And, when the outpour-

---

[36] Some had previously been printed in the *Elim Evangel* or published with photographs by R.E. Darragh, *In Defence of his Word* (London: Elim Publishing Company, 1932).

[37] Letter: George Jeffreys to E.J. Phillips on 20 and 26 Jan 1933 where he requests a copy of Donald Gee's book on spiritual gifts and any others Phillips might get hold of.

ing occurs there are effects upon human faculties including upon the ear (the sound of wind), the eye (the fire), and the vocal organs (speaking in tongues) and also an effect upon the waiting world.

He then offers a chapter, unusual for its time, on the personality of the Holy Spirit and is quite clear that the Spirit has personal faculties like the ability to speak, see, and hear as well as emotions and a will but; in addition, the Spirit is eternal, omnipotent, omniscient, and omnipresent, and so divine; in this way Jeffreys places himself firmly in the centre of Trinitarian Pentecostalism. In the same chapter, he deals with terminology and argues that the four terms 'baptism', 'filling', 'outpouring', and 'gift' are interchangeable and deduces this from the fact that the terms are used to refer to the same experience.[38] Taking the term 'baptism' as it is used in Acts 1.5 he has no difficulty in showing that it applies to the day of Pentecost where it is described as an outpouring and a gift as well as a filling. He concludes, 'therefore the same Pentecostal experience was termed a *baptism*, a *filling*, an *outpouring*, and a *gift*'.[39]

With regard to the purpose for which the gift is given he delineates two main schools of thought: 'one holds that the definite reception of the Spirit after conversion is identical with an experience called sanctification'. This experience is received after conversion by which the person 'is delivered from what is called inbred sin'.[40] The other school of thought claims that 'the person is made a new creature in Christ, but he is cleansed from all sin by the blood of Christ, and that he receives the subsequent gift of the Spirit to empower for service. We belong to the second school.' The Spirit empowers but it is the blood of Christ which sanctifies.

Then follows a discussion of tongues as an initial sign of the baptism in the Spirit and Jeffreys argues that the various signs given in the book of Acts mean that the 'claim based upon precept and example that tongues is the initial sign of the baptism is not valid, because it is not stated to be the example of Acts 4, nor in Acts 8'.[41] The position that baptism in the Spirit is indicated by *one* of the gifts of the Spirit but not necessarily by speaking in tongues has

---

[38] Jeffreys, *Pentecostal Rays*, p. 31.
[39] Jeffreys, *Pentecostal Rays*, p. 32.
[40] Jeffreys, *Pentecostal Rays*, p. 35.
[41] Jeffreys, *Pentecostal Rays*, p. 37.

remained the Elim position to this day and was held by Jeffreys for the rest of his life.

Jeffreys continues to hold his position about the distinction between the Spirit of Christ and the Holy Spirit, the former being responsible for regeneration and the latter for empowerment. He then launches into a long comparison, rarely if ever found in other Pentecostal literature, between 'three baptisms' found in the New Testament. The first of these is the baptism into the likeness of the death of Jesus which is 'a deep spiritual experience of identification with Christ in his death' and described in Romans 6 and held forth as 'an incentive to holy living'. This baptism is 'the immediate normal experience of a person when justified'.

The second baptism is by immersion in water and here Jeffreys follows the line taken by Baptists since the time of the Reformation. Baptism symbolises death, burial, and resurrection and its mode is total immersion in water and occurs after conversion and as an ordinance, like the Lord's Supper, instituted by Christ himself. It is an ordinance indicating the love of Christ towards the sinner and the love of the believer towards the Saviour.

The third baptism is that with the Holy Spirit and here Jeffreys examines the events of Pentecost and then Ephesus (Acts 19) and shows that believers are baptised by immersion in water and subsequently receive the Holy Spirit. The only exception occurs at Caesarea (Acts 10) when baptism in the Holy Spirit preceded baptism in water. He provides a summary of his position in tabular form showing who carries out the baptism, who is the subject of the baptism, and the element of baptism.[42] In the case of the baptism in the Holy Spirit it is Christ who baptises, the believer who is baptised, and the element into which the believer is immersed is the Holy Spirit. Jeffreys confirms his analysis by referring to the Old Testament events (or types) that parallel the teaching of the New Testament.

There is more to be said about baptism in general and Jeffreys, in an analysis of baptism in water unto repentance, in water into the name of the Trinity, and in one Spirit into one body (1 Cor. 12.13) shows that the word '*into* clearly shows that the subjects were bap-

---

[42] Jeffreys, *Pentecostal Rays*, p. 83.

tised in the different elements because of their previous state'. For instance, those baptised into repentance had already repented before they were baptised. Similarly in 1 Cor. 12.13 'believers were baptised in the Spirit because of their state as members of the body of Christ' and this is because believers are 'incorporated into the body of Christ when they receive Christ the Saviour'.[43] This is consistent with Jeffreys' view that there is ultimately only one church and membership of it follows from reception of Christ himself. There is inconsistency, however, between Jeffreys' teaching on the Spirit of Christ and the Holy Spirit since he is prepared to acknowledge at this point that the Holy Spirit *is* responsible for regeneration,[44] a position he had previously denied on the grounds that the Holy Spirit was not given till the Day of Pentecost.

Writing about the gifts and fruits of the Spirit, nevertheless, Jeffreys attributes the fruits to the Spirit of Christ and the gifts to the Holy Spirit.[45] Regarding the miraculous gifts of the Spirit in 1 Corinthians 12, Jeffreys comments on each one of them. The word of wisdom is 'a supernatural giving of a word of wisdom to believers by revelation'[46] and is needed 'in times of testing and crisis'.[47] The word of knowledge is 'not the knowledge that is acquired through mind-training at a seminary'[48] and differs from the word of wisdom in that 'it miraculously supplies the mind with knowledge of things'.[49] Faith is not saving faith which the sinner exercises but is a special enduement that 'seems to come upon certain of God's servants at times of great need'.[50] The gifts of healing lead to gradual recovery and are distinct from miracles which 'were used for the purpose of convincing people of the truth'.[51] The gifts of healing do not imply that everyone will be healed because on one occasion Jesus himself 'only healed a few sick folk' and 'marvelled at their

---

[43] Jeffreys, *Pentecostal Rays*, p. 216.

[44] Jeffreys, *Pentecostal Rays*, p. 217.

[45] Jeffreys, *Pentecostal Rays*, p. 115.

[46] Jeffreys, *Pentecostal Rays*, p. 120.

[47] Jeffreys, *Pentecostal Rays*, p. 121.

[48] Jeffreys, *Pentecostal Rays*, p. 121.

[49] Jeffreys, *Pentecostal Rays*, p. 122.

[50] Jeffreys, *Pentecostal Rays*, p. 124.

[51] Jeffreys, *Pentecostal Rays*, p. 127.

unbelief'.[52] This wonderful gift does not preclude 'all believers lay-ing hands on the sick' or elders from anointing with oil. Discerning of spirits concerns 'the discernment of spirits of a supernatural order' and interpretation of tongues follows from an exercise of the gift of tongues within a church.[53]

The gift of tongues itself requires more extended treatment. Jef-freys begins as usual in the Old Testament and has no difficulty in showing servants of God in that dispensation 'frequently experi-ence physical manifestations as they came under the power of God'.[54] This is the context he lays down for speaking in tongues and here he notes the believers on the original day of Pentecost be-haved 'exactly like those who had come under the intoxicating in-fluence of strong drink'.[55] Paul, writing to the church at Ephesus must have been 'accustomed to spiritual intoxication' because he exhorts the believers there not to be drunk with wine but to be filled with the Holy Spirit (Eph. 5.18). At Caesarea the Holy Spirit came upon the Gentiles assembled in the home of Cornelius the centurion. Miraculous languages spoken by them were a 'tangible manifestation beyond question or dispute, whereby an all-wise God had set His seal upon the Gentiles in a sovereign act that could not be withstood'.[56] It is this speaking in tongues by the Gentiles that enabled the 'traditional prejudices and age-long beliefs of an entire race' to be swept away before incoming power and allowed the 'im-pregnable wall of partition that stood between nations for centu-ries' to fall at the sound of the 'wonderful tongues'.[57] So, although Jeffreys does not invariably tie speaking with tongues to baptism in the Spirit, he does say 'speaking in tongues was certainly a most fre-quent sign of the baptism the Holy Spirit in the days of the Apos-tles'.[58]

He then cites other passages in the New Testament and notes that both prayer and worship may be conducted in tongues (1 Cor. 14.15). He includes a section answering the question 'are tongues

---

[52] Jeffreys, *Pentecostal Rays*, p. 126.
[53] Jeffreys, *Pentecostal Rays*, p. 128.
[54] Jeffreys, *Pentecostal Rays*, p. 134.
[55] Jeffreys, *Pentecostal Rays*, p. 140.
[56] Jeffreys, *Pentecostal Rays*, p. 141.
[57] Jeffreys, *Pentecostal Rays*, p. 142.
[58] Jeffreys, *Pentecostal Rays*, p. 142.

divine or satanic?' and proposes several tests including the lifestyle of present-day believers who speak in tongues to demonstrate the wrong-headedness of those who oppose the practice.[59] Finally he notes the utility of speaking in tongues and suggests that they confirm the ministry of believers, in exceptional cases convince foreigners, magnify God, edify believers, edify the church, and are a sign to unbelievers. Over seven pages he provides examples of speaking in tongues in languages unknown to the speaker that have an impact on the hearers, and in most cases, he cites his sources. He ends with a lengthy description taken from Dean Farrar's book *Darkness To Dawn* describing a very early Christian meeting in the days of the Emperor Nero during which glossolalia occurs.[60] He ends:

> Dean Farrar in this description of the meeting among the Christians at Rome has given in the main an accurate account of the happenings at a present-day meeting where the same Holy Spirit is poured forth.[61]

A whole chapter is devoted to the gift of prophecy. The main thrust of this chapter is to deny the validity of the 'set prophets' who govern churches in some branches of Pentecostalism. The three bodies Jeffreys refers to and names are: (1) the Catholic Apostolic Church, the outcome of the 1830 revival and connected with Edward Irving; (2) the Apostolic Faith Church, with headquarters at Winton, Bournemouth, which has come into existence since the present outpouring of the Spirit; (3) the Apostolic Church, with headquarters at Penygroes, South Wales, which was formed after a secession of its leaders from the Apostolic Faith Church. And there are others of much less importance. The second and third of these groups believe in the establishment of an office of a 'set prophet … through whom messages of guidance can be given to their adherents'.[62] These messages 'claim to be the spoken word of God,

---

[59] Jeffreys, *Pentecostal Rays*, p. 150.

[60] F.W. Farrar, *Darkness and Dawn or Scenes in the Days of Nero* (New York: Longmans, Green & Co, 1897). Jeffreys appears to have slightly misquoted the title.

[61] Jeffreys, *Pentecostal Rays*, p. 170.

[62] Jeffreys, *Pentecostal Rays*, p. 173.

and as such are infallible'.[63] Moreover, 'if any follower reveals the least uneasiness concerning the accuracy or wisdom of the message uttered, he is sometimes warned of fearful impending dangers'.[64]

Jeffreys examines the function of prophecy in the book of Acts with reference to Agabus in Acts 8 and is scathing about the notion that the New Testament Church was guided by prophecy. The practice is 'positively dangerous'.[65] The main purpose of New Testament prophecy is to comfort, exhort, and edify the church. Even Edward Irving, a remarkable man, 'erred in relying upon prophetic utterances for guidance'.[66] The failures of the church Irving established should 'sound a warning note to all who participate in the great revival of today'.[67] Yet the so-called Apostolic churches of the 1930s appeared to be a physical replica of the church established by Irving.

Prophetic utterances can come from the human mind. Any overemphasis upon the set prophets and enquiring of the Lord leads to the 'paralysing of all reasoning faculties, and the abandonment of all righteous judgement'.[68] Rather, prophecy is intended to edify, exhort, and comfort and many examples of this can be found. In summary:

> The true pattern of the church of Christ is in the New Testament, and in that pattern there is no room for any such system as 'enquiring of the Lord'; neither is there any room for the setting up of an 'infallible' prophetic office for guiding or controlling the church.[69]

Jeffreys also gives attention to healing in the local church and makes a distinction between Jas 5.14, 15 and Mk 16.15-20. So the promises of Mark apply 'more to an evangelistic work when the message needs confirming'.[70] The evangelist is deputed to preach to 'the outsider, and on the authority of these verses he lays hands on

---

[63] Jeffreys, *Pentecostal Rays*, p. 173.
[64] Jeffreys, *Pentecostal Rays*, p. 173.
[65] Jeffreys, *Pentecostal Rays*, p. 176.
[66] Jeffreys, *Pentecostal Rays*, p. 184.
[67] Jeffreys, *Pentecostal Rays*, p. 184.
[68] Jeffreys, *Pentecostal Rays*, p. 186.
[69] Jeffreys, *Pentecostal Rays*, p. 192.
[70] Jeffreys, *Pentecostal Rays*, p. 233.

the sick, regardless of the particular person's faith or obedience and the signs follow'.[71] When the evangelist moves on 'the signs cease'. But in the church, it is a different matter and the believer is 'clearly taught to comply with certain conditions' with the result that healing in the church only follows when Christians render continued allegiance to the Scripture and may be chastised if they fail in this duty. If healing services are conducted in the local church on campaign lines

> outsiders may continually come to be prayed for and not be healed, for the simple reason that the gift of healing, set in the church, it should be ministered along Church lines, and not expected as a sign which seems to be given to confirm the evangelistic message.[72]

In short, the gift of healing has a different function in an evangelistic context: it is a sign confirming the gospel that is proclaimed; in the church, administered by others, healing is part of the ministry of a holy community and given to believers who are obedient in their discipleship.

Conclusion

The theology Jeffreys published at the turn of the decade had been hammered out in numerous preaching engagements. It was direct, clear, logical, and based almost entirely on Scripture. Jeffreys displays a fine ability to deduce a theological position from apparently contradictory texts; and, though he can appear dogmatic, he is for the most part only dogmatic in the service of clarity. His theology is intended to be an explanation and defence of the gospel that he preached and in most of the books there is a dialogical section where he deals with objections to his views and thereby shows himself to be willing to listen to those who saw things differently from himself.

It may be asked whether Jeffreys attempted to aggrandise himself by attributing exceptional gifts of healing to his own ministry.

---

[71] Jeffreys, *Pentecostal Rays*, p. 233.
[72] Jeffreys, *Pentecostal Rays*, p. 233.

There have been commentators who have wondered whether the prominence given in the *Elim Evangel* to Jeffreys' own healing ministry had the result of diminishing any rising evangelistic stars who might have challenged his own pre-eminence.[73] Yet his distinction between the evangelist whose preaching is 'confirmed' by signs and the elder or pastor who prays for those who are sick within the congregation according to James 5 is a valid one. Scripture appears to present more than one theology of healing and it is notable that there is no reference to anointing with oil in Mark 16[74] while there is in James 5.[75] The question of whether Jeffreys was excessively protective about his dominant position within Elim needs to be considered later.

There is nothing in these books about church government apart from the reference to the error of introducing 'set prophets' into church life. There was a background discussion with E.J. Phillips by letter while the last book was being written about the advisability of introducing within an assembly a 'set interpreter' of tongues to whom the pastor might turn if utterances in tongues were given out in public meetings.[76] Phillips advised him against this and Jeffreys largely took the advice. The interpreter of messages in tongues should be a member of the assembly and 'those in authority could acknowledge an interpreter for a certain period, and then change'; that is, no individual should be appointed as the interpreter on a permanent basis.[77] There is no reference to the relationship between elders and deacons or between a pastor and elders or, indeed, the question of whether elders and pastors have the same office. There is no discussion about the ministry of women or about the ownership of buildings or the relationship between separate congregations and the overarching denomination to which they belonged. Perhaps this is because Jeffreys did not consider these matters to be purely theological. In any case they were to surface soon enough as the 1930s progressed.

---

[73] James Robinson, *Divine Healing: The Years of Expansion 1906–1930* (Eugene, Or: Pickwick, 2014), p. 127.

[74] Though apparently anointing with oil occurs in the ministry of the disciples who had been sent out by Jesus in Mark 6.

[75] And this is the conclusion Robinson, *Divine Healing*, pp. 127, 128 reaches.

[76] EJP to GJ, 27 Feb 1933.

[77] Jeffreys, *Pentecostal Rays*, p. 237.

There is also no discussion about eschatology apart from the general belief in the near return of Christ and the deteriorating social situation that confirmed this. It is true there is reference to the rapture and the expectation that the church will be lifted from the earth before the arrival of the Antichrist and the Great Tribulation. In this sense Jeffreys appears to be in line with much Pentecostal belief about the order at endtime events. There is no discussion of British Israelism or reference to the Jewish people and any role they might have in the future. Nor is there speculation on the millennium or the rebuilding of the Temple in Jerusalem or other less important matters like whether Pentecostals should eat pork, observe the Sabbath, and so on. Such matters were left to the *Evangel* and to shorter articles. These books represent the mature theological thought of Jeffreys, and it is remarkable that between January 1933 and sometime in the summer he managed to complete *Pentecostal Rays* in the midst of his many other duties and engagements. When Jeffreys is compared with a later generation of Pentecostals who had the advantage of tertiary education, knowledge of Greek, extensive time to study, and better access to evangelical scholarship, his theological achievement may rightly be included in the Pentecostal canon. As far as his own generation is concerned what he writes is as good as anything written by any other Pentecostal who lived in the first part of the 20th century.

12

CAMPAIGNS AND COMPLICATIONS

Introduction

This chapter is concerned with the years 1931–1933. Elim still viewed international events through the lens of biblical prophecy. Elim preachers saw a correlation between events on the world stage and their pre-millennial interpretation of Scripture. Some of them saw the British Empire as a vehicle designed by God to take the Protestant gospel across the world. Any weakening of the Empire would be to the detriment of this vision. And then, standing in contrast to the faith of the British Empire stood the militant atheism of Soviet Russia with its political ploys and communistic agents seeking to overthrow democratic governments with revolutionary violence. The British intelligentsia of the 1930s were notoriously blind to the faults of Stalin's Russia with the result that left-wing journalism conveniently ignored the famines in the Ukraine and all the terrors of a totalitarian state.[1] Elim writers seemed unaware of journalistic or intellectual justifications for communism but they recognised atheistic propaganda when they saw it, and it was this which attracted their attention and informed their worldview.

Behind or in reaction to communism, fascism darkened European life. Mussolini had come to power in 1922 and thought of himself as revivifying the glories of Rome. Here the British intelligentsia were perceptive though, at the end of the period covered by this

---

[1] Roberts, *History*, p. 214.

chapter, Hitler won an election for the Chancellorship of Germany and rapidly and ruthlessly moved against his political opponents and Jewish businesses and families. For part of this period E.J. Phillips was the editor of the *Elim Evangel*; and, probably because he himself was of Jewish extraction, the *Evangel* seems especially sensitive to the plight of Jewish people in Nazi-controlled territory.

Both in Germany and elsewhere in Europe male unemployment rose. The US stock exchange crash of 1929 had damaging repercussions across the entire Western world. In Germany reparation payments weighed down the economy and allowed nationalist politicians to blame the Versailles Treaty of 1919 for the misery of the unemployed. In Britain there were small numbers of Communists but their message was largely sidelined by the press and the BBC. The United Kingdom suffered from a post-war economic malaise as raw materials from the old Empire became more expensive, jobs were exported overseas, sterling dropped in value; and conventional economics, if anything, made the situation worse. In 1931, in response to an official report,[2] unemployment benefit was cut by 10% and much hated means testing (that is, bureaucratic checks to test whether an unemployed man qualified for financial assistance) was reintroduced.[3] By 1933 there were 2.5 million unemployed in Britain and whole industries – especially shipbuilding in the north-east of England – were standing idle.

Occasionally Elim writers, particularly James McWhirter one of the Revival Party, drew historical parallels with the time of Wesley.[4] Rather than trying to interpret the 1930s by reference to prophecy, McWhirter reflected on how Britain had changed during Wesley's ministry and after it. For 50 years Wesley had travelled an average of 8,000 miles a year from town to town, and his gospel message gradually permeated the whole of society. Prison and educational reform followed and evangelical philanthropy began to have a political bearing as it did in the abolition of slavery through enactments

---

[2] The May Report of 1931. See Roy Jenkins, *The Chancellors* (Basingstoke: Macmillan, 1998), p. 296.

[3] http://www.nationalarchives.gov.uk/cabinetpapers/themes/unemployment-assistance.htm; see also http://www.nationalarchives.gov.uk/education/resources/thirties-britain/monster-demonstration/, showing a public demonstration against Means Testing in 1932.

[4] *Elim Evangel* 12.2 (9 Jan 1931), p. 27.

in the British Parliament. Whether this historical parallel was valid or whether other factors might have accounted for social ameliora-tion is beside the point. McWhirter saw the changes brought about by Methodism as similar to the changes that might be brought about by George Jeffreys and the Foursquare Gospel. This justified the long-term institutional building of Elim ideals and the diverting of energy from the alarmism of Pentecostal adventism.

1931: Pressing Forward in Ulster and Yorkshire

The cut in benefits paid to the unemployed was among the measures taken by the government to get a grip on the economic situation. There had already been a General Election in 1929 but turbulence in the markets and the political realm provoked a further crisis and another General Election: the votes cast in 1931 resulted in a National Government that replaced Labour. High unemploy-ment spread misery widely because the families of the unemployed suffered and they, in their turn, had nothing to spend in local shops and pubs. As far as the practicalities of Elim were concerned, un-employment implied low offerings in meetings and a tendency for campaigns to generate a loss. In the circumstances the willingness of Elim leaders, and George Jeffreys in particular, to push ahead is remarkable and bold. They really did act 'in faith' and this was espe-cially so when Jeffreys returned at the beginning of 1931 to Ulster, a province where competition for jobs or benefits exacerbated Protestant/Catholic animosity. It may be argued that a dire eco-nomic situation predisposes desperate human beings to embrace the gospel of hope – an explanation for Jeffreys' success that depends upon a 'deprivation theory' which assumes that what people lack in worldly goods they make up for in spiritual realities.[5] Yet such an explanation would not account for the triumphs Jeffreys enjoyed along the wealthier south coast of Britain. Ulster received Jeffreys with open arms.

The Irish churches had felt a sense of grievance at the failure of Jeffreys to give more of his time to them. While the churches in the

---

[5] R.A. Anderson, *Vision of the Disinherited: The Making of American Pentecostalism* (Oxford: Oxford University Press, 1979).

rest of Britain had grown, Ireland had remained relatively static.[6] True, Jeffreys had returned for Christmas conventions but now he gave three weeks to the province. The meetings in Belfast eclipsed anything previously seen there. 'Extraordinary scenes have been witnessed in the Ulster Hall, Belfast, during the past ten days'.[7] Memories of the early days of the Elim Band were rekindled[8] and by February the *Evangel* could report in its telegram style:

THE FOURSQUARE REVIVAL IN ULSTER IS SPREAD-ING ALL AROUND AND NUMBERS ARE BEING CON-VERTED IN THE VARIOUS REVIVAL CENTRES. PRIN-CIPAL GEORGE JEFFREYS IS AT THE CITY HALL, AR-MAGH, WHICH IS PACKED TO CAPACITY, AND RE-MARKABLE REVIVAL SCENES ARE WITNESSED. THE QUIET CITY IS STIRRED BY THE POWER OF GOD AND THE NEWS OF SO MANY CONVERSIONS AND HEALINGS TAKING PLACE IS SPREADING LIKE WILDFIRE.[9]

Forty miles from Belfast, Armagh was Roman Catholic heart-land.[10] It was perhaps the first time the Foursquare Gospel had bro-ken out of the indigenously Protestant zones of Ulster.[11] The re-port continued with a description of the emotional effects of reviv-al beyond the city hall where the preaching took place.

THE WORD OF GOD IS ASSUREDLY PROVING ITSELF TO BE SHARPER THAN ANY TWO-EDGED SWORD AND IS ACCOMPLISHING ITS OWN GLORIOUS WORK WITH GRAND RESULTS. THE LIVING WATERS ARE RUNNING DEEP AND THE COMMUNITY IS PASSING THROUGH A CONVICTING AND HEART-SEARCHING TIME.

---

[6] EJP to GJ 17 Oct 1933. 'The people think they are neglected while we are pushing ahead in all other parts of the British Isles. Of course this is true – there has been practically no advance in Ireland for ten years or more.'

[7] *Elim Evangel* 12.4 (23 Jan 1931), p. 49.

[8] *Elim Evangel* 12.4 (23 Jan 1931), p. 52.

[9] *Elim Evangel* 12.8 (20 Feb 1931), p. 114.

[10] *Elim Evangel* 12.13 (27 Mar 1931), p 194.

[11] *Elim Evangel* 12.10 (6 Mar 1931), front cover.

If the community was passing through a 'heart-searching time', this may be a reference to adjustments in long-standing Protestant/ Catholic antagonisms. The atmosphere was tearful rather than triumphalist.

> ONE REALISES THE POWER OF GOD OUTSIDE THE MEETINGS ALSO. PERSONS CONVICTED IN THEIR HOMES ARE SENDING FOR THE MINISTERS TO LEAD THEM TO THEIR SAVIOUR. THE MELTING POWER OF THE CROSS MAKES SINNERS WEEP OPENLY, WHILE BELIEVERS WEEP FOR JOY. APPEALS FOR REVIVAL MEETINGS POUR IN. PRAY ON.[12]

Although reports of revival scenes stirred the hearts of Elim people all over the British Isles, it proved much more difficult, as events were to show, to build a system of church government that was equally acceptable everywhere. Many of the laity in Ireland had Presbyterian and Brethren roots and consequently expected lay involvement in the leadership of assemblies. The default Elim position created ill will. Headquarters could install a pastor able to govern the congregation without conceding much ground to the wishes of the congregation. This situation was only worsened when the headquarters in August 1931 appointed a District Superintendent for Ireland who actually lived in London; he was too far away to hear grass roots concerns. By 1933, as we shall see, the Irish situation had deteriorated and provoked disagreement between Jeffreys and the headquarters staff, especially Phillips.

Crossing to England, Jeffreys continued breaking new ground although he also returned for conventions or special weekends to places where he had previously drawn huge crowds. He was in Southport (12-30 April) starting small and ending with 600 conversions.[13] He intended to return to Blackpool where he preached from a boxing ring in 1926; but, whether by accident or design, his nephew, Edward Jeffreys, had set up a rival tent in the same field. To avoid newspaper tittle-tattle, and despite the fact that 'money had been spent in advertising, electric cable laid and chairs were on their

---

[12] *Elim Evangel* 12.8 (20 Feb 1931), p. 114.

[13] *Elim Evangel* 12.23 (5 June 1931), p. 352; Canty, *Unpublished*, p. 122.

way' George withdrew to the Isle of Wight while sending Pastor Hulbert and the boy preacher Frank Allen to fill his place and draw the crowds.[14] The Isle of Wight was thoroughly evangelised and over 100 accepted Christ.[15] While in the south of England Jeffreys was able to open a new Tabernacle in Portsmouth and a month later one in Leeds.[16] He opened the Kensington Temple in London on 31 July[17] and the same month laid a foundation stone in Worthing and another in Belfast.[18] By 9 August he was ready to start in Sheffield[19] although, 'in response to the appeals by many who had taken rooms in Blackpool especially for the campaign' Jeffreys preached at the August Bank Holiday week-end services.[20]

These were busy times. The revival in Nottingham continued unabated and annual engagements at the Royal Albert Hall were also discharged with panache. The Easter Monday events appear to have been just as good as in previous years and the *Evangel* was able to report the 'Premier meeting place of the British Empire packed from floor to ceiling with over 10,000 men and women'[21] and noted that 'Principal George Jeffreys had a wonderful reception when he stood before this immense congregation, a reception worthy of an ambassador of the King of Kings'.[22] The national press again reported without obvious criticism. Later the *Evangel* could speak of a 'nine-hour queue for religious rally in spacious town hall' in Birmingham and a Whit Monday meeting where 'the building was stormed by enthusiastic Foursquare Gospellers until every available corner was filled'.[23] The Crystal Palace was booked for 12 September after the 'glorious revival at Sheffield' counted 1,000 conversions.[24] Leaving Pastor Hulbert in Sheffield Jeffreys transferred to

---

[14] *Elim Evangel* 12.23 (5 June 1931), p. 360.

[15] *Elim Evangel* 12.26 (26 June 1931), front page.

[16] *Elim Evangel* 12.25 (19 June 1931), inside cover; on 30 May, *Elim Evangel* 12.26 (26 June 1931), p. 401.

[17] *Elim Evangel* 12.29 (17 July 1931), Advertisement; *Elim Evangel* 12.30 (31 July 1931), p. 481.

[18] *Elim Evangel* 12.32 (7 Aug 1931), p. 498.

[19] *Elim Evangel* 12.32 (7 Aug 1931), inside cover.

[20] *Elim Evangel* 12.34 (21 Aug 1931), p. 536.

[21] *Elim Evangel* 12.18 (1 May 1931), p. 276.

[22] *Elim Evangel* 12.18 (1 May 1931), p. 278.

[23] *Elim Evangel* 12.24 (12 June 1931), p. 369.

[24] *Elim Evangel* 12.36 (4 Sept 1931), p. 568.

Glossop and later to Huddersfield. All these activities were interspersed with reports of the big London meetings and the news that old church buildings were being bought up.[25] The Glossop meetings were highly successful and this, like Nottingham, was a centre of Methodism and Free Church activity going back many years. The telegram style related:

> THE FOURSQUARE REVIVAL FIRE THAT STARTED IN SHEFFIELD SOME MONTHS AGO AND WHICH BURNED ITS WAY TO GLOSSOP AND HUDDERSFIELD, HAS NOW BROKEN OUT WITH INTENSIFIED FORCE IN THE INDUSTRIAL TOWN OF HALIFAX.[26]

The Trinity Road Baptist Church was packed and meetings then moved over to Barnsley, an indication that all these old northern towns, relatively close to each other, were being impacted individually and cumulatively. This, in December on the front cover of the *Evangel*, was described as a 'Yorkshire revival'. Cartwright calculated that Elim's 70 congregations in 1928 had soared to 153 by 1933.[27]

At the end of the year when Jeffreys shared his Christmas reflections with his readers, his meditations poetically noted, 'within doors the light from the Yuletide log will fall upon the pages of subconsciousness, and records long thought to be illegible will be clearly read beside the Christmas fire'.[28] He recalled the trials and triumphs and remembered how when Elim began 'the truths of divine healing and the baptism of the Holy Ghost were shunned almost everywhere' and that the Elim Band set out at a time when 'extravagances and excrescences' were 'rife' and any kind of organisation was condemned by Pentecostals. He saw Elim as having been established 'with its scripturally controlled churches' and 'its sane presentation of the Foursquare Gospel message'.[29] He mused on the 'pathway so clearly mapped out for us by a loving Heavenly Father' and the establishment of a movement that demonstrated God's faithfulness. He saw miracles of healing graciously given 'in

---

[25] *Elim Evangel* 12.43 (23 Oct 1931), front cover.
[26] *Elim Evangel* 12.48 (27 Nov 1931), p. 761.
[27] Cartwright, *The Great Evangelists*, p. 112.
[28] *Elim Evangel* 12.51-52 (25 Dec 1931), p. 801.
[29] *Elim Evangel* 12.51-52 (25 Dec 1931), p. 802.

confirmation of the Foursquare Gospel message'[30] and the discarded crutches, iron belts, and other medical aids as eloquently testifying to the supernatural. Referring to local congregations he ponders:

> It would have been much easier to leave the revival centres to look after themselves, but the Shepherd heart kept beating so loudly that we were constrained to choose the more difficult pathway in order to consolidate the work of God entrusted to our charge.[31]

He listed the 12 outstanding features of the Elim movement. These included 'strict adherence to Scriptural rule and authority', 'Christ-like regard for all other Christian bodies' (and here he stretches out an ecumenical hand to evangelical groups) as well as miracles of healing and the condemnation of fanaticism and extravagance. He ends by marvelling at the great 'world-wide Elim Foursquare Gospel family' with its Overseers, Members of Council, Divisional Superintendents, Ministers, Evangelists, Foursquare Gospel Missionaries, Editors, College Staff, Students, Church Offices, Sunday School Superintendents, Teachers, Scholars, Crusaders, Cadets, the Staffs of Holiday and Healing Homes, and those in the Printing, Publishing, and Correspondence School departments. All in all he appears to be a thankful man without regrets and at peace with himself and his co-workers.

Themes in the *Evangel* 1931

The whole Elim movement was reflected in the pages of the weekly *Evangel* which acted as a news sheet and advertising forum as well as a printed pulpit for consolidating existing beliefs or exploring contentious questions. Modernism was routinely attacked[32] and teetotalism supported: Elim people were told that they should not drink at weddings because 'married life was all the happier without wine or champagne'.[33] There was sane teaching on spiritual gifts in development of a tradition within British Pentecostalism that was shared with Assemblies of God and took note of the *charismata* outlined in

---

[30] *Elim Evangel* 12.51-52 (25 Dec 1931), p. 802.
[31] *Elim Evangel* 12.51-52 (25 Dec 1931), p. 802.
[32] *Elim Evangel* 12.5 (30 Jan 1931), p. 65.
[33] *Elim Evangel* 12.5 (30 Jan 1931), p. 67.

1 Corinthians 12 and 14, treating each of the nine separately. There were further discussions of the Second Coming and a finger pointed towards the Jewish race which was seen as the symbolic 'fig tree' of prophecy. Their re-gathering was a sign that the tree was budding.[34] There was reference to Palestine and Zionism in an extract of a speech by Lloyd George at the Zionist Federation of Great Britain.[35] Lloyd George spoke about the mandate giving the Jews a national home and the transformation of the country by Jewish immigrants: 'Zionism has brought to an old land, a renowned ruined old land, new wealth, new energy, new purpose, new initiative, new intelligence, a new development and new hope'. Zionists saw in the resettlement of the Jewish people in Palestine a fulfilment of biblical prophecy as well as a solution to stubborn European anti-Semitism.

Of German and Soviet militarism, it was said that 'the Soviet government has just received ten miracle all-metal planes with a cruising speed of 220 miles an hour'[36] while Germany was talking about war and its new fascist leader was able to report an increase of 38,500 registered members of his party.[37] At the time, Mussolini appeared to be more important than Hitler and the disagreement between Mussolini and the Pope was viewed as foreshadowing prophetically predicted quarrels between the antichrist of military Rome and papal power.[38]

Nearer to home the national financial crisis resulted in the formation of a National Government and praise was given to ministers who had shown that 'noble self-sacrifice in the face of tremendous opposition' to act in the interests of the country rather than their own party. The electoral stampede away from the Labour Party was met with the exhortation that 'we are truest to our land when we are truest to God', a sentiment that avoided entering the fraught world of party politics.[39]

---

[34] *Elim Evangel* 12.5 (20 Feb 1931), p. 113.
[35] *Elim Evangel* 12.18 (1 May 1931), p. 288.
[36] *Elim Evangel* 12.19 (8 May 1931), p. 294.
[37] *Elim Evangel* 12.21 (22 May 1931), p. 325.
[38] *Elim Evangel* 12.26 (26 June 1931), p. 410.
[39] *Elim Evangel* 12.38 (18 Sept 1931), p. 598.

One shock event that saddened all Elim supporters was the sudden death of William Henderson at the age of 52.[40] Henderson, who had been with Jeffreys from the beginning, was known as a stable and good man whose advice, had it been available in the years that followed, might have changed Elim's history.

1932: Campaigning in Scotland and Heighted Expectations of the Second Coming

Against a background of political tension in Europe and high unemployment in Britain, English church attendance continued to decline. For example, a census of church attendance on a selected Sunday in York showed that, after an increase in the population from 48,000 in 1901 to 72,000 in 1935, church attendance had fallen from 35.5% in 1901 to 17.7% in 1935. The largest decline was among Nonconformists though Anglicans were almost equally affected. Only the Roman Catholics managed to hold their numbers. When these figures are compared with levels in Scotland, the joining of the United Free Church with the established presbyterian Church of Scotland produced a united presbyterian church that, in 1930, claimed the allegiance of 26.2% of the population. In short, Christianity in Scotland was numerically stronger than in much of England.[41]

Jeffreys, in addition to his Easter and Whit Monday gatherings at the Royal Albert Hall, continued to book the Crystal Palace. Around these three big London celebrations which were fixed in the diary, the bulk of his campaigning was moved north to Scotland. He preached in Glasgow for the New Year convention and then Greenock, Perth, Ayr, Portobello, Dundee, and Edinburgh.[42] He made trips to Ulster for conventions and went down to the Brighton Dome for what had become an annual event but his main church-planting energy was directed to Scottish churches. These welcomed his ministry wholeheartedly and the *Evangel* was able to publish admiring reports of healings, baptisms, crowds, converts, and religious fervour. The Caird Hall in Edinburgh was taken for a third week and by the middle of the year the front page of the

---

[40] Cartwright, *Evangelists*, p. 109.
[41] John Stevens, *British Society 1914–1945* (Harmondsworth: Penguin, 1984), pp. 362, 369.
[42] *Elim Evangel* 13.51-52 (25 Dec 1932), p. 818.

Evangel reckoned on over 1,300 conversions in Scotland.[43] The Member of Parliament for Dundee,[44] Edwin Scrymgeour, contributed an article about the revival there and congregations were established and buildings bought. By October, as an indication of commitment as well as enthusiasm, up to 400 converts from Dundee visited the Edinburgh meetings and Jeffreys had to move to the 2,200 seater Usher Hall for the last six days of his campaign.[45] In Edinburgh itself 800 conversions were reported and a cinema in Dean Street that became a permanent Elim Tabernacle was purchased.[46]

There was one fruitful foray south into the Spa Fields church in Finsbury, London,[47] but continuous concentration upon Kensington Temple where Jeffreys was able to leave McWhirter and Darragh to carry on his revivalism and build up the Elim Crusaders organisation, which was mainly composed of young people.[48] At Easter, Kensington Temple, and four other London churches – Clapham, Croydon, King's Cross, and East Ham – were coordinated in preparation for the big Royal Albert Hall meeting on Easter Monday.

Towards the end of the year Jeffreys returned to Glossop and took part in a consultation with the Northern District of Elim (covering all the way from Birmingham to Dundee). The three days of meetings had no formal agenda. In addition to talking about the future organisation of the movement the topic of British Israelism was broached. Jeffreys proposed that Elim should 'admit the identity', a phrase meaning 'admit the identity between British people and the ten lost tribes of Israel'.[49] No decision was made but the scene

[43] *Elim Evangel* 13.24 (10 June 1932), advertisement; *Elim Evangel* 13.24 (24 June 1932), front cover.
[44] He lost his seat in the 1931 General Election.
[45] *Elim Evangel* 13.41 (7 Oct 1932), front cover.
[46] *Elim Evangel* 13.43 (21 Oct 1932), front cover; *Elim Evangel* 13.44 (28 Oct 1931), front cover.
[47] *Elim Evangel* 13.7 (12 Feb 1932), p. 104.
[48] *Elim Evangel* 13.10 (4 Mar 1932), inside front cover. McWhirter had inaugurated the Elim Crusader Movement seven years earlier, *Elim Evangel* 13.5 (29 Jan 1932), p. 74.
[49] Cartwright, *Evangelists*, p. 121.

was set for a full debate at a ministerial conference the following year.[50]

Themes in the *Evangel* 1932

Warnings of the impending Second Coming of Christ increased in frequency. There was an article on the subject in February, three in May, two in June, two in August, and one in September. Some of these were general and made deductions from the world situation. Corry, who was not a scientist, wrote an article about science and the invention of 'death rays' (by which he appeared to mean radiation) that showed how human capacity to destroy was ramping up.[51] There was no exegesis of Scripture here but on 6 May, Henry Proctor, a regular contributor, provided a long and detailed set of calculations based on the Book of Daniel and, using a chronological scheme incorporating the Islamic Hegira (AD 622) as a starting point and then running forward 1295 years arrived first at 1917, when Jerusalem was liberated from Turkish rule, and then at 1934 when the temple in Jerusalem might be rebuilt.[52] He thought 1934 marked the beginning of a new era and the final crisis would end in 1957. It seems that the rapture of the church could occur at any point.

Further general discussion continued in August with a declaration that Armageddon would precede the coming of Christ. Postmillennialists had pinned their hopes largely on the League of Nations but this, as the Japanese invasion of Manchuria a few months previously had shown, was utterly helpless to curb war. War was rooted in human lust and the appearance of death rays and a red Napoleon in the East completed the fearsome prophetic picture.[53] The following week readers were told again about the signs of Christ's speedy return: the budding fig tree; distress among the nations; worldwide evangelism; spiritual apathy and spiritual decay; spiritual awakening and alertness in the true church; men's hearts failing them for fear; rapid travel; and a form of godliness without any spiritual power.[54] A month later Proctor renewed his calcula-

---

[50] Cartwright, *Evangelists*, p. 111.

[51] *Elim Evangel* 13.6 (5 Feb 1932), p. 81.

[52] *Elim Evangel* 13.19 (6 May 1932), p. 289.

[53] *Elim Evangel* 13.32 (5 Aug 1932), p. 507.

[54] *Elim Evangel* 13.33 (12 Aug 1932), p. 521.

tions using Daniel. 'It seems clear therefore that we are coming swiftly to the end of the times of the Gentiles' and 1934 would be the last year of this period after which 'there will be signs in sun and moon and stars'.[55] Even without Daniel, warnings were to be found in the Book of Revelation for those interpreting it along historicist lines, that is, who saw its symbolism as speaking of future world events. Both McWhirter and John Leech taught on the topic to packed congregations at Kensington Temple in June of that year.[56]

1933: Itinerating and Preparing for Change

Jeffreys returned to Ulster at the start of 1933 and found the situation there far worse than before. Many of the people who had joined Elim churches earlier now appeared to have left, and there were complaints about headquarters.[57] There had been public prayers asking God 'to smash the secret society at headquarters and save the work from Popery';[58] prayers that all too clearly indicated how distant headquarters seemed – as far away as Rome and just as inscrutable. Jeffreys became convinced that the only way to satisfy the disenfranchised congregations was to install a system of local church government. This would remove power from the headquarters and also relieve headquarters of some of its financial duties or, strictly speaking, transfer some of Jeffreys' fund-raising burdens onto the churches themselves.

When he wrote to Phillips with his pessimistic assessment of the situation, he explained that rules agreed in England were being ignored. The congregations were expected to find treasurers and secretaries to deal with their finances; but, almost in every case, these were handled by the pastor alone who had the authority to choose church officers. Consequently the local leaders became 'monuments … strutting about in the churches, a stumbling block and a positive hindrance to any progress in the church' because they did not feel

[55] *Elim Evangel* 13.38 (16 Sept 1932), p. 596.
[56] *Elim Evangel* 13.25 (17 June 1932), p. 393.
[57] This observation appears to come from GJ to EJP, 23 Oct 1933 and is found in Hudson, *Schism*, p. 169.
[58] GJ to EJP 23 Oct 1933.

accountable to anyone.[59] Congregational loyalty was non-existent because members had nothing to do apart from listen to sermons.

Phillips replied soothingly to Jeffreys because he thought the circumstances far less serious. The best solution would be to 'deal with individual situations as they were discovered, to stay with existing local church government framework and ride out the storms of controversy'.[60] And, though Jeffreys knew the situation on the ground in Ireland, Phillips had been a pastor there before 1920 and revisited in 1931. The church at Portadown offered an opportunity to test out new methods of government. Jeffreys suggested that the present pastor should remain and that any private gifts he received should be paid towards the outstanding debt on the building. The local secretary and treasurer should function properly and pay the pastor and ensure that surplus money was used to defray the debt on the building – the point being that money need not be sent to headquarters but should be shown to have a benefit for local people who were the ones who gave it in the first place. After a year the church should be given a financial report and could vote local officials into position and, if he were willing to stay, retain the pastor.[61] Jeffreys would raise funds for the new building and he and Phillips would remain as trustees and hold the building on behalf of the Alliance.

Although Phillips deferred to Jeffreys as the leader of Elim, he refused to become a co-trustee and opposed local trustees while the church was still under the direction of the Clapham headquarters. But Jeffreys could not introduce a local government scheme without Phillips because it required the preparation of extensive documentation. This impasse left the situation unresolved, and unwittingly battle lines between Jeffreys and Phillips had been drawn. The topic was put on the agenda for the ministerial conference in September.

In February 1933 Jeffreys went back to Wales to celebrate his birthday with his family. His sister's birthday fell on nearly the same

---

[59] GJ to EJP 23 Oct 1933.

[60] I am grateful to Neil Hudson for access to his doctoral thesis and for the many insights he brings.

[61] Hudson, *Schism*, p. 67.

date as his own and they often celebrated together.[62] While he was at home he wrote to Phillips saying that he was feeling bad and had boils.[63] On 22 March he wrote again saying, 'very much cast down with these boils. Can scarcely hold up my head.'[64] In December 1937 Jeffreys collapsed dramatically and was placed under urgent medical care.[65] He was found to be suffering from diabetes. One of the symptoms of diabetes – an early warning sign – is the outbreak of skin infections including, particularly, boils.[66] Given, also, that diabetes often goes undiagnosed for many years, it is reasonable to speculate that Jeffreys began to suffer from diabetes from 1933 onwards. We do not know which type of diabetes he had or whether he took medication or simply tried to control the condition by exercise and diet. His willingness to accept 'natural healing' may indicate that he managed his health for a number of years before his collapse. The symptoms of his illness would have been a feeling of tiredness with additional susceptibility to minor infections. We do not know how all this played out in his private life but it is evident that from 1933 onwards he rarely held prolonged crusades and his sermons may have become shorter. There is no indication that he suffered from erratic moods or mental confusion although the condition may have caused him to be more observant of his daily routine than previously. However he handled the situation, and whether he recognised what was happening before his collapse, his lifestyle, where he lived in a caravan for several weeks a year with other members of the Revival Party, would have given him little opportunity for privacy. The outer circumstances of his life over the next few years make it reasonable to assume that Jeffreys began to feel unusually tired and, without realising that illness was debilitating him, that he tried to deal with this by cutting back on his demanding schedule.

The year began as usual with preaching in Ulster and from there Jeffreys travelled across to the City Temple, Glasgow before cam-

---

[62] Cartwright, *Evangelists*, p. 116.

[63] GJ to EJP 28 Feb 1933.

[64] Cartwright, *Evangelists*, p. 117.

[65] Cartwright, *Evangelists*, p. 142.

[66] http://www.diabetes.org/living-with-diabetes/complications/skin-complications.html (accessed 5 Feb 2016).

paigning in Aberdeen. Considerable success occurred as over 250 people were converted and 55 baptised in water.[67] James McWhirter took over when Jeffreys went south to Bradford. Within the year's programme the Royal Albert Hall was as usual given top priority and as usual Jeffreys preached to three gigantic congregations and baptised over 100 candidates in water, held a healing service, and celebrated communion. John Leech KC and E.C.W. Boulton were given the honour of leading in prayer, and again telegrams were sent to, and replied to, by the King.[68]

Jeffreys opened a church in Reading and preached down in Brighton again. The main innovation to the year was a south coast tour Jeffreys made throughout May using his trailer caravan and with the Revival Party to bring organisation and music.[69] They visited the Isle of Wight, Exeter, Plymouth, Portsmouth, Hove, Worthing, Brighton, Eastbourne, and Exeter. Many of the stops were simply for a weekend or for an evening but they rallied the people and drew crowds and in many instances conversions occurred and services were packed.

Jeffreys had arranged to go to Switzerland from the 10-18 June and reports in the *Evangel* and photographs record over 200 conversions and many healings. Sermons were translated into French and German and many nationalities attended including Swiss, German, French, Polish, Italian, Spanish, and Scandinavians as well as citizens from the USA.[70] It was this success in Switzerland that appears to have led Jeffreys to decide to set up his World Revival Crusade (about which more later) as an agency that would handle bookings and funds from overseas to support his tours and the expenses of his revival team.

He returned to the UK and preached at a convention in Bangor, Ireland, in July and then prepared for four services at the Crystal Palace. Everything started with a morning healing meeting and the first afternoon meeting would be for water baptism with a further healing meeting in the late afternoon. Finally, at 6.30, the service climaxed with a communion service. The ground plan of the Crys-

---

[67] *Elim Evangel* 14.16 (7 Apr 1933), p. 243.
[68] *Elim Evangel* 14.18 (5 May 1933), pp. 273, 285.
[69] *Elim Evangel* 14.17 (28 Apr 1933), p. 264.
[70] *Elim Evangel* 14.26 (30 June 1933), front page.

tal Palace was sufficiently complex and the area sufficiently large to allow 25 smaller meetings and lectures to take place including one by John Leech interpreting biblical prophecy from a historicist standpoint and another by Charles Kingston from a futurist standpoint. The two views differed in their expectation of the future that Christians would pass through. Leech saw signs of Christ's near return in world events focused on Britain and Palestine while Kingston, one of the few older and experienced ministers within Elim, was less willing to equate contemporary events with the symbolism of Revelation.[71] There were lectures on Palestinian customs, and there was choral singing.

In September, Jeffreys erected his big tent in the fairground at the port city of Hull and saw over 1,000 conversions – so many, that a new church was opened. After this he returned to Ireland for a healing crusade before the first full ministerial conference at Clapham. The deliberations were not reported in any detail in the *Evangel* which only went so far as to say that despite disagreement, the tone was friendly and courteous. The discussion of local church government took centre stage and the impression given is that Jeffreys encouraged criticism of the current system. He had been working 'from morning to night trying to get some shape [in] the local church working arrangements, model deed, and other things'.[72] During the five days of the conference schemes were proposed, revised, amended, and then abandoned.[73] Elim governance was already complicated since there were three categories of churches. The largest group were centrally governed from headquarters but there were personally governed churches under a minister who had founded a congregation and there were locally governed churches under deacons. Cartwright assigned 89 churches to the first category and 90 to the other two groups combined.[74] The big block of churches that were centrally governed comprised those founded by

---

[71] Kingston spoke of the budding of the fig tree – the flourishing of the land of Palestine after Jewish immigration – as the main sign of the second coming: *Elim Evangel* 8.17 (1 Sept 1927), pp. 257-61.

[72] Cartwright, *Evangelists*, pp. 118, 119.

[73] Cartwright, *Evangelists*, p. 119.

[74] These were the figures in 1938 but they would have been similar enough in 1933 to show what sort of difficulties confronted the conference. Cartwright, *Evangelists*, p. 119.

Jeffreys.[75] Any attempt to transfer the centrally governed churches into one of the two other categories was bound to be problematic. For a start, which of the two other categories should predominate and then, once the shifting of category had taken place, how was the whole new enterprise to be held together as a common and unified denomination? Who would own the properties and pay the mortgages, especially since all the terms of repayment had presumed the central system? More than this, should the locally governed churches remain exactly as they were or did their categorisation need alteration in some way? No decisions could be agreed. Beyond all the purely administrative and technical details the thorny subject of British Israelism was raised again, and again rejected by the majority of ministers. Jeffreys returned to Scarborough for a crusade and finished the year with a week at Ashford in Kent.

Themes in the *Evangel* 1933

If anything, articles on the Second Coming increased in frequency. There was one in January where belief in pre-millennial rapture was underlined: however bad the situation became, the church could expect to be snatched to safety. A premillennial chart setting out prophetic events in a diagram and used by the Elim correspondence course was published in February and there was another article on the Second Coming in March, and a further article in April.[76] At the Easter Monday convention at the Royal Albert Hall Jeffreys himself spoke on the Second Coming.[77] Eschatology again featured in May when the prophetic words of Ezekiel were interpreted to indicate Russia would attack Jews in Palestine.[78] For those who wondered what would happen to the earth after the rapture of the church, an article in June assured them that the Holy Spirit would continue to work in the world as he had done before the present outpouring.[79] Signs of the Second Coming were underlined in July and an article in August pointed out that John Wesley accepted the reality of the

---

[75] I have not been able to check the details of the founding of each congregation. If Jeffreys did not found them all, he founded the majority.

[76] *Elim Evangel* 14.8 (24 Feb 1933), p. 123; *Elim Evangel* 14.13 (31 Mar 1933), p. 218; *Elim Evangel* 14.14 (7 Apr 1933), p. 221.

[77] *Elim Evangel* 14.15 (14 Apr 1933), p. 225.

[78] *Elim Evangel* 14.19 (12 May 1933), p. 293.

[79] *Elim Evangel* 14.24 (16 June 1933), p. 376.

millennium.[80] Reference to eschatology appeared in lectures in the Crystal Palace and a further article on the Second Coming appeared in October and another in November. The rebuilding of Palestine and the gathering of the Jews under the 'splendid protection of Great Britain' was seen as sufficient proof of the soon-coming of Christ. And finally in December a new note was struck,

> We agree that prophecy speaks of war in the near future. But we believe that if the whole world would turn as a man to God, and in true penitence seek his gracious forgiveness, and be renewed in heart and mind, God would repeal those words and give us 'peace in our time'.[81]

Hitler's consolidation of power in Germany was brought to the attention of Elim readers with a report that 17 million voters had supported him and his fascist party.[82] Even in France Jews were at risk. And then, in what seems a volte-face, the *Evangel* carried a strange article by Gerald Winrod with strong anti-Semitic undertones attempting to justify Hitler's persecution of German Jews: fascism was the only answer to communism and the Jews were responsible for communism.[83] This appears to have been an ill-judged editorial attempt to provide a balanced coverage of world events. Winrod, a maverick American evangelist, was soon dropped and nothing else of his was printed.

Reflection

Although we do not have any precise medical information about Jeffreys' health or any letters from colleagues or friends commenting on his well-being, it is reasonable to bear in mind his likely, if fluctuating, physical impairment. It is possible that, because of the way events unfolded in the 1930s, he would in any case have campaigned less; but, if his energy levels quietly declined, he may have become averse to the strenuous demands of prolonged crusades. Apart from one more successful campaign in 1934, his great reviv-

---

[80] *Elim Evangel* 14.32 (11 Aug 1933), p. 497.
[81] *Elim Evangel* 14.49 (8 Dec 1933), p. 772.
[82] *Elim Evangel* 14.12 (24 Mar 1933), p. 182.
[83] *Elim Evangel* 14.43 (27 Oct 1933), p. 675.

alistic days were behind him. It is true he preached at large meetings and continued to see conversions in response to his evangelistic appeals but the campaigns when he continued day after day and then week after week, often holding more than one service a day, appear no longer to have been sustainable. The rising momentum of campaigning brought about by a sudden dramatic healing that drew the crowds and stirred a whole city or district could only occur if the meetings were stretched out over several weeks.

Jeffreys had raised the matter of British Israelism in 1932 and again at the conference in 1933.[84] It was a matter of importance to him and he pressed the topic on his colleagues even when they politely rebuffed him. Only 16 of those present 'accepted the identity' and it was agreed that the doctrine 'should neither be preached nor attacked in our churches'.[85] Undaunted, he was to ensure that the topic was formally debated in 1934. Although there are no explicit articles or letters on the connection between BI and the Second Coming of Christ, a scenario can be constructed that may have existed in the minds of BI adherents. They believed the British Empire was the embodiment of divine promises and the means by which the light of the gospel could be spread across the world. More than this, the British Empire was the protector of Palestine and the returning Jewish people. The strength of the Empire was guaranteed by the promises and power of God working behind world events and 1934, if the calculations of expositors of the book of Daniel were correct, was going to be the culminating year that might see the return of the Lord. If this return were for the rapture when the church would be removed from the earth, then the remaining Jews would be left in the residual structure of the British Empire to face the betrayal and predations of the Antichrist before their final rescue when Christ returned from heaven with his saints to inaugurate the millennium.

Although Jeffreys was genuinely concerned about the condition of the Irish churches and believed self-government would help to rescue them from deterioration, he was also aware of the financial implications of transferring ownership from headquarters (and the

---

[84] From this point forward, British Israelism will be abbreviated BI.

[85] *Conference Minutes* (22 Sept 1933). The photo shows over 60 ministers present, *Elim Evangel* 14.41 (13 Oct 1933), p. 648.

legal structures of the Alliance) to congregations with their own trustees. On one hand, he clearly believed the Second Coming of Christ was imminent; and, on the other hand, he made provision for suitable buildings and the future development of Elim as if the return of Christ was still a distant prospect. What did it matter who owned buildings if the congregations that would have worshipped in them were raptured?

We might say that there was an inner contradiction in Jeffreys that would make him indecisive in the years to come. Or was he simply acting astutely by covering every eventuality and preaching fervently on the Second Coming while preparing his churches for the long haul? He made it clear on many occasions that, although he believed the British-Celtic people were descended from or assimilated with the lost tribes of Israel, salvation could not be secured simply by birth and must be obtained by faith in Christ. In this sense his BI beliefs were irrelevant to his preaching but in the sense that they informed his wider worldview, they were very relevant indeed.

There is a piece of evidence that might give a clue to Jeffreys' intentions. The two topics of BI and self-governance of churches were discussed at three consecutive conferences. Was it chance that the topics appeared on the same agenda or, as headquarters staff and particularly E.J. Phillips began to fear, was it part of a clever plan? Did Jeffreys want to enable the churches to come out from under the control and protection of the headquarters into a self-governing condition so that they would be open to receive teaching on BI? Or, to put this another way, was Jeffreys already willing to lead churches out of Elim for the express purpose of turning them into BI congregations? Seen in this light his tour of the South Coast churches might be viewed as preparatory to a decisive moment when the congregations would have to decide whether they were loyal to Elim or loyal to him.

13

THE 1934 MINISTERIAL CONFERENCE

Introduction

While the European situation darkened, the British Empire struggled with the largest territory of the Raj, India. Resistance led by Gandhi and others weakened imperial confidence. At home, Elim was entering a period of turbulence and 1934 was one of the decisive years. Its governance was changed, Jeffreys' final great crusade was held, and the ministerial conference made important theological judgements.

British Israel

The ideas of BI had been known for years, possibly centuries, and only gradually came into prominence in Britain towards the end of the Victorian era.[1] They were ideas that fitted comfortably with the running of the British Empire and many of those who held them had a part to play in its expansion or maintenance.[2] Military and other personnel were sympathetic to the belief that the Empire was not merely an imperialistic or commercial venture but was worthily carrying forward the great work of God.

---

[1] Eric M. Reisenauer, 'British-Israel: Racial Identity in Imperial Britain, 1870–1920' (PhD, Loyola University Chicago, 1987).

[2] E.g. Lord Fisher, First Lord of the Admiralty (1904–1910). Cf. Reisenauer, *British-Israel,* p. 365.

Despite depending almost entirely upon the tenets of Protestant Christianity exponents of BI were careful to avoid sectarianism or any sense of wanting to set up alternative and competitive religious structures.[3] In a formal statement, the British Israel World Federation declared,

> The B.I.W.F. is a non-sectarian and interdenominational body which seeks to make a constructive presentation of Christian truth without competing in any way with the work which the Churches are doing themselves.[4]

The Federation wanted to influence church strategy through their central belief that Britain-Israel was a servant nation to carry the gospel to the ends of the earth.

> The greatest spiritual awakening that has ever been will come with a realisation of our identity with Israel.[5]

These words were written by James McWhirter, a member of Jeffreys' Revival Party, and published in 1937. They indicate that it was necessary for Britain to realise its identity, to become aware of its racial descent and its historic destiny, and that once this awareness had been granted, spiritual benefits will rapidly follow. A 'national revival' – the title of one of the chapters in McWhirter's book – would break out. He believed, 'when our national privilege is understood it will beget in us a sacred sense of responsibility. The result will be a transforming reaction from materialism to a new spiritual life.'[6]

Here in a few words is the latent driving force behind Jeffreys' persistent propagation of BI teaching. Despite prevaricating with Elim in the 1930s, he retained a strong desire to impart to his converts a belief in what he took to be their new racial identity. There

---

[3] John Wilson, 'The Relation between Ideology and Organization in a Small Religious Group: The British Israelites', *Review of Religious Research* 10 (1968), pp. 51-60.

[4] *National Message* (10 Apr 1937), Quoted by Wilson, 'The Relation between Ideology and Organization in a Small Religious Group: The British Israelites', p. ?.

[5] James McWhirter, *Britain and Palestine in Prophecy* (London: Methuen & Co, 1937), p. 80.

[6] McWhirter, *Britain*, p. 80.

is a fault line here between the public declaration of the solidity of the Foursquare Gospel and the shadowy enticements of BI doctrine. McWhirter wrote of Britain's honourable role in translating and distributing the Bible across the world[7] and of the inevitable drift of historical events implied by BI. By contrast Jeffreys himself appears in his public statements at this stage in his life to have maintained his evangelical theology as completely separate from any BI beliefs he held; he always insisted salvation was always a matter of grace and never a matter of race.[8] In this way he remained within the Pentecostal fold and the bounds of evangelical orthodoxy. In his public statements to Elim he only asserted BI should be seen as one among several legitimate interpretations of the Book of Revelation – as if he were asserting an optional and minor doctrinal variant.

Jeffreys himself believed his ancestors migrated from Palestine to Wales. In a personal letter in 1935, Phillips spoke of a planned visit to Palestine, 'We will actually cross the Suez Canal quite close to where your self-claimed ancestors crossed …'[9] We do not know whether Jeffreys' claim to descent from the northern ten tribes was vital to his personal identity since, in claiming Israelite heritage for himself, he was also claiming it for thousands of other British, Welsh, and Irish people and, in this respect, claiming nothing that would distinguish him from others. Writing later, and making no secret of the fact, Jeffreys explained that he had been introduced to BI teaching by John Leech in about 1919.[10]

Leech (1857–1942) had come to know George Jeffreys during those early pioneering days in Ulster. Leech was an unusual addition to Pentecostal ranks because he came from an altogether different social and educational circle. He identified with Pentecostalism early enough for Alexander Boddy to invite him to speak at the Sunder-

---

[7] McWhirter, *Britain*, pp. 81, 82
[8] http://truthinhistory.org/the-israel-question.html (accessed 13 Feb 2016).
[9] EJP to GJ 31 Jan 1935.
[10] GJ to EJP 1 Dec 1934, 'My attitude towards B.I. today is what it has been for fifteen years', http://www.ensignmessage.com/archives.html#october06 ['The Israel Question'] (accessed 16 Feb 2016), 'I accepted the view of the Israel School in the early days of my Elim ministry. That eminent barrister-at-law, Mr John Leech, MA., LL.B., K.C., introduced me to this School nearly 40 years ago (about 1920); and I have remained in it ever since.'

land conventions in 1913 and 1914. He had high-flying credentials from Trinity College, Dublin, and was the Plunkett Gold Medallist for oratory in the field of legal debating. He was a member of the bar of Ireland, had 'taken silk' as a King's Counsel and was senior Crown prosecutor for County Longford and chairman of the Incorporated Council of Law reporting for Northern Ireland. He judged at Belfast Recorder's Court and the County Court of Antrim.[11] As was pointed out earlier (chapter 4) he was preaching in Ulster during the Easter 1916 uprising in Dublin and so escaped the violence of what was effectively a civil war before Partition in 1922. Moving away from the Republic and up to Ulster he became Commissioner for the Reconstitution of District Electoral Divisions of Northern Ireland and was known and deeply disliked by the Roman Catholic community for what were seen as gerrymandering decisions. By drawing up the electoral boundaries so that the Roman Catholic vote was largely concentrated in a few constituencies, he was able to ensure the continued political dominance of Protestantism.[12]

Not only was Leech a highly able man, he was also politically calculating and effective, even when his decisions were unpopular and lacked natural justice. His dealings with the Roman Catholic minority in Ulster still rankle with historians of the province.[13] Yet British Israel teaching, which Leech was absolutely committed to, contained a curious sub-theme whereby Canaanite peoples were represented in Ireland through Roman Catholics. The belief was that, although the lost tribes of Israel had emigrated and some had found their way to Ireland, a few Canaanites had arrived as well so that, just as Israel was at war with Canaan, so Anglo-Israel was at war with Catholicism.[14] Although Leech's decisions in Ireland have no direct bearing on his relationship with Elim or George Jeffreys, they do indicate the kind of man he was: forceful, manipulative, and willing to act repressively if he felt he had religious justification.

---

[11] This information is taken from Hudson, *Schism*, p. 199.
[12] Tim Pat Coogan, *Ireland in the Twentieth Century* (London: Arrow, 2003), p. 305.
[13] John O'Brien, *Discrimination in Northern Ireland: Myth or Reality?* (Newcastle: Cambridge Scholars Publishing, 2010), pp. 10, 11.
[14] Reisenauer, *British-Israel*, pp. 398, 400.

The senior leaders of Elim all knew Leech or, at least, had heard him preach, pray publicly, or were aware of his connection with their movement. Phillips spoke with him early in 1934 and was able to report to Jeffreys:

> [Leech] is probably remaining on with the BIs half time. He will be their legal advisor, and remain on the Executive and lecture occasionally ... he made it perfectly clear he could not compromise on the subject of BI, and he could not tie himself in any way not to preach it.[15]

By then Leech was 77 years old and had moved to London near the Elim Clapham headquarters.[16] Evidently Leech was employed by the British Israel Federation and functioned as their legal adviser, as a lecturer and served on their Executive. His role in connection with Elim was similar. He acted as legal adviser (although not as solicitor), spoke at Elim's Bible College on more than one occasion,[17] took part in national events like the Crystal Palace celebration in 1933, and felt himself at liberty to preach about BI in Elim churches whatever anybody else might say. Despite his prominence in Elim, he remained a member of the Church of Ireland[18] and so had no right to attend Elim ministerial conferences. As we shall see, he did attend the 1934 conference and can only have done so as result of private arrangements made by Jeffreys.

We do not know how frequently Jeffreys and Leech met since, although Phillips tells Jeffreys when he sees Leech, Jeffreys does not pass information the other way. Whereas letters between Jeffreys and Phillips show their relationship to be, for the most part, warm to the extent that they gave each other nicknames – Phillips called Jeffreys 'Prince' (short for Principal) and Jeffreys called Phillips 'Cardinal' (because he had been a pastor in Armagh for a short time).[19] In letters to each other Phillips and Jeffreys always referred

---

[15] EJP to GJ 13 Feb 1934.

[16] EJP to GJ 2 Nov 1933, 'You may be surprised to know Mr Leech has bought a house in Park Hill'.

[17] Hudson, *Schism*, p. 201.

[18] Hudson, *Schism*, p. 199.

[19] Maldwyn Jones, 'An Analysis of the Role of E.J. Phillips and an Assessment of his Leadership in the Establishment of the Elim Movement as a Coherent Christian Denomination' (MA, Bangor University, 2011), p. 13.

to 'Mr Leech' indicating respect rather than warmth. Nevertheless, because of the way the 1930s unfolded, it is probable there were unrecorded meetings between Jeffreys and Leech over the two topics in which the older man was expert: BI and constitutional change.

One further piece of information about Leech's character is telling. In 1935 Phillips reported to Jeffreys:

> Mr Hathaway says he is already having some trouble with Mr Leech, some of our Ministers refusing to have him. It has created difficulty in several churches. For example: he is announced for a BI campaign in Barking ... naturally it will draw our people to the BI meetings.[20]

Leech was willing to campaign on the doorstep of an Elim church. He did not seem to care whether he inflicted damage on a congregation by sowing dissention in its ranks – he 'created difficulties in several churches'. There appears to be a counter-cultural obduracy in Leech, and to his admirers he was a courageous hero; just as he stood with Elim against traditional Irish Presbyterianism in the early years, now he is willing to stand against Elim and with BI.

The Deed Poll

The disquiet in Ireland made Jeffreys and Phillips realise the governance of Elim needed to be democratised. Instead of a system where Jeffreys governed the movement with only an advisory group to assist him, a Deed Poll was drawn up to transfer power to a group of nine people. This painstaking exercise involved Jeffreys fully. He wrote to Phillips on 25 February saying, 'I've gone carefully through the notes made in black ink on the three documents which I enclose'. A day later he wrote again noting or accepting other amendments. There were questions about the exact name of the group, the role of evangelists, retired ministers, the difficulty about giving voting power to the General Conference, and other matters of this kind in a document that ran to at least 36 pages. Jeffreys agreed to, 'let Ministerial Conference elect President of Coun-

---

[20] EJP to GJ 7 Feb 1935.

cil who will also be President of Ministerial Conference'.[21] Although Jeffreys viewed the General Conference,

> more as an advisory one which could give us guidance if we so desired ... Is it not possible to make a simple rule to show that the Executive Committee can decide from time to time the composition of the General Conference? In any case I leave you to decide the matter.[22]

The long and short of the business is that Jeffreys was fully involved in drawing up the documentation of the Deed Poll and in considering all its implications, although he did leave several final decisions to Phillips. In this instance Phillips saw how the General Conference needed a publicly defined membership and could not be fluidly composed in response to *ad hoc* decisions of the Executive.

On 1 March Phillips told Jeffreys, 'I had nearly four hours with Counsel yesterday afternoon, plus an hour with our own solicitors'. Counsel must be John Leech, and this shows that Leech himself was also fully immersed in all the detail of the Deed Poll and so were Elim's solicitors who, presumably, checked the consequences of transferring the control of property to the Executive.

The Deed Poll was signed on 10 April 1934.[23] Jeffreys later reported his hesitation before putting pen to paper, asking whether the autonomy of local churches would be affected and was assured by Phillips that it would not.[24] Jeffreys signed and there is a photograph of him doing this. It was a significant moment in the development of Elim's constitutional governance and transferred control of the whole movement and all its assets to an Executive Council of nine men, of whom Jeffreys appointed three, two (Jeffreys and Phillips) were *ex-officio* and four were elected from the annual Ministerial Conference which became the final seat of authority. Out of

---

[21] GJ to EJP 26 Feb 1934.

[22] GJ to EJP 26 Feb 1934.

[23] The nine who signed were: George Jeffreys, E.J. Phillips, R.E. Darragh, James McWhirter, R. Gordon Tweed, E.C.W. Boulton, W.G. Hathaway, Joseph Smith, and Percy Corry.

[24] Noel Brooks, *Fight for Faith and Freedom* (Southampton, UK: Revival Library, Kindle edn, 2014), loc 689. The question asked was, 'Is there anything in here to prevent local government in our churches?' The book was published in 1950.

the nine, Jeffreys could count absolutely on the votes of four people (himself and his three appointees) so that he only needed to secure the vote of *one* other person to ensure a majority. Presumably he believed this would be a foregone conclusion with the result that his own control of the movement would remain unimpaired.

Noel Brooks, in his book *Fight for the Faith and Freedom* written some 15 years later, saw the signing of the Deed Poll as a desperate mistake. The Poll 'legally swallowed up all the undisclosed trust church and house property that had previously been held by individuals' and 'by signing the deed poll the nine ministers made themselves the legal governors of all Elim Alliance churches, pastors, properties and finances throughout the British Isles'.[25] In Brooks' view the churches should have been consulted and the failure to do so resulted in a form of totalitarian clerical control.[26] Whether this was so or not – and it hardly seems to be so since there were now *elected* ministers on the Council – the document was only drawn up after careful consideration and with the full involvement of Jeffreys and his primary legal advisor, John Leech.

Reporting the Year in the *Evangel*

The private constitutional deliberations were invisible to ordinary Elim ministers and congregations. The churches continued as before. The *Evangel* now reported that ministers would have the title 'Rev' inserted in front of their names though some might prefer the title 'Pastor' – a hint ministers were edging closer to the mainstream clergy.[27] Articles about the scientific and archaeological evidence for the Bible were printed and there is surprisingly well-informed comment about armaments and the relative military strength of nations.[28] In January Jeffreys took his faithful Chrysler to the ancient city of York and began a campaign that soon counted over 700 conversions[29] and by the end of March this number had risen to 1,400.[30] While revival broke out in York, Jeffreys opened buildings in Birmingham, City Temple Cardiff, and later carried out a

---

[25] Brooks, *Fight*, loc 46.
[26] Brooks, *Fight*, loc 48.
[27] *Elim Evangel* 15.1 (5 Jan 1934); *Elim Evangel* 15.2 (12 Jan 1934), p. 26.
[28] *Elim Evangel* 15.3 (19 Jan 1934), pp. 36, 43.
[29] *Elim Evangel* 15.11 (16 Mar 1934), front page.
[30] *Elim Evangel* 15.13 (30 Mar 1934), p. 195.

baptismal service in Scarborough where he laid a foundation stone.[31] McWhirter preached a crusade to Kensington Temple and five churches were coordinated for an Easter Convention in London before the big meetings at the Royal Albert Hall. Jeffreys opened a fifth tabernacle in Belfast and made a summer trip with nine of the Revival Party to Switzerland (3-24 June: Berne, Zurich and Basel) resulting in 2,300 conversions.[32]

In June Jeffreys took a full page in the *Evangel* to explain the constitutional changes to readers:[33]

> Expansion is impossible without wise adjustment and revision of existing arrangements ... The Constitution of the Elim Foursquare Gospel Alliance has now been set out in a Deed Poll which has been duly enrolled in the Supreme Court of Judicature. Thus in the event of the home-call of any of its present leaders, suitable and satisfactory provision has been made for the continuance of the activities of the work.

Expansion of the movement and continuity in the event of the death of leaders are given as the prime reasons for the new system of government.

> The whole Movement is now governed by an Executive Council which is elected by the Ministerial Conference. A new Trust Corporation is being formed for holding property in trust, and, as in the past, no Church building for which any money has been subscribed or given will be held by any individual personally.

This statement showed how a democratic process had been added, though in respect of buildings it verged on the misleading. Everything would continue 'as in the past' with the addition of a 'new Trust Corporation' and no church building could be held by an individual; but, as will become apparent, there were several important buildings that were held by two people which, if one of them died, would then of course be held by one person alone.

---

[31] *Elim Evangel* 15.18 (4 May 1934), p. 273; *Elim Evangel* 15.18 (11 May 1934), p. 289; *Elim Evangel* 15.20 (18 May 1934), p. 315.

[32] *Elim Evangel* 15.24 (15 June 1934), front cover; *Elim Evangel* 15.26 (29 June 1934), front cover.

[33] *Elim Evangel* 15.24 (15 Jan 1934), p. 379.

The personnel of the first Executive Council includes those same tried and trusted Ministers who have stood loyally by my side through the years, and whose faithful ministry has so largely contributed towards the success of the Movement as a whole. The other eight members are Pastors E.J. Phillips, E.C.W. Boulton, W.G. Hathaway, R.E. Darragh, James McWhirter, Robert Tweed, Joseph Smith, and P.N. Corry.

There is nothing here about the proportion of appointed members to elected members or any reference to *ex-officio* membership. Readers would assume that all members of the Executive were elected but this was not so.

The Field Superintendent is our beloved brother, Pastor W.G. Hathaway, whose loyal and devoted service has gained the respect of all who have worked side by side with him for years at Headquarters. Practically all the other offices remain unchanged, and all come under the jurisdiction of the Executive Council.

The Headquarters Committee, which is responsible for the control of the work between the sittings of the Executive Council, consists of Pastors E.J. Phillips, E.C.W. Boulton, and W.G. Hathaway.

The last two paragraphs cover pastoral and administrative arrangements.

To all intents and purposes Elim continued to steam ahead. A large baptismal service was held in the college grounds with sunny photographs showing crowds on the grassy banks,[34] Jeffreys visited Leeds for a weekend and preached twice on Saturday and three times on Sunday and held healing services[35] and his preaching continued to be 'masterful and dramatic' with warnings of the Battle of Armageddon at the end of the gospel age.[36] Campaigns were announced for Bangor, Ireland, at the end of July, and then in Winton, Dorset, at the start of August before ten days in Barking and the huge Crystal Palace meetings on 18 August. There was prolifer-

---

[34] *Elim Evangel* 15.25 (22 June 1934), p. 392.
[35] *Elim Evangel* 15.26 (29 June 1934), p. 402.
[36] *Elim Evangel* 15.28 (13 July 1934), p. 434.

ating Elim missionary work overseas[37] while an editorial by Boulton spoke presciently of the beating of the drums of war again.[38] Jeffreys visited the large industrial city of Manchester in September in a crusade organised by McWhirter. There were said to be 1,800 conversions after preaching first at the Piccadilly Theatre and then in packed rallies at the 3,200 seater Free Trade Hall[39] though, unreported in the *Evangel,* Canty noticed that Manchester, which was intended to be the greatest campaign of his life, 'did not quite come off' and that the flow of Jeffreys' eloquence faltered for the first time – perhaps a sign of hidden stress or worsening diabetes.[40] Even so, an Elim church was planted in Manchester.

The *Evangel* printed a long and thoughtful article on sanctification by Jeffreys in which he argued for its beneficial effect on the body.[41] Later in the year R.E. McAllister, a distinguished Canadian Pentecostal, wrote about natural and spiritual laws and pointed out how taking a 'very radical stand against physicians' had little merit. Rather, 'I have met scores of people who were under the doctor's care and yet received supernatural healing from God'.[42] Such articles are consistent with the theory that Jeffreys had begun to recognise his own illness and was open to medical treatment. There is never any trace of an aggressive anti-doctor position in his writings and he at no time condemned those who helped alleviate human suffering – like nurses.

In December the *Evangel* was forced to deny 'an unfounded rumour' that Elim was supported by many wealthy backers and had no need of financial support. 'We wish to make clear that this is entirely untrue' and in fact 'the work is in greater need financially now than ever before'.[43] It is easy to see how such a rumour could start. Jeffreys' own lifestyle brought him sweeping into town in a large car, he took his entourage on foreign tours, and possessed the capacity to raise huge sums of money to buy buildings outright. He

---

[37] *Elim Evangel* 15.30 (27 July 1934), p. 465.

[38] *Elim Evangel* 15.31 (3 Aug 1934), p. 490.

[39] *Elim Evangel* 15.42 (19 Oct 1934), p. 666.

[40] Canty, *Unpublished,* p. 125.

[41] *Elim Evangel* 15.41 (12 Oct 1934), p. 643; *Elim Evangel* 15.42 (19 Oct 1934), p. 657.

[42] *Elim Evangel* 15.50 (14 Dec 1934), p. 787.

[43] *Elim Evangel* 15.50 (14 Dec 1934), p. 794.

seemed to enjoy the benefits of wealth, and association with senior members of the judiciary like John Leech would only have increased this suspicion.

The 1934 Ministerial Conference

The five day conference began on the morning of Tuesday, 18 September, and according to later voting figures about 130 people were present including ministers, probationers, wives, and, significantly, John Leech.[44] At Jeffreys' insistence the conference debated BI; and, in a later note, Phillips recalled that the discussion was forced on the conference 'under threat of resignation'.[45] Having been defeated in 1932 at the conference of the Northern Division Jeffreys must have met privately with Leech to agree a new strategy. Leech was going to make the case for BI to the whole conference and to answer questions from the floor. Everyone was to be exposed to his persuasive rhetoric. So he put his case on Tuesday morning before the conference turned to other business for the rest of the day. The whole of Wednesday was again devoted to the topic. At first Leech was questioned and then Leech's debating opponent was given an opportunity to put the case against BI before himself being questioned from the floor. The procedure was symmetrical in that both speakers were given uninterrupted time to make their first presentations and both speakers were subjected to detailed questioning by their audience.

Leech was a debater and advocate with a fearsome reputation. He was capable of marshalling information expertly and speaking cogently and his years as a barrister had only polished his eloquence.[46] Originally Percy Corry, the Dean of the Bible College, was programmed to put the anti-BI case to the conference; but, at the last moment, and for unknown reasons, Corry withdrew. It was left to E.J. Phillips at ridiculously short notice to take his place and

---

[44] Cartwright, *Evangelists*, p. 121.

[45] Hudson, *Schism*, p. 341.

[46] In 1940 he wrote *Israel in Britain*, a point-by-point rebuttal of W.F.P. Burton's pamphlet *Why I do not Believe the British-Israel Theory*. Whatever one thinks of Leech's conclusions, there is no doubt that, even towards the end of his life, his polemical abilities remained intact.

speak on Wednesday morning. Good authority reports that Phillips was up all night preparing his address.[47] He had no opportunity to study the topic in detail but was forced to rely upon his innate analytic ability and his general stock of biblical knowledge. The odds were stacked against him and the future of Elim rested in the balance.

We have handwritten notes made by Phillips after the event and possibly the notes he used to speak from at the time. There are also handwritten jottings made by someone else during the debate and these allow us to reconstruct some of the main lines of argument and the questions put to the protagonists.[48]

The debate was conducted courteously; and, as far as we can see, Jeffreys himself made no contribution to it, presumably because he anticipated Leech would win the day handsomely. Jeffreys must have hoped that his own apparently neutral stance would prevent any bad feeling within Elim and shield him from possible accusations of procedural bias.

Leech was entirely confident in the case he advanced and this added to his rhetorical persuasiveness. He knew Elim ministers present would only be convinced by biblical arguments so that, although the BI Federation had accumulated a range of other supporting material, this was almost entirely absent from the discussions on those two days. Leech needed to establish two central points:

1. That the ten northern tribes of Israel were never reunited with the two southern tribes of Judah after the reign of Solomon, and as part of this proof the terms 'Israel' and 'Judah' were never synonymous;

2. The ten northern tribes had made their way to Britain and settled in the British Isles in the remote past.

The first point is addressed in Phillips' later rebuttal. The second was connected with the text of 2 Sam. 7.10 that speaks about the settlement of Israelites in their own place from which 'they shall be

---

[47] I have this information from John Glass, then General Superintendent of Elim Churches.

[48] These are held at the Cartwright Centre at Regents Theological College, Malvern, and the debate below is constructed from them.

moved no more' and where they will live safely. Leech argued 'the place' referred to Britain and the text proved conclusively the lost tribes, having arrived, would never leave. The question-and-answer session probed this assertion.

Kingston began by turning attention to 2 Sam. 7.10 and the words, 'they shall be moved no more from this place'. He pointed out that other Scriptures state the Israelites, the whole of the tribes, are to be brought back from the lands where God had scattered them. If 'this place' refers to the ten tribes of Israel, how do the BIs explain what was happening? The Jewish people should remain in Britain and not move any more.

Leech replied, 'There is no Scripture which says the whole of them are to be brought back to Palestine. They will be brought back into Palestine one of a city and two of a family. They are going back by representation just as Members of Parliament do.'

Rudkin then asked, 'Do you maintain that ... 2 Samuel refers to the ten tribes being moved across Europe and planted in the British Isles? you say the British Isles is the place?' Rudkin wanted a clear statement from Leech about his central contention. Leech replied, 'God gives no dates on when it was to be done ... They came as God moved them and gathered them and he planted them in the appointed place'. Rudkin replied, 'the Scripture says after they were planted they were not afflicted. We had terrible affliction from the Romans.' His point was that the words of 2 Samuel were *not* fulfilled with regard to the population of Britain.

Leech dealt with this by saying,

> The last were the Normans in 1066 and from that date we have never been invaded. Napoleon planned invasion, the Spanish Armada had also planned an invasion; the Kaiser had his liners ready to invade us, and none of them came off. God's word has kept true.

Here Leech ignores the chronological point that the ten tribes, if they had settled in Britain, would have settled *before* the Norman invasion.

Corry queried the proper interpretation of 2 Sam. 7.10 by asserting, 'the appointed place is not only Palestine but all that land from the river of Egypt unto the Euphrates; then they will be moved no more'.

Leech simply denied Corry's statement by saying, 'that is entirely incorrect … My friends are under a wrong impression when they say the Promised Land necessarily stretched from the river of Egypt to the Euphrates.'

Robinson followed up by pointing out 'the French possess part of the Euphrates and Iraq' which was land outside the territory controlled by the British Mandate. Leech confidently asserted, 'we will possess it'.

McEvoy returned to the topic of the ten tribes and their presumed lifestyle in Britain, 'Suppose ten tribes came to these islands of ours, did they continue to keep the law of Moses?'

The exchanges show ministers were sceptical of the historical narrative of BI and posed questions Leech could not answer. Leech's chronology would have placed the Israelite migration to Britain in prehistoric or pre-Roman times, and this showed Leech's application of 2 Sam. 7.10 to Britain to be flawed. Britain is not the appointed place spoken of in the text. Equally, if other Jewish groups around the world continue to be differentiated from the surrounding population by the observance of the Mosaic law, it makes little sense to suppose that the ten tribes, by the time they arrived in Britain, had lost all trace of mosaic practices.

Leech's convictions shaped his understanding of the British mandate too. 'We are entitled to Palestine by virtue of conquest' he said,

> But like fools, not knowing who we were we took a Mandate, which means nothing because we were there already, and we are going to stay there. We took a mandate from the League of Nations. I say that merely shows the truth of that Scripture 'blindness in part has happened to Israel'.

The text about blindness refers to the failure of Jewish people to accept Jesus and is nothing to do with the land of Palestine.[49] But Leech applies the text to a political decision made by Britain since Britain, in his mind, is Israel. It took Phillips to point out, 'Mr Leech begins his argument by begging the question. He began by saying that we are entitled to Palestine; that is arguing in a circle.'

---

[49] Romans 11.25

When Phillips was given the platform to present his case we are in a better position to reconstruct his arguments from the notes he left.[50] He argued that Judah and the Israelites are one and many of the ten tribes joined the two tribes before the Babylonian captivity because they were all within one empire (see 2 Chron. 11.13). Here he is contradicting the first of the propositions Leech had attempted to prove and providing Scriptural evidence against it. He refers to 1 Chronicles 9 where Israel and Judah are mentioned together and to Ezek. 9.9 that charges the abominations committed in Jerusalem during the Babylonian captivity 'against Israel and Judah together'. The point here, and made by reference to Scripture, is that the ten tribes of the north were subsequently assimilated into the southern tribes around Jerusalem. Phillips put it this way:

> I have tried to establish that the people who are called Jews today constitute practically all the 12 tribes of Israel, not that they are just a few of them, that they are scattered all over the world as Jews, and the final gathering to Palestine is a gathering of what we call Jews today.

Phillips' remarkable performance carried the day. Most of his speech was built on Scripture but he also made a practical and contemporary case against BI teaching by pointing out how it diverted attention from things that really mattered, especially the evangelistic work by which Elim had been so successfully been built up. He went so far as to say that there is 'no end to rubbish preached' by young workers especially who have only been fed on British Israel literature and he asserted that 'our people would not be satisfied with identity only' but required teaching on Pentecostal matters including the experience of the Holy Spirit. More than this, the acceptance of BI teaching by Elim would 'double opposition' since the movement would find herself criticised for Pentecostal distinctives and for its propagation of BI.

There was already factionalism in congregations exposed to the BI message. Wholesale adoption of BI would open the door to splitting the denomination on other subjects over which Christians disagreed. The official adoption of BI was terribly risky and 'all for

---

[50] These are held at the Cartwright Centre at Regents Theological College, Malvern.

something of little value even if true'. BI had no part in the Great Commission of Mt. 28.19 or the 'faith once delivered to the saints' (Jude 3). He wanted to put Leech on the spot by asking, 'if we are convinced that to preach BI in our churches would split them, would you advise us to keep it out?' He wanted Leech to choose between denominational unity or BI. Finally, Phillips argued the miracle of the regathering of the Jews in Palestine and fulfilled prophecy to this effect would be completely overshadowed by BI teaching. More than this, any reference in Scripture to the 'bride of Christ' was likely to be transferred from the church to Israel only. In short, there was no advantage to Elim in preaching BI except that it would draw in a few BI adherents and allow them to 'spread their strange beliefs'.

When the vote was taken, and the conference was asked whether it accepted, rejected, or was neutral about BI teaching the results were:

Voting on British Israel teaching at 1934 Ministerial Conference[51]

Category of voter	Accept	Reject	Neutral	Total
Ministers - members of Conference	13	44	21	78
Ministers - not of Conference	0	1	1	2
Probationers - under Direct Government	2	12	7	21
Sisters in Ministry	0	5	2	7
Wives of Ministers or Probationers	1	11	9	21
John Leech	1	0	0	1
Category not marked on Voting Paper	0	0	1	1
TOTAL	17	73	41	131

The figures show that each category of voter rejected BI teaching and that of the total number of votes cast only 17 or 13% were in favour. Given that John Leech was granted a vote even though he was not a permanent member of the conference, the result was even more resounding. All the members of the Revival Party could be expected to vote with Jeffreys, and when these are subtracted, it is evident that only nine other ministers who were members of the conference were in favour of the BI position. Consequently, the conference agreed that BI 'should neither be preached nor attacked in any Elim church under Direct Government, nor should any Elim

---

[51] Taken from Hudson, *Schism*, p. 205.

minister appear on a British Israel platform'.[52] The churches not under Direct Government would, however, be allowed to promote the BI doctrine of identification 'within certain limits'.

The results of the voting were embarrassing to Jeffreys – he had seen his champion defeated – but he was allowed to keep the figures secret from all the other ministers (the minute for this item concluded with the comment 'at the request of the Principal the result of the voting was not announced to the meeting'). This strange procedure indicates the power of Jeffreys over the gathering or the sensitivity of Phillips and other members of the Executive to his feelings. Presumably none of the other members of the conference realised quite how small the BI minority was and this may have emboldened Jeffreys to bring the matter up the following year. It is true that the agreement about the extent to which BI teaching might be taught in churches under local government was vague and might need clarification, especially since Phillips later came to see the BI faction as agitators.

Post-Conference Rumblings

The conference had managed to preserve the unity of the Spirit but if Phillips and other elected members of the Executive hoped that a line could be drawn under the topics brought to the surface in the debate, they were sadly mistaken. Courtesies were maintained, letters exchanged and the *Evangel* regularly published; and, by spreading out the year's activities or offering more than one article on the same bit of 'old' news, a full and productive programme of events appeared to be in train. And yet Jeffreys was beginning to dream up new schemes which Phillips soon interpreted as being attempts to circumvent the decisions of conference.

We do not know whether Jeffreys produced these schemes by himself or after consultation with Leech. Already by early in September Jeffreys had made a proposal that there should be two conferences, one for the section A or Direct Government churches and another for everyone else. He even wanted to duplicate headquarters, a proposal that would have institutionalised the incipient divisions within the movement and made it much easier for one section to be hived off in its entirety.

Meanwhile, as ministers were moved around within the Central Government churches from one congregation to another, destabilisation was felt. There appeared to have been fanatical spiritual gifts operating in some places, perhaps because ministers were not settled long enough in one congregation to cope with extravagant Pentecostal behaviour.[53] There were reports of seething discontent in the churches as people wanted to gain admittance to Elim but found they could not.[54] Exactly why this was is raised in a letter by Phillips to Jeffreys about his, Jeffreys', refusal of churches. 'We are accepting new workers at the rate of one a fortnight and we need more. We are accepting new churches into section A.'[55] Eventually on 13 December Phillips wrote,

> The crux of this problem is that you are asking for these churches to be run as a group with separate headquarters. We discussed it several times and on each occasion, everyone has been emphatic that it would be impossible to set up a separate group for local government or to have separate headquarters. We all feel that it should be run from headquarters like every other section of the work.

And then he added,

> If there is any possibility of your agreeing to the new local government section being run as every other section of the work from headquarters, then I think we should meet and try and solve the problem.

The suspicion of Phillips and others was that Jeffreys wanted to increase the power of local government and correspondingly decrease the power of central government for one purpose only – to propagate BI teaching in the locally governed churches which he might then hope to draw away after himself. By the middle of December Jeffreys replied to Phillips and wanted his own group to work with, even though he had objected to a similar East Essex group with Kingston. Despite strenuous efforts to maintain harmony, tensions were becoming difficult to suppress.

---

[53] W.G. Channon to GJ, undated, but taken to be 1934.
[54] GJ to G. Hathaway, 15 Nov 1934.
[55] EJP to GJ 11 Dec 1934.

282   *George Jeffreys*

Added into all this were financial complications and manoeuvres. Phillips wrote to Jeffreys about tax liability on three churches being set up under the trusteeship of particular individuals: Glasgow Temple and Kensington Temple each for Darragh and McWhirter.[56] Such arrangements were contrary to the public report of the consequences of the Deed Poll in April of that year. A month later Phillips wrote to Jeffreys again about 'trio trusts' and their difficulties.[57] What appears to have been happening was along these lines: as the salaries of Elim ministers in centrally governed churches were fixed by headquarters, large congregations often gave more money than they spent. And this was especially so if the mortgages on their buildings were either paid for or small. It is easy to imagine how a congregation of 400 people who were giving generously and whose building was in good condition and who supported their pastor at the level recommended by headquarters would generate a surplus. This surplus was paid to Elim headquarters and from Elim headquarters was paid to the trustees of these churches. So, in effect these churches were supporting between one and three invisible beneficiaries.

No doubt, because they were made by Phillips, the arrangements were entirely legal but unquestionably they were used to favour members of the Revival Party and later, in his Will, Jeffreys justified what he had done by declaring that, whereas other denominations provided pensions for their ministers, he had not been able to do so. So members of the constantly-touring Revival Party (who could not also be pastors of congregations) effectively ended up with good salaries for the rest of their lives from the churches of which they were trustees. McWhirter was in this position in relation to Kensington Temple, which perhaps explains why he preached there more than other members of the Revival Party.

On 28 November the Executive met to discuss a scheme put forward by Jeffreys for the local government of churches. It appears that those who paid a shilling a week towards the church might have a vote in the affairs of a local congregation. At the Ex-

---

[56] EJP to GJ 29 Oct 1934.
[57] EJP to GJ 16 Nov 1934. These involved three trustees. The trusts had to cover buildings held under Scottish and English law, which varied. On the death of their trustees the buildings could revert to Elim.

ecutive Council meeting the scheme was discussed and Phillips recalled the occasion in a written aide-memoir in 1940:[58]

> All elected members were present. Next day I wrote [to the]
> Principal: 'Every one expressed surprise at the proposal to intro-
> duce a form of government which strikes at the very root of the
> Deed Poll, and asked why it was not suggested before we spent
> hundreds of pounds and months of discussion on the Deed
> Poll. The next thing I was faced with was this: Everyone who
> was present said they felt it was a means to introduce B.I. into
> the work. I did not breathe a single word about B.I. I found a
> very strong opposition from this point of view.'

All the elected members of the Executive were present. These men
would not have automatically accepted whatever opinion was advanced by Jeffreys.

> G.J. replied Dec. 4th: 'In order to avoid any possible misunder-
> standing between us, I assure you as members of the Executive
> that my motive in seeking to launch a plan for these Local Gov-
> ernment churches is not to provide ways and means to introduce
> this teaching into these churches.'

Tellingly, Phillips went on:

> I confess to you I did not accept that assce [assurance]. Events
> later proved it was right. A week or two after, in drafting the
> rules, I put in a clause that questions of doctrine outside the
> Fundamentals should be decided by the Executive. There was a
> deadlock.

It is possible to interpret these events in Jeffreys' favour, but only
just. Did other matters apart from BI cause the deadlock? Yet, the
giving of an assurance which Phillips 'did not accept', even if he
kept his thoughts to himself, tells of a crumbling of trust, a trust
cemented over 15 years of brilliant collaboration.

> So on 21st Dec., 1934 at an Executive meeting I proposed a res-
> olution that there should be liberty to preach B.I. in L.C.G.

---

[58] Hudson, *Schism*, appendix 2 and described as E.J. Phillips' unpublished
hand-written notes presented to the 1940 Ministerial Conference.

churches unless & until it spread to a stage when the Council felt it would be a menace to the rest of the work. The whole situation changed. G.J. shewed [*sic*] his pleasure & the scheme was launched with his blessing. About 3 yrs later, (Spring of 1937) G.J. admitted that he introduced L.C.G. for purpose of making an outlet for B.I. Any wonder [it has] not prospered?

The releasing of the deadlock once the new rules allowed the teaching of BI in Local Government churches received Jeffreys' blessing points only one way. It was becoming increasingly obvious to the elected members of the Executive that BI was the favoured doctrine to which all administrative change was subordinated.

The Executive's nerves or suspicions about BI can hardly have been quietened when Leech was appointed to teach at the Bible College in December 1934.[59] They must have assumed Jeffreys wanted the next cohort of Elim ministers to be soaked in BI doctrine.

Reflection

The 1934 ministerial conference marked the first open rebuff Jeffreys had experienced within Elim. Until that point, he had been charismatically and legally in complete charge of the movement built up around his ministry since those early days in Ulster in 1915. In the beginning he and his small Evangelistic Band had shared food and money, prayed together, slept under the same roof, and become friends as well as successful campaigners. The 1934 signing of the Deed Poll transferred legal power away from Jeffreys although, because of the way the Executive Council was composed, he must have anticipated life continuing much as before. He thought he could rely entirely on Phillips to do his bidding even though Phillips had stood up to him in the past. He must have anticipated that the elected members of the Executive would defer to him on important decisions. Even so, if Phillips and the three appointees Jeffreys could make were all in agreement, the Executive would have a majority in favour of any proposal Jeffreys might make.

---

[59] *Elim Evangel* 15.51 (25 Dec 1934), p. 807.

We must assume the resistance to Jeffreys' British Israel scheme at the ministerial conference came to him as a nasty surprise. He had prepared the ground by enabling Leech to lead the charge and speak to everyone. He fully anticipated that Leech, who had persuaded him about the validity of BI doctrine, would persuade everybody else. We do not know why Corry backed down at the last moment and refused to make the case against BI. Without any evidence at all, we might speculate that pressure had been brought to bear on him. What nobody seemed to have anticipated was how effective Phillips would be. He was perpetually in the office and weighed down with practical tasks and a multitude of duties. True, he had come to Christ and been a pastor for a short while but his gifts were so evidently in the back room that Jeffreys must have been amazed at his capacity to rebut Leech and articulate the weaknesses of the BI case to conference.

One of the possible explanations for Jeffreys' behaviour was that he was insulated from ordinary ministers and ordinary believers by his encircling Revival Party. They were a quasi-family to him and one opinion (put by Phillips at the end of the decade) was that they were likely to pander to him and flatter him.[60] Jeffreys only occasionally met strong-minded people who questioned him and one of these, as he knew, was Phillips ... but Phillips was in the office buried under a mound of paperwork and mostly tied to a typewriter.

At a later point Phillips described BI teaching as 'an infatuation' rather than a theory susceptible to disproof. One of its attractions was that it had a following among upper-middle-class men and women. The granddaughter of Queen Victoria, the Princess Alice, Countess of Athlone, was the patron of the British-Israel World Federation[61] and there appears to have been something in Jeffreys' character that found the social elite especially appealing.

Jeffreys was undoubtedly a complex man whose insecurities were well concealed. There is correspondence between him and Phillips over Percy Parker's review of *Pentecostal Rays*. Parker used the word 'simple' and meant this as praise to an author who could write so clearly about a complicated subject. Jeffreys complained, 'Our ene-

---

[60] E.J. Phillips' notes presented to Annual Conference General Survey – Tuesday Afternoon 21 Nov 1939. Taken from Hudson, *Schism*, Appendix 1.

[61] Reisenauer, *British-Israel*, p. 168.

mies Pentecostal and otherwise will be delighted to know that the book is only by a simple evangelist and not even by a third-rate teacher'.[62] Phillips had to mollify Jeffreys by explaining that the review was a good one and the description of the book as being written in 'powerful and simple language' was complimentary.[63]

Jeffreys, despite his intelligence, went out to work without any secondary schooling whatever and must have occasionally felt his deficiencies in the company of men like Leech who had all the advantages of university education. Whether Jeffreys would still have been a convert to BI even if he had received higher education can never be known but at least he might have been equipped with the capacity to critique. Leech himself was never an historian or scientist or even a linguist. As a lawyer and classicist, he extracted meaning from texts and built logical arguments from them; and, as a preacher, this is essentially what Jeffreys did also. We can understand how Jeffreys felt unable to combat Leech's confident speeches about ancient British history or the racial composition of the British people since Leech had immersed himself in late Victorian ethnology. These racial speculations look amateurish and tendentious to the modern reader – but then much 19th century science appears flimsy to the 21st century scholar who can ascertain racial characteristics with amazing precision through DNA. What Leech offered was a way of interpreting the world and facing the future – even fighting for the future – that appeared to add a vital dimension to Pentecostal revivalism.

We cannot be sure of the inner workings of Jeffreys' mind during the rest of this decade. It is no longer possible to interview members of the Revival Party, and private correspondence Jeffreys had with other people apart from Phillips at the headquarters was destroyed by Albert Edsor, his pianist and chauffeur, who survived him by more than 25 years. Like an iceberg floating on the water there is much more below the surface than above, but at least we can see where the iceberg went; we can examine the decisions Jeffreys made and the actions he took and, from these, attempt to discover what he truly thought and felt. If there are discrepancies be-

---

[62] GJ to EJP 17 July 1933.
[63] EJP to GJ 18 July 1933.

tween what Jeffreys said and what he did, we can look for reasons why and make a judgement on whether Jeffreys' explanation of his actions is more credible than those who came to disbelieve him. The following chapters take us over the rough seas to come.

14

1935–1937: THE GATHERING STORM

Introduction

Over the next three years the disagreements between the Jeffreys loyalists and others in Elim were for the most part kept hidden. They emerged at the meetings of the Executive Council and during the ministerial conferences and might be traced in the correspondence between Jeffreys and Phillips. As far as ordinary members of the congregations were concerned, everything continued much as before: Jeffreys preached to large crowds, the *Elim Evangel* was published on time and weekly, the main public events of the year continued as usual at the Royal Albert Hall and at the Crystal Palace and Jeffreys himself wrote a letter to all Elim members everywhere in the Christmas edition of the *Evangel*. True, he was enjoying success in Switzerland and to a lesser extent in France but his visits to these countries occupied only two or three weeks of the year. Phillips continued as Secretary-General with an immense workload of correspondence and the Revival Party was also stable (although McWhirter married in 1936[1] and so began to take a backseat). Behind all this normality the baying for war in Germany and Italy could be heard in the distance.

One of the striking features of the *Evangel* concerned its clear-sightedness of political events in Europe. Atheism in Russia was rampant and on the rest of the European stage Mussolini appeared

---

[1] Edsor, *'Set Your House in Order'*, p. 20.

as significant a figure as Hitler. His declarations were increasingly outlandish. The state was to become totalitarian and to swallow up the church: 'our formula is this: everything in the state, nothing outside the state, nothing against the state'.[2] Once Abyssinia had been invaded and put under Italian rule, all British missionaries were expelled.[3] Italy was said to be interfering with the British mandate in Palestine and Mussolini's desire to revive the Roman Empire seemed an ominous fulfilment of Dan. 2.40-43.[4] Given the eventual military performance of Italy after 1939, and the dictator's grisly end and the exposure of his body as a public spectacle, Mussolini's grandiose claims appear in hindsight to be ridiculous. At the time they appeared the words of a visionary statesman. In Germany Hitler developed the art of reassuring people with solemn promises he later broke. But the British press and the liberal elite were all too ready to be reassured and few seemed to notice the perversion of Christianity being visited upon the German church and the implications of this for the national values now driving Germany. 'Adolf Hitler is the real Holy Ghost', claimed Dr Kerrl, chairman of the Prussian Diet.[5] Or as Nazis in the Saar declared, 'Hitler is a new, a greater and a more powerful Jesus Christ'.[6] The Jewish lineage of Christ was denied by Dr Goebbels, Minister of Propaganda: 'Christ cannot possibly have been a Jew. I don't have to prove that scientifically. It is a fact,'[7] and German people were urged to suppress humanitarian love in words that echoed the philosophy of Fredrick Nietzsche:

> you must fight in the true spirit of anti-christ against the last remnant of the heritage of Christianity in our Nordic race and free yourselves from the Jewish-Christian conception of compassion and loving your enemies.[8]

---

[2] *Elim Evangel* 18.24 (11 June 1937), p. 378.
[3] *Elim Evangel* 18.20 (14 May 1937), p. 314.
[4] *Elim Evangel* 18.35 (27 Aug 1937), p. 554.
[5] *Elim Evangel* 17.3 (17 Jan 1936), p. 37.
[6] *Elim Evangel* 18.24 (11 June 1937), p. 378.
[7] *Elim Evangel* 17.3 (11 Jan 1936), p. 37.
[8] *Elim Evangel* 17.5 (31 Jan 1936), p. 67.

No wonder Pastor Martin Niemoller, one of the founders of the Confessing Church which resisted Nazification, reported 'Christ Himself is regarded as a public enemy in Germany'.[9]

The *Evangel* eventually formulated an answer to the European situation. Yes, there would be war but this would be ended by the return of Christ and the Church would be rescued from tribulation.[10] More than this, or perhaps prior to this, the church needed to work as hard as it could for revival since revival could possibly avert terrible events. Jeffreys went so far as to declare that dictators were *frightened* of revival.

> What we want in this country is a return to God and the birth of the mightiest revival we have ever seen. If such a revival were to break out in our land it would strike more terror in the hearts of dictators who are anxious to capture our land than all the battleships and armaments we could ever have.[11]

Elim churches, then, should dedicate themselves by financial giving and ceaseless activity and in this way, stand up for the faith and the Foursquare Gospel.[12] Because war itself was an evil and a sin[13] and even if the bearing of arms was a matter of Christian conscience,[14] there was no defeatism within the leadership or wringing of hands in the face of prophetic inevitability. The church should intensify its quest for widespread revival.

In Britain as a whole, politics entered a phase of stagnation even if there was a change of Prime Minister in the summer of 1935 and a General Election in the autumn of that year when Stanley Baldwin was returned as head of a national government. Elim may have welcomed an experienced hand on the tiller while watching Europe goose-step towards fascism.[15] The Archbishop of York, William Temple, a leading Anglican who later became Archbishop of Canterbury, broadcast on the BBC and placed hope in the League of Nations, a toothless international body marked by passivity and

[9] *Elim Evangel* 18.32 (6 Aug 1937), p. 506.
[10] *Elim Evangel* 16.1 (4 Jan 1935), p. 11.
[11] *Elim Evangel* 18.24 (11 June 1937), p. 369.
[12] *Elim Evangel* 18.52 (24 Dec 1937), p. 817.
[13] *Elim Evangel* 16.46 (15 Nov 1935), p. 722
[14] *Elim Evangel* 16.46 (15 Nov 1935), p. 728.
[15] *Elim Evangel* 16.46 (15 Nov 1935), p. 730.

failure.[16] Its attempts at guiding disarmament involved long-winded committee meetings in Geneva and three years of discussion on such topics as what actually constituted an offensive weapon.[17] Temple along with most Anglicans at the time appeared to have no eschatological vision and could not see the return of Christ as being on the horizon.

He and other members of the church did better in an attempt to offer moral support for unemployed miners who marched all the way from Jarrow to London in protest at unemployment and poverty.[18] By contrast, Baldwin declined to see them, there were exchanges in the House of Commons, misleading statistics were quoted by the government to suggest unemployment was falling, a rally was held in Hyde Park and the men, without having achieved anything of substance, returned home by train to a rapturous reception. Paralysis, political and economic, gripped most of the governing class with the result that the appointment of Neville Chamberlain as prime minister in May 1937 appeared to complete the symbolism of limping ineffectiveness.

Elim, along with other Pentecostal churches, felt unable to speak with authority on poverty and unemployment and refused to be deflected from evangelism to trade unionist activism. Where they did enter the realm of finance, they became caught up, as we shall see, with teaching about the necessity of tithing or appeals for money to pay off the debts on their buildings. And there were murmuring questions about how wealthy Jeffreys really was.

1935

The year began with a report on a revival in Manchester and then, at the end of January, came the first *Evangel* headlines of the year featuring Jeffreys. He had been in Ulster for the Christmas celebra-

---

[16] *Elim Evangel* 16.40 (4 Oct 1935), p. 628.

[17] Malcolm Muggeridge, *The Thirties: 1930–1940 in Great Britain* (London: Weidenfeld and Nicholson, 1940, 1989), p. 133.

[18] Temple was president (1908–1924) of the Workers' Educational Association. He was chairman of an international and interdenominational Conference on Christian Politics, and Citizenship held in 1924. See also F.A. Iremonger, *William Temple: Archbishop of Canterbury, his Life and Letters* (London: OUP, 1948), p. 440.

tions and travelled across to Glasgow for the New Year convocations. Jeffreys, as Crusader-in-Chief, praised the Elim Crusaders for their many types of service to prisons and hospitals and in choirs and open air meetings. The Crusader movement was for young people and provided organised avenues of Christian service as well as a way of associating the young with Jeffreys directly. He then opened tabernacles at York and Romsey before news of his visit to Aberdeen: the correspondent delighted in the rich Welsh accent of Jeffreys and the Irish brogue and humour of McWhirter. There followed an announcement that the Revival Party would travel to Palestine for a tour. 'No party is more worthy of this change and rest since ... their busy life ... [is] taxing both spiritual and physical strength to the utmost'.[19] So, leaving on 21 February for five weeks, the Revival Party together with Percy Corry and E.J. Phillips set off on a pilgrimage with spiritual and educational overtones.

In May the *Evangel* gave a full account of the tour which started at the pyramids of Egypt and turned north by rail to Palestine. Each member of the party wrote a piece that combined tourist impressions with spiritual reflections. Most arresting is the piece by Jeffreys himself who was obviously moved by his view of Jerusalem from the Mount of Olives and this led him to an imaginative meditation on the turbulent history of the city over which Jesus wept.[20] He evoked the destruction of the city left a smoking ruin by the Roman Legion that destroyed the walls and burnt the temple. He called to mind the recapture of the city by General Allenby in 1917 and was able to 'listen with delight to the story of a most reliable eye-witness of the scenes that transpired when the British troops entered into the city' and the emotions of children dancing in the streets and the kisses to the hands of the soldiers and the flowers showered upon them. For Jeffreys this moment was the culmination of a 2,520-year period predicted by Scripture counting from Israel's first dispersion from the city in 604 BC. 'God, by fulfilling the prophecy at the exact time and in the right place, has put into our hands a mighty weapon against the forces of Higher Criticism and Modernism'.

[19] *Elim Evangel* 16.5 (15 Feb 1935), p. 106.
[20] *Elim Evangel* 16.18 (3 May 1935), p. 280.

Beyond this Jeffreys recalled the period of stress and perplexity ushered in by the Great War (1914-1918) and reflected on the final struggle over the city and military conflict on the Plain of Megiddo:

> I had seen the Union Jack flying over Government House in the Holy City and I had watched the smart and happy contingent of British soldiers marching through its streets to the place of worship on Sunday morning. Were these the forerunners of the British troops that will soon be called upon to defend Jerusalem, and might they see Christ coming in a cloud with great glory to deliver just when all hope is gone? It's difficult to see how any other empire can ever hold the Mandate for Palestine.

Returning to England Jeffreys campaigned in Darlington and Middlesbrough and saw over 400 conversions in the latter.[21] By the end of the month the *Evangel* felt it necessary to publish a page-long rebuttal of claims that Jeffreys was rich. It is true, the rebuttal admitted, that Jeffreys had bought a home for his mother and sent her money to live on; he had merely acted as a good son would. He lived modestly at the back of Park Crescent up to 1926 and in 1935 his personal bank account stood at £30 while the Revival Party only had money to pay the rent on a hall for one good campaign. Readers were assured he had 'no investments of any kind' except part ownership of a house in London.[22]

Such reassurances would only have been made in the light of persistent rumours. One must assume the article was published at Jeffreys' request. He had lived in cramped circumstances in Park Crescent, Clapham, and in his caravan during revivals tours but perhaps it was the foreign travel as well as his refined manner that gave rise to suspicious comment. In private, letters were exchanged with Phillips showing the trio trust deeds were being drawn up for Darragh and McWhirter (on Kensington Temple and Glasgow) while Tweed was given sole trusteeship of the Blackpool building.[23] These established congregations with large, almost mortgage-free buildings would have provided steady income for the trustees. The letters indicate that Jeffreys himself held the sole trusteeship of a

[21] *Elim Evangel* 16.24 (14 June 1935), p. 379.
[22] *Elim Evangel* 16.26 (28 June 1935), p. 410.
[23] EJP to GJ, 20 June 1935; GJ to EJP, 20 June 1935.

Brighton church from which he appears to have derived £103 quarterly.[24] None of this is to deny his relatively modest personal income.[25] Large sums were collected during campaigns and large sums were spent during campaigns. As for the expensive church buildings, it is important to note in the light of what was to happen later that the trust deeds discussed in these letters ensured all the properties would, on the death of trustees, revert to Elim.[26] Having said this, and having denied Jeffreys was a rich man, his two bank accounts on 7 June 1935 held between them £3,271, that is, about ten times the average salary of a male school teacher. One must assume that the statement made in the Evangel's article on the 28 June (mentioned above) was only correct because the personal accounts had been almost completely emptied into the World Revival Crusade account.[27]

There were evangelistic meetings in Sheffield and an editorial praising Elim's system of central government both in the buying of buildings and in the rotation of ministers. By August an editorial was reporting the Executive wanted to clear 'all our existing commitments' by which they meant paying off mortgages on all buildings.[28] The push must have come from Jeffreys himself to coincide with the Elim's Coming of Age or 21st year in 1936. There was no grassroots financial clamour here. August printed reports of Jeffreys' meetings in Lincoln with 100 conversions and of revival fer-

---

[24] EJP to GJ, 19 July 1935. The mortgage on Brighton was down to £1,355 (EJP to GJ, 16 Nov 1934) and EJP anticipated it would soon be paid off. Jeffreys received £103 quarterly and £61 each was paid to Darragh and McWhirter two years later (EJP to GJ, 17 Sept 1936).

[25] As the BBC website gives the average annual wage in the 1930s as around £200, Jeffreys would have been in receipt of double this from his trusteeship of the Brighton church, http://news.bbc.co.uk/1/hi/wales/4203686.stm (accessed 31/3/16). Similar figures for average wages are given by A.L. Bowley, *Wages and Income in the United Kingdom since 1860* (Cambridge: Cambridge University Press, 1937), pp. 113-14. I say that Jeffreys' income was 'relatively modest' because the average salary of a male school teacher was £312 per year. See *Whitaker's Almanac* (1938), p. 452 (accessible on Google Books).

[26] EJP to GJ 19 July 1935.

[27] Maldwyn Jones, *An Analysis of the Role of E.J. Phillips and an Assessment of his Leadership in the Establishment of the Elim Movement as a Coherent Christian Denomination* (MA, Bangor University, 2011), p. 51. The information comes from an interview with Desmond Cartwright on 18 May 2011 as well as from paperwork. E.J. Phillips completed Jeffreys' tax returns for him and must have left notes behind.

[28] *Elim Evangel* 16.34 (23 Aug 1935), p. 538.

vour in York with 110 water baptisms; and there had previously been meetings in Scunthorpe and a new Elim church had been planted in Middlesbrough.[29] Shortly afterwards Jeffreys returned to York while a new Elim church was established in Lincoln. In September Jeffreys spoke to vast crowds at the Crystal Palace[30] and the *Evangel* carried articles and photos together with the report of his highly successful campaigns in France at La Havre and Rouen.[31] In October there were accounts of revival fires burning in France and Switzerland[32] and an unprecedented request that month from the Executive willing to hear from non-Elim churches that wanted to hold crusades, perhaps as a way of bringing wavering churches into the Local Government scheme. By the autumn a front page of the *Evangel* claimed 12,000 converts in Switzerland with signs and wonders following Jeffreys' ministry.[33] Later that year he preached at Bristol where 100 conversions were claimed.[34] The contrast between overwhelming success abroad and comparatively meagre results in England was noticeable: it provided justification for a new organisation. Jeffreys decided to found the World Revival Crusade quite separate from Elim and with its own financial arrangements as well as its own literature and outreach.

An anonymous report on the autumn's ministerial conference noted that ministers often 'made unselfish decisions involving sometimes more labour and responsibility for themselves in order better to meet the need of their people', coded wording pointing to the financial hardships confronting some pastors.[35] Even so, an ordination service at Kensington Temple for a new intake of pastors took place accompanied by a large photograph of all the ministers together.

By the end of the year Boulton, as editor, announced 24 new Elim churches had been established in 1935 and printed a map showing where they all were.[36] The Bible College was successful,

---

[29] *Elim Evangel* 16.35 (30 Aug 1935), front page, p. 555.
[30] *Elim Evangel* 16.39 (27 Sept 1935), p. 609
[31] *Elim Evangel* 16.39 (27 Sept 1935), p. 609.
[32] *Elim Evangel* 16.42 (18 Oct 1935), p. 657.
[33] *Elim Evangel* 16.45 (8 Nov 1935), p. 712.
[34] *Elim Evangel* 16.49 (6 Dec 1935), front cover.
[35] *Elim Evangel* 16.46 (15 Nov 1935), p. 723.
[36] *Elim Evangel* 16.51-52 (25 Dec 1935), p. 803.

publications were booming and gramophone records of Elim music and sermonettes were selling. The correspondence course was attracting students and all seemed well. Admittedly the World Revival Crusade raised qualms in the minds of perceptive Elim leaders like Phillips who saw it as a potential rival to Elim but for the time being no objections were voiced, or not voiced loudly. And there were questions behind the scenes about the governance of the Irish churches which still continued unsettled. On Christmas Day Jeffreys meditated on the whole year highlighting the emotions evoked by his visit to Bethlehem. 'Standing in the vicinity of the manger the meditation of my heart centred round the marvels of the Incarnation and its resultant effects upon the human race.'[37]

1936

Elim was determined to celebrate its 21st year. Regardless of the national economy or the international situation the Coming of Age would be joyfully acclaimed. Jeffreys, with the Revival Party, would make a series of preaching tours; the scenes of his earlier triumphs would be revisited and old loyalties rekindled. The United Kingdom was divided up to allow as many congregations as possible to attend a Jeffreys meeting: for instance one of the tours lasted seven weeks and took in 35 churches.[38]

Jeffreys announced:

> I shall also (DV) be touring the Churches, and shall thus meet my people face to face through the land during the year ... let me at this time make a direct appeal to one and all to give their hearty support to the JUBILEE FUND ... all financial responsibilities would very soon be lifted from our shoulders and we would feel free to extend our borders.[39]

There is a hint here that Jeffreys was inviting adulation and shifting the perception of the relationship between himself and ordinary Elim members. These were now 'my people'. It is the possessive pronoun that raises an eyebrow. Would Jeffreys as a younger man

[37] *Elim Evangel* 16.51-52 (25 Dec 1935), p. 801.
[38] Canty, *Unpublished*, p. 126.
[39] *Elim Evangel* 17.6 (7 Feb 1936), p. 90.

have spoken like this or would he have preferred to speak about 'the Lord's people' or even followers of the Foursquare Gospel? The single word may be over-interpreted though later, when troubles had come to a head, Jeffreys' grand British tour looked to members of the Executive Council as if it was designed to refresh his popularity in preparation for a triumphant exit from Elim leading all 'his' people behind him.

Coupled with this was the appeal for cash to be poured into the Jubilee Fund to lift financial responsibilities from 'our shoulders' (there is a worrying Royal 'we' here). The implication was that Jeffreys alone had to be the fundraising machine to keep all Elim accounts in balance. There is no recognition of the role of local pastors sustaining congregations and encouraging the people to give and there was a puzzling statement about only extending 'our borders' once the debt was paid off. Jeffreys seemed to be saying there would be no more church planting and no more expansion until the current crop of churches had all been paid for; the cycle of campaigning, congregational planting, and buying buildings that had been so satisfactory for 21 years was under threat unless everyone emptied their pockets and settled the mortgages within a year.

At the time, and in the happy knowledge of what had been achieved, a grand effort and financial reinvigoration might seem perfectly reasonable. Yes, let's pay the debts and prepare ourselves for the next leap forward and the next round of revivalistic successes. If our beloved Principal wants his burdens eased, let's do all we can to help him. Jeffreys, surrounded by his compliant Revival Party, had the trappings of contemporary celebrity. Huge crowds hung on his every word and newspapers splashed photographs of his big campaigns. The *Evangel* regularly projected his fame and ministry, and printed testimonies of healings added awe to the adulation that surrounded him.

On his 47th birthday George was presented with an illuminated address signed by the staff and senior officers at Elim headquarters.[40] At the big meetings in Royal Albert Hall a second illuminated address was presented to Jeffreys signed by 11 laymen who represented the 209 Elim churches in Britain. The man chosen to present

---

[40] Cartwright, *Evangelists*, p. 131.

the scroll on the big occasion was John Leech, the same man who had been so roundly defeated in his presentation of BI at the 1934 conference. The scroll read,

To Principal George Jeffreys

We, Beloved Principal, the undersigned, on behalf of the Elim Foursquare Gospel churches in the British Isles, wish to place on record our deep appreciation and heartfelt gratitude to God for the great service you have, through his grace, rendered to the people of these lands. Twenty-one years ago you were led to the shores of Ireland and gave that Island the honour of being the cradle of what is today one of the greatest religious awakenings of modern times. We have viewed with thankfulness the establishment of the Elim Bible College and the great company of preachers you have ordained to the ministry of Christ. We have watched with joy the extension and progress of the work in our own land and in other lands, and we have seen the answer to our prayers in the multitude of lives and homes which have been transformed under your ministry.

As an apostle, you have pioneered the full gospel message and established churches in the largest cities and towns of the British Isles.

As an evangelist, your ministry has been signally owned and blessed of God. Through your faithful proclamation of the old-fashioned gospel you have led countless thousands to Christ.

As a preacher and teacher, you have stood uncompromisingly for the Word of God, your exposition of the Sacred Scriptures have enriched our minds and hearts.

As a leader, you have stood like a bulwark in the midst of back-sliding and departure from the faith.

Kindly receive this address at the Coming of Age celebrations in the Royal Albert Hall, London, as a token of our sincere regard for your past and as an assurance of our prayerful interest and loyal support for the future, as you continue to follow our Lord and saviour, Jesus Christ.

The Lord bless thee, and keep thee

the Lord make his face shine upon thee, and be gracious unto thee:

the Lord lift up his countenance upon thee, and give thee peace
– Numbers 6.24-26 *Whit-Monday, June 1st, 1936*[41]

The wording here is sincere and appropriate. Later Christian historians might wonder at the word 'apostle' in the address; but, if an apostle is a person who has the ability to plant churches where none existed before, Jeffreys may rightly claim such a gift at this stage in his life. We may wonder about the effect these presentations might have been on Jeffreys' psyche. He never appeared to lack confidence but would he now become overconfident?

In February that year Jeffreys had published an article in the *Evangel* entitled 'What is the World Revival Crusade?' and answered:

… It is a world-wide bond of fellowship between ourselves and those we have been privileged to lead to Christ in different parts of the world … After much prayerful meditation … To meet the crying need we were convinced that the only possible way of keeping contact with such multitudes [in Switzerland] was by forming a world-wide fellowship which would include all … With this end in view we have formed the World Revival Crusade, and have set apart Kensington Temple … as the Crusade centre of intercession at a definite time each day throughout the year … When the Principal is ministering elsewhere he will be kept in constant touch with the healing Centre, and prayer requests sent to the Temple will be laid before the Throne at his Revival and Healing campaigns.[42]

So the World Revival Crusade is a 'bond of fellowship between ourselves and those we have been privileged to lead to Christ' intended to strengthen the link between individuals and Jeffreys while providing a location in London to which prayer requests might be sent. Even miles away Jeffreys' prayers were deemed specially efficacious, and we see in embryo organisation-building practices taken up twenty or thirty years later by other healing evangelists. There is no mention here of any other churches that might be attached to the

---

[41] *Elim Evangel* 17.51-52 (25 Dec 1936), p. 802.
[42] *Elim Evangel* 17.7 (7 Feb 1936), p. 99.

World Revival Crusade or any funds that might be diverted into it or the complete financial control Jeffreys would exercise over it.[43] It is presented purely as a connective network.

Afterwards Jeffreys toured Scotland including Aberdeen, Dundee, Dunfermline, Edinburgh, Kilsyth, Greenock, Ayr, and Glasgow and reported 40 decisions for Christ in Edinburgh[44] and in Glasgow more than 200 conversions.[45] In Blackpool, where the Jubilee Temple had opened, 120 people were converted and the *Evangel* was glad to print a story of an Anglican bishop who acknowledged genuine healings in Jeffrey's ministry.[46] The Albert Hall meetings were packed and 1,000 healings were enjoyed[47] before Jeffreys turned south to Bournemouth and opened another tabernacle and then north to Carlisle, Darlington, Middlesbrough, Barnard Castle, Scarborough, and Sunderland where hundreds of decisions for Christ and healings occurred. In June the *Evangel* speaks of the 'triumphant tour' with 'packed buildings, hundreds converted and healing miracles'[48] and there is 'great joy everywhere, revival fervour'[49] and there are meetings at Huddersfield, Sheffield, Bradford, and later in Southend-on-Sea, Nottingham, and Ipswich before visits to Lincoln, Doncaster, Cardiff, Neath, Swansea, Llanelli, and enthusiastic crowds greet Jeffreys in the Principality of Wales. Jeffreys launches an Irish campaign in Belfast where his 'big tent is besieged and amazing revival scenes' follow[50] with 200 conversions and many healings taking place and in September it is reported that 'never before has the city been stirred by such a revival, with its miracles of healing, signs and wonders'.[51] Only at the larger Crystal Palace meetings might there have been a greater impact. There Crusader banners were unfurled and Jeffreys told the inspiring story of Elim

[43] Taken from Hudson, *Schism*, p. 218.
[44] *Elim Evangel* 17.9 (28 Feb 1936), front cover.
[45] *Elim Evangel* 17.12 (20 Mar 1936), front cover.
[46] *Elim Evangel* 17.15 (10 Apr 1936), p. 234.
[47] *Elim Evangel* 17.18 (1 May 1936), p. 283.
[48] *Elim Evangel* 17.23 (5 June 1936), front cover.
[49] *Elim Evangel* 17.24 (12 Feb 1936), front cover.
[50] *Elim Evangel* 17.35 (28 Aug 1936), front cover.
[51] *Elim Evangel* 17.37 (11 Sept 1936), p. 579.

to the attentive crowds[52] and a huge double page photograph shows his wondering audience.

Less glowingly the Jubilee Fund had realised 'just over 10% of our total commitments', which was something of a disappointment.[53] The Ministerial Conference started straight after the Crystal Palace weekend. The ministers agreed:

> they would proclaim a national week of prayer and supplication before God, throughout all the church. They believed as a result of waiting upon God in this manner, the way would be open for a great forward move in evangelising the districts around about their churches and in the adjoining districts and villages … That in this way a great national revival could be brought about.

And they went on to say,

> We were reminded … of the inscription in the Parish Hall, Fulwell Road, Monkwearmouth, Sunderland, 'when the fire of the Lord fell it burnt up the debt'.[54]

In short, the reason for prolonged prayer and supplication was more than the hunger for revival; it was a desire to boost financial flow to the Jubilee Fund. At that point the fund only stood at £6,870.[55] This insistence upon raising money to pay off the debt – and it was a debt upon buildings that the Building Societies were content to allow to be paid back in the normal way over a period of years – had serious consequences for the funds available for ministers. In effect, money was switched from ministerial salaries into buildings. Both Canty and Cartwright point out the fundraising led to genuine ministerial hardship,[56] and this at a time when the unemployed Jarrow marchers made their long trek south to an unsympathetic government in London.[57]

---

[52] *Elim Evangel* 17.39 (25 Sept 1936), p. 611.
[53] *Elim Evangel* 17.39 (25 Sept 1936), p. 618.
[54] *Elim Evangel* 17.40 (2 Oct 1936), p. 637.
[55] Cartwright, *Evangelists*, p. 130.
[56] Canty, *Unpublished*, p. 128; Cartwright *Evangelists*, p. 141.
[57] Phillips' notes of a report to the Ministerial Conference on 1 Nov 1939 include:

> Cry of financial crisis just because a/cs shewed [*sic*] loss of £104 in year when Jubilee Fund raised nearly £7,000. All sorts of schemes drawn up & G.J. even

The apparently disconnected storms buffeting Elim became part of one big storm. The appeal for money, first presented as a special coming-of-age effort, now began to be interpreted as a crisis threatening the future expansion of the movement. Within this storm disagreements over the validity of BI complicated decision-making. Years later Phillips saw the 'financial crisis' as an exaggeration perpetrated by Jeffreys for the sole purpose of detaching groups of churches from the body of Elim – or at least for opening them up to BI doctrine. Yet the psychology of the main protagonists inclined them to interpret the relevant financial spreadsheets differently. Jeffreys himself had a strong aversion to debt of any kind and Jones suggests this stemmed from his working-class Welsh roots; he grew up in a culture where debt was deeply feared and regarded as sinful.[58] For Phillips, from a middle-class background, the borrowing of money for property and its repayment over time was perfectly normal practice. It was nothing to worry about provided a regular income could be guaranteed.

The disposal of funds was in the hands of Elim Headquarters since church collections from all the centrally government churches were sent there. The arrangements were intended to equalise ministerial salaries but with the effect of keeping the unmarried ministers at a permanent disadvantage because they were not provided with houses whereas married ministers were. Jeffreys wrote to Phillips,

> Personally if I were in section A it would be a sore point with me to be doomed to lodgings eternally simply because I felt called to the unmarried state, more especially if I had to send money home to a mother or sister dependent upon me, knowing that this was from the reduced allowance granted me because I was unmarried![59]

---

considered selling Elim Woodlands. As a result of decisions then made some mins [ministers] have been practically starving while we have been paying money off mortgages when mortgages were arranged for 15 yrs & cd easily have been pd out of church surplus, & lenders didn't want it back, & need not have been pd for 15 yrs - or not at all if the Lord came back before then.
Taken from Hudson *Schism*, Appendix 1.
[58] Jones, *An Analysis*, p. 47.
[59] GJ to EJP 19 Mar 1936.

This was a reasonable point though while funds were at full stretch and while collections were being directed to pay down the debt, the position of unmarried ministers was hardly likely to improve.

Further financial discussion took place behind the scenes. Jeffreys wrote to Phillips, 'we regard the "stock in hand" in the trio returns[60] last year as belonging absolutely to the Crusade'[61] (i.e. the World Crusade account), which was fair enough since it meant the Revival Party pooled its expenses at least while it was together though once McWhirter married he presumably took his payments to set up home with his wife. And then Albert Edsor, the pianist, was put onto a salary (at Jeffreys' request) and so Phillips had to deal with his tax returns and was at the same time asked to seek charitable status for the World Revival Crusade accounts.[62] A draft letter from Hathaway planning for 1936 proposed the Revival Party would go through 'as many churches as possible' in the Coming of Age tour while dealing with its own travel and catering costs. It would also pay for advertisements in local newspapers but asked to retain the collections at the services 'to go to their campaign fund', a procedure bound to cream cash from churches to the detriment of ordinary pastoral salaries.[63]

When a generous donation of £1,000 reached Elim, Jeffreys directed Phillips to use the money for paying down the mortgage of Kensington Temple.[64] In other words Jeffreys was making sure that the big churches with trustees belonging to his own inner circle were at the front of the queue when it came to paying off debts. This preferential treatment for large key congregations runs against the grain of a shared financial burden. The spare money from Kensington Temple would have found its way through the 'trio returns' into the World Revival Crusade account where it remained under the direct and private control of Jeffreys.

On 9 December 1936 Jeffreys wrote to Phillips asking to be released from his responsibilities at Elim. This seems to be the first

---

[60] These are the tax returns on the three big churches, Glasgow, Blackpool, and Kensington Temple that Jeffreys 'gave' to his inner circle by nominating them as the trustees of the buildings.

[61] GJ to EJP 5 Apr 1936.

[62] EJP to GJ 21 Apr 1936.

[63] Hathaway, draft letter Apr 1936.

[64] GJ to EJP 23 Aug 1936.

time that he revealed how burdensome he found his work. 'I shall be released from what I feel is a burden. Be more free to follow my spiritual calling.' He did not intend to walk away from Elim, only to be released from the business side of the organisation. Phillips went to see him the same day and learnt more of Jeffreys' anxieties: he was worried about the debts on buildings; he was concerned about local trustees and the pain ministers would feel if the movement split but he might be prepared to stay on as a 'spiritual father' under certain conditions. His letter was confidential and only for the eyes of the Executive Council and what he wrote should not be seen as an ultimatum.[65]

On 15 December Jeffreys sent four pages of proposals for the restructuring of Elim. All the Direct Government churches could be assigned to one of two sections. The self-supporting churches would be placed in a 'Jubilee Concentration' and the remainder, which were weaker and less established, in a 'Forward Movement'. All future churches would be placed in the Forward Movement. Once all the buildings in the Forward Movement had been paid off, all the churches could be joined together and run as a before as a single entity. As for his own position, he declared:

> I have no thought of leaving the work, on the contrary, I have every intention of going ahead with you all, in spreading the glorious work of deepening the confidence we have in each other.[66]

More than this, he wanted to give the new Executive Council the chance to formulate its own policy without any interference from him.

> Let me say from the depths of my heart that no leader could be surrounded by a more devoted, self-sacrificing, and trustworthy band of men than those who surround me. It is this knowledge that prompts me to hand over the work without the thought of settling the terms for the withdrawal of myself.

All this appeared magnanimous though with oddities mixed in. What did Jeffreys mean by 'spreading the glorious work of deepen-

---

[65] Cartwright, *Evangelists,* p 134. I have followed Cartwright's account without modification.

[66] Cartwright, *Evangelists,* p. 135.

ing the confidence we have in each other'? Was confidence 'in each other' so weak that he, as a renowned international evangelist, should spend his time preaching from public platforms to deepen it? And why should he want to make changes to the structure of Elim and *then* take a back seat. His proposal does look like an ultimatum; he would only withdraw once the self-supporting churches had been separated from the rest. But if he did this, how should the 1935 Conference decision restricting BI be applied? Did Jeffreys intend to hive off all the best churches to his new World Revival Crusade? And, if the self-supporting churches were in a separate organisation, would they continue financial support to the weaker churches? Surely not.

Without entering into argument and speculation Phillips simply made two objections to the proposal: first, it would involve extensive and expensive alterations to the Deed Poll; and, second, it would divide Elim into separate groupings that might, without any central governing authority, drift apart. More than this all the best and most effective pastors would be in the Jubilee churches and all the inexperienced and untried ministers would be in the other group who would hold the future of Elim. As for Jeffreys' desire to resign, the Executive Council was troubled: 'there is not the slightest doubt that it would be a real blow to the work'.[67]

In the pages of the *Evangel* the year ended with reports of Revival Party meetings in Guernsey and Camberwell and of the disastrous fire that reduced the Crystal Palace to a tangle of twisted metal girders; it has never been rebuilt.[68] In the Christmas edition Jeffreys spoke of his early days in Wales when 'the Baptism in the Holy Ghost with signs following separated me from friends and loved ones' and how 'hemmed in on every hand' he had felt 'utterly forsaken' until 'the Vision came ... I was called to attempt that which seemed impossible'.[69]

---

[67] Cartwright, *Evangelists*, p. 136.
[68] *Elim Evangel* 17.50 (11 Dec 1936), p. 794.
[69] *Elim Evangel* 17.51-52 (25 Dec 1936), p. 801.

1937

Although, in the afterglow of the celebrations for the 21st year of Elim's history, the evangelistic and healing campaigns continued, the most important events of the year took place out of public sight and behind the pages of the *Evangel* and concerned negotiations between Jeffreys and the Executive about the future complexion of the work. In essence he threatened to resign unless British Israel teaching could be introduced to the churches. There were nuances and qualifications to the twists and turns of the argument as letters passed backwards and forwards between Jeffreys and headquarters. As the fog cleared, the positions held by the two sides of the debate became visible. The Executive did not want Jeffreys to leave and Jeffreys did not want to stay if he could not preach BI.

A new element in the debate, however, became more prominent that year. Jeffreys insisted on, and later claimed divine revelation for, a revision to the governance of Elim. No longer should church buildings be owned by Elim but by the congregations whose offerings bought them. This dispute about governance permeated letters and ministerial conferences and eventually spilled out publicly. It seemed disconnected from teaching on BI but was not since, in locally governed churches, there was no ban on its preaching. If all Elim became locally governed, all Elim would be open to preaching on BI. So here lay an interpretive fault line and in the years to come the supporters of Jeffreys insisted that his position was nothing to do with BI doctrine and everything to do with his reforming zeal to democratise the ownership of church buildings. To his supporters, Elim was in bondage to an undemocratic centralised control; to others, Jeffreys had become obsessively distracted from his primary role as a supremely gifted evangelist.

Buckingham Palace held its own secrets. The Abdication crisis of 1936 had been concealed from the general public in a way that would not now be possible. The press had treated the Royal Family with kid gloves and suppressed any hint of scandal almost until Edward VIII's abdication broadcast. He explained he could not bear to live apart from the woman he loved; and, since she was ineligible to be his wife, he must give up the throne. She was a double divorcee and though Edward, before his marriage, had shown a concern for the unemployed miners of South Wales, Baldwin as

prime minister upheld conventional morality and was better at dealing with matters of this kind than he was at handling the economy.
Edward stepped down with the minimum of fuss and the new king,
George VI, his younger brother, was scandal-free and happily married with two young daughters, Elizabeth and Margaret, whose faces
adorned the front cover of the *Evangel* in January 1937. Whatever
Jeffreys and others thought about connections between the British
Royal Family and British Israel teaching on the house of David,
there was no denying that the new family were set to enjoy the nation's affections. An editorial said, 'We would have wished that it
had been otherwise … we must bow to that which has transpired,
recognising in it the permissive will of God … we pray for the new
king and his gracious Consort'.[70]

Meanwhile Elim members were urged, 'let us as a people devote
ourselves more desperately than ever to the work of revival. We can
render the nation no greater service than this'[71] and shortly afterwards there was an article on 'the coming world war'.[72] Jeffreys attended a Crusader rally in February 1937 only a month before the
letters page was opened up and laid bare the concerns of ordinary
Elim members in print for the first time. There were questions
about whether Christians should attend educational films and little
support for such an idea was given: the weight of opinion was
strongly separationist[73] and later there were questions about whether Christians should save money.[74] After all if cataclysmic world
events were shortly to take place, what use was a little money in the
bank? Correspondents wrote in to say that Christians should tithe
first and then save and if they had no children should make a will in
favour of Elim. Emphasis on tithing must have been part of the
drive to raise money and pay off mortgages on church buildings,
especially as further letters asserted the tithe was owed and must be
paid.[75]

---

[70] *Elim Evangel* 18.1 (1 Jan 1937), p. 10.
[71] *Elim Evangel* 18.2 (8 Jan 1937), p. 26.
[72] *Elim Evangel* 18.3 (15 Jan 1937), p. 33.
[73] *Elim Evangel* 18.11 (12 Mar 1937), p. 10.
[74] *Elim Evangel* 18.14 (2 Apr 1937), p. 222.
[75] *Elim Evangel* 18.20 (23 Apr 1937), p. 262.

A coronation number of the *Evangel* celebrated 'a momentous day in history' and Jeffreys' exulting article repeated 'God save the King' many times and connected the cry with the Old Testament words (1 Sam. 10.24) when the new king was revealed. Reference was made to the regalia of the British king kept in the Jerusalem chamber lined with cedar wood from Lebanon. The Coronation Oath made direct reference to Protestantism, 'I will, according to the true enactments which secure the Protestant Succession to the throne of my realm, uphold and maintain the said enactments to the best of my powers, according to the law'.[76] And Jeffreys asserted,

> The people over which British kings reign have been chiefly responsible for preaching the message of the Bible to the whole world. It is therefore fitting that the Bible should hold so prominent place in the Coronation service.

There was fervent patriotism here as well as an echo of Ulster Protestantism. In May photographs of Princess Elizabeth and Princess Margaret were again on the front cover of the *Evangel* in an issue devoted to the Sunday School and in the same issue held a strangely juxtaposed discussion of whether church would have to endure tribulation and 'the time of Jacob's trouble'.[77] Readers were assured that since the Feast of Trumpets preceded the Day of Atonement, the church would be rescued: the trumpets symbolised the rapture while atonement spoke of tribulation.

In June the Revival Party were at the Guildhall Southampton for 'two mighty meetings' and Jeffreys spoke again of the capture of Jerusalem in 1917. He can see no hope for the world until the return of Christ.[78] Letters discuss whether Christians should keep the Sabbath, another indication of the separationist strain. October contains a report on the fifth annual ministerial conference. Rumours of Jeffreys' possible resignation had leaked out:

> ... But it was not long before the Principal and the Executive Council were able to prove that these fears were unfounded.

---

[76] *Elim Evangel* 18.19 (7 May 1937), p. 302.
[77] *Elim Evangel* 18.22 (28 May 1937), p. 346.
[78] *Elim Evangel* 18.24 (11 June 1937), p. 369.

There had been for example a rumour that Principal Jeffreys would consider leaving the Elim movement to start another work and that for this reason he was seeking to be released from being President of the Executive Council ... Regarding another rumour, viz.: bringing in the teaching of British Israelism into the Elim movement, it was made perfectly plain at the conference that Principal Jeffreys never wanted to make the identity of the Anglo-Saxon peoples with Israel a plank of Elim's platform. The official attitude of the Direct Government section of the Elim movement to this teaching can be seen in the following Resolution passed at the Ministerial conference in 1935 ... Neither to propagate nor to attack it in any Direct Government Church.[79]

Articles drew attention to Fascist Italy and saw 'both Communism and Fascism, those two political ideas which today are making a bid for world supremacy, as mutually antagonistic to Christianity'.[80] Finally in his Christmas message Jeffreys issued 'a call to prayer and a call to sacrifice ... from the Principal to his people' but included a striking statement in the light of his later intransigence.[81] He wrote,

All who embraced the message were blended into one family, so that when one church building was acquired in one town, it belongs just as much to the other members of the family in another town.

Yet, having characterised the current system of mutual ownership as one where all church members owned all buildings, he continued with little elaboration,

In a growing Movement like ours, the time has come when people of each new place must provide their own home and all churches be self-supporting ... We have inaugurated an Elim Debt Clearance Fund.

Before such an appeal one might have expected the income and expenditure of the whole of Elim to have been fully aired in the Ex-

---

[79] *Elim Evangel* 18.42 (15 Oct 1937), p. 667.
[80] *Elim Evangel* 18.51 (17 Dec 1937), p. 810.
[81] *Elim Evangel* 18.52 (24 Dec 1937), p. 817.

ecutive Council before being discussed at the ministerial conference. Someone in these bodies would have surely wanted to consult the Building Societies to obtain their expert opinions. They provided the mortgages and had the most to lose in the event of defaults. Instead, and without the trigger of any obvious threat, the quest for fresh funds stemmed almost entirely from Jeffreys.

As we have said, the most formative exchanges of the year took place out of the public eye. Letters at the beginning of the year between Jeffreys and Phillips forced the clarification of plans for the World Revival Crusade. Jeffreys is evasive on key issues and the suspicion he is starting a rival to Elim appears well founded. When questions arise about the observance of the ban on BI – which is neither to be attacked nor defended and about which the churches are to remain neutral, a long letter from Jeffreys to Phillips asked what constitutes neutrality. Jeffreys attempted to show that neutrality is a contestable concept and exists only in the eye of the beholder. To this in February Phillips replies,

> We note your very embracive definition of neutrality, and I'm sure you must agree with us that it would be quite impracticable to adopt this in Elim. Furthermore we cannot believe for a moment that you would be prepared to bind yourself in this way.[82]

Phillips continued:

> With this hope of a solution to the problem shattered, it seems to us that you have left us only two alternatives, viz: that you cease to be leader of the Elim work, or that liberty on the subject of BI is given in all our churches.

> After very careful consideration, it is our considered opinion that either of these courses would split the work.

Here Phillips is officially communicating with Jeffreys as the movement's Secretary-General and speaking on behalf of the Executive Council.

On 23 February Jeffreys is writing to Phillips,

---

[82] EJP to GJ 23 Feb 1937.

I do not see the necessity to refer to BI again, except to say that your attitude to the subject does not change my decision to be released from the present leadership ...

A week later Jeffreys is saying that he is willing to continue as leader and to shoulder the debts once reform policy is agreed.[83]

Phillips replies starkly,

We have now been brought to this position. We are either to accept your resignation or to alter our policy on the question of BI. After careful consideration the Executive Council is not prepared to accept responsibility for deciding on either alternative – we are not prepared to accept your resignation, and we are not prepared to change the policy with regard to BI decided upon by the Ministerial Conference of October, 1935.[84]

The Executive ponders the resignation of Jeffreys. Perhaps this might be avoided by re-defining his job? Legal advice rules this out: the only way Jeffreys could resign the Presidency would be to resign from the Alliance. Similarly, he could not resign his right to appoint nominees to the Executive without resigning from the Alliance, 'for the insertion of this power in the constitution suggests that it is for the benefit of the Alliance'.[85]

These fundamental disagreements between colleagues are highly stressful and on 30 July 1937 E.J. Phillips' health gave way. He suffered from a lung condition (probably tuberculosis) that required convalescence for nine to twelve months.[86] Treatment in those days before antibiotics involved bed rest and a lengthy stay in a sanatorium. So, although he can read and occasionally dictate letters, Phillips misses meetings of the Executive Council and the Ministerial Conference. Jeffreys promptly moves into the office and takes up the duties of the Secretary-General, a decision that makes no sense if he is the chief fundraiser and he fundraises by preaching at large meetings. While he is in the office Jeffreys examines the accounts carefully and, with the finance department, adds up the total amount of money owing on all the buildings. At the end of Octo-

[83] GJ to EJP 1 Mar 1937.
[84] EJP to GJ 3 Mar 1937.
[85] Letter to EJP from Bulcraig & Davis, 4 Mar 1937.
[86] Cartwright, *Evangelists*, p. 141.

ber he reaches a figure of £44,818. He overlooks the value of Elim's assets – they amounted to over £200,000 – or the £4,000 owed on ministers' houses, which could be sold off in emergency.[87]

In 7 September Phillips, from his bed, dictated a letter to Boulton, Hathaway, Corry, Kingston, and Smith forewarning of the line Jeffreys will take at the forthcoming Conference: he will make a play on neutrality, on conscience, on being free to preach anything that is not contrary to the fundamentals, on the 'ban' on BI, for freedom to preach BI but not against.[88] In the 1934 Conference he was 'quite definite that BI should not be preached in our churches'.[89] The candour of the letter reveals the close team relationship between members of the Executive opposed to Jeffreys. They believe they know exactly what he is doing and want to block him. He will attempt to sway the Conference to open the way for BI teaching despite repeated decisions to the contrary after lengthy debates and formal voting.

Although the conference attempted to defuse the growing crisis – and it had to face the publication of James McWhirter's pro-BI book, *Britain and Palestine in Prophecy*, published by Methuen in August of that year – the movement was shocked to the core when Jeffreys himself collapsed just before Christmas. The medical cause of this was his diabetes.[90] He appears to have succumbed to a diabetic coma brought on by overwork and stress. Jeffreys was in hospital for about a month but the Movement was rallied by calls to prayer in telegrams to churches that brought with them an outpouring of genuine affection for him. With Phillips and Jeffreys ill, other Elim leaders steadied the movement as well as they could; but, in addition to all the internal worries, the tensions generated by mili-

---

[87] Cartwright, *Evangelists*, p. 142.

[88] EJP's letter of 7 Sept 1937 to Boulton, Hathaway, Corry, Kingston, and Smith: 'I would remind you that the Principal proposes to press for freedom to preach BI, but not to preach against. I need not comment on all this.'

[89] EJP's letter of 7 Sept 1937 to Boulton, Hathaway, Corry, Kingston, and Smith: 'The Principal denies that he has changed his policy. Please refer to the papers in my leather bag. You will find typed out four or five remarks by the Principal in the 1934 Conference. These were extracted by Miss Dalton from the verbatim report. He was quite definite then that BI should not be preached in our churches.'

[90] Edsor, *'Set Your House in Order'*, p. 23.

tary and para-military activity in Europe dampened optimism. Jeffreys was only able to return to work in April 1938.[91]

Reflection

The conflict between the Jeffreys and Phillips has been viewed as a classic sociological struggle between the charismatic leader and the desk-bound bureaucrat but that perception of events is inadequate.[92] Jeffreys was certainly a charismatic leader in the sense that he possessed preaching and healing *charismata* as well as faith to undertake enormous and risky ventures. He was also willing to immerse himself in the practicalities of finance, buildings, publicity, and constitutional legality. Phillips, by contrast, was gifted with a capacity to draft, read, and understand contracts, accounts and debating procedure as well as a thousand practical matters. More than this he was a capable preacher and debater as his performance in the 1934 conference showed. Each was charismatic in different ways and both wielded constitutionally conferred power. When the two men worked together they made a formidable team but when they disagreed it was another story. The correspondence shows they made a huge effort to maintain Christian affection for each other; and, though their letters sometimes became formal, they never lose civility. Undoubtedly Jeffreys spent more time and energy after 1934 on matters of governance than he had previously. Had he continued to preach in the second half of the 1930s with the same commanding authority and fervour he had demonstrated earlier, the great national revival he was hoping for might have come about. Yet, whenever Jeffreys is criticised for deviating from his evangelistic calling, there have been those who have run to his defence by arguing that he remained entirely faithful to his original vocation and that he was as great a preacher in the second part of his life as he was in his youth.[93]

As we have said, Jeffreys began to insist his true indictment of Elim concerned its form of government, and that British Israel

[91] Canty, *Unpublished*, p. 128.
[92] B.R. Wilson, *Sects and Society: A Sociological Study of Three Religious Groups in Britain* (London: Heinemann, 1961), p. 52.
[93] Edsor, *Set Your House*, is the best example.

doctrine was irrelevant to this. What is clear, and what the documentary evidence reveals, is that Jeffreys in the years from 1932 onwards made a number of contradictory statements about British Israel teaching and its place in Elim. Sometimes he agrees to mention it no more and to abide by the decision of the Conference and at other times he appears to forget his earlier statements. As a young man he had been completely dedicated to the Elim cause and careful to keep his word; and, because he did this, the team he worked with trusted him. In the 1930s this transparency began to cloud over though no one can say whether fluctuations in his insulin levels brought about by diabetes had any part to play in this. The final years of the 1930s play out the drama of Jeffreys' relationship with the Elim.

15

FALSE HOPES

Introduction

Neville Chamberlain was the Chancellor of the Exchequer of the National Government in the years from 1931 to 1937. The National Government had been elected to solve the social and economic problems confronting the United Kingdom following the 1926 General Strike and the financial crash of 1929. Unemployment and domestic hardship soared as huge industries came to a halt and thousands of working men were laid off. Shipyards stood idle and heavy industry contracted. The Labour Government was out of its depth and imposed financial stringency with little political imagination. In response to the crisis and after a General Election the politicians arranged themselves into a National Government with a Labour Prime Minister and a Conservative cabinet in an effort to combine the best of both political philosophies. Chamberlain as Chancellor of the Exchequer presided over finance; and, though he had an excellent track record as Lord Mayor of Britain's second city, Birmingham, his cast of mind appears to have been essentially administrative and his character self-righteous and prickly. He was reluctant to spend money on armaments and, when Germany began to agitate against the provisions of the Versailles Treaty, accepted the passive policy of appeasement initiated by the National Government. The treaty had made Germany liable to huge payments to the Allies, especially to the French, to cover the cost of the First World War. In a poisonous climate fomented by Nazi thugs, reparations were blamed for German unemployment and economic stagnation; anger, bitterness, and a sense of national humiliation fostered circumstances exploited by Hitler. He legitimately won an election in 1933 and became Chancellor. He then broke the terms of Versailles and began rearming Germany, a policy that quickly restored Teutonic pride by putting men back to work by creating jobs in armaments factories. Across the water in Britain, the National Government viewed these developments with concern but appeared to think the best way to avoid another war was to do nothing.

Appeasement involved giving Germany what Hitler demanded in the hope that, with each concession, he would be satisfied. In 1937, in violation of international law, he simply annexed the neighbouring independent country of Austria. By 9 July 1938 the British government was sufficiently alarmed to issue gas masks to its civilian population. Meanwhile German threats against smaller states grew, this time against Czechoslovakia. In response to the emergency, Chamberlain, now Prime Minister, flew to Munich at the end of September to meet Hitler. He and his adviser Horace Wilson were, in the words of the diarist Harold Nicolson, like 'two young curates entering a pub for the first time'; they were naïve and incapable of reading the situation.[1] They trusted they had reached a binding settlement by accepting the swallowing up of Czechoslovakia as the limit of Hitler's territorial ambitions; and, with Hitler's signature on a piece of white paper, Chamberlain returned home in triumph believing his diplomacy had secured peace.

> ... He read to the waiting crowds and newsreel cameras the famous document signed by Hitler that morning. When he reached the passage about the determination of 'our two peoples never to go to war with one another again', his voice was almost lost amidst the jubilant cheers. He then boarded the Royal car to be transported slowly through the ecstatic crowds to an official welcome ... At Buckingham Palace he acknowledged the acclamation of the assembled throng from the floodlit balcony flanked by his wife and the Royal couple ... he made his way to Downing Street. Despite the cold, damp and blustery conditions, the

---

[1] http://www.historytoday.com/reviews/neville-chamberlain#sthash.8ELT-SyvJ.dpuf (accessed 16 Apr 2016).

crowd shouted deliriously until he appeared at a first-floor window to proclaim that he had returned with 'peace for our time'.[2]

The *Evangel* like everyone else was won over and wrote in a glowing editorial,

> The whole world owes a lasting debt of gratitude to the British Premier for his undaunted and unprecedented efforts to save Europe from self-destruction. No one has made a more valuable contribution to the cause of peace than Mr Chamberlain. In the face of possible misunderstanding he launched upon his great adventure of salvation, determined to go to all possible lengths to avert war, and spare the world the horrors of international strife. Words cannot express our admiration of the man who has so nobly given himself the task of securing a peaceful solution to the problems which threatened to plunge the world into chaos.[3]

When the agreement was debated in the House of Commons two days later it was Churchill who punctured the facile optimism engendered by it.

> The German dictator, instead of snatching his victuals from the table, has been content to have them served to him course by course.[4]

First Austria and then Czechoslovakia had been consumed. More than this,

> I believe the Czechs, left to themselves and told they were going to get no help from the Western Powers, would have been able to make better terms than they got.[5]

The Times reported that Churchill had 'treated a crowded House [of Commons] to prophecies which made Jeremiah appear an op-

[2] Robert Self, *Neville Chamberlain: A Biography* (Aldershot: Ashgate, 2006), p. 1.
[3] *Elim Evangel* 19.41 (14 Oct 1938), p. 650.
[4] http://www.winstonchurchill.org/resources/speeches/231-1930-1938-the-wilderness/101-the-munich-agreement (accessed 18 Apr 2016).
[5] http://www.winstonchurchill.org/resources/speeches/231-1930-1938-the-wilderness/101-the-munich-agreement (accessed 18 Apr 2016).

timist' and referred patronisingly to his 'dismal sincerity'.[6] Yet within two months of these fraught scenes in Parliament the first kindertransport train bringing Jewish children from Berlin arrived in London. Within a year, war broke out between Britain and Germany and the British Empire, by which Jeffreys and Leech set so much store, received blows from which it never recovered.

1938

The year opened with Jeffreys in hospital and evidently in a serious condition. Less publicised was the condition of Phillips who was still out of action while convalescing slowly. So, between January and April, the leadership of Elim was depleted and inactive. An editorial announced,

> The Principal has for some time been wholeheartedly desirous of a great move forward and was, with the Executive Council, planning definitely for this, but the strain which he has undergone has prevented him at present putting this into effect … The Principal appreciates very much the letters and telegrams of sympathy and enquiry which have come from all quarters during this time of test, and for the response already made to his appeal to all who have been blessed under his ministry to share the financial burden.

Heavy use of Christian biographies filled the *Evangel* which had little to report in the way of evangelistic campaigns – although a brief mention of Percy Brewster's meetings at Eastbourne was made.[7] In January a sympathetic editorial spoke about the 'burden of making suitable provision for the ever-increasing number of converts who have been won for Christ' and in February 'readers will be glad to know the Principal is making steady progress towards recovering, and prayer is being answered on his behalf'. And by the end of the month an editorial announced, 'We are believing that this year's meetings at the Royal Albert Hall will once again bring

---

[6] William Manchester, *The Last Lion: Winston Spencer Churchill: Alone, 1932–1940* (Boston: Little, Brown and Company, 1982). [taken from Google books and without page numbers].

[7] *Elim Evangel* 19.6 (11 Feb 1938), p. 93.

together a vast crowd of the Lord's people to participate in this pageant of Pentecostal power and Glory'. The Executive Council must have asked themselves whether to book the Royal Albert Hall or to cancel meetings for that year. Meanwhile by March 'gifts to the Elim Debt Fund continue to come in from churches and from individuals' and at the end of March a double page article on tithing continued to press the financial theme. By now James McWhirter was also ill and readers were informed that he had been advised to take a long sea voyage and so was planning to travel with his wife to Australia. McWhirter was a highly competent organiser who served with the Revival Party and his absence was felt later in the year.

There was a Foursquare demonstration in Birmingham on 9 March. Jeffreys was well enough to come onto the platform of the afternoon service although others preached. In April an editorial drew attention to Russian show trials and a suspicion that the confessions of prisoners were extracted by torture, which implied the communist state was 'governed by torturers'. In the same issue the Elim Publishing Company was reported to have paid a dividend of 6.25% and 20 probationers were accepted as ministers and set aside for ordination at Easter in the Royal Albert Hall. And then, by the middle of the month, two conventions were announced in London with services to be 'conducted by Principal George Jeffreys'. It appeared that the worst was over for Jeffreys and that his health and strength were returning. There was a round-up of news from the churches and crowds in Birmingham where Jeffreys and the Revival Party ministered before they opened a building in Croydon.[8] The end of April carried the first article of the year by Jeffreys and entitled 'God answers prayer'. He wrote,

> The wave of prayer that swept over our churches in response to the SOS call to intercession in the form of those telegrams sent forth on New Year's Day, brought me back from the gates of death,[9] and here I am, feeling as fit as ever, penning these lines for the *Elim Evangel*. The threatened financial crisis with its ap-

[8] *Elim Evangel* 19.15 (15 Apr 1938), p. 238.
[9] Cartwright, *Evangelists*, p. 143, reports Robert Darragh and Albert Edsor (at some time in mid-January?) were wakened by a policeman and called to Jeffreys' hospital bedside at 6 am after his condition worsened.

parently inevitable upheaval which brought about my physical breakdown has been miraculously averted.[10]

No doubt these words were sincerely written but there is an element of myth-making about them: Jeffreys had collapsed as a result of the heavy financial burden but was raised up by the faithful prayers of God's people. The implied moral is that if God's people wish to keep Jeffreys physically fit they must lighten the financial burden by giving even more generously than before. There is no mention here of diabetes or of medical opinion. Financial demands rather than disharmony at the ministerial conferences have brought Jeffreys to the point of death and nothing is said about the 21 years of ceaseless travel or the lack of proper rest. Nothing is said, either, about prayer for the healing of Phillips or McWhirter.

Jeffreys then goes on to speak well of the newly elected Executive Council which, presumably, met without Phillips since he was still ill. 'Personally, I feel the right men are in the right place' and he went on to commend them in the confidence that they will 'wholeheartedly engage in the necessary reforms of the work'.[11] He writes about this some nine years later, and the passage needs to be quoted in full.[12]

> Then came the sudden illness of the Secretary-General followed closely by mine, and I believe that under the circumstances it had to be, in order to bring about the opportunity for an exacting examination of ourselves and the rapidly growing organisation.
>
> In my illness I had an experience which revealed the things I would have to suffer in the oncoming struggle to free the churches from the legal system that bound them and which had made it impossible for them to obey the word of God. There was the cunning misrepresentation, the half-truth propaganda, and the delusive reasonings of those who would seek to undermine my influence and even try to blot out my name as founder and builder of Elim. The dangers of the system were many, and what I saw made me determined, regardless of cost, to reform it

---

[10] *Elim Evangel* 19.17 (29 Apr 1938), p. ?.

[11] *Elim Evangel* 19.17 (29 Apr 1938), p. 267.

[12] It was written in about 1947 since it continues 'Nine years have passed …'. See Brooks, *Fight for Faith and Freedom* (Kindle edn, 1950), loc 563.

or to renounce it and to deliver as many churches as possible from its Babylonish bondage.

To fully explain the experience I had would be difficult; all I can say is, 'whether in the body or out of the body I cannot tell'. It seemed as if the Elim organisation was judged before the bar of God and condemned. That experience showed me how very wrong it was to be a leading governor in a legal clique of clerical governors over Elim pastors, people and property. I was only too glad to get back to the Bible for church government, in which there were no legal central governors![13]

In the same passage he continued,

Within the secret constitutional walls of the Elim Executive Council, the governing body, I also heard the command, 'Set your house in order', and regardless of consequences, my one desire was to live to reform the movement. God, I believe, raised me up from the gates of death to witness against all such systems, and to warn students, pastors and churches of their subtle dangers.

The phrase 'whether in the body or out of the body I cannot tell' comes from 2 Cor. 12.3 and is used by the apostle Paul speaking of a mystical revelation he received. He is taken up into the 'third heaven' and Jeffreys felt himself lifted up in a similarly mysterious way to receive a revelation that Elim was under the judgement of God. This revelation contradicts the joyfulness of the Coming of Age presentations given only a couple of years before.[14] There was no hint then that Elim was somehow under judgement because its constitutional arrangements were so wicked.

The other text that spoke to Jeffreys told him to set his house in order, a command given to Hezekiah (Isa. 38.1) and referring to the making of will and other preparations for death. Here Jeffreys re-

---

[13] I am assuming this experience occurred in 1938 as it is recorded as having taken place when both Jeffreys and Phillips were ill at the same time. Other writers (e.g. Hudson) have dated it in 1937 and it may be there were two spiritual experiences, one in each year because of the separate reference to the 'Set your house in order' occasion.

[14] His Christmas letters in the *Evangel* are infused with thankfulness to God and the 'Elim family'.

ceived the text in a way understood by Pentecostals and others who believe God speaks to them through the Bible with meanings beyond its original context. Setting his house in order is interpreted by Jeffreys as a divine requirement for constitutional change and he says here he received this command 'within the secret constitutional walls' of the Executive Council.

The judgement of private revelations in Pentecostal churches is normal, though easier in theory than in practice. There are clear instructions about the weighing or testing of charismatic gifts in the first Corinthian epistle.[15] There is also a reference to 'testing' prophecy in Thessalonians.[16] Biblical principles, regardless of individual circumstances, call for the evaluation of spiritual gifts by more than one person and yet, without searching hard, exceptions to this rule can be found. Paul receives a vision of a Macedonian man and gathers that he must go with his companion across the sea to Greece.[17] Jeffreys was a sufficiently mature Pentecostal to understand the principles as well as the exceptions. One might have expected him to submit his revelation to other members of the Executive Council asking them to weigh it. But this was not Jeffreys' way and he had been in command of Elim for a long time and acknowledged as the pre-eminent leader. Phillips questioned his judgement on practical matters; but, if Jeffreys insisted on a course of action, Phillips would give way.

The revelation had the effect of preventing Jeffreys from backing down. He insisted that he had no choice and that he must reform Elim come what may. The debate is lifted above normal reasoning and argumentation to an entirely different plane when one person among a conference of ministers or an Executive Council believes he has received a private and irresistible divine command. Regardless of the damaging consequences to himself or others, Jeffreys felt obliged to press for reform.

Jeffreys wrote the account of his divine revelation years after the events described. He embeds his recollections within the drive to reform a system of 'Babylonish' control but makes no reference here to finance or debt. Perhaps putting his house in order included

---

[15] 1 Corinthians 14.29.
[16] 1 Thessalonians 5.20.
[17] Acts 16.9.

the settling of all debt. In any event, there is a lack of clarity here about what the divine revelation required and no explanation of why Elim should be judged so harshly when, in a string of his Christmas messages in the *Evangel*, Jeffreys had been so thankful for what had been achieved and so grateful to all the Elim staff who had helped him. There is no single incident that switches the light off and turns the brightness of blessing into dark anxiety about divine judgement. The sudden reversal of direction follows a series of decisions Jeffreys himself had made dating right back to the earliest Elim constitutional documents. At no point had other people foisted on Jeffreys or Elim a system of governance they had unwillingly received. Even the Deed Poll, whose validity Jeffreys later questioned, was willingly signed by him and endorsed as a legal enactment that would guarantee the continued existence of Elim in the event of the deaths of key personnel.

What we can say is that Jeffreys emerged from his three or four months of severe illness (though he had diabetes for the rest of his life) with a determination to reform Elim and pay down the debt on buildings. In the *Evangel* for the 29 April 1938 he highlighted the debt and, at first, confined plans for reform to the Executive Council or the Ministerial Conference. He told readers that £6,500 had been given in six months and the debt was now reduced to £37,500 while also noting what had not been noted before – that Elim held property to the value of about £200,000. He then sought to show the revival party was living modestly so as to assist the debt-reduction program.

> It is not generally known that no member of the revival party receives a salary from the headquarters central fund; each works under the 'World Revival Crusade' which is entirely supported by the free-will offerings that are given definitely to its own funds by God's people. From the very commencement of the year each member of the revival party was determined to live on a minimum allowance in order to allow as much as possible to go towards extinction of the Elim debt. When I say that in addition to board and lodging, the total allowance amounted to £325 for the year, our readers will readily understand that this sum between five men [meant] living on a minimum. But the Revival party were more than compensated by the fact that through

prayer and works they contributed substantially towards the reduction of the debt of Elim.[18]

He also gave a clue about why he felt the Elim financial position
was so burdensome. 'During the last year deficits paid to non-self-
supporting churches amounted to almost £3,000', which in plain
language means pastoral salaries in churches unable to support their
pastors received a top-up from the headquarters fund.[19] It was this
constant need to supply the shortfall in pastoral salaries that Jeffreys
found irksome and adds a further line of explanation about the fu-
rore he was creating over debt. Once mortgages were paid off, congregations would find it simple to pay their pastors and he and the
surplus-generating congregations would be free of financial obliga-
tions to them. So long as pastoral salaries were set by headquarters,
the weaker pastors were being carried by the others and by contributions made to central funds by Jeffreys. If there had been no central salary scale and no financial support for them, the weaker pastors would have been starved out of their pulpits or become part-
time ministers – a position familiar to numerous struggling nonconformist congregations. So, even though the World Revival Crusade
insulated Jeffreys from financial flows inside Elim, he still wanted
the weaker churches to succeed.

The Easter meetings at the Royal Albert Hall were carried off
triumphantly. Jeffreys preached three times and a youth choir of
1,250 sang at each service. Whatever the ongoing effects of diabetes on Jeffreys, the *Evangel* was able to report healings of 27 cripples
and 10 blind people as well as 25 cured of cancer.[20] Despite these
public demonstrations of Jeffreys' prowess and his return to public
life, he contributed an editorial pursuing his financial theme. 'For
some years I have been deeply concerned about subsidising non-
supporting churches' but as a result of all the money so generously

---

[18] The information in this paragraph was no doubt strictly true even if misleading. We do know Albert Edsor had been awarded a salary (see GJ to EJP 19
Mar 1936). If it was not paid from the headquarters fund, it must have been paid
from World Revival Crusade offerings or from the pooled money generated by
Glasgow, Kensington Temple, Blackpool, and Brighton congregations and available to the trustees of these buildings who happened to be members of the Revival Party. (*Elim Evangel* 19.17 [29 April 1938], p. 267).
[19] *Elim Evangel* 19.17 (29 Apr 1938), p. 267.
[20] *Elim Evangel* 19.18 (6 May 1938), p. 282.

given 'non-supporting churches have become self-supporting'.[21] He wanted to place responsibility for pastoral salaries squarely on each congregation, a laudable aim that would coincidentally make it easier for congregations to cut the umbilical cord linking them to headquarters and through which they were accustomed to receive financial nourishment.

By June Jeffreys was able to report that £13,646 had been cleared from the debt since October 1937[22] and a note advertised the annual Ministerial Conference for 12-16 September. In July Jeffreys was in Colwyn Bay in North Wales campaigning with his big tent and by the end of the month 400 converts were gained. Seventy Crusaders from Northern Ireland came over to sing, healings occurred, and by August the number of converts had risen to 550.[23] Despite this evidence that Jeffreys' campaigning zeal was unimpaired and his ability to stir whole communities remained intact, no Elim church was established in Colwyn Bay. We do not know why this was so but the lack of McWhirter's organisational ability or the absence of any help from Phillips on the buying of buildings would have told. Alternatively, Jeffreys may have wished to avoid taking out a mortgage on a new building if the converts were unable to raise enough money for its outright purchase. And then, by September, there was a report of an outpouring of the Spirit in Portsmouth and 450 conversions and a further article by Jeffreys showing that the balance of the debt was now down to £25,141. He also said, 'After due consideration the Executive has approved the scheme whereby a portion of the debt will be charged to a House Property Fund, having its own income and assets'.[24] This was probably at the insistence of Phillips who, throughout Jeffreys' financial appeals, had been stung by the implication that his handling of Elim finances was incompetent.[25] It was Phillips who was able to point out that over £4,000 was owed on ministerial houses rather than church buildings. The words 'the Executive has approved the scheme ... House Property Fund' disguises the fact that actually the

---

[21] *Elim Evangel* 19.18 (6 May 1938), p. 282.
[22] *Elim Evangel* 19.23 (10 June 1938), p. 379.
[23] *Elim Evangel* 19.32 (5 Aug 1938), p. 488.
[24] *Elim Evangel* 19.35 (2 Sept 1938), p. 555.
[25] EJP to GJ, 29 June 1938.

debt on church properties was £4,000 lower than Jeffreys had been claiming.

Again, almost certainly because Phillips was now back in action, clarifications were made. 'The Executive, together with myself, wish to make it perfectly clear that none of the debts were incurred by paying deficits to churches. The debts were all incurred in acquiring properties for the work.'[26] In other words, the debts were exactly related to property and not related to pastoral salaries which is what 'paying deficits to churches' must imply. By 9 September 660 conversions in Portsmouth were reported before Jeffreys and his party went on to London's Westminster Central Hall, now the regular autumn venue in the absence of the Crystal Palace. At the end of the month the *Evangel* carried a photograph with the caption 'World Crusade Meeting at Westminster Central Hall' which was an unusual title given that this was an Elim meeting.[27] The growing prominence of the Word Crusade organisation is signalled. But what of the 1938 ministerial conference which, unlike conferences in previous years, is not reported at all in the *Evangel*?

The 1938 Conference

Jeffreys wrote to the members of the Executive Council on 1 August 1938 asking them to consider several items before he arrived. First, he was keen that any unintended criticism of Phillips conveyed by his article of April 29 should be removed. His tone is gracious and humble. He is prepared to halt his appeal for money while rectification is made. Second, he is concerned about the Irish work since, when debts were pooled, the 'book-debts' were wiped out. So 'it is most essential that the Executive states definitely what proportion of the actual debt is now charged against the Irish work'. Third, Blackpool Temple: 'here it would be well for the Executive to decide what proportion of the debt should be charged against Mr Tweed, seeing that all debts have been pooled' (Tweed was the sole trustee of Blackpool Temple).

The last two items deal with proposed changes to the constitution of Elim. Would the Executive recommend the conference should:

---

[26] *Elim Evangel* 19.35 (2 Sept 1938), p. 555.
[27] *Elim Evangel* 19.38 (23 Sept 1938), p. 597.

(a) bring all qualified ministers into the conference under Direct Government?

(b) develop the Foursquare Gospel churches with its groups under an all-inclusive presbytery?

If (a) I would like to know exactly what are the essential qualifications for membership of the ministerial conference.

He went on to say that this has to do with his recommendation for the future. He wanted to know whether 'the Elim Foursquare Gospel Alliance is to be a group in the all-inclusive body, or to be the all-inclusive body itself?'[28]

Hudson points out that 'both schemes were in fact directed to the same end, that is to create a larger single body which would be identified as the Elim church' and he goes on to explain,

the basic difference between the two schemes was whether the existing Direct Government scheme was to be enlarged, or whether that could be dismantled and all the churches be administered on a new, equal footing.[29]

If the scheme (a) were to be operated successfully then the Direct Government ministers needed to be willing to share the rights they already enjoyed with another, equally large, group of ministers. In Hudson's words,

These rights included a share in any gifts to the movement, eligibility for the opportunity to propagate their work in the *Elim Evangel*, a right to determine the nature of the future training of ministers and the right to change pastorates with those in larger churches. In return, the General Conference ministers would have to commit themselves to be governed by the Executive Council.[30]

However, scheme (b) had advantages since 'the Direct Government conference would not run the risk of being weakened' and more than this the 'newly enfranchised groups would not be disappointed

---

[28] The quotations and information here come from Jeffreys' letter of 1 Aug 1938 to the Executive Council.

[29] Hudson, *Schism*, p. 253.

[30] Hudson, *Schism*, p. 253.

if they discovered that the Executive Council's interest was mainly directed to the Direct Government churches because of their existing relationships'.

Key to both schemes, however, was the enfranchising of the lay representatives. Attendance (and perhaps membership) of the Ministerial Conference would be widened to include lay participation and Jeffreys considered himself to be 'in honour bound to consider the welfare of both ministers and people in the changes that are being proposed for the future of Elim'.[31] Moreover, early in August Jeffreys had written round to all ministers explaining his desire for constitutional change including his desire for lay representation.[32]

Jeffreys obviously prefers option (b), the one that dismantles the category of Direct Government churches as it was then legally defined. So this option has the effect of rendering void the 1934 Conference decision forbidding the propagation of BI in Direct Government churches. There will be no more Direct Government churches since all the churches would now to be brought together into a new body that for the first time includes lay representation. In Hudson's words, 'all the churches [would] be administered on a new, equal footing'.[33]

The Conference met and 'it was evident that as a result of the statement being read, there was a desire that the Ministerial Conference should have more power'. Yet, the following day, the mood changed when 'Phillips pointed out that there were many practical areas over which the Conference could not have authority, i.e. the acceptance of new churches, property deeds, Elim Trust Corporation business and the operation of the model trust deed'. At this point the proposal was changed 'whereby instead of the Ministerial Conference becoming the governing body, the Executive Council would delegate certain powers which would be mutually decided upon'.[34]

---

[31] GJ to Executive Council, 1 Aug 1938.

[32] Letter entitled 'To members of the Ministerial Conference' and with a pencilled date of 1 Aug 1938.

[33] Hudson, *Schism*, p. 253.

[34] Hudson, *Schism*, p. 254. He is quoting *Conference Minutes* (12 and 13 Sept 1938).

Jeffreys objected so strongly to this turn of events that he 'read the Conference an ultimatum stating that the Conference must introduce a new legislative body with the lay representation or else he would have no alternative but to resign in six months' time'. More than this he would 'go to the churches on this issue and tell them why he had resigned'. The Conference, now tense, took a vote 'to indicate whether people believed that there was a strong demand for lay representation'. In the event only eight were in favour, and four of these were from Ireland. Nevertheless, the following morning 'Jeffreys presented his own proposal that the Ministerial Conference should include lay representation and become the supreme legislative body'. The conference debated but voted 'no'. The very people who had followed him so respectfully had defeated Jeffreys, the charismatic leader. The next morning Jeffreys withdrew his threat to resign if lay representation was not introduced.

The Conference had stood its ground and refused to bend to Jeffreys' demands even when he employed the nuclear option of threatening resignation. Jeffreys did not expect to be denied. He had ordained many of the ministers at the conference and they deeply respected him and many loved him. However, 'by their voting they chose to stand with Phillips and his declared opposition against lay representation which he believed would cause trouble for the ministers'.[35]

The switchback ride at Conference left everyone shaken and uncertain of the future direction of the Movement. A month later Jeffreys suggested, 'relationships between those on the Executive Council had become so strained that it was imperative that the problems be resolved'.[36] Presumably the Executive was split between a pro-Jeffreys faction made up of his own nominees and the rest. Phillips welcomed the prospect of a 'real spiritual meeting' to resolve their differences provided nothing that was said would later be repeated outside.[37] The meeting took place and the attempted Christian conciliation may have prevented personal animosity but did nothing to create unanimity. Letters from Jeffreys explaining what he wanted were circulated to the churches and so Phillips cir-

---

[35] Hudson, *Schism,* p. 256.
[36] GJ to EJP 9 Nov 1938 from Hudson, *Schism,* p. 256.
[37] EJP to GJ 11 Nov 1938.

culated replies. By now disagreement had spilled over from the Executive to the Conference and from the Conference to the churches. It was impossible to pretend all was well.

As if Elim needed reminding of what it would lose if Jeffreys resigned, he visited Nottingham at the end of the year and recorded 800 converts; there was no one else in the country who could have done this.[38]

Reflection

The international events reported in the national press were correctly read by Elim leaders as pointing to an inevitable war. In this they were assisted by their eschatological expectations. What they did not foresee was the sudden collapse of Jeffreys and the long slow illness that debilitated Phillips. Jeffreys presumably was glad to climb into the driver's seat in the office and to examine the accounts and then to place his own construction on them to the effect that there was a huge crisis facing the Movement, a crisis that required dramatic action and implied gross miscalculations by the headquarters staff and particularly Phillips.

This is not to say that Jeffreys *pretended* to be alarmed by the figures but it does seem he was unable to understand how and why mortgages work. Nor, given his repeated insistence on preaching about the second coming of Christ, is it easy to appreciate why mortgage repayments were so urgent. If he believed an impeding period of biblical tribulation would disadvantage Christians in debt, he never said so publicly. His behaviour is consistent with a desire to break up Elim and to take as many churches as he could into a new denomination. His behaviour is also consistent with a generalised anxiety without any grand plan in mind, especially if he was given contradictory advice by Leech on one side and the Revival Party on the other.[39]

The interpretation of his actions is divergent: at least two men wrote at length arguing Jeffreys' paramount concern was for consti-

---

[38] Cartwright, *Evangelists*, p. 147.
[39] We have no record of correspondence between Leech and Jeffreys or of advice given by the Revival Party. We do know Jeffreys continued to keep in touch with Leech who was an astute constitutional manoeuverer.

tutional reform along democratic lines, and everything else being incidental to this.[40] Others see Jeffreys using every stratagem to weaken the structure of Elim in order to prise free churches he could later fill with BI teaching. What is clear is that the later denunciations of the Elim governmental system by Jeffreys ignored the democratic process at the Conference. His claim that the Executive Council held all property in its grasp through the exercise of a tyrannical dictatorship failed to acknowledge the role of the annual Ministerial Conference and the voting that took place there on an entirely reasonable basis; and on this basis Jeffreys found his proposals defeated. It is true that the Executive Council drew up the agenda but the process of debate and voting was a model of democratic polity. A fair hearing was given to those who held contrasting views, accounts were presented, minutes taken, and prayer and worship were part of the proceedings. The question of lay leadership that Jeffreys raised to the top of the agenda, and which seemed to have been resolved, was to recur compellingly the following year.

---

[40] Albert Edsor and Noel Brooks.

16

1939: RELUCTANTLY AT WAR

Introduction

Throughout the year the international situation worsened. The accession of Phillips to the editorship of the *Evangel* brought a greater realism and engagement with the public events than was the case under Boulton. 'This old world is in the throes of a great agony just as God has foretold'.[1] Although Chamberlain had promised peace, his words appeared increasingly delusory. Britain was to find itself at war in September, less than 12 months after Chamberlain's paperwaving return from Munich. For the first nine months of the year an uneasy peace held.

Mixed Signals

Jeffreys baptised candidates in Wimbledon early in the year and, after the death of Pastor Newsham in a car accident, wrote appreciatively of him and spoke at the funeral.[2] He took the Revival Party up to Carlisle and the local newspaper reported 1,500 people gathered on two Sundays and 500 nightly.[3] There was also news of revival fire in Sheffield with Percy Brewster and 280 converts at Hull with John Woodhead.[4] Presumably because he knew the writing was on the wall, Phillips was determined to publicise other evangelists

---

[1] *Elim Evangel* 20.1 (6 Jan 1939), p. 5.
[2] *Elim Evangel* 20.5 (3 Feb 1939), p. 65.
[3] *Elim Evangel* 20.8 (24 Feb 1939), p. 116.
[4] *Elim Evangel* 20.8 (24 Feb 1939), p. 122.

than Jeffreys. In Germany the imprisonment of Pastor Niemoeller prompted an exposure of Nazi hypocrisy: 'when necessary, Herr Hitler can talk about his fervent desire for peace ... Yet if a minister because of his religious belief prays for peace, it is a misuse of the pulpit, and an offence against the State'.[5] Further, mean-spirited persecution of the Jews continued: 'In Mainz the town council for the last two years cut gas and electricity from Jewish houses'.[6] Against this deteriorating situation a report of Jeffreys in Carlisle revealed what he was preaching,

> Principal Jeffreys made a special appeal for all churches to unite in a spiritual revival, which, he said, would turn back the sorrows of war, just as the revival under the Wesleys turned back the tide of revolution in their day.[7]

Two hundred converts were registered in Carlisle although Brewster saw 450 decisions in Sheffield.[8] For the first time there were bigger headlines and great results from an evangelist other than Jeffreys reported in the *Evangel*. Meanwhile Jeffreys announced a cumulative total of £21,274 had been received and the outstanding balance in the debt fund was down to £18,626.[9] Small amounts came with notes from the faithful poor showing how the appeal made by Jeffreys reached into the hearts of the old and impoverished. And then, in March, an editorial reported, 'Under the threat of superior force, Prague yielded to Germany, and Czechoslovakia is no more' and the exclamation 'surely the significance of world events should drive us to our knees for the victims of inhuman outrage' – words that must have come from Phillips' heart.[10] In April the Royal Albert Hall meetings passed successfully and then Jeffreys preached in Birmingham before it was reported that on Good Friday 'on the day when Christians universally commemorate the crucifixion of our Lord, and without any previous warning, Italy invaded Albania'.[11]

---

[5] *Elim Evangel* 20.9 (3 Mar 1939), p. 130.
[6] *Elim Evangel* 20.9 (3 Mar 1939), p. 136.
[7] *Elim Evangel* 20.11 (17 Mar 1939), p. 161.
[8] *Elim Evangel* 20.11 (17 Mar 1939), p. 171.
[9] *Elim Evangel* 20.12 (24 Mar 1939), p. 187.
[10] *Elim Evangel* 20.13 (31 Mar 1939), p. 202.
[11] *Elim Evangel* 20.16 (21 Apr 1939), p. 250.

If the hearts of ordinary people were not 'failing them for fear', there was an underlying anxiety across the land. The *Evangel* published an article on 'why I am a pre-millennialist' that spoke of the rapture of the church before the millennium while an editorial repeated the 1935 conference resolution favouring pacifism, and it did so despite objections from Jeffreys, who wanted the whole matter discussed by the Executive.[12] Phillips went ahead and published this pacifist statement anyway:

> The General Conference of the Elim Foursquare Gospel Alliance … believes the church of Jesus Christ is called out from the world to preach the gospel of salvation and peace to all men [is] based on spiritual principles which are incompatible with the Christian's participation in war.[13]

A kind of theological fatalism infected some believers and an editorial found it strange that such people refused to pray for peace because tribulations and war are foretold.[14] An article on the rapture of the saints was printed and a leaflet campaign begun encouraging believers to evangelise with tracts.[15] Whatever else might be said about them at this point in their history, Jeffreys and the Executive Council could not be accused of fatalism: they plunged into frantic literary activity.

Jeffreys spent July and August in a tent crusade in Worthing on the south coast. The conference was due to start in September. Before this the Executive Council had given Jeffreys permission to circulate his ideas for changes to Elim's system of government to the Movement. He printed a seven-page paper and posted this out to 100 ministers. He included in the envelope a list of questions to find out what changes they wanted and he asked them to reply personally to him. The Executive Council did not see these papers before he sent them out and on the same day (11 July, 1939) the

---

[12] *Elim Evangel* 20.16 (21 Apr 1939), p. 250. Cartwright, *Evangelists*, pp. 148, 149. Cartwright suggests Phillips wanted to help any Elim conscientious objectors brought before tribunals. The tribunals accepted religious people whose denominations officially took a pacifist position.

[13] *Elim Evangel* 20.13 (31 Mar 1939), p. 193; *Elim Evangel* 20.19 (12 May 1939), p. 298.

[14] *Elim Evangel* 20.26 (30 June 1939), p. 410.

[15] *Elim Evangel* 20.15 (14 Apr 1939), p. 235.

Council sent out their own proposals. By the end of July, half the ministers had replied to Jeffreys and he then followed up with a further paper which the members of the Executive Council regretted because it contained inaccurate statements. When this happened Jeffreys immediately wrote another letter to the ministers and this evoked a reply from the Executive on 15 August. The Executive were still reluctant to conduct business through an attritional war of public correspondence and said so, but this only resulted in further circulars. Jeffreys went so far as to publish selected minutes of the Executive Council meeting of 22 May. This meeting agreed that he should send out a list of his proposals to the ministers; it also agreed that he should show them a draft of these proposals before sending them out, and this he did not do.[16]

The European Conference in Stockholm

While Hitler blitzkrieged countries adjacent to Germany, persecuted Jews, formed an alliance with the fascist Mussolini, and engaged in outrageous propaganda, the Scandinavian countries of northern Europe stood on the sidelines. They had been neutral in the First World War and soon after the Reformation had embraced a Lutheran form of Protestantism. Baptists and Methodists were welcome there and the original 20th century Pentecostal outpouring of the Holy Spirit had started in Norway through the ministry of T.B. Barratt. The Swedish Pentecostal movement was led by Lewi Pethrus, originally a Baptist, whose aversion to denominational organisation was absolute. He was pastor of a huge congregation in Stockholm – the largest in the world at the time – and, at the suggestion of Donald Gee, a leading light in British Pentecostalism who served with Assemblies of God, called a European conference.

Unlike British Pentecostal conferences, there was no voting or decision-making. Instead, the conference considered a series of questions on which speakers could share their opinions. Everyone could learn and consensus might gradually shift one way or another. The conference ran from 7 to 12 September with consideration of the set questions during the day and big public evening meetings. Approximately 15,000 people attended including members of the Swedish Royal family and Jeffreys was asked to preach each night in

---

[16] See Cartwright, *Evangelists*, pp. 151, 152.

the big tent, something he did with distinction. Over 70 delegates
from Britain came and a photograph of the gathering shows Jeffreys sitting next to Howard Carter with other Elim and Assemblies
of God leaders in the line-up. Gee reported:

> On the night of Monday, June 12th, the great conference
> reached its climax with a Communion Service in the tent in
> which 8,000 believers participated, each of them in some way
> connected with the Pentecostal movement, and gathered from
> every corner of Europe. It was an unforgettable occasion, and
> provided a sacred memory for the dark years that lay ahead ...
> On that Northern summer night those baptised by one Spirit in-
> to one body tasted for a few brief hours the unassailable serenity
> of the great company which no man can number to have found
> eternal peace through the blood of His Cross.[17]

The sermons and speeches of contributors were transcribed and
eventually printed in Swedish in *Europeiska Pingstkonferensen in Stockholm, den 5-12 Juni 1939*. Jeffreys was impressed by the shape of
Swedish Pentecostalism and later came to see it as an ideal. His
analysis of church government, away from the backdrop of British
Pentecostalism, reveals his ability to appreciate the advantages of
differing systems. The Assemblies of God was more loosely organised than Elim and gave each congregation autonomy while making
collective decisions at its own conference. Jeffreys could see the
benefits of this system while also partially defending the central
government of Elim. He quoted a text and elaborated,

> 'For first of all, when ye come together in the church, I hear that
> there be divisions among you; and I partly believe it'. 1 Cor 11:18

> Note the word: 'For there must be factions among you.' In the
> English Bible we have the word 'heresy', but a well-known au-
> thority in the case of the New Testament Greek original text
> gives a completely different interpretation of the original, which
> means that there must be 'differences of opinion' in the gather-
> ing. For me personally, I am convinced that as long as we live on
> this earth, there will be differences of opinion among us con-

[17] Gee, *Wind and Flame*, p. 177.

cerning the truths that are not fundamental, but I also believe that God can give us so much of Christian mercy, that we have respect for each other's beliefs. No two men are created exactly alike. Some people have a legalistic or rational orientation, while others are of an emotional type; however, both can be used by God.

He continued,

There must be room for different opinions in a Christian church development, and the one who is loving enough to respect his brother's views on non-essential things.

His willingness to entertain a variety of opinions is praiseworthy and unforced. Strangely, only a few years later, he seems to have forgotten all this. At the time he characterised the two main Pentecostal systems prevalent in Britain and affirmed both had been blessed by God. There was no single definitive organisational system to which Pentecostals were obliged to submit. On the contrary, the systems may be 'more a matter of method than a matter of principle'. He is clear on these points:

Let us now look at the differences that appear to exist among Pentecost directions in England. The two most important things are the doctrine and organization, and these issues are also those that concern our brothers in other countries. Therefore, I would like to say to our British brethren, that we need to regulate these conditions in their home country, if we shall be able to be of help to our foreign brethren …

When we come to the question of organization, so there is a difference between the two movements in Britain. 'Elim Foursquare Gospel Alliance' has a highly centralized executive, while the 'Assemblies of God' takes a decentralised confederation … God has blessed both camps … Is it possible that our troubles are more a matter of method than a matter of principle?[18]

At the end of his speech Jeffreys held out a hope for Pentecostal unity in Britain and then across the world. Ultimately, unity is to be

---

[18] These translations from the Swedish have been made either by Google translate or Bing translator.

found in Christ, he argued, and as Christians grow closer to Christ they will grow closer to each other.

Such warm feelings and such idealistic hopes hinted at a grand reconciliation in Elim. On returning to British soil and a nation now preparing for war, however, good intentions gave way to a harder realism. The turning point of Jeffreys' year was to be played out at the annual Ministerial Conference and in circumstances that would have been comic had they not been tragic.

The 1939 Elim Conference

Jeffreys had threatened to resign the previous year if his demand for lay representation went unheeded. As a persuasive measure Jeffreys took Phillips over to Ireland to hear the Irish churches first-hand. They wanted lay representation and Phillips 'explained that this had been rejected in the past because of a fear that erroneous doctrine, specifically BI, would infiltrate the movement'.[19] Jeffreys had responded, 'My error has to go, or I must go with my error' indicating that he had more or less made up his mind to leave unless he could persuade Elim to accept an infusion of British Israel teaching.[20] Nevertheless he told Phillips that he would be prepared to make it legally impossible for BI to be introduced or taught in Alliance churches. Later, Phillip bluntly told Jeffreys to his face that there would be fewer problems if Jeffreys were willing to release some of his power. This appeared to surprise Jeffreys but he responded by proposing to withdraw as President of the Executive Council and offered to stand for election on the same basis as any other minister. He would even withdraw his nominees and give further assurances about making it legally impossible for BI to be introduced to the churches. In return, he asked for lay representation and an acceptance the Irish would be welcome to their own separate governing body linked to the Elim Alliance.

The Executive sent out a letter to ministers again asking for their views on lay representation, and arguments were put forward in favour of the scheme including the information that it proved possi-

---

[19] Hudson, *Schism*, p. 257.
[20] Hudson, *Schism*, p. 257.

ble in Ireland and would avoid a split between Ireland and England. Against the scheme it was argued that a minority from Ireland should not dominate the Elim work, ministerial safeguards would be of no use if power was given to laymen and that ministers would be treated with disrespect; more worryingly, lay people would enable the introduction of British Israel teaching.

Hudson's analysis points out the reasons for disallowing 'lay representation reveal the ministers' own sense of insecurity in their positions'.[21] Jeffreys asked to see the correspondence containing the soundings of ministers and Phillips refused. Given that Jeffreys was the founder of the movement and on the Executive Council, this high-handed behaviour can only be explained by assuming trust had vanished. Hathaway, who acted as a peacemaker when he could, explained that Jeffreys' policy of disregarding the Executive leadership appeared to spring from his desire 'to impose upon the movement policies which appear to be neither acceptable to ministers nor to the work'.[22] Here then was the rub: lay representation engendered by Irish churches functioning in a culture more sympathetic to BI would set policy for the whole movement and eventually override the main body of pastors and the Executive Council – that appears to have been their fear.

In August Jeffreys circulated letters to ministers and these were rebutted by others from headquarters. On 3 September Britain and Germany found themselves reluctantly at war. Along with other offices Elim's headquarters were evacuated from London to Glossop out of range of Germany bombing. Public transport was interrupted, families worried about those who joined the armed forces and air raid wardens checked homes for the effectiveness of their blackout. The annual Conference had to be postponed (the Deed Poll allowed this for 21 days) but Phillips had to use a stratagem to do this, and did so twice. Hathaway, acting on Phillips' instructions, met with another minister to agree the delay. The Conference was eventually held from 24 November to 1 December 1939.

The circulating letters (including one from Jeffreys in pamphlet form called The Pattern) and their replies had taken their toll of

---

[21] Hudson, *Schism*, p. 259.

[22] Hudson, *Schism*, p. 269 taken from letter Hathaway to Jeffreys, 29 Aug 1939.

everyone's patience. Phillips had written to Jeffreys telling him in advance of the issues that would be raised. In particular, Jeffreys had criticised the absolute power of the Executive Council without making the conference aware that the system he condemned was of his own design.[23] Originally, when the Deed Poll was drawn up, Jeffreys suggested that he should have four nominees on the Council (which would have given him an automatic majority) and the Executive reduced this to three. Jeffreys' complaints about the power of the Executive Council looked hollow in the light of the powers he himself had wished to exercise. He would also explain that Jeffreys had outlined a scheme in 1937 for reducing the Ministerial Conference to 40 members even though the Deed Poll made this unconstitutional. He would press the charge against Jeffreys of fomenting unrest and dissatisfaction within the Movement by constantly proposing unnecessary changes. Most pointedly he would ask Jeffreys why he had not carried out his promise to transfer properties held in his own name to the Elim Trust Corporation; why he discouraged any evangelistic campaign apart from his own; why he continually attempted to inflict his will on the Council and why, in his attempts to make Elim more accountable, he had established the 'one-man government' of the World Revival Campaign.

Jeffreys must have been shocked at this forensic dissection of his inconsistencies and manipulativeness and indicated he did not want to attend. Eventually he agreed to so by remaining at 10, Clarence Road, Clapham, while the Conference assembled in Woodlands next door. This almost farcical situation made discussion and any meeting of minds well-nigh impossible. The ministers, who were understandably worried about their families and congregations, sat in one building while Jeffreys with his advisors (among whom John Leech was surely counted) sat in another. Messages were sent between the two. One assumes the ministers were in no mood to be trifled with: Jeffreys appeared unwilling to face the criticism Phillips had warned him of.

---

[23] Hudson, *Schism*, p. 263.

The 1939 Elim Conference: Phillips Speaks

The notes of Phillips' speech have survived and enable us to reconstruct what he said.[24] Essentially he offered an historical overview of the business and constitutional side of Elim from 1919. The absence of Jeffreys himself may have made it easier to speak without restraint. On Tuesday afternoon 21 November Phillips delivered an account of continual change and inconsistent demands that flowed into the headquarters offices for years. This was not a personal attack on Jeffreys although criticism of his numerous schemes could not but create a bad impression. When Phillips arrived in Belfast in 1919 there were no accounts, no list of properties, and no formal organisation. The first Constitution was drawn up in 1922 by Jeffreys without consulting Overseers and was amended two years later before being replaced by another Constitution in 1925 which was itself superseded by a new Constitution in 1929. A period of reflection and discussion followed until the Deed Poll was drawn up in 1934 and yet, in 1938, Jeffreys was agitating for a new Deed Poll. On average, then, a new Constitution had been drawn up every three years.

Apart from this Phillips wanted to 'mention the type of thing we have had to contend with'. In 1928 there was a proposal to take over a property at Paternoster Row which Phillips, his brother, and Mr Henderson had examined and strongly advised against. Jeffreys overruled all of them and the result was that after two years the Movement withdrew from the property and had to pay a loss of over £1,500 to avoid public bankruptcy proceedings. About the same time Jeffreys insisted on founding a new journal, the *Foursquare Revivalist*, and Phillips and his brother pleaded with him not to embark upon it. Jeffreys prevailed and everyone did their best to make it a success but it proved a 'fiasco' and closed. About the same time Jeffreys pressed for shops all over the country and started one in Brighton but within a few years he wanted to wash his hands of them and even got rid of the Publishing Company and said it should not trade at all.

---

[24] These are given by Hudson, *Schism*, in his appendix 1 as well as held at the Cartwright Centre at Regents Theological College, Malvern. The notes use abbreviations, e.g. 'wd' for 'would', but where quotations are given the words are written in full here.

In 1929 he started more sections of the work against the advice of headquarters that always believed that unity was required for strength. Since then all sorts of concessions had been demanded in an attempt to bring all sections of the work together. In the same year the Divisional Superintendent system was launched and worked splendidly until 1934 when Jeffreys scrapped it against the advice of headquarters. Why was this? Simply because Jeffreys wanted to get rid of one or two of the District Superintendents and thought scrapping the system would be the easiest way to do it. The result of this was Ireland was left without anyone in authority and there was now open rebellion there.

Regarding British Israel teaching, agitation began first in 1932 and discussion of it was forced on the Conference. In 1935 veiled threats were made that Jeffreys would leave if BI were not given liberty. The resolution was passed and Jeffreys promised not to bring the matter up again. Yet he still pressed hard for the next three years under the cry 'liberty of conscience'. However in 1937 he said he was prepared to drop all prophetic teaching if we would do the same. 'I have on me a letter from GJ dated January this year in which he was prepared to make it "legally impossible for British Israelism to be taught in any Alliance Church" provided we grant lay representation'. So was this really a matter of conscience?

Then there was the 'shilling a week' scheme. The first phase of this obsession was that the Executive Council be elected by all church members paying a shilling a week. After weeks of arguing this was dropped. Was this, Phillips argued, really according to biblical pattern?

And then there was the Local Church Government (L.C.G.) scheme brought in after 1934. The shilling a week idea was incorporated into that by proposing only members paying a shilling a week to their church should have the right to vote at local church meetings. The whole idea turned out to be an utter failure and the ministers of the churches involved now blame the Executive for leading them up the garden path although the Executive were only following Jeffreys' instructions. The Executive had met in November 1934 to discuss the scheme and all the elected members were present. Afterwards Phillips wrote to the Principal,

> Everyone expressed surprise at the proposal to introduce a form of government which strikes at the very root of the Deed Poll,

and asked why it was not suggested before we spent hundreds of pounds and months of discussion on the new Deed Poll. The next thing I was faced with was this: everyone who was present said that they felt it was a means to introduce BI into the work.

So on the 4 December Jeffreys replied,

> In order to avoid any possible misunderstanding between us, I assure you as members of the Executive that my motive in seeking to launch a plan for these local government churches is not to provide ways and means to introduce this teaching into these churches.

Phillips went on, 'I confess to you I did not accept this assurance. Events prove it was right' and he went on to explain how he was

> drafting rules for these churches and put in a clause stating that questions of doctrine outside the Fundamental truths accepted by Elim should be decided by the Executive. Immediately there was deadlock. So on 21 December 1934 at an Executive meeting he proposed a resolution that there should be liberty to preach BI in L.C.G. churches unless and until it spread to a stage when the Council felt it would be a menace to the rest of the work.

As soon as this happened the whole situation changed and Jeffreys showed his pleasure and the scheme was launched with his blessing. About three years later (the Spring of 1937) 'GJ admitted that he introduced L.C.G. for the purpose of making an outlet for BI'. Was it any wonder, Phillips asked, that the scheme has not prospered?

He went on to cover the financial crisis from 1937 onwards. The crisis was said to have occurred because the accounts showed a loss of £104 in a year when the Jubilee Fund raised nearly £7,000. Jeffreys drew up all kinds of schemes and even considered selling Elim Woodlands (where they were then all sitting). And then, making a point that would have registered heavily with the conference he said,

> As result of decisions then made some ministers have been practically starving while we have been paying money off mortgages when mortgages were arranged for 15 years and could easily have been paid out of church surplus, and lenders didn't want the money back, and need not have been paid for 15 years – or

not at all if the Lord came back before them. All this money was taken out of the Ministers' pockets.

We do not know what effect this disclosure had on the listening ministers though, obviously, any who had been reduced to the breadline would have been emotionally affected and many of them were unlikely to have known that Jeffreys himself was the sole trustee of a number of churches. The contrast between their own hardship and the comfortable circumstances enjoyed by Jeffreys and his inner circle – whatever the *Elim Evangel* might have said – must have sent them reeling.

Phillips continued: in 1938, Jeffreys introduced the lay representation scheme accompanied by an ultimatum that he would resign if it were rejected. 'When pressed by Pastor Boulton he said he would do this even if it split the work from top to bottom', and he made this statement when only four ministers in Great Britain and four in Ireland knew of a desire for lay representation in their churches. Even so, at the end of the conference in 1938 'we passed resolutions proposed by GJ, he said he was satisfied, and thought they had brought about "real unity of policy"'. Yet, as late as July 11, 1939 he was *still* pressing for a lay representation scheme.

As far as Ireland was concerned he pressed for lay representation at the 1938 Irish conference although, since then, he had been pressing for Irish property to be held by an Irish Executive while opposing the same arrangements in the rest of the United Kingdom. How can it be right that the Irish Executive should hold property but the Executive in the rest of the United Kingdom should not? It was, Phillips said, 'enough to make angels weep'.

And now there is a request for elders and deacons to be introduced in every church, this is to take priority over everything else. Phillips had been through his files and 'found literally scores of schemes drawn up by GJ' that troubled us for years. 'You have had a dose for only four months' he told the listening ministers, meaning that they had been subject to a literary avalanche from Jeffreys for the four preceding months.

During the last year or so pages & pages have come from him trying to prove there was a financial crisis in the work, that the debt was going up when it was going down by thousands of pounds, and a host of other things he doesn't understand.

If Jeffreys had been pressing for only one thing then the Movement could to have given way for the sake of peace but 'it is something different every year' so that the fact is he is 'not fighting for a principle', but fighting for his own way with 'every scheme that comes into his head'. And all this has come about because 'unfortunately of latter years GJ has ceased to consult headquarters. He has around him admirers and flatterers. If they were true friends they would point out his failures.'

Phillips ended his speech by saying that there was now unrest and dissatisfaction among ministers and churches which was sapping the very life of the Movement. He had submitted more than enough evidence to show that Jeffreys was totally unfitted for the business side of the work and he, Phillips, did not blame Jeffreys because 'any doctor will tell you that the symptoms of his illness are just those revealed in his correspondence'. Apart from this he is out of his depth in matters of organisation and business. In Acts 6 the Apostles call seven men to do the business side of the work while they devoted themselves to prayer and ministry of the Word. If

> the Principal would only take his hands off the government of the work we would forget the past and I believe there would be a new lease of life for Elim. We could 'solve the Irish problem' and would be glad if Jeffreys would remain as head of the work 'with no more to say as to its government than King George VI has to the government of this land'.

We would gladly work with him and 'I believe once more the blessing of God would rest on the Elim work which we love and for which we have almost given our life's blood'.

We do not know whether Phillips sat down to stunned silence or a round of applause but we feel the current of emotion beneath the recital of tortuous events. He speaks as a man who, to no financial advantage for himself, has put his brilliant business brain and all his energies at the service of Elim and of George Jeffreys personally, and found himself wondering if he has sacrificed in vain.

The 1939 Elim Conference: Decisions are Reached
The Conference was protracted because Jeffreys insisted on absenting himself from the debate. A delegation was sent from the conference to him, he replied, and a delegation then came back, and another group, appointed by Jeffreys, functioned as his representa-

tives at the Conference. The cumbersome procedure allowed Jeffreys to sit out of sight with his lay advisers around him and to avoid haste.[25] For everyone else, the process was tedious but they went to work and debated the eight points set out in Jeffreys' letter to the ministers in the correspondence circulating beforehand.[26] By the end the Conference agreed:

1. The Ministerial Conference, not the Executive Council, would become the governing body with the inclusion of accredited lay pastors with five years ministerial experience;

2. A property board would be established to oversee the future purchase and selling of property, this board would include three laymen;

3. Lay representation would be introduced if this was approved by two-thirds of the Conference;

4. Presbyteries would be established if there was a similar demand;

5. A diaconate would be set up in every church;

6. The Principal would be relieved from his obligation and a Book of Order would be instituted.

---

[25] Cartwright, *Evangelists*, p. 153, considers Jeffreys did not know really what he wanted.

[26] The eight points were (taken from Hudson, *Schism*, p. 269):

1. The Ministerial Conference to be the governing body of Elim, with the Executive Council being the functioning arm of the Conference.

2. District Presbyteries to include an equal mix of ministers and lay representation.

3. Lay representatives to be included into the Conference.

4. Mortgages to come under the control of the Governing Body, with legal exemption being granted to those who had previously controlled them.

5. A sustentation fund to be established for disabled, widows and orphans; a subsidy fund to be established for poorer churches.

6. A Book of Order to be made available to everyone to show how the Movement was governed.

7. Each church to have control of its property under the Model Trust Deed, and so jointly own the church with the Movement.

8. Each church to have elders and deacons.

7. The Trust Deeds of churches would be executed by the Elim Trust Corporation, but 'no building be sold or mortgaged without the approval of the majority of church members'.

8. The Ministerial Conference would decide matters of doctrine, not local churches.[27]

The one stumbling block was the Model Trust Deed which Jeffreys' advisers wanted more time to consider. Jeffreys asked for 28 days to give his final views to the Conference and at this point patience snapped. A vote was passed by 79 of the 94 present stating:

This Ministerial Conference, having gone to the limit in their attempts to meet the Principal's demands are determined at the expiration of seven days from the date of this resolution to withdraw all the concessions agreed upon and to abide by the Deed Poll in 1934, unless the following conditions are complied with by the Principal during the said seven days:

1. That he sign an agreement embodying the terms agreed at this Conference.

2. That he limit the number of laymen he consults on these matters to 6.

3. That he undertake not to contend against the Constitution of the Alliance by means of circular letter, printed matter, or organised effort.

On Friday morning 30 September Jeffreys came in and read a statement to the Conference announcing his resignation from the Alliance and from the Elim Church as a whole. After handing in a written notification and kneeling down to pray for the ministers, he left. Appreciations were profuse and attempts were made to keep him on board with a nominal role in charge of the Bible College or as the moderator of the Conference; and, in fact, news of his resignation was not at first released to the Movement. All this was to no avail and to all intents and purposes the break had been made. There was to be no reconciliation, no joint campaigning, no sharing of assets or meetings, no return to the good old days, no warmth

---

[27] Hudson, *Schism*, pp. 269, 270.

and no trust. There were attempts by individuals to build bridges and an apparent compromise for a few months in 1940; but, in essence, the relationship between Jeffreys and Elim was fractured beyond repair.

At the heart of the matter is the question of why Jeffreys resigned *even after he had secured almost everything he wanted.* And the answer may lie in the wording of the Conference resolution that prevented the churches being opened up to BI teaching. So, for instance, the Ministerial Conference and not local church was to decide matters of doctrine. In this way, whatever lay leadership in local churches might or might not accept, it was the Conference itself that laid down the lines and limits of Elim's doctrinal position. And, to the same effect, Jeffreys was asked not to contend against the constitution of the Alliance. This would prevent him from campaigning to draw churches away from Elim and into any new organisation.

If this analysis is correct, then the principle of lay leadership which Jeffreys had insisted upon and which later became his rallying cry, was actually secondary to the advancement of BI doctrine. Other analyses are, of course, possible including that Jeffreys was deeply reluctant to transfer the properties of which he was a trustee into the Elim Trust Corporation since, by doing so, he would lose control of substantial and valuable assets.

After the 1939 Elim Conference

The ministers must have dispersed with heavy hearts. True, there was a faint hope Jeffreys might accept a continuing role in Elim unrelated to business matters and so, on 5 December, a circular letter from headquarters said,

> Principal George Jeffreys, who for some time has intimated his desire along these lines, has resigned from the Executive Council, and is thus released from the business side of the work. This will free him more fully for his spiritual ministry in the work of the Lord, which God has so signally blessed in the past.[28]

---

[28] Cartwright, *Evangelists*, pp. 154-55.

Any hopes this paragraph might soften attitudes vanished to almost zero when, a few days later, Jeffreys published a pamphlet *Why I resigned from the Elim Movement.* This was too much for the Executive who, on 20 December, published, *A Reply.* The arguments on both sides will be examined in the next chapter.

Jeffreys slips out of sight to readers of the *Evangel.* Having exchanged a fusillade of paper, dissension continued on the ground. Elim church buildings were now closed to Jeffreys and so he hired public halls and announced meetings in local newspapers. In Carlisle 'a misleading notice' was placed right next to the advertisement for Elim's Sunday night meeting.[29] Similarly in York Jeffreys hired a hall and put the local pastor in a quandary when, in the face of disagreement by some of his members, he disputed Jeffreys' claims. Despite this, the church survived. According to Cartwright the main places where Jeffreys drew crowds to himself were in those towns where he had held follow-up campaigns not long before the split. Carlisle, Nottingham, Portsmouth, and Worthing were notable in their loyalty to Jeffreys; so were congregations he or his friends held in trust: Brighton, Blackpool, Glasgow, and Kensington. The total number of Elim Alliance members who left with Jeffreys was less than ten; and, when they left, they lost their ministerial status and this made them eligible for military service.[30]

In these early days of war 'the effect of the blackout has been, generally speaking, to limit our evening expeditions to those dictated by duty'.[31] Doing their duty for Elim people meant attending weeknight and Sunday services, and these attracted large numbers. The *Evangel* urged caution about prophetic interpretation of the Bible while encouraging churches to declare the gospel unmistakably when soldiers at nearby training bases attended church parades.[32] The first death of a London Crusader chorister occurred in December after his ship was sunk.[33] There was no reference to Jeffreys in the Christmas *Evangel* but the last issue of year included up-

---

[29] Cartwright, *Evangelists*, p. 155.
[30] Cartwright, *Evangelists*, p. 156.
[31] *Elim Evangel* 20.42 (20 Oct 1939), p. 666.
[32] *Elim Evangel* 20.46 (17 Nov 1939), pp. 725, 730.
[33] *Elim Evangel* 20.49 (8 Dec 1939), p. 778.

lifting articles promising a great outpouring of the Spirit and the harvest of converts at the end of the age.

Reflection

There are puzzles about Jeffreys' departure from Elim. After eight or nine days of protracted debate with Jeffreys only vicariously present, fences were nearly mended and the efforts of constructive peacemakers were on the brink of a reform package to satisfy its founder. The 1939 Stockholm Conference indicated the European stature of Jeffreys and his analysis there of systems of church government is perceptive and rational. Phillips was also a rational individual not given to emotional tantrums of any kind. At the Stockholm Conference Jeffreys refers to arranging each local assembly in the New Testament pattern but he also went on to say, 'this means looking to get some kind of assurance that we retain our property' which demonstrates he was conscious that property disputes would arise when systems of church government changed. So, whatever else might be said about lay leadership, ownership of property mattered to Jeffreys: if he were to leave, he needed to take property with him. If he were to stay, he needed to ensure congregations that later fell out with Elim would not forfeit their properties.

Even so, the resignation at the 1939 conference must have been rendered more probable by Phillips' devastating opening speech. The mystique of Jeffreys was stripped away and he was shown as a demanding and inconsistent boss capable of making costly mistakes. The financial appeals made to Elim by Jeffreys diverted money away from the pockets of the pastors at the conference. They, when they heard what had happened, must have been less inclined to vote for Jeffreys despite their admiration for his campaigning abilities. Many of them were beholden to Jeffreys for their pulpits and a number of them were conscious of their need to accept the stipulations of headquarters. When Phillips showed them their own livelihoods were being downgraded by the Jubilee Fund, they must have found it easier to vote against Jeffreys and in favour of any proposition that Phillips put. Or turning this the other way, Jeffreys by his financial behaviour was alienating the very people whose votes could help him defeat headquarters.

We do not know who was advising Jeffreys at this time. John Leech remained in the shadows. He and Jeffreys retained a good relationship right up until Leech's death in 1942. When criticism of Leech was mooted, Jeffreys had written to Phillips showing a protective loyalty.

> If they penalise him [Leech] because of anything I have suggested, it is only the grace of God that can save the iron from going into my soul, and it is only love for the churches I have, through Grace, founded that will enable me to suffer … such an affront to a true and tried brother and friend of Elim's of twenty years standing.[34]

If indeed Leech was one of those who offered advice to Jeffreys in 1939, we can wonder what the outcome of events would have been without the influence of the man who was such a staunch pillar of the British Israel Federation.

---

[34] GJ to EJP 1 Dec 1934. Quoted by Hudson, *Schism*, p. 202.

17

PAMPHLETS, PROMISE, AND PARTING

Introduction

Britain was now at war and after all the waiting, hoping, praying, and diplomatic negotiation the foundations of ordinary life shifted. Substantial and heart-rending preparations were made for the evacuation of children from areas of greatest danger. German bombers could not reach to the west of Britain because their fuel tanks would not carry them that far and so inner city children, mostly from London, said goodbye to their mothers and were sent to families on farms, villages, and seaside resorts. There are photographs of children carrying their gas masks and little suitcases and with a name tag attached as, holding the hands of a policeman or air raid warden, they board trains headed for safety.

In the months following the 1939 Conference, Jeffreys acted in a way giving evidence for the suspicion that he had planned his departure to coincide with the founding of a new denomination. The new *Pattern* magazine was launched quickly. A selected group of ministers and churches were ready to pack their bags and leave with him once the green light was given. 'Fellowship centres' or embryonic congregations under the title Believers' Commonwealth Fellowship had already come into being. These could be rebranded and connected with the departing ministers. And, on the other side of the fence, others who thought everything was all over must have included the staff of the *Elim Evangel* since, from January 1940 onwards, Jeffreys' name and photograph disappeared from the masthead.

The First Two Pamphlets

As mentioned in the previous chapter Jeffreys distributed a pamphlet *Why I resigned from the Elim Movement* shortly after the 1939 Elim conference and within two weeks this was answered by *A Reply* on 20 December. The tone of both these documents was level and without excessive recrimination or personal animus. If repairs were to be made, they would have to be made quickly.

Jeffreys began by stating, 'for some years I have been at variance with the system of church government in Elim' and went on to give a brief overview of the history of the movement and its organisation. He pointed out that the governing body of the Alliance was the Executive Council consisting of nine ministers and before his resignation he was a permanent member of this Council and had the power to appoint three other members. All this is uncontentious. He then explains that the directors of the Elim Trust Corporation were the same as the nine ministers of the Council; they 'control the vast accumulation of Alliance property in Great Britain and Ireland'. And then, turning to the Deed Poll signed in 1934, he explained there is 'a clause which gives power to the Executive Council to compel any person who holds property in trust for the Alliance' to sign a property over to the Trust Corporation. This also is uncontentious.

He explained he made proposals to the Ministerial Conference in 1938 to amend the Deed Poll so as to introduce lay representation and a balanced government of ministers and layman on a 50-50 basis that could delegate power from time to time to the Executive. Then, in 1939 he presented the Ministerial Conference with a modified scheme and four months before the conference eight points of reform (listed in the previous chapter). The majority of these were granted or partially granted but disagreement on the final point centred on the 'reasonable control of its own church property, under a proper Model Trust Deed, so that the building would be held jointly by the Church and the Governing Body of the Movement'. When the Conference tried to negotiate the clauses of this deed, breakdown occurred.

After his resignation, Jeffreys consulted with his lay advisers that afternoon and came up with eight subsidiary points that should be included in the Model Trust Deed. The last of these stipulated, 'A

majority vote of the church to reject or accept any change in doctrine and procedure proposed by the governing body'. It therefore
envisaged the local church could accept or reject the doctrines of
the movement of which it was part. The deep appreciation of Elim
ministers for Jeffreys and their warm words are included in the
pamphlet before a brief summary of reasons for his exit.

Elim's *Reply* also opens with a discussion of the movement's organisation although it includes information that Jeffreys had omit-
ted. It points out how Jeffreys himself had written glowingly of the
1934 Constitution of Elim. At that time he asserted 'we can face
the future with renewed confidence in Him who has so wonderfully
led us thus far, assured that the hand of God holds yet greater
things in the coming days'. The text goes on to reveal the attempt
by Jeffreys to introduce British-Israel teaching to Elim and the debate that occurred in 1934 and the resolution passed in 1935 when
ministers agreed that 'for purpose of preserving unity' it shall treat
the teaching of British-Israel in the same way as is the custom with
other matters on which there is an acute difference of opinion, viz.:
neither to propagate it nor to attack it'. Despite this, the pamphlet
noted the BI dispute led friends of Elim to lament the cessation of
Jeffreys' pioneering campaigns and the diversion of his energies
from evangelistic preaching to the production of constitutional
schemes.

The 1939 Conference faced a different set of demands from
those made in 1938. Negotiations broke down partly because Jeffreys did not attend and partly because he asked for powers to be
granted to each local church 'and yet *was unable to state the extent of
those demands*' (original italics).

> Although there was ample opportunity in the months preceding
> the Conference for the Principal to consult his advisers to for-
> mulate their suggestions, they were not asked to do so until the
> day after the conference when the ministers had left.

It is no wonder that Conference lost patience.

So far as the Model Trust Deed was concerned, the reply pointed out Elim's method of holding property in a Trust Corporation
was similar to that used by other denominations and that the surplus offerings from churches had been used to build the work up to
the extent that many churches would not have been in existence

unless the surplus offerings from wealthier churches had enabled this. Equally the surplus offerings were used to support ministers: 'many of our Pastors and Evangelist in poor districts or small churches are subsidised by the Central Fund provided by the balances from the larger churches'. And finally the whole notion of allowing doctrine to be decided jointly by the local church and the governing body would have opened the door to endless unnecessary friction.

A Push for Reconciliation and Reform

The possibility of reconciliation between Jeffreys and Elim seemed to be a technical matter that, with time and patience, could be resolved. If the wording of the Model Trust Deed could be revised, Jeffreys would surely return and any ministers and congregations who has left Elim or were on the brink of doing so could be brought back into the fold of the Alliance. There were already different categories of church (Direct Government, Local Government) within the Elim Alliance so that the option of creating one or more new categories to accommodate differences of opinion seemed within touching distance. Over and above these possibilities Elim acted rapidly in the early months of 1940 to speed up the democratisation of representation. A letter from E.J. Phillips dated 18 January 1940 outlined the Executive's proposals for constitutional reform and included a voting paper with a stamped addressed envelope to allow a formal response within a week. The letter admitted that big churches were in the balance; Southampton, Worthing, Portsmouth, and Nottingham had already decided for Jeffreys while Birmingham and others had decided the other way. To help the waverers the letter explained the Executive now accepted a 50/50 split between clergy and laity at the annual conference and the lay representation at District Presbyteries.

A Unity Conference, arranged by Ludwig Naumann, was called for 22-25 January 1940. Here Elim, Assemblies of God, and other Pentecostals might meet and agree to work together or, at least, not to work against each other. Within the ambit of this conference Jeffreys met the headquarters officers. He felt the goodwill on all sides, commenting, 'it was a touching moment and one that can never be forgotten as one after another from the different movements offered their services as mediators between the two sides of the situa-tion in Elim'.[1] Less than a month later a day of prayer for all Elim ministers was held on 6 February at the Bible College before two days of face-to-face meetings between Jeffreys and the Executive Council on 9-10 February. At the end of these meetings, a break-through appeared to have been achieved; time and patience ap-peared to have been rewarded. Most of the changes Jeffreys had previously asked for were accepted. In Hudson's words:

> The Conference would consist of an equal number of ministers and laymen. The District Presbyteries would have the same pro-portional representation. Headquarters officers would be voted into office by postal vote. The property board would consist of three ministers and three laymen. A chairman would be elected who would have a casting vote. A Model Trust Deed would be given to each church. There would be quarterly church meetings; elders and deacons would be confirmed/elected every two years; each church would have a representative at Conference; a per-centage of offerings, not exceeding 10% would be sent to head-quarters; until the debt was cleared 80% of a church's surplus funds would be allocated to the Debt Fund, the rest would be placed in the Ministerial Subsidy Fund; no church property would be sold without two-thirds of the church members voting for it; the Model Trust Deed would include the Fundamentals; stationing of ministers would only happen after consultation with local church officers; changes in the Model Trust Deed would require the vote of 75% of both the local church and the Conference; any disciplinary actions would be based on Matthew 18:15-17.[2]

A democratic enhancement at each level – the local church, the District Presbytery, and the Conference – had been agreed in re-sponse to the Phillips' letter of 18 January. Church property was now more obviously in the control of congregation[3] and the Model

---

[1] G. Jeffreys, 'George Jeffreys Comments on the Unity Conference', *The Pat-tern* 7 (Feb 1940). Taken from Hudson, *Schism*.

[2] Hudson, *Schism*, p. 282.

[3] I am not clear whether the Direct Government churches were affected but the tendency within Elim was for local congregational control of more buildings.

Trust Deed could be altered, although the proportion in agreement needed to reach 75%. Surely now after all the discarded amendments and proposals and hours of drafting and debate, the wounded Elim body might be healed. The two full conferences of 1938 and 1939, the Unity conference of January 1940, the consultations with lay advisors and collective prayer had all played their part and the set of Mutual Recommendations acceptable to Jeffreys and to Elim (as set out above) could now become the formal basis for new constitutional machinery, and the agreement between the parties was circulated round the churches in a printed newsheet in February 1940.[4]

And then without warning all these hopes were jeopardised when Jeffreys conjured a new requirement into being and circulated it in a pamphlet. On 17 May, 1940, Hathaway wrote round to all ministers explaining that Jeffreys now wanted all supplementary doctrines to be decided by the local church.[5] Hathaway, who had a record as a peacemaker in the ongoing dispute, could only interpret the demand as motivated by the desire to propagate or allow British-Israel teaching, saying, 'we are therefore faced with this new situation and these vital doctrinal issues which have been at the root of our troubles are now being brought to the fore'.

His letter went on to give six reasons why a central governing body was better able than a local church to determine doctrinal standards:

1. If local churches decided doctrine there was a possibility that local churches could be led into error. Pentecostal denominations were begun as a safeguard simply because many early Pentecostal groups had strayed into erroneous doctrine.

2. Practically all Pentecostal groups decided doctrinal standards centrally.

---

[4] The pamphlet *Unity in Elim: Mutual Recommendations* was published and circulated by Elim in February 1940. It opened, 'Elim friends all over the country will rejoice to know that as a result of negotiations between Principal George Jeffreys and the Elim Executive Council, agreement on recommendatons for unity has now been reached'.

[5] He had issued a pamphlet on the subject.

3. There is no New Testament precedent for local church making these decisions. Acts 15 is an example of a centrally governed Conference.

4. Young and immature assemblies could be swayed by erroneous doctrines. Therefore, it was better to allow the maturity of a central governing body to determine doctrine. If local churches decided doctrine the inevitable result would be schism.

5. Therefore, it was better to allow the maturity of a central governing body to determine doctrine.

6. If local churches decided doctrine the inevitable result would be schism.[6]

The special Elim Conference met from 20-24 May, 1940, in its new expanded format with 75 ministers, 75 lay representatives and about 50 other ministers, probationers and church leaders present. Churchill had become Prime Minister ten days before and injected resolution and realism: he had made his declaration, 'I have nothing to offer but blood, toil, tears and sweat' to the House of Commons.[7] It was not a time for the faint-hearted. The Conference began by facing Jeffreys' new requirement head on and resolved,

> In view of Principal Jeffreys' pamphlet concerning supplementary doctrine, we now consider the questions of supplementary doctrine and British Israelism before proceeding with a consideration of Mutual Recommendations.[8]

It is agreed that all those present could take part in the general discussion on whether 'matters of doctrine outside the Fundamentals [should be] decided by the Governing Body or otherwise'. As might be expected wide discussion followed and many people spoke. In the end it was agreed that 'all questions of doctrine outside the Fundamentals be decided by the Governing Body, with liberty of expression for differing interpretations of prophecy in the

---

[6] Hudson, *Schism*, pp. 282, 283.

[7] http://www.churchill-society-london.org.uk/BdTlTrsS.html (accessed 27 Apr 2016).

[8] *Minutes of the Elim Conference* (May 1940).

churches'. The vote was close with 83 in favour and 72 against.[9] This surely met Jeffreys' perennial concern since BI was customarily classified as a form of prophetic interpretation. By a narrow margin, he had secured the option to teach what he wanted.

The Conference then considered the Mutual Recommendations. Unsurprisingly they resolved as a Conference to accept these since February's groundwork had been done, though they made a number of minor amendments. For instance, lay representatives should be at least 25 years of age and have been with Elim for five years. The Executive Council should be elected by postal vote, each church should have elders or deacons or both and the deacons should be appointed or confirmed every two years. Until the present debt of the Alliance had been cleared up and after ministers' minimum salaries had been made up all surplus offering should go into the Debt Fund.

There was a desire 'in the interests of unity that Principal Jeffreys should return to the Movement', as was his wish, as an Evangelist rather than as Moderator.[10] It was agreed by a huge majority that 'Principal George Jeffreys be asked to withdraw his resignation as President of Elim Church Incorporated, and return in that capacity'.[11] Jeffreys intimated his acceptance of the proposal and verbally withdrew his resignation from Elim. All seemed well and celebration seemed justified.[12]

There were discussions regarding the future of *The Pattern* magazine and of the World Revival Crusade and

> Principal Jeffreys stated his willingness to bring both *The Pattern* and the World Revival Crusade under the supervision of the Governing Body when the decisions of the present conference were put into effect. It was also agreed that meanwhile no fellowship centres under the Believers Commonwealth Fellowship should be started in any town or city where there is an Elim church.[13]

---

[9] *Minutes of the Elim Conference* (May 1940).

[10] *Minutes of the Elim Conference* (May 1940).

[11] *Minutes of the Elim Conference* (May 1940).

[12] A report of the Conference was given in the *Elim Evangel* 21.24 (10 June 1940), p. 379.

[13] *Minutes of the Elim Conference* (May 1940).

Finally the Unity Conference proposals were considered. These appear to have involved better communication between Conference and congregations. The Elim Conference agreed to issue to the churches a general statement of the decisions it had made, and this statement was to be drawn up by a committee of two ministers and two laymen. In this way the good news of the reconciliation between Jeffreys and Elim should be publicised. Following this it was agreed that all proceeds of the World Crusade boxes to the foreign missionary work be devoted to Elim foreign missions. Additionally, the agreements made at the Presbytery meeting in Belfast in December 1939 between the Executive Council and the Irish Presbytery were approved. It was agreed that a Provident Association for future Elim ministers as well as their widows and dependents should be established and it was agreed that the next annual Conference be held along the lines of the newly revised Constitution and be convened for September 1941. It was also agreed that efforts should be made to extend Elim by fresh evangelism. Finally the conference sent a telegram to the King, grateful for his call to a day of prayer on Sunday 20 May, but also respectfully requesting he should consider closing cinemas, places of amusement, and public houses during that day.

Relationships Sour and Dissolve

Soon after the conference in May and the National Day of Prayer called by the King, the 'miracle of Dunkirk' unfolded. The British Expeditionary Force sent across the Channel to fight alongside the French army was outmanoeuvred and driven back to the coast abandoning large amounts of equipment in its retreat. The British and French armies were wedged apart by the German forces and there was every prospect that over 330,000 British soldiers would be encircled and captured. Yet, extraordinarily, Hitler delayed his advance and unwittingly gave an opportunity to hundreds of boats sent across from the British coast in a marine evacuation of astonishing proportions. Pleasure steamers, military vessels, fishing boats, and any other seaworthy craft shuttled backwards and forwards to bring the exhausted men home. In the skies overhead the Royal Air Force provided substantial cover although several ships were bombed and sunk. In this atmosphere of the national deliverance surely Elim's problems could be forgotten.

Yet in August 1940 Jeffreys published an article in *The Pattern* outlining objections made to him by churches that had become aware of problems and loose ends left over from the successful Conference in May. Jeffreys claimed these problems had been brought to his attention by the churches. The objections were that the Conference could become a small body of men with extensive powers since Conference numbers would be set each year for the following year; no church or minister was assured of the right of representation at the Conference; surplus offerings were to be used at the direction of the Conference; a Stationing Committee could remove a pastor if a confirmatory vote were not taken by his congregation every two years; churches would be obliged to accept supplementary doctrines decided by the Conference and the subsidy of smaller churches by larger ones could continue indefinitely.[14]

These objections seem slight and insubstantial compared to the problems already solved. All could have been raised and discussed at any future Conference and addressed by minor amendments. The Executive Council rebutted Jeffreys in a circular sent to members of the conference with these words:

> It is perfectly clear that the Principal is treating the Elim Conference of May 1940 ... In the same way as he treated the Ministerial Conference and the Executive Council in previous years, and is refusing to accept the decisions of an overwhelming majority.[15]

Jeffreys would not take this lying down and sent a reply to the diaconates of all Elim churches. Until now most arguments had been between Jeffreys and ministers or conferences but now he spoke directly to lay people in charge of the finances of local congregations, people whom he must have believed would be sympathetic to his rhetoric. These were the people who flocked to his meetings and listened spellbound to his sermons. Jeffreys disclosed his emotional pain:

> I cannot tell how deeply I feel over the circular letter sent out by the Executive Council, a letter which seeks to re-commence a

---

[14] Hudson, *Schism*, p. 286.
[15] Hudson, *Schism*, p. 286.

controversy over personalities. Such a letter is uncalled for at any time, but especially at a time when our Movement is troubled over organisational problems which must of necessity be attended to, and, when the world is bleeding from its war wounds.[16]

Jeffreys, in appealing to the diaconates through *The Pattern* magazine, proposed a revision of the Local Church Government rules within the Elim Alliance. At the same time he tried to explain why he had not signed over the trust deeds he held. He was legally bound to return the churches of which he was a trustee to the Elim Trust Corporation but he claimed that he had not done so at the request of the churches who wanted to examine drafts of an amended Deed Poll. This was all too much for the Executive who sent their own letter to the deacons making the simple point that Jeffreys had broken the word he had given at the May 1940 Conference. And, indeed, there were 200 witnesses to what he had agreed to there so Jeffreys could hardly deny what he had said. Jeffreys made an attempt to shift the focus of attention by writing,

> I would say, that the Executive Council is entirely wrong in making it appear that the present dispute in Elim is between myself and themselves or the conference. The real trouble is between 'the powers that be' in Elim on one side, and a substantial section of the Elim Movement on the other.[17]

In November Jeffreys wrote his final letter of resignation from the Elim Church Incorporated claiming that no changes had been made since his resignation a year before. Many of the points he made were the same as those he said the churches had raised with him in August – a similarity that leads Hudson to believe that Jeffreys put his words into their mouths rather than the other way round.[18] Next he sent letters to the diaconates confirming his resignation and containing words likely to cause a quarrel between minister and deacons,

> The responsibility of guiding your church aright is now upon your shoulders, and if I am not one with you in policy I am one

---

[16] Hudson, *Schism*, p. 287.
[17] Hudson, *Schism*, p. 287.
[18] Hudson, *Schism*, p. 285.

with you in heart through the old Gospel that has meant so much to us.[19]

Reflection

So George Jeffreys, founder, builder, and star of Elim, resigned finally in November 1940 never to rejoin. The psychological effects of this parting felt like bereavement. Jeffreys had many Elim colleagues and had endured privations and opposition in those pioneering early years; the ties between him and his co-labourers ran deep. He could now no longer rely on the almost superhuman efficiency of Phillips or the goodwill, prayers, and generosity of thousands of Elim believers. He could no longer visit Elim buildings he had helped to buy and whose foundations stones he had in many cases laid. The projection of his ministry through the pages of the *Elim Evangel* now ceased and all the goodwill that he had accumulated now began to disperse and even turn against him. What had begun as a private disagreement between himself and Phillips or himself and other members of the Executive Council had become a public dispute over property.

Although Jeffreys consistently thereafter presented the dispute as one about church government, this insistence is hard to maintain in the light of the numerous changes made by Elim in response to his pressure and criticisms. Elim was willing to listen, adapt, revise, and change. It did not bear the marks of dictatorship or clerical elitism (as he later maintained) – even if the Executive Council could be pedantic or slow to decide. The argument, as it continued on into the 1940s, chewed over the details of the ownership of church buildings, especially those held by private trusts where the trustees were members of Jeffreys' inner circle. Essentially, he refused to sign these churches over to Elim once he left even though he was legally obliged to do so, and he could only maintain his moral right to refuse his signature on the grounds that the churches were not reformed along the lines he required. 'I will sign off the buildings, once you reform the constitution or model trust deeds or procedure', he might have said, 'Until you do that, I will retain my trus-

---

[19] Hudson, *Schism*, p. 288.

teeship'. Legally he had no right to do this but he knew that Elim would not take him to court, and he knew this because New Testament stipulations speak strongly against litigation between one Christian and another.[20] It is even arguable the consistent demand Jeffreys made for church reform was a displacement activity consciously or unconsciously designed to shield him from having to surrender the valuable buildings he had acquired.

It is psychologically strange after all the debate in 1938 and 1939 and then the three meetings in 1940 (the Unity Conference, the two-day meeting between Jeffreys and the Executive, and the May conference) that, within four months, Jeffreys was agitating for the further change that eventually led to his departure. It is difficult to think of any other Christian leader of a domination who would have made such a decision after having secured so many concessions from the denomination he formed. It is difficult to understand why Jeffreys resigned in the light of the relatively minor additional points of dispute he raised in August 1940. His behaviour is not calculating, rational, or constructive; it is strangely emotional and there are signs of deep pain in his later almost obsessional written attacks on Elim – some 20 pamphlets were printed on either side, many of them repetitive, up until 1946.

Having brought his argument into the open, Jeffreys had associated with other Pentecostal denominations at the Unity Conference in January 1940. He had been touched by the offers of mediation; but, when the final break took place in August 1940, the majority of Pentecostals outside Elim lost patience with him. This is not to say that Jeffreys became a pariah but he no longer had the confidence of other Pentecostals nor was given the place of honour he might otherwise have taken. The statesmanlike role he might have occupied during and after the 1939–1945 War was lost to him and he was reduced to being a marginal figure even though he continued to attract crowds when he preached evangelistically in the British Isles and elsewhere.

---

[20] Matthew 5.24; 1 Cor. 6.1.

18

THE PHONEY WAR IS OVER

Wartime Britain

War changed the pattern of life for everybody living in the British Isles. The great cities were affected by huge bombing raids, with London as the most heavily pulverised target but with other cities, especially after 1940, receiving an explosive pounding as well. The London Blitz occurred from September 1940 until May 1941 with aerial bombardment for 76 consecutive nights apart from 2 November when weather conditions ruled it out.[1] The carnage was horrific and far greater than found in any peacetime accidents. On the first night 430 civilians died and 1,600 were seriously injured while thousands more were made homeless.[2] The mainline train terminals were put out of action on the first night and there was inconvenience and obvious suffering. The raids could last for 12 or 14 hours and people would have to sleep, eat, and excrete in their shelters. Altogether approximately 43,000 civilians in Britain were killed in 1940 and 1941, with a further 17,000 in the remaining years of the war. Half the deaths (nearly 30,000) were in London.[3]

Some 79 stations in the Greater London area became *de facto* shelters and at the peak of the bombing over 170,000 people were

---

[1] Angus Calder, *The People's War: Britain 1939–1945* (Kindle edn; London: Jonathan Cape, 1969), loc 3415.

[2] Calder, *People's War*, loc 3407.

[3] Calder, *People's War*, loc 4933.

sleeping in the underground system.[4] When bombs fell the fire service and the air raid wardens who had been appointed for each local area coordinated rescue attempts to dig people out of fallen buildings, remove bodies, and repair water and gas mains as well as electrical wiring. It took time to coordinate the wardens with the local police and local government employees and to provide temporary accommodation for those who were numbed by the loss of their homes or loved ones.

Beyond this there were symptoms of panic in a flood of hasty marriages, a boom in the sales of wills, and indications of people hoarding sugar and petrol. The blackout was rigidly and strictly enforced with fines for those who allowed any light out into the street. This led to accidents as people fell into canals or bumped into walls. Food prices had risen by a seventh by February 1940 and the price of clothing by a quarter.[5] By the summer of 1940 rationing was introduced to all the main commodities including food, tea, clothing, and petrol though this was not as unpopular as might have been expected since the effects of rationing were seen to be fair. Until then people had been incensed by the sight of rich people turning up in their cars and buying up butter or other goods from poorer areas. In this way, the war equalised social conditions and created an atmosphere of communal help and support and for the first-time British people could be found talking to complete strangers on buses and trains.

Normal working hours shot up. People were expected to go from 8 am to 7 pm seven days a week and almost everyone worked even longer.[6] There was full employment and wages continued to be paid, and increased, and overtime was available on Sundays so that, if workers found themselves too exhausted to reach the office or factory, they would often make sure that they missed the midweek day rather than the Sunday. Gradually Ernest Bevin, a staunch trade unionist who, in the coalition government, had wisely been put in charge of organising the workforce and given enormous legal powers, managed to redeploy engineers to the manufacture of aircraft munitions and to ensure the entire country was geared up for its

---

[4] Calder, *People's War*, loc 3974.
[5] Calder, *People's War*, loc 1410.
[6] Calder, *People's War*, loc 2464.

war effort. Something like 30% of the working male population ended up in the Armed Forces[7] and there were 'reserved occupations' (like working in a shipyard or farming the land) which were obviously necessary for the war effort even if they did not involve frontline engagement with the enemy. Indeed, for the first part of the war the military were largely stationed in the UK defending Britain's strategic assets and coastline from anticipated invasion.

In addition to the redeployment of working people to thousands of new jobs created by the war, internal migrations occurred. Altogether about 213,000 unaccompanied children were evacuated in the summer of 1940 although when the London Blitz occurred there were still half a million children of school age in the metropolitan area.[8] Other adults moved away to safer areas; and, indeed, for a short time in 1939 after war was declared it was still possible to leave the country and escape to the United States, which the very wealthy and assorted members of the artistic community like the poet W.H. Auden did.

Revival campaigning was sharply affected. Expenditure on petrol for private motoring ran at a mere 6% of pre-war levels[9] and another figure shows petrol imports to have dropped between 1940 and 1943 by over 65%.[10] This was an era of austerity made worse because postal services were disrupted by the loss of staff and telephones disrupted by damage to lines. Faith in God did not obviously drop and Winston Churchill had said, 'There are times when all men pray'.[11] Only one person in 20 was ready to profess atheism[12] and at the start of the war, before military call-up would take full effect, churches were packed even if big meetings on a grand scale were now impossible.

The Pentecostal churches had learnt a lesson from the First World War. Assemblies of God in its 1924 Constitution accepted conscientious objection with the result that all its ministers were exempt from military service and the same applied to Elim minis-

---

[7] Calder, *People's War*, loc 7099.

[8] Calder, *People's War*, loc 2717.

[9] Calder, *People's War*, loc 7015.

[10] Calder, *People's War*, loc 6067.

[11] http://www.ibiblio.org/pha/policy/1941/410622d.html (accessed 31 May 2016).

[12] Calder, *People's War*, loc 10638.

ters. Jeffreys and his Revival Party were mostly too old for the first
wave of conscription (although, by leaving Elim, Albert Edsor was
at risk of call-up for a while). Attitudes against conscientious objection were softer in the Second World War than they had been in the
First: then about 30% of conscientious objectors had been imprisoned whereas from 1939 only 3% suffered in this way.[13] Archbishop
William Temple recognised conscientious objection as an authentic
vocation and popular opinion was less jingoistic than previously
although a number of high-profile conscientious objectors like the
philosopher Bertrand Russell, who had been imprisoned in the First
War, had changed their minds by the time the Second War started:
the Nazi party was an unmitigated evil and had to be resisted even
by force. This position was held by Temple who saw military service
as the lesser of two evils.[14] Pentecostal pastors accepted that conscription was a matter of conscience and would support young men
and women in their congregations whether or not they decided to
join the forces. Congregations were not generally divided over this
testing issue and there were non-military jobs like becoming an air
raid warden which could be done without breaking Christian pacifist principles.

What the Pentecostal churches may have been unprepared for
was the soaring popularity of the cinema and of pubs and other
forms of entertainment during the war. The strong separatist doctrine preached by Jeffreys and other leaders of Elim was difficult to
maintain when every week some 25 or 30 million cinema seats were
sold[15] and pubs became a natural venue for battered community life.
Beer was watered down to make it stretch further and this had the
effect of reducing its alcoholic content and slightly mitigating
drunkenness. There was a desire to carry on as normal and enjoy
life as long as it lasted. Sexual activity increased, as measured by the
number of marriages contracted, many of them in haste, and as

---

[13] Calder, *People's War*, loc 11078.
[14] Temple said, 'We are involved in an entanglement due to the sin of mankind, including our own, in which the best thing we can do is still a bad thing.
None the less, it is right to do it because it is the best possible. And so we have to
do it and be penitent', Calder, *People's War*, loc 10854.
[15] Calder, *People's War*, loc 8127.

measured by a rise in sexual transmitted diseases as well as in the birth of illegitimate children.[16]

It is against in this dire situation that the increasingly bitter dispute between Elim and George Jeffreys must be seen. From one perspective, the arguments appear trifling and petty against a background of burning buildings, crowds of homeless people, and the overwhelming suffering of bereaved or wounded individuals including children. From the comfort of an armchair in the 21st century the reader may want to cry out to the quarrelling churches that they should have diverted their energies to humanitarian aid for their fellow Britons. From another perspective, the arguments are an indication that ordinary life struggled to go on as before. While the bombs rained down, people continued to go to work, to be paid, to go shopping, cook and eat, to have children and to buy and sell buildings. For those with British-Israelite leanings, the United Kingdom was invincible: there was no possible way that Germany would invade or defeat the British people.[17] In these circumstances the war was fated to turn out as it did with a victory over Nazi Germany. And if this was the *necessary* outcome, then argument over buildings and land was sensible in the light of the peace that would eventually dawn.

Even so, it is alarming to read how many of the cities where Jeffreys had campaigned were struck by heavy bombing raids. Raids were particularly targeted at the southern ports. Portsmouth suffered its 37th raid on 11 March, 1941 when

> Another attack on the docks, shipyards and factories sent 193 high-explosive bombs – many of them as heavy as 5,500 1bs – 46,000 incendiaries raining down on the town. Fires were started in fuel storage depots and at the Royal Naval barracks … On 17

---

[16] Calder, *People's War*, loc 6888. Juliet Gardiner, *Wartime: Britain 1939–1945* (London: Headline, 2004), pp. 555, 556.

[17] Calder, *People's War*, loc 2333 'Everyone with the exception of the quartermaster, a British Israelite, whose readings of the Pyramids left him no room for doubt that, despite all appearances of disaster, Britain would be victorious'. British Israelism beliefs, in addition to the migration of the lost tribes to Britain, included the idea that the measurements of the pyramids of Egypt contained a coded prophecy about chronology.

April Portsmouth was attacked again, and again the docks burned, electricity supplies were cut, houses destroyed.[18]

The same kind of destruction was seen in Southampton, Cardiff, Birmingham, and even Nottingham. It is a testimony to the stability and tenacity of the first generation of Elim people that they hung on to their faith right through explosive tribulation as it poured down upon them.

War between Jeffreys and Elim

If Germany and Britain found themselves at war after the heady hopes of the Munich Agreement, an uncanny similarity was found in the Jeffreys-Elim relationship. After the intense negotiation and effort to bring Jeffreys and Elim back together again in May 1940, the ultimate departure of Jeffreys at the end of the year signalled the start of open conflict. The tone of the documentation changes. Jeffreys became more strident and Elim became more willing to show how Jeffreys has twisted and turned over the years. There are roughly three phases in the dispute. First, there were general contentions over the wording of Elim's new constitution, and the criticisms Jeffreys made of it, and these were followed by his own counterproposals and justification for remaining outside Elim. Second, there are disputes over particular buildings and congregations. Third, the debate eventually moves out beyond Elim to the point where Jeffreys criticised any joint ventures affecting European Pentecostals, and this is the stance he maintained to the end of his life.

Because there were no face-to-face meetings between Jeffreys and the Elim conference or the Elim Executive in the years that followed, communications were indirect and sometimes by pamphlet, sometimes by open letter, and sometimes by an article either in the *Elim Evangel* or in *The Pattern*. There do not appear to have been any Elim letters sent out to the Pattern churches although there are letters sent by Jeffreys to the Elim churches. The first shots of his literary campaign had raised the consciousness of lay people because by May 1940 the Elim Executive admitted there were now demands for lay representation. There is a flurry of

---

[18] Gardiner, *Wartime*, pp. 417, 418.

printed material in 1940 and 1941 and then a period of relative quiet until 1945 when Jeffreys once again escalated the dispute.

Jeffreys had two sets of relationships from 1940 onwards. Within his own circle and those who had left him or joined him in the Bible-Pattern Fellowship he maintained the sort of collegial friendships he had known in the early days of Elim. The first wave of defectors from Elim, including Jeffreys himself, drew a line round themselves and considered they were fighting for religious freedom against a dictatorial Elim system. They felt themselves to be a small and brave band struggling against a tyrannical opposition. By 1942 Jeffreys had 45 congregations associated with him and he set them up with local and national linkages and an annual conference.[19] This is not to say that the local churches were run identically since these were much more obviously financially and spiritually autonomous and great emphasis was given to this: some called themselves Free Elim congregations. But there were overarching connections between the churches that gave them an identity and a coordinating committee as well as annual meetings and *The Pattern* magazine with a circulation of around 2,250 copies per fortnight – though this later dropped.[20] The magazine took many of the stylistic features of the *Elim Evangel* although it was obviously smaller both because of the wartime paper rationing and the diminished constituency. Jeffreys himself was still called 'Principal' and his Revival Party continued to tour and preach as it had done in the early 1930s.

The other set of relationships that Jeffreys maintained was oppositional. Here he continued in his antipathy to the Elim Executive and accused them at various times of being 'governors' or a 'priestly' elite and made the point that his quarrel was not with the ordinary people but with the headquarters and its officers. The fusillade of pamphlets he issued undoubtedly detracted from his evangelistic work although there is also evidence he found difficulty in main-

---

[19] *The Pattern* 3.8 (mid-Apr 1942), p. 1.

[20] A financial statement in the Cartwright Archive at Regents Theological College, Malvern, shows the cost of printing *The Pattern* for October 1949 and the number of sales. There were 1,900 sent to the churches and 700 individual subscriptions. By 1950 the number sent to the churches had dropped to 1,650.

taining the heavy schedule of meetings;[21] and, on top of this, wartime conditions depleted resources so that his activities were in any
case trimmed back. Even so, Elim remained a reference point for
Jeffreys and he never forgot it or sought humble reconciliation.[22]

Pamphlets

The pamphlet war was damaging to both sides and, as is often the
case in inter-church argument, caused numbers of people to walk
away from both sides. Later in the 1970s when new Pentecostal and
charismatic churches were formed, successful congregations grew
in major cities where painful partings from Pentecostal congregations had occurred. It is possible that there were residual memories
of revivalistic meetings in cities like Sheffield, Birmingham, and
Hull. Yet it was necessary to make the dispute public since both
sides were appealing to average congregational members. Jeffreys
needed the votes of ordinary members to form new congregations
for the Bible-Pattern or else to keep them in the Bible-Pattern once
their pastors had taken them out of Elim. Elim needed to appeal to
ordinary members to justify their severance from the 'beloved Principal' whose magnetic ministry had brought so many people to
faith. Usually the pamphlets avoided personal attacks; but, in some
of them, hard feelings are apparent and it was Jeffreys who was in
the firing line; the Elim pamphlets were almost entirely anonymous
and so could not attract personal criticism.

Elim published a leaflet in August 1941 setting out information
about its new constitution and this was rapidly rebutted by Jeffreys
in *Elim's New Constitution* as well as *The Rights of The Local Church* and
Elim's New Constitution in the Light of Scriptural Principles.[23] The critique
made by Jeffreys of the new Elim constitution amounted to eight
points: the church would not have a voice or vote in the dismissal
of church members; the church will not have a voice or vote in the
initial choice of its elders; the church was not assured of voting

---

[21] *The Pattern*, 3.2 (mid-Jan 1942), p. 2, 'During the latter years the Principal
has lost much of his physical strength in his tremendous fight for religious freedom in the Churches he had founded'.

[22] I am told he did meet E.J. Phillips late in life for what was presumably a
personal rapprochement.

[23] Earlier pamphlets print a date of publication but many later ones have to
be dated from their internal evidence.

representation at the annual conference if the number of churches rose above 125; the church was not assured that its views would be presented at the conference by its minister and representative; the church would not have the right to dispense its own surplus offerings; the church would not have the right to reject erroneous doctrine; the church would not have a voice or vote in the choice of its pastor, its retention of its pastor, in the salary it has to pay its pastor or in the dismissal of its pastor; the church could be turned out of its building if it does not abide by Elim rules. An expansion of these points followed in *The Rights of the Local Church* and *Elim's New Constitution in Light of Scriptural principles,* which contains 12 points of criticism. The essence of Jeffreys' case is that the local church is supreme, and its supremacy is expressed by its democratic congregational system that guards it against external system of control. The church – by which he means the members of the congregation – have the right to confirm or deny decisions of the diaconate, to decide on the salary of their pastor, and to elect their elders by a show of hands. When acting together with other churches, one governing body should be formed of ministers, honorary pastors, and lay representatives but the local church should have the right to consider all agenda items presented to the governing body or its district presbyteries in advance. This governing body should give the churches and ministers 'as much freedom as possible to conform to the Scriptural Pattern'. In effect, Jeffreys advocated hyper-congregationalism.

Church Property: An Important Notice, focused on ownership of buildings and contains the words 'Since my resignation from Elim I have made it known that I would sign any church property over to the Elim Trust Corporation … If the congregation concerned would send me a resolution requesting me to do so'. And he went on to say, 'it is only right that I should warn all Elim Alliance Pastors and Churches throughout Great Britain and Ireland of the bondage that still exists under the amended Elim Constitution, dated 14 January 1942'.

Elim's reply is in *The Rights of the Local Church: George Jeffreys' Eight Points Analysed* and in *A Disgraceful Document.* In the first, in a point-by-point rebuttal, the biblical texts used by Jeffreys to justify his critique are shown to be capable of interpretations quite different from the ones he gave. Elim was able to show that the system Jef-

freys criticises was one that he himself set up or that Jeffreys had
changed his mind radically. For instance, 'as late as 1939 Mr Jeffreys
contended that an elected diaconate in each local church was unnecessary, and opposed the proposal in future to elect deacons'. In a
section entitled 'an appeal for unity' the pamphlet asked Jeffreys to
submit his views, contentions, and arguments to a gathering of
Elim churches in the same way that the early church resolved its
crisis by coming together for a conference in Jerusalem to discuss
the applicability or otherwise of the Mosaic law to Gentile converts.

The most scathing reply to Jeffreys comes within *A Disgraceful
Document* that reminds readers that Jeffreys had promised to relin-
quish his trusteeship of several churches and properties at the end
of 12 months from 1 July 1942, except where any church passed a
resolution to the contrary. It goes on, 'it is also an effrontery for Mr
Jeffreys to offer to sign over in a year's time property for which he
admits he did not pay, and which he tells us belongs to people who
gave the purchase money' and continues,

> Mr Jeffreys knows full well that apart from any promises of any
> character, with conditions or without conditions, he is bound by
> the Trust Deed which he himself signed to relinquish his trus-
> teeship of these buildings. No hedging about the Law or the
> Church can alter his moral obligation.

And then in response to the accusation that Elim is governed by a
'priestly dictatorship', points out that the new governing body …

> is composed of elements from local churches, brought together
> in a common fellowship for the common good of the work.
> Moreover it is untrue to say that Elim church members have no
> say in the government of the work, for they appoint the lay rep-
> resentatives to the conference; and any insinuation that church
> members have no control over the affairs of their Church is dis-
> proved by the fact that the deacons who are in charge of the
> church and all its departments are elected by the church mem-
> bers.

Whoever wrote the Elim pamphlet is clearly stung by Jeffreys because he says, 'The whole list of suggestions is a gross and unright-
eous libel, belying the actual facts of the situation.' Libel can be the
ground for court judgements and the attitude of both parties to law

had earlier been laid out in Elim's *Should a Christian Go to Law?* and answered by Jeffreys' *The Church and the Law: Which?* Elim noted that 1 Corinthians 6 admonished believers to allow themselves to be defrauded rather than to go to court against other Christians. However it carefully distinguished the situation envisaged by St Paul from one where Christians were accountable for *other people's belongings.*

> While we may and in certain cases should allow ourselves to be defrauded rather than to take legal action, there is no scripture to warrant our standing by and allowing others to be defrauded, for whose interests we are responsible.

The Deed Poll signed in 1934 bound the members of the Executive Council to exercise their office 'for the benefit of the Alliance and not otherwise' (clause 23). Jeffreys himself had invoked the law when he caused the deed poll to be enrolled in the Central Office of the Supreme Court of Judicature in 1934. Consequently the Elim conference of ministers and laymen passed a resolution with an overwhelming majority authorising the Executive Council to take 'such steps as might be considered necessary to ensure that the rights of Elim church members and their buildings were properly safeguarded'. Such safeguards would include court action.

Jeffreys replied with what might be seen as great cunning or great wisdom by contending, 'the Elim governors are acting against the interests of the people in withholding such a Trust Deed from the churches' and by 'such a Trust Deed' he meant one that would allow local congregations to own their buildings and deploy their own financial resources as they wished. He maintained that he would willingly act according to the majority vote of the members of each church – in other words he *was* acting for the benefit of Elim people once they demonstrated what they wanted by voting. He went on to say that the methods being employed by Elim were 'not Christian, neither are they British. It seems as if Elim's unscriptural organisation has been, and still is, in the grip of the spirit of Babylon (confusion) and that those who are party to it are urged to act against their own better judgement.' By arguing his case before the churches and all readers of his leaflets he was showing how he would defend himself in court. Presumably, his confidence in the case he was making would have been fortified by the advice of John

Leech. In such circumstances there is no surprise in discovering neither side ventured into the legal arena or stood before a magistrate.

Buildings

Particular buildings were more than symbols of disagreement.
Struggles over abstract principles and constitutional wording solidi-
fied into struggles over precious bricks and mortar and the attendant surplus finances of established congregations.

Worthing

The case of the Worthing church shows that by the autumn of
1941 the gloves had come off. Jeffreys was doing his best to pull
churches out of Elim into his new organisation. Worthing had
moved into the orbit of the Pattern early on; but, when the pro-
Jeffreys pastor accepted a call to Blackpool, a new man was drafted
in and he examined the claims of both sides and decided to stay in
Elim. He was offered a minimum salary with Elim so long as he
brought the congregation with him, which he did. This apparently
caused consternation in Pattern ranks and Jeffreys went down to
Worthing to try to repair the breach. He held a public meeting (12
November 1941) at which about 200 people were present of whom
47 were from Worthing. Two pamphlets were issued, one by the
Pattern side and the other by Elim which lamented the inaccurate
reporting authorised by Jeffreys.[24]

> The report suggests that the Worthing people present were
> unanimous for the Pattern. If the writer of that report was at
> the meeting, he must have known that a large number of
> Worthing people present were absolutely opposed to the Pattern.
> What are the facts? At the beginning of the meeting Mr Jeffreys
> asked all who belonged to Worthing to stand, and 47 people
> stood. This included the pastor and church officers and others
> who at that meeting definitely opposed the Pattern. It was there-
> fore perfectly obvious to every thinking person present when Mr
> Jeffreys at the end of the meeting asked those who wanted a Pat-
> tern church at Worthing to stand, and he again counted 47, they
> could not have been the same 47 who stood at the beginning.

---

[24] The Pattern published *The Elim Headquarters and The Worthing Church* and
Elim published *Worthing and Elim: Exposure of a False Publication.*

Whatever the mathematics of that occasion, Jeffreys was undoubtedly fostering division.

Portsmouth

On Sunday 7 December, 1941, a tug-of-war over the ownership of a building took place between Elim and the Bible-Pattern church. The congregation had been in existence since 1927 and had benefited from visits by Jeffreys over the years. It had purchased a building and, in accordance with normal Elim practice, had sent surplus money to headquarters for spending elsewhere in the movement. Its pastor was Robert Mercer, a staunch follower of Jeffreys who had been in his circle since the early days in Ireland.

When Jeffreys made his demands for self-government and first resigned from Elim in December 1939, the congregation stood with Jeffreys. After May 1940 when reconciliation seems to have been reached, the Portsmouth church strengthened its ties with the rest of Elim but then, 'when Jeffreys resigned a second time the Portsmouth Church followed his lead and decided as a Church not to recognise the Constitution of Elim'.[25] Indeed when Jeffreys formed the Bible-Pattern church fellowship, leaders of the new movement influenced a number of churches to secede from Elim and join the new group although Portsmouth was late in doing so. By this time there was a division within the congregation between those who wanted to stay in Elim and those who wanted to join the new movement. The deacons who were pro-Elim were voted out and replaced by pro-Pattern men. As a result many of the original members left the church and went elsewhere.

On 7 December 1941, five Elim ministers from London arrived in Portsmouth and installed a new pastor in the building which, as they pointed out, belonged legally and morally to the Elim Foursquare Gospel Alliance. The fact that the taking of the building occurred on a Sunday morning when a communion service was due to be held and in the presence of a police officer, who had been brought along in case of trouble, aroused anger in the Pattern group and confirmed their worst fears about the strong-armed dictatorial nature of the Elim Executive.

---

[25] Taken from a leaflet *Elim and Portsmouth* published by Elim.

Letters were exchanged between the two groups, one from Elim dated 31 December 1941 and a reply on 13 January 1942. The letters dealt with minor financial matters concerning money in missionary boxes and the electricity bill and the value of the furniture in the house of the minister. For the most part these were resolved simply enough but the Pattern church refused to send the balance of the offerings taken in the church up to the date of Jeffreys' second resignation on 12 November 1940. Mercer and others replied,

> The church is not prepared to give any of its surplus offerings, as these are reserved for local purposes in accordance with the Resolution of June 3, 1940; neither is the Church now prepared to give the 10% for administration until their Church Building is restored to them.[26]

These disputes illustrate the painful nature of the split within Elim brought about by Jeffreys' resignation. Some of the dispute descends to petty details while other parts of it are diffused with high principle. The local church in this letter says that 'all that our congregation asked for were proper Title Deeds to the Church property they had paid for'[27] which is an apparently just claim; but what it fails to note is that other members of the congregation who had supported Elim had by then left so that the claim that this particular congregation had paid for the entire building is misleading. In addition, the congregation that paid for the building knew very well, or its church officers knew very well, that the building belonged to the Elim Foursquare Gospel Alliance and surplus monies were being sent to Elim headquarters for dispersal elsewhere. The Pattern congregation took its stand on a principle of local church government even though this principle contradicted the Title Deed of the church and its own earlier practice. Elim were correct in saying it had a legal right to the building, and the moral case made by *The Pattern* was messy because the original congregation was no longer intact.

---

[26] Letter to W.G. Hathaway of the Elim Foursquare Gospel Alliance from R. Mercer and ten deacons dated 13 Jan 1942, first published in *The Pattern* 3.3 (Feb 1942), p. 7.
[27] Letter to W.G. Hathaway of the Elim Foursquare Gospel Alliance from R. Mercer and ten deacons dated 13 Jan 1942.

This unhappy episode, however, whatever the rights and wrongs of the individual case, shows how the resignation of Jeffreys from Elim and his subsequent repudiation of the system he had originally advocated caused misery to many hundreds of ordinary Christians who had followed his lead and given their money so readily in response to his revivalistic preaching.

Glasgow

The dispute over Glasgow City Temple followed now familiar lines. Presumably Elim (in documentation we do not possess) claimed the building back under the terms of the legal agreement made between the Temple's trustees and Elim. The three trustees were Robert Darragh, James McWhirter, and George Jeffreys who had left Elim and therefore forfeited their right to the building. However, as Jeffreys pointed out in a pamphlet published on 1 January 1943 the trustees had raised the money to purchase the Temple – presumably through their campaigning in the 1930s – with the result that Jeffreys felt himself justified, despite the terms of the trust deed, in holding on to the building. He asserted the whole congregation 'claim from the Trustees and Elim Governors a proper Trust Deed with local trustees for their Church building' in the expectation that the new deed would 'for ever prevent any Governor or Governors outside the Temple forcing objectionable rules upon the congregation'. The demand Jeffreys made, then, was that until Elim changed the deed in line with the wishes of the congregation and its officers, he would not surrender his trusteeship. And there the matter stood for many years in permanent deadlock.

London, Kensington Temple

The story of Kensington Temple is more tortuous but similar in many respects. The building had belonged to the Congregational Church and Stephen Jeffreys preached an evangelistic and healing campaign there in 1921 (see chapter 5). George bought the building in 1930 and the two trustees were Robert Darragh and James McWhirter during the period of their lifetimes. Again Elim wanted the building but the trustees refused to return it unless changes were made to the proposed trust deed along the lines Jeffreys had

by now developed.[28] The Elim Executive was not prepared to modi-
fy their standard trust deed but in the late 1950s Robert Darragh
died and left James McWhirter as the only trustee. McWhirter,
whose theological views had now broadened, was prepared to sell
the building back to Elim despite objections from Bible-Pattern
ministers.[29] So in the end Elim acquired the Temple as a base for
many of its London operations and in the second part of the 20th
century it became one of the city's mega-churches.

Reflection

Within the Bible-Pattern organisation Jeffreys remained the beloved
Principal, the leader, the evangelist, the chairman, and the main
speaker; outside the Pattern organisation he was an irritant, a trou-
bler of the churches, and yesterday's man. Even without assessing
the rights and wrongs of the dispute with Elim, the Pattern organisation functioned as a support network and financial base for his
ministry. It is too much to claim that he was consciously trying to
recreate the material conditions of his early ministerial life or that
John Leech was a father figure to him in the Irish years who became
a father figure to him in the 1940s. For one thing, Leech died in
1942. Nor is it more than speculative to argue that Jeffreys had a
psychological need to place himself as the leader of an embattled
minority. If one turns everything round and views the events of the
1940s and beyond from Jeffreys' perspective, a more positive assessment of the last 20 years of his life emerges. He *did* champion
religious freedom and in a messily executed reform broadened the
basis of Elim's collective decision-making. He would have resisted
any of the heavy shepherding that marred the later charismatic
movement or some of the exaggerated claims to be heard among
apostolic neo-Pentecostals, and faint echoes of his words may still

[28] See the leaflet *Kensington Temple, London*, presumably written by George Jeffreys but without his name on it and without a date. His name was probably left
off because he was not a trustee and so had no right to dictate terms. Darragh
was close to Jeffreys and would have acted as Jeffreys asked.
[29] Jack Hywel-Davies, *The Kensington Temple Story* (Crowborough: Monarch,
1998), p. 39. Hywel-Davies states George Jeffreys was also a trustee but I think
this unlikely because he does not name himself in *Kensington Temple, London*,
whereas he does name himself in the leaflet about Glasgow City Temple.

sometimes be heard today. Elim, despite its struggles and pain, emerged as a better denomination in the post-war period than it would otherwise have done.

Genuine anger runs through the early Elim pamphlets. Jeffreys had voluntarily and thoughtfully entered into contractual arrangements with four big congregations that, at the time, and without the glare of publicity, brought financial benefit through the diversion of surplus church funds to a small number of trustees of whom he was one.[30] Once he left Elim, he was contractually obligated to surrender these buildings but he refused to do so, arguing that he was acting in the interests of the congregations within the buildings he retained. Jeffreys maintained that he was acting in the interests of these congregations and many others by preventing them being dispossessed by Elim. Yet, any normal reading of the situation would place Jeffreys firmly in the wrong. If we assume Jeffreys was not double-minded and that he genuinely believed he was standing up for defenceless congregations, we can only admire his resolution. If we assume Jeffreys was acting in his own interests (by accruing the surplus income from the four selected congregations) while pretending to act in the interests of others, we can only marvel at the self-deception involved. Jeffreys' friends and his inner circle, with the possible exception of James McWhirter, remained loyal to him and endorsed his account. Letters or articles by his friends repeat the arguments made by Jeffreys with little or no deviation; and, after his death, Albert Edsor fiercely defended his memory and reputation and destroyed correspondence and accounts relevant to the post-Elim period.

As we shall see in the next chapter, Jeffreys continued his evangelistic meetings up and down the country as far as wartime conditions allowed. The dispute with his former Elim colleagues, though pursued obsessively, only occupied a part of his heart and mind.

---

[30] Glasgow, Blackpool, Brighton, and Kensington Temple were the four big congregations that provided income for the trustees in Jeffreys' inner circle. The majority of the other congregations sent their surplus offerings to Elim Headquarters for distribution within the movement, including to pastors whose congregations could not afford the minimum salaries.

19

1940–1945: STARTING ALL OVER AGAIN

War Continues

The invasion of Britain by German forces required command of the air. From July until the end of October 1940 the 'Battle of Britain' was fought by fighter pilots and ground air defences that gradually asserted their supremacy over the German air force, the Luftwaffe. Once Hitler realised control of the air could not be achieved, he called off invasion plans; and, by May 1941, the blitz on London was scaled back. Bombing continued over other cities but the immediate crisis had passed. In September 1941 the British Eighth Army was formed and sent by ship to fight Rommel in North Africa. In December 1941 the Japanese, without a declaration of war, attacked the American fleet at Pearl Harbour, and this shook American public opinion, silenced neutral and non-interventionist voices, and brought the United States into the war. Once the United States and its vast industrial resources were placed on a war footing, Churchill was convinced Hitler could never win. Moreover, in the summer of 1941, having turned away from Britain, Hitler made the strategic mistake of invading the Soviet Union and sending at least two armies and multiple panzer groups to capture valuable oil regions. His troops were not prepared for a long campaign and not clothed for the icy snows of the Russian winter.[1] Germany found three-quarters of its forces locked into combat on the eastern front.

---

[1] Anthony Beevor, *Stalingrad* (Harmondsworth: Penguin, 1999).

As British forces were now no longer solely concentrated on defending their coastline, the Royal Air Force stretched its wings into the bombing of German heartlands; and, with American personnel and armour, the balance of the global conflict tipped in favour of the Allies.

Even after 1941 bombing raids persisted over selected British cities, and civilians continued to die. Food and other imports were reduced by the U-boat campaign in the Atlantic but the population acclimatised itself to the new realities. American troops arrived in Britain in large numbers in preparation for the Normandy landings on 6 June 1944. On a vast fleet of vessels with their assorted landing craft 160,000 troops crossed the English Channel on the first day; and, although at least 10,000 were killed within 24 hours, the landings were completed. The German army found itself fighting on two fronts. Bombing continued in both directions as German cities were flattened and Britain was subject to the new terror of flying bombs launched from Peenemünde on the north east coast of Germany. Although the British population could not dismiss its fears, it also developed a kind of cheerful fatalism as ordinary life continued. Full employment, a diet of home-grown food, a collective purpose, and gradually rising hope enabled Jeffreys and his Bible-Pattern Fellowship to operate along lines similar to, but on a smaller scale than, the Elim of the 1920s.

Beginning Again

Although the infrastructure of Britain took a heavy pounding during the war years, travel was possible by road or rail. During much of 1940, Jeffreys appeared ready to rejoin Elim after the intense discussions at the start of the year and the conciliatory Elim conference in May. Even so, Jeffreys published monthly issues of *The Pattern* magazine with the result that his exit from Elim has the appearance of being pre-planned – although a more charitable explanation would be that after his first resignation from Elim he was simply keeping the new magazine going in case the peace talks came to nothing. Jeffreys turned to a group of advisers after the conference in May and they appear to have persuaded him to impose new conditions on Elim. The upshot of this is that Jeffreys' inconsistency was at least partly due to the multiplicity of voices he allowed to influence him. It may be, of course, Jeffreys was indecisive and forgot what he had previously agreed but the impression given by his writings is the opposite. He appears to have remembered much, though not all, of the zig-zag discussions of the 1930s and he rarely writes as if he holds an opinion tentatively.

So, when the break with Elim became final, he began the enormous task of building a new denomination. His preaching activities in the 1940s show him to have given high priority to the acceptance of new congregations, the support of congregations that had come out of Elim and the support of groups (often with his encouragement) that had split away from Elim congregations. He spoke of himself as 'standing with' factions that had seen the precious truth of ecclesiastical liberty. He found himself building his new denomination while insisting, loudly and clearly, that each congregation was autonomous. There was a paradoxical element to this: he wanted to organise and pull together congregations over which he had no legal or constitutional control. Any central denominational committees he created had to be advisory only. His own magnetism and name were the greatest assets he could deploy.

While he was engaged in setting up his Bible-Pattern Fellowship he was also engaged in a running battle with Elim and one that quickly turned nasty. During 1940, when reconciliation appeared possible, comment was relatively restrained but from 1941 onwards both sides pushed hard. This is not to say that personal insults or scurrilous comments were part of the discourse. The tone was firm and pointed but not abusive. Very quickly Jeffreys cast himself in the role of the defender of church liberty, and he did this by insisting on constitutional and legal safeguards for all congregations. They were to hold their own buildings absolutely, to have the power to appoint their ministers and deacons and the capacity to discuss in advance any national agenda that might be prepared by the denomination to which they belonged. To draw the contrast between the Bible-Pattern Fellowship and Elim, he had to cast Elim as dictatorial, even tyrannical, and unchristian. He developed an oratory invoking the ancient city of Babylon as the paradigm of all priestly control systems. The more he did this, the less likely Elim were to concede to his demands or his rhetoric.

An unforeseen consequence of his dispute with Elim was his willingness to accept other congregations and ministers into his orbit. A distinct ecumenical tone can sometimes be heard, and this contrasts strongly with the occasionally strident language he used in the 1930s.[2] He speaks of revived Christians working together free from the shackles of denominational control. He draws upon the example of Swedish Pentecostalism and of Lewi Pethrus to substantiate the case he is making and so, perhaps in recognition of this, Pethrus responded by publishing a supportive piece in *Herald of Faith*.[3] To this both E.J. Phillips and Donald Gee responded with letters of their own, letters telling Pethrus he only knew one side of the story and ought to publish a correction.[4]

Travels

In each of the years of the war Jeffreys preached in about 20 different places. The four congregations whose surplus income flowed to the World Revival Crusade and thence to funds in Jeffreys' control (Glasgow, Blackpool, Kensington Temple, Brighton) were big venues and consistent locations for his preaching. He was at Brighton every year from 1940 to 1945, Blackpool in three of those years, at Glasgow for all of them, and Kensington Temple on multiple occasions. He gave time to Carlisle (that soon transferred from Elim to the Bible-Pattern Fellowship) and to Portsmouth and Nottingham. The city where he preached most frequently throughout the war was London because of its multiple locations – Barking, Caxton Hall, Clayton, East Ham, Fulham, Orange Street (Leicester Square), Upper Norwood, Westminster Central Hall, and Westminster Chapel. He was in Wales and preached in Cardiff three times, Newport, Penarth, and Swansea twice as well as Cwmtwrch, Pontypool, and Upper Tumble. On the east coast he visited Hull twice and Scarborough twice. On the west he was in Liverpool, Southport, and Bristol twice each. Of the northern industrial towns he visited Halifax in successive years and Middlesbrough, Huddersfield, Barnsley, Sheffield, and Newcastle. In the south he was in Dorking, Bournemouth, Boscombe, Worthing, Portsmouth, Heathfield, Southampton, and Brighton.

---

[2] *The Pattern* 4.8 (mid-Apr 1943), p. 3.
[3] *The Pattern* 2.11 (June 1941), pp. 5-8.
[4] Pethrus claimed that Jeffreys' departure from Elim had nothing to do with BI.

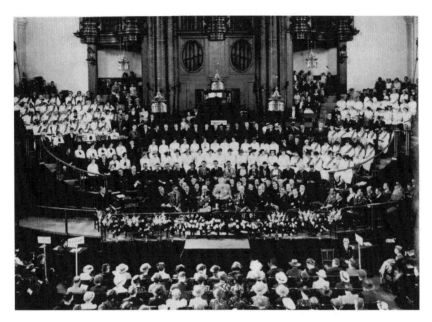

Jeffreys Preaching in Westminster Central Hall c. 1950

An older, greyer Jeffreys continues to preach at Easter in London, this time in
Westminster Central Hall. He maintains the format adopted in the 1930s when
he annually hired the Royal Albert Hall. A choir is visible behind him and in the
attentive congregation the ladies are visible wearing hats. The scene speaks
of order and dignity, which was the hallmark of Jeffreys' Pentecostalism.

As the war continued, his preaching and travel showed no sign
of abating. Scotland heard him many times partly because of the
pull of Glasgow City Temple and, partly, because life was less disrupted by the Luftwaffe north of the border. The most poignant of
his campaigns was in Coventry, close to the machine tools industry,
when he set up his big tent in the summer of 1940 as part of an
old-style campaign.[5] He claimed 200 converts but must, like the rest
of the country, have been shocked by the 515 bomber raid on 14
November 1940 when the heart this picturesque city and its cathedral were set ablaze and hundreds of deaths ensued.[6]

Perhaps older and wiser, or perhaps more desperate, Jeffreys was
willing to share the limelight with the preachers who had joined him

---

[5] *The Pattern* 1.7 (July 1940), inside cover.
[6] Juliet Gardiner, *Wartime Britain 1939–1945* (London: Headline Book Publishing, 2004), pp. 350-54.

in the Pattern fellowship. James McWhirter was always a popular man in the pulpit as well as an imaginative contributor to *The Pattern*. Other names appear like, Gwilym Francis, a Welsh evangelist and the Pattern Fellowship's secretary, and, surprisingly, members of the Jeffreys family. Stephen Jeffreys, now infirm, joined George as did Edward, Stephen's son. Meanwhile John Leech, an old man now, was president of the Fellowship and a dignified figurehead as well as treasurer. Percy Parker, one of Elim's stalwarts, had defected with Jeffreys and found himself as editor of *The Pattern* and charged with looking after the correspondence course. All these were part of the pool of preachers who helped stabilise the congregations they accumulated – there were 20 in March 1941 and 45 a year later[7] – but there is evidence too of switching around from pastorate to pastorate so that, for instance, Noel Brooks was at one point in Bristol and another time in Scotland, which suggests that Pattern congregations were not entirely settled.[8]

BI Themes
Running as an underground current in the theology of Jeffreys was the doctrine of BI. Elim, in common with classical Pentecostal denominations across the world, had no time for what they took to be a fanciful although relatively harmless doctrinal aberration. Having set up the Bible-Pattern Fellowship and its magazine, Jeffreys was free to publish articles supporting British-Israel. He always maintained, however, that British-Israel teachings were a species of prophetic interpretation concerning the national destiny of Israel/Britain. During the 1930s he had repeatedly argued that adherence to one or other school of prophetic interpretation was a matter of conscience. He was as good as his word in *The Pattern*. He allowed British Israel writers to be published; but, equally, allowed rebuttals to be printed as well. *The Pattern* magazine in this respect was unusual as a Pentecostal publication because it contained an ongoing debate within its pages. True, the last word normally went to the British Israel side and true, too, the implications of British-Israel teaching generated unusual Scriptural exposition – though

---

[7] *The Pattern* 2.4 (mid-Feb 1941), p. 1 and *The Pattern* 3.8 (mid-Apr 1942), p. 1.

[8] *The Pattern* 2.11 (June 1941), p. 4 and *The Pattern* 3.5 (Mar 1942), p. 3.

always indicative of ultimate British victory in the war. However, at
no point did Jeffreys compromise his evangelical theology: individual regeneration was always necessary for salvation.

Early on the magazine set out three articles on the ten lost tribes,
each of the same length but defending different positions and the
final one saying that the ten tribes of Israel did not return from
captivities and so by implication were in a position to migrate across
the world to Britain.[9] Another article on the topic appeared a month
later and in July 1940 Jeffreys himself said, 'many Spirit-baptised
leaders believe that … the revelation of a hitherto hidden Israel is
closely linked to the outpouring of the Spirit in the last days'.[10] In
August McWhirter asks rhetorically whether a successful invasion
of Britain was possible and answers robustly 'never!'

> The ground of our hope for Britain's immunity to invasion is
> because she is Israel. If she is *not* then her immunity has been really good fortune, which may be turned by the Nazi hordes. The
> confidence that no foreign foe will over-run our land is the hope
> only of those who believe that Britain is Israel. The spiritual joy
> of this conception is only second to the Church's 'blessed hope'
> of the Lord's return.[11]

This long article asserts there is a biblical promise of a home for
the Jewish people outside the land of Palestine and the identification of the home with the British Isles 'is now an epic story of Israel-Britain's history. These are the isles North-West of Palestine so
often addressed by God through Isaiah the prophet.' All this serves
to reassure and protect us 'at this moment of grave anxiety'.[12]

A month later McWhirter is writing on 'national repentance' and
says that we are now experiencing 'the birth pangs of a new day
which is about to dawn, when the kingdoms of this world shall become the kingdoms of our God and his Christ'.[13] And he discerns
'signs, not only of a stirring and awakening of the national conscience but of a seeking after and acknowledging of God in a new

[9] *The Pattern* 1.3 (Mar 1940), pp. 10, 11.
[10] *The Pattern* 1.7 (July 1940), p. 8.
[11] *The Pattern* 1.8 (Aug 1940), p. 6. Original emphasis.
[12] *The Pattern* 1.8 (Aug 1940), p. 7.
[13] *The Pattern* 1.9 (Sept 1940), pp. 6, 7.

way'. In keeping with the right of reply an article by Mr Naumann refutes McWhirter's earlier claims scathingly:

> Mr McWhirter has like many other British-Israelites failed in correct exegesis of Scripture, and in logical and proper approach to his subject. Thus he has not even raised the standard of the efforts of British-Israel apologists. He has added another danger by his remarkable statement that we are automatically immune from invasion and thus possibly weakening the efforts of prayer warriors and believers.[14]

McWhirter never replied to this indictment. At the end of 1940 Mr Llewellyn Williams, President of the British Israel Federation, weighed in with his assessment of the situation: 'Satan is making his last desperate bid for world domination … By their action in making war on Christian civilisation, the Axis powers are against Christ, and are, therefore, a manifestation of the Antichrist.'[15] This was followed in February 1941 by Lt Commander Macmillan asserting strongly that the Anglo-Celtic-Saxon peoples are the remnant of Israel.[16] Pushing the logic yet further was an article entitled by Percy Parker's question 'Is America Manasseh?' – the implication being that the American people may be the tribe of Manasseh just as Britain is Israel.[17] Taking the theory even further, *The Pattern* asks whether Iceland is actually the tribe of Benjamin.[18]

A new line of speculation opens when *The Pattern* gives space to the notion that the Great Pyramid of Egypt is referred to in Scripture, 'In that day there will be an altar to the Lord in the heart of Egypt, and a monument to the Lord at its border. It will be a sign and witness to the Lord Almighty in the land of Egypt' (Isa. 19.19-20).[19] A so-called 'pyramid publication' was advertised and we are told 'many are interested in the pyramid' and its teaching, though with the caveat, 'many are very careful not to be dogmatic' and this is followed by the assertion that the year 1941 was 'an outstanding

---

[14] *The Pattern* 1.9 (Sept 1940), p. 12.
[15] *The Pattern* 1.12 (Dec 1940), p. 14.
[16] *The Pattern* 2.3 (Feb 1941), p. 4.
[17] *The Pattern* 2.3 (Feb 1941), pp. 6, 7.
[18] *The Pattern* 2.8 (mid-Apr 1941), pp. 4, 5.
[19] *The Pattern* 2.13 (July 1941), p. 9.

year in Biblical and Pyramid prophecy' because the dimensions of the Pyramid are secret signs of future events.[20]

By January 1943 *The Pattern* was carrying an advertisement for a book arguing Germany's doom because 'Germany is Esau'. Fortunately, even from the British Israel point of view, balancing comment was available. Maynard James argued,

> We have become pagan again and are being justly judged for our national and church sins' and went on to say 'the mere preaching of British Israelism as a popular lecture only feeds our national vanity ... our only hope in this dark hour of Jacob's trouble is national repentance.[21]

John Leech died in 1942 and was replaced as president of the Bible-Pattern Fellowship by Lt Cmdr D.H. Macmillan who combined ardent BI with anti-Catholicism. For Macmillan Roman Catholicism was wrong to declare that she was the new Israel since it is actually God's Protestant Remnant People who are predominantly the elect of Israel.[22] By 1944 he is declaring, 'Pattern Christians' must be 'free of the degrading clutches of the world over the work of the Spirit' and that 'from military, naval and air supremacy God is going to turn Britain to a spiritual power in the service of mankind' but then 'the pagan hordes of unregenerate humanity impelled by demon power will seek to destroy Britain's power by conflict in and near the Land of the Mission of Israel and of Our Lord Jesus' and that as a consequence 'we must stand by and rally round Principal George Jeffreys'.[23] This cast the Bible Pattern Fellowship into a heroic role preparing Britain for its further spiritual service while being ready for renewed and vicious attack. In the circumstances, rallying round George Jeffreys is the answer.

Organisation
By April 1941 Jeffreys was able to report on the 'first district gathering of regular Ministers, Elders and Deacons from Elim Free churches and others in the Fellowship'.[24] Between two and three

[20] *The Pattern* 3.4 (mid-Feb 1942), p. 9.
[21] *The Pattern* 3.9 (May 1942).
[22] *The Pattern* 2.7 (Apr 1941), pp. 10, 11.
[23] *The Pattern* 5.1 (Jan 1944), pp. 3-5.
[24] *The Pattern* 2.7 (Apr 1941), p. 1.

hundred ministers and laypeople gathered in Portsmouth where they formally resolved to 'place on record their determination to promote and extend the work of the Bible-Pattern Church Fellowship' and their willingness to negotiate with the Executive Council of Elim. They also resolved, 'owing to the deadlock in the dispute between the Governing Body of the Elim Alliance' all churches in sympathy with the 'principles of the Bible-Pattern Fellowship to link up with the Fellowship'.[25] In this way they brought into existence a 'district assembly' that became one of several across the country that would fit into a national body in due course. In short, Jeffreys was establishing a loose-knit national church organisation with regional or district components. It was loosely controlled by a smaller Church Fellowship Coordinating Council which, in 1941, took the decision not to make legal moves unless Elim forced the issue.[26]

In the first year the new Fellowship was internally debating its exact terms of reference so that, even in 1941, discussion about: (1) the holding of property and control of finance; (2) the rejection of erroneous doctrine; (3) stationing ministers; and (4) the church council were still unclear. Despite the claims of the Fellowship that it was strictly following biblical guidelines, Mr J. Lindsay, writing in the pages of *The Pattern*, pointed out, 'There's no pattern in the Scriptures as to the method of acquisition or holding of property'. Central bodies, just as much as local bodies, can hold property and he pertinently asks, 'did not the central body bear the liability, and was it not the gifts of many who are members of other churches and of some who never were, or are not now, in fellowship, that helped procure the property? Is the congregation the same today as that which originally advances most of the money?' And so, 'Are the present users, therefore, morally entitled to hold the building?'[27] Such questions are devastating in the light of the persistent claims of Jeffreys and others that the Elim Executive was controlling properties over which they had no moral right. Yet, it is to the credit of Jeffreys and the Pattern Fellowship that they were willing to allow foundational debate of this kind within the pages of their jour-

---

[25] *The Pattern* 2.7 (Apr 1941), p. 1.
[26] *The Pattern* 2.22 (mid-Nov 1941), p. 4.
[27] *The Pattern* 2.7 (Apr 1941), p. 9.

nal. Answering, Lindsay, Parker offered a defence of the new Fellowship by asserting that all the money had been given because of 'confidence in the Foursquare Gospel message' and, crucially, 'confidence in the Leader of the Foursquare Gospel work'.[28] In other words, the money given to buy the Elim churches was *only* given because people had confidence in George Jeffreys and his preaching. This is a large claim. It certainly cannot be proved and it ignores the contributions of every other Elim minister and officer. As a moral justification, it is precarious.

Local gatherings similar to the one in Portsmouth were set up in Stockport[29] and Nottingham[30] and elsewhere. New congregations had been established by a resolution of those present, as had occurred in Dundee.[31] After a year a National Assembly was brought into being and Jeffreys addressed it at an Easter Monday service in Westminster Central Hall, London, in 1942. He declared,

> In my opinion there are certain principles in the out-working of the Pattern Constitution that need stressing in order to safeguard the glorious liberty our unfettered Ministers and Free Churches are enjoying. I prayed that in the working arrangements of the Fellowship not one member shall have any selfish motive or vested interest to protect.

> Counting on the all-sufficiency of God:

> (1) we should prevent the Pattern Fellowship and its various departments from entry into the world of organised and commercialised religion. Our job is not material business but spiritual. It is to preach the Gospel of Christ and to establish churches that are self-governing, self-supporting and self-propagating.

> (2) we should see that there is no man-made Constitution to bind Ministers or local Churches to the Pattern Fellowship. The binding link between ministers and churches with the Fellowship must be fellowship and nothing else. It is the Biblical way of holding believers together in united service.

---

[28] *The Pattern* 2.9 (May 1941), p. 11.
[29] *The Pattern* 2.11 (June 1941), p. 3.
[30] *The Pattern* 2.10 (mid-May 1941), p. 1.
[31] *The Pattern* 2.20 (mid-Oct 1941), p. 3.

(3) we should keep out of debt, so that no member of the Pattern Fellowship shall ever be burdened with any financial responsibility ... Let us not forget that spiritual Ministers have become fettered by binding them to man-made Constitutions and Rules, until they have become slaves to a cruel bondage and shepherds without shepherds' hearts.[32]

Signing Over

Jeffreys published in *The Pattern* magazine many critical comments on Elim and many elucidations of the Bible-Pattern position. He or his supporters maintained that, since the pages of the *Elim Evangel* were no longer open to him and because the Elim congregations had been told to close their doors to him, he had no choice but to make his views and appeals known in the pages of his magazine.[33] In 1944, in a six-page article, he published a list of all the properties he was finally signing over to Elim. He was able to do this, he said, having received a satisfactory indemnity; and, by signing the properties over, he was severing the remaining legal links between himself and the churches he founded throughout Elim. The article lists at least 44 tabernacles and halls and 11 houses. Some are held under the Elim Trust Corporation and others by what has been called the Elim Pentecostal Alliance Council and others under the Elim Model Trust Deed. He also transferred over £810 of Edinburgh Corporation 2.5% stock.[34]

He pointed out, 'there would be no layman in the Elim Conference and no elected deacons in the Elim churches if the ministers now outside Elim had not fought for them', a claim that is correct although it assumes that he would not have been able to introduce these changes by working within the Elim conference system which he dominated for many years. He also, as a kind of parting shot, says,

If the Elim Pastors, Lay Representatives, Elders and Deacons have been deceived by the make-believe of the wordy amended

---

[32] *The Pattern* 3.8 (mid-Apr 1942), p. 5.
[33] *The Pattern* 3.1 (Jan 1942), p. 6.
[34] *The Pattern* 3.8 (mid-Apr 1942), p. 5.

Elim Constitution of 1942, and the Ulster brethren by the Irish Code of Laws, it is not our fault.[35]

The long list of valuable properties comes as a surprise. These were all over the country and represented the material fruit of his ministry in the 1920s and early 1930s. One might suspect that he was attempting to bargain with Elim to secure the four key properties of Glasgow, Brighton, Blackpool, and Kensington Temple in exchange for all the rest although this is never expressly stated. It is a watershed moment and the exact timing of it must surely be due to more than the provision of an indemnity. By October 1944, in another long article on the subject and another subheading 'Is it too late to unite?', he suggests the Elim movement could be preserved if each Elim church were given a model trust deed that protected the Elim fundamental truths, the percentage income given to headquarters, the requirement to keep the church building in good repair and to pay a proportionate share of the pooled debt, and if safeguards were given to the local churches to protect their ability to choose their own pastors, then, even at this late hour, a reconciliation would be possible.[36] Although what he says is reasonable and conciliatory, it is amazing that all the complicated articles and pamphlets about the legal differences between the Pattern and Elim are apparently bridgeable by eight simple conditions. Had Jeffreys made his offer four years previously, and had he stuck to it, legal impediments would surely have been removed. But by 1944 everyone had moved on and damage had been done to friendships and hope.

Campaigning

The war in Europe ended on 8 May 1945. It was not feasible to campaign in the war years. Big meetings were possible and conventions were held but the huge crowds that streamed into meetings night after night in Birmingham or Cardiff in the 1930s were never going to materialise. Although there are reports of revival scenes in Southampton (April 1940) or even in an air raid shelter in Nottingham (September 1940) and although Jeffreys continued to preach evangelistically, he often also spoke about the Bible-Pattern Church and the advantages of its new constitution. In September 1941,

---

35 *The Pattern* 5.8 (mid-Apr 1944), p. 11.
36 *The Pattern* 5.19 (Oct 1944), p. 7.

when he was in Cardiff, the headline is 'Reformation fires are burning! Revival flames are kindling!' It was the twin topics of revival and reform that he preached. In 1943 he spoke at a large hall in the centre of Barnsley at a well-filled weekend and shortly afterwards returned to Birmingham for three days; at the end of the year 1,000 people were present at a meeting in Hull (December 1943). On Easter Monday in Westminster Central Hall (April 1944) there were 45 decisions for Christ and crowded meetings at Barking and Lancaster in July 1944. In November of that year 700 were present in Hull and 600 in December 1944 in Nottingham. The numbers are impressive but never reach the heights of the pre-war era. Consequently reports of converts are also smaller, 20 or 50 people at a time.

Reflection

Jeffreys was frenetically active in the war years, perhaps more active than he had been in the lead-up to 1939. He seemed galvanised by the challenge of starting again from the beginning and he threw himself into preaching, organising, attending conferences, writing pamphlets and articles, and, presumably, raising money. He had the old Revival Party round him. They used the car and the caravan while petrol was available but eventually travelled by train.[37] There was a reference to a long train journey in January 1940.[38] One can admire the energy of Jeffreys although by January 1942 the strain was beginning to tell. 'During the latter years the Principal has lost much of his physical strength in his tremendous fight for religious freedom in the churches'.[39] He is sometimes portrayed as a victim of his convictions: Parker reported, 'he's been forced to resign twice'[40] and elsewhere the reclaiming of church buildings by Elim is seen as an affront to good Christian people who are turned out into the street.

At times there are hints that the Bible-Pattern Fellowship and Jeffreys himself are leading Britain into an eschatological future;

---

[37] Edsor, *'Set Your House in Order'*, p. 193.
[38] *The Pattern* 1.1 (Jan 1940), p. 8.
[39] *The Pattern* 3.2 (mid-Jan 1942), p. 2.
[40] *The Pattern* 3.1 (Jan 1942), p. 6.

they are at the forefront of a spiritual battle for freedom while Britain's identity as the new Israel waits to be revealed. This heightened expectation leads to highly speculative theology derived from the British Israel position. If Britain is Israel and America is Manasseh and Germany is Esau and Iceland is Benjamin we are in the realm of the fantastic. And when any kind of credence is given to the great Pyramid as a prophetic symbol whose mysterious dimensions are indicative of the future, the Foursquare evangelical certainties publicly proclaimed by Jeffreys begin to fade into the background. There is a flirting with these outlandish ideas but they never take over or assume centre stage. They show Jeffreys is associating with the fringe of Pentecostalism in his desire to build a new movement.

And within the British-Israel psyche two competing positions co-exist. On one side Britain *cannot* be invaded because she is Israel; on the other, because she is Israel, she *can* be subject to divine judgement unless as a nation she repents. Jeffreys appears not to embrace any of the extremities of British-Israel thinking and the more colourful ideas are expressed by others, including McWhirter, who is part of the Revival Party. If there is any softening towards Elim or lessening of demands for reform, we might wonder if the simpler approach of 1944 stems from the departure of John Leech from the scene. This, in itself, is speculative and we have no inside information to confirm or deny it. If the articles Jeffreys writes can be judged by their tone rather than their content, we might detect a lessening of tension once he signs over the Elim properties and is no longer responsible for raising finance for new congregations and pastors. And, if he is more relaxed, this would explain his reconciliation with his brother Stephen who worked with him as he had done when they were young. George himself was never purely a gospel preacher because he always encouraged prayer for healing while spinning out organisational schemes with another part of his psyche, but his life simplified. Even during the dark days of the war his gifts remained undiminished and his evangelistic drive constant and once VE day dawned, Jeffreys made plans to take the ferry over to Ulster.

20

POST-WAR EVANGELISM AND MARGINALISATION

Peace and Austerity

Victory in Europe was secured on 8 May 1945 over a week after Hitler's death. The celebrations in London saw crowds wandering round the city 'on shop-fronts, up lamp-standards, singing and shouting'.[1] Guardsmen might be seen in paper hats, flags were waved and bells were ringing. Churchill delivered a short speech at 3 pm from 10 Downing Street that was heard across the land through radios and innumerable loudspeakers. There were spontaneous cheers and two days of holiday.

The Labour Party decided not to remain in the coalition government and so Churchill led a caretaker administration until the general election of 5 July. He had expected to win with a reduced majority. The results, when they came, were a landslide for Labour and Churchill was ejected from office. Labour had proved itself competent within the coalition cabinet of the war and had embraced the Beveridge reforms that supported old-age pensions, the National Health Service, and what became the welfare state. It also was enthusiastic about the 1944 education reforms which promised better education for everyone with access to managerial jobs for those who succeeded in the new selective school system.

---

[1] David Kynaston, *Austerity Britain 1945–1951* (London: Bloomsbury, 2007), p. 6.

Labour energised a programme of house building and civic repair although food rationing continued. There was undoubtedly a black market operating behind the careful bureaucratic procedures now extended beyond the conditions of wartime emergency. Town planners bulldozed their way over local objections to reconstruct soulless town centres. Labour approved nationalisation of industry so that the docks and coal mines passed into national ownership with increased pay for dockers and miners. The railway system was repaired, the football league resumed, and an FA Cup competition took place in 1945–1946.[2] Horse racing restarted and 'almost everyone, it seemed, was hungry for escapism'.[3] New clothes, theatre tickets, and meals in posh restaurants became the goal of people who felt the right to enjoy themselves and yet, as the post-war exuberance subsided, many people found themselves pinched: 'we're so short of everything'.[4] By 1947 the Labour honeymoon was well and truly over. Rationing continued. Demobbed soldiers were looking for work or, if skilled, were dispossessing women of the factory jobs they had now mastered. Teenagers were perceived to be out of control. The huge financial cost of the war had reduced the resources of the comfortable middle class and prepared conditions for political criticism of continuing national austerity.[5]

On 6 August 1945 a huge American aircraft dropped an atomic bomb on the city of Hiroshima and almost instantly killed 80,000 people. Three days later Nagasaki was bombed and 40,000 people died. The Japanese government, which had intended to fight on, rapidly surrendered. The world entered the atomic age and newspapers reported the immense power unleashed by nuclear fission. Deaths by radiation followed the destruction of extensive swathes of Japanese property; and, without much imagination, thoughtful people understood how the combination of an atomic bomb and the rockets fired at London at the end of the war threatened the human race. Pentecostal Christians with strong imaginations could foresee the ravages of Armageddon on the horizon and the words of Scripture speaking of fiery conflagration (2 Pet. 3.9).

---

[2] Kynaston, *Austerity*, p. 94.
[3] Kynaston, *Austerity*, p. 84.
[4] Kynaston, *Austerity*, title of chapter 4.
[5] Kynaston, *Austerity*, p. 144.

The practical consequence of the end of the war for Jeffreys and the Bible-Pattern church was an improvement in travel. Jeffreys could now go west to Ireland or east to continental Europe. Ordinary people could expect a summer holiday and might converge for a camp convention in the Lake District. Pentecostals more widely asked themselves what they could do to alleviate suffering in continental Europe. If Britain was in a bad condition, central and eastern Europe were worse. Once prosperous cities were disfigured by piles of rubble, bullet-marked facades, and broken windows. There were stateless persons, refugees and starvation immediately after 1945; and, if this were not enough, the icy winter of 1947 was bitterly severe.

1945–1950: Jeffreys Battles On

Once the war was over, Jeffreys made plans to travel to his heartland in Belfast; but, before this, he preached in London. At a VE Day (Victory in Europe) service of praise and thankfulness people arrived from all over London and faraway parts of the UK where Jeffreys preached and in this way, he drew his followers together by finding the words and symbolism appropriate to their religious understanding of Allied victory;[6] beer and dancing in the street were not fitting for Bible-Pattern people. In April he had held his crowded Easter Monday meetings in Westminster Central Hall and issued 'a solemn call to church and nation' that must have included an appeal for Pentecostal unity as a precursor to extensive revival.[7] Although 66 conversions were registered, the wider appeal served only to set the tone of high seriousness that would become Jeffreys' hallmark over the next few years. On one hand, he continued in his efforts to extend the number and influence of the Bible-Pattern Church Fellowship; and, on the other, he made overtures to Elim – although always with the condition that the buildings he would hand back must be granted trust deeds safeguarding local autonomy. He met a blank wall of resistance. Elim itself was set on post-war expansion and Jeffreys' efforts were thwarted by Elim's de-

---

[6] *The Pattern* 6.24 (mid-Dec 1945), p. 8.
[7] *The Pattern* 6.8 (mid-Apr 1945), p. 9.

mands for the return of the buildings they legally held. In Nottingham, for instance, Elim installed its own pastor into the large building it owned, as it had a perfect right to do, and the Bible-Pattern congregation moved out and convened itself in a hired motor showroom.[8]

Returning to the theme on Whit Monday, 'Jeffreys gave a short but powerful discourse on the dangers of the anti-scriptural central control of local assemblies, which opened the eyes of those present from other Pentecostal bodies, to the truth'.[9] He and others gathered to talk about their concern for the work of God because the stress on local government of churches was uppermost in his mind. This was particularly so when the Barking congregation was asked to leave its building or, in the words of *The Pattern*, 'Elim Governors force another congregation on the road'.[10] Despite formal resolutions and letters of protest from the biggest names in the Bible-Pattern organisation, little happened. Complaints that the Elim church was withholding the kind of trust deeds Jeffreys wanted for the disputed congregations received a polite brush off. Phillips wrote to say that the Elim conference that year did not have time to consider the Pattern's grievances.

In the summer of 1945 Jeffreys was preaching at Gravesend in Essex before launching out in Barking where he was setting up one of his own congregations in competition with the Elim congregation already there. He did the same in August in Cardiff and was able to report 222 conversions and admits, 'we no longer stand for central dictator-government over the people of God', which is the nearest he comes to any kind of apology for setting up the Elim system he is now attacking.[11] It is tempting to read the campaigns in Barking and Cardiff, which would threaten the unity of existing Elim congregations, as retribution for Elim's policy of reclaiming its buildings; this was not behaviour that would win him friends in the wider Pentecostal movement.

National politics were of little interest to Jeffreys and there are few comments in his writings about contemporary events. Yet, in

---

[8] *The Pattern* 6.8 (mid-Apr 1945), p. 5.
[9] *The Pattern* 6.11 (June 1945), p. 3.
[10] *The Pattern* 6.12 (mid-June 1945), p. 6.
[11] *The Pattern* 6.19 (Oct 1945), p. 6.

June the front cover of *The Pattern* printed a large photo of the king and queen standing with Churchill: underneath was a caption quoting the speech Churchill made in the House of Commons before moving a vote of thanks to the monarch.[12] Meanwhile McWhirter's fertile mind seized on the atomic bomb as a sign of the times.[13] Having seen the rise of fascism and the threats of Hitler and Mussolini as a sign of the times, the Jeffreys circle of preachers now shifted their focus to a different sign. Their preaching began to be shot through with alarmist undertones and the threat of atomic war was a theme that Jeffreys would develop in the coming years. In this he was not alone: the philosopher and Nobel prize-winner, Bertrand Russell, published *Has Man a Future?* in 1961 at the start of a period of anti-nuclear agitation.[14] Jeffreys merely preceded Russell by a decade.

In the autumn of 1945 Jeffreys made the familiar journey to Northern Ireland and filled the Royal Hippodrome with 2,600 listeners; nearly 250 conversions were recorded and 100 people stood to testify to healing. *The Pattern* reported, 'from the Royal Hippodrome the Party carried the revival flame to the Ulster Stadium, Belfast, a large boxing and skating rink near the city centre, and again the same scenes of enthusiasm were witnessed – a packed building long before the announced time ...'.[15] By the end of the year Jeffreys has been to Brighton, London, Southampton, Portsmouth, Boscombe, Barking, and parts of Scotland. Cardiff is described as 'an Acts of the Apostles revival' and a visit to Glasgow as an 'old-time revival'.

Jeffreys had not lost his power to draw a crowd. His trip to Northern Ireland is a further indication that he was starting from the beginning again, and the most likely explanation of his strategic purpose is that he intended to draw as many of the Irish churches as he could into the Bible-Pattern fold. He must have been extremely disappointed that Elim appeared to have thwarted him by making constitutional adjustments to meet the concerns of the Ulster churches. Consequently, Jeffreys failed to build a big new Northern

---

[12] *The Pattern* 6.11 (June 1945), front cover.
[13] *The Pattern* 6.16 (mid-Aug 1945), front cover.
[14] Bertrand Russell, *Has Man a Future?* (Harmondsworth: Penguin 1961).
[15] *The Pattern* 6.23 (Dec 1945), front cover.

Irish base of loyal congregations. By the summer of next year, he wrote dismissively about the accommodation Elim had made with the Ulster congregations after noting that, while the deeds of the Irish churches are now kept in the Ulster bank, their content has hardly altered: 'the Irish Executive Council and the Irish conference are reduced to a nominal status owing to the legal control held over them by the Elim Governors'.[16] There is a provocative thrust here that implicitly challenges the Irish to break free of their English masters. In the end the records show a Bible-Pattern congregation at Portadown in Ulster but no mass defections despite the huge and grateful crowds.[17]

In 1946 Jeffreys established an annual calendar of events that he maintained, with minor variations, for the next decade or so. He was determined to preserve his key church bases and service them as often as he could. He preached in London at an Easter Monday event at Westminster Central Hall and this continued for the rest of his life. He remained an evangelist at heart and made appeals for conversion at most of his large meetings and would usually carefully count the numbers who responded. He prayed for those who were ill, and this is partly what drew the crowds. He retained his marvellously mellow and musical voice and his Revival Party remained loyal to him with one exception. In 1947, McWhirter, who was married, started to distance himself from the Jeffreys' entourage and their theology. Marriage in and of itself drew McWhirter away from the tight circle of the Revival Party.

In an autobiography published in 1983 McWhirter wrote, 'rather than meandering through my experiences, let me put it in a nutshell; from ultra-fundamentalism to liberal evangelicalism'.[18] Expanding on this:

> [my] journey covered nearly 30 years … What started it was a week's visit to the headquarters of the World Council of Churches in Geneva in 1947. It was a mental conversion. I took

---

[16] *The Pattern* 7.14 (mid-July 1946), p. 5.

[17] Compare http://www.elimchurchireland.com/elimministriesireland with http://thebible-patternchurch.blogspot.co.uk/2013/10/portadown-pattern-bible-pentecostal.html (accessed 28 July 2016).

[18] James McWhirter, *Every Barrier Swept Away* (Cardiff: Megiddo Press, 1983), pp. 11, 12.

with me all the prejudices, suspicions and fears engendered by my fundamentalist training. Briefly it taught me that the ecumenical movement was building the apostate church of the last days. The building material was the powerless churches with the outward form of godliness. They were creating the great organisation for false Prophet [*sic*] who with the Man of Sin and the Antichrist are, according to the Futurist school of thought, to run the world together, prior to the Second Advent of Christ.

He visited its offices in Geneva and found the World Council of Churches more committed to the fundamentals of the faith than his theology had led him to expect. He experienced a kind of conversion and spoke of happiness and that an ability, 'to breathe the fresh air of tolerance, in an escape from stifling intolerance, was exhilarating ... My most interesting ecumenical experience was in Rome'.

McWhirter did not break with Jeffreys in a blazing row; and, as we shall see the working relationship continued on a new basis. Meanwhile the revised Revival Party continued to support the now familiar preaching tours. Roughly speaking Jeffreys would spend time in London, often at Kensington Temple, sometimes for a weekend or a convention, ensure that he was always present on Easter Monday in Westminster, and then travel to the north where he would visit Bradford, Stockport, Halifax, and Blackpool or other congregations in the counties of Yorkshire and Lancashire. He would revisit Glasgow and make this the base of his operation in Scotland before returning for a summer tour in France or Switzerland and sometimes in Scandinavia. He would include Northern Ireland and Wales in his itineraries and in the autumn, use his big tent to campaign near a large city in an attempt to gather a congregation that might form a new Bible-Pattern church. At some point he returned to his old congregations on the south coast of England, usually in August. Greater crowds attended his meetings on the continent than those in Britain and he continued to lead the Bible-Pattern church, and presided over its annual discussions and a week's teaching at Bowness in the Lake District.

There is a timeless, almost *déjà vu*, quality about Jeffreys' public life at this point. *The Pattern* magazine published several old articles of his that had been first written in the late 1930s and they continued to use old photographs of him so that he looked younger than he really was.[19] When the front cover of the December 1946 issue of *The Pattern* was printed, a photograph of Jeffreys with his team shows him to be thinner, greyer, and noticeably older. He was now in his mid-50s and we do not know what steps he was taking to mitigate his diabetes. His preaching schedule would have tired a younger man and his only concession to age appeared to be his unwillingness to accept prolonged campaigns more than once or twice a year.

By 1946 Pentecostal leaders were beginning to travel and organise themselves again. A preliminary conference was held in Paris in 1946 to plan for the World Pentecostal Conference in Zürich in May 1947. There had already been connections between returning missionaries and British Pentecostals and the annual conferences of British Pentecostal denominations were enjoying renewed contact with their mission fields. Elim sent additional workers overseas to a range of countries while British Assemblies of God took large missionary offerings in the immediate post-war period. There was increasing recognition of the value of Pentecostalism to the extent that in 1945 the Elim London Crusader Choir was invited to broadcast on the BBC, and this was followed by a second broadcast in 1946.

Jeffreys had preached memorably at the Stockholm conference in 1939 on the eve of war. He was now one of the speakers invited to Zürich in 1947 along with representatives of Elim and Assemblies of God. When the conference settled to business, and in the face of moving reports of the humanitarian needs within war-ravaged European countries, 'a serious division of opinion soon arose over the method to help them'.[20] Large Scandinavian Pentecostal churches consistently opposed organisation above and beyond local assemblies because they feared controlling mechanisms would be introduced. But how to offer practical help without breaching this principle? The Scandinavians had adopted a system where they met annually to discuss topics without any intention of reaching conclusions; the British and American Pentecostal churches met at their conferences precisely in order to come to decisions, and they did so by voting. In the end, a solution was found by des-

---

[19] *The Pattern* 7.11 (June 1946), p. 3; *The Pattern* 7.12 (mid-June 1946), p. 3.
[20] Gee, *Wind and Flame*, p. 222.

ignating the Basel church in Switzerland 'an international centre for co-ordinating relief work'[21] so that practical supplies could be funnelled through this local church without breaching any Scandinavian scruples; and, it must be said, scruples George Jeffreys now shared. But he went well beyond the Scandinavians, and for different reasons: while they saw no organisation beyond the local church in the pages of the New Testament, Jeffreys saw a horrific vision of a false church at the end of the age.[22] His address to the Zürich conference was published in *The Pattern*:

> Many believe that, according to God's word, the day is fast approaching when organised religion, whether it be Catholic or Protestant, is going to be stripped of all its pretence, and be shaken to its very foundations. This belief is sufficient to justify our attitude towards central control …

> We, as free churchmen, are convinced that there will always be friction in any committee that consists of representatives from central governing bodies that are empowered by law to control the pastors, people, finance and properties of their churches, and representatives from free churches that govern themselves. The two principles are diametrically opposite each other. There should be safeguards, for there are many dangers … [23]

What runs through Jeffreys' separatist argument and drives it is an eschatological fear, a deep pessimism. Other Pentecostals did not share that fear and their broader engagement with the realities of human suffering in post-war Europe made the concerns of Jeffreys look myopic. He had every right to use the pages of *The Pattern* to highlight his own sermon to the conference but he may not have realised the extent of deprivation in Belgium or Germany because his own preaching tours took him to relatively unscathed parts of Europe. Switzerland, as a neutral country, had been entirely untouched and southern France, despite German occupation, witnessed no Allied landings or bombing raids. Elsewhere, especially in Germany itself and in Belgium and those vast tracts of land where

---

[21] Gee, *Wind and Flame*, p. 222.
[22] Revelation chapters 17 and 18.
[23] *The Pattern* 8.12 (mid-June 1947), p. 6.

thousands of fighting men had manoeuvred and fought, the civilian population was deprived of food and medical supplies and the growth of children had been stunted.[24] To his credit Fred Squire of the Full Gospel Testimony (a small Pentecostal denomination in Britain) collected supplies from churches and organised lorry loads of relief for Europe. He had little time for Jeffreys and his portentous rhetoric.

Instead of prioritising humanitarian aid, Jeffreys pursued his own quest for a form of Pentecostal unity. He wanted to propagate Scandinavian-style Pentecostalism in Britain as a way of diminishing the importance of other kinds of church government. So in September 1947 G.I. Francis, the secretary of the Bible-Pattern fellowship, sent out a letter to the Executive councils of all the other Pentecostal denominations in Britain. It attempted to build upon the appeal by James Salter, the veteran Congo missionary, at the close of the Zürich conference in May of that year. The letter wanted to 'consider as a fundamental basis for unity, that each local church be assured of freedom to declare the whole counsel of God; to appoint its own Pastors, Elders and Deacons; to control its own church funds; and to own and control its property'. By May 1948 the Bible-Pattern men received their answer. Elim was simply 'not prepared to co-operate in calling a conference to consider any particular type of church government as a fundamental basis for unity among Pentecostal churches in this country' and Assemblies of God would not attend unless everyone attended. The Apostolic Church would also only attend if everybody did and a small group, the Council of the United Apostolic Faith Church, did not believe that the 'four freedoms' constituted an acceptable basis for unity. Bluntest of all was Fred Squire's Full Gospel Testimony which merely said that it would not be possible to take part in the suggested conference. The Bible-Pattern initiative fell on stony ground and Jeffreys, obviously disappointed, ended his report with a sideswipe at the 'secrecy of the Babylonish system of church government'.[25] The truth was that the other Pentecostals did not want to work with him and Jeffreys was being marginalised.

---

[24] http://www.audrey1.org/biography/23/audrey-hepburns-statement-to-the-united-nations (accessed 4.8.2016).

[25] *The Pattern* 9.9 (May 1948), p. 4.

Noel Brooks, one of the leading lights of the Bible-Pattern movement, had written a book, *Fight for the Faith and Freedom: George Jeffreys – Revivalist and Reformer*, in 1941 that was persistently advertised in the pages of *The Pattern*.[26] The book portrayed Jeffreys as a great revivalist and a courageous reformer and, like the earlier book by Boulton published in 1928, covered the ministry of Jeffreys up to that point in his life. Jeffreys was happy to be seen as a reformer and sometimes referred to himself in this way.

Although the painful schism between Jeffreys and Elim had resulted in substantial reforms to the Elim Constitution, Jeffreys now made his demands for local church autonomy a central feature of his ministry. He was not prepared to 'live and let live' or to accept that the New Testament contained variously interpretable guidance on church government and none at all on the ownership of property. When a National Pentecostal Conference met in August 1948 with the purpose to 'keep the unity of the Spirit in the bond of peace and further the proclamation of the whole counsel of God by cooperative effort',[27] Jeffreys reported that the Bible-Pattern church fellowship at its Blackpool conference in September 1948 could not recommend becoming part of the new organisation called 'the Pentecostal Fellowship of the British Isles' on account of the 'grave danger' of a central bureau.[28] Only when all assemblies in all groups in the national conference were assured of the rights for which Jeffreys was campaigning would he accept membership. This created a stand-off: he invited everyone to join his group in the name of unity, and they refused; others started a unity group, and he refused to join it because it would not make his preferred form of church government compulsory.

In pressing for a Scandinavian model of church government the Bible-Pattern had invited over a trio of Scandinavian preachers who answered questions at the Bible-Pattern convention at Bowness in the summer of 1948. The following year Jeffreys pressed on with his attempts to change the culture of British Pentecostalism. He

---

[26] E.g. *The Pattern* 9.9 (May 1948), p. 4. The book remains available on Amazon.

[27] *The Pattern* 9.19 (Oct 1948), p. 5. R.G. Tweed and G.I. Francis attended for the Bible-Pattern.

[28] *The Pattern* 9.20 (mid-Oct 1948), front cover.

persuaded the London churches to hold a monthly United Pentecostal rally to strengthen 'all the Pentecostal people in this great city, who were standing for the Biblical principles of free churches'.[29] He reported in April 1949 on a tour of 'free Pentecostal churches' up as far as Glasgow.[30] Lewi Pethrus joined the group with two Scandinavian pastors who then went down to Blackpool, Halifax, and Nottingham and later other towns and cities. Pethrus, however, is featured on the front cover of *The Pattern* magazine and joined Jeffreys for his Easter Monday services at Westminster Central Hall.[31] Pethrus spoke at the meetings and combined with Jeffreys in praying for those who were ill, and there are multiple photographs of the event to enhance publicity. The association between Jeffreys and Pethrus added credibility to the push for autonomous Pentecostal congregations held in a loose association.

All this followed a meeting the previous year between teams from the Bible-Pattern and Assemblies of God in Britain. This was a ground-clearing discussion intended to improve relationships. The Assemblies wanted to know why Jeffreys, after coming out of Elim, had not joined AoG rather than starting a new Pentecostal grouping. This is a perfectly reasonable question given that the Bible-Pattern mode of government was almost identical with that already adopted by Assemblies of God. Jeffreys replied that the Pattern had been founded during the war when a long discussion about theological fundamentals was not feasible. And it is true that Assemblies of God took a slightly firmer line on evidence for baptism in the Holy Spirit than the Bible-Pattern would have done. The two groups agreed they could work together (whatever their differences on BI) since their methods of church government were so similar.[32]

In May 1949 the second World Pentecostal Conference was held, this time in Paris. Jeffreys did not attend and is not mentioned at all in reports of the event but Robert Tweed and Gwilym Francis for the Pattern were both there. Tweed reported on disputes about organisation in Paris similar to those in Zürich. Pethrus, who was present, objected to the formation of any permanent body and ex-

[29] *The Pattern* 10.3 (Feb 1949), p. 10.
[30] *The Pattern* 10.8 (mid-Apr 1949), front cover, p. 5.
[31] *The Pattern* 10.10 (mid-May 1949), front cover, p. 3.
[32] *The Pattern* 9.1 (Jan 1948), p. 3.

plained, 'it is a centralisation of the Pentecostal movement that we fear'.[33] An elaborate agenda had been prepared but after two days this was scrapped in favour of a manifesto or declaration to be approved by voting with acclamation rather than by ballot. In this way the conference completed its business. An advisory committee was appointed and Donald Gee was confirmed as having complete control over the publication of the new magazine, *Pentecost*. Tweed concluded,

> these points might certainly give rise to questionings, but so long as the Conference has no executive or legislative power, I do not think there is much to fear, and furthermore the 'Free Churches' are very strong and would soon withdraw from the Fellowship if the matter was pressed.[34]

A further report was given by Francis who focused positively on the big public gatherings and worship.

Less than a month later Jeffreys took his customary hard line. His article on the Paris conference was subheaded, 'bondage and freedom in a worldwide organisation of organisations'. He maintained, 'a grave injustice is being done to the thousands of Pentecostal assemblies and pastors throughout the world if they are being made unsuspecting parties of this world-wide organisation without their proper consent'. And he went on to explain why he and others would remain firmly outside:

> Our Bible-Pattern church fellowship was founded in the British Isles soon after the separation from Elim and we are more determined than ever that, by God's grace, we shall never be inside any national or world-wide Pentecostal organisation that does not make freedom of biblical assemblies crystal clear and the basis of its fellowship.[35]

Reading between the lines it appears Jeffreys swayed the Bible-Pattern conference and overrode the favourable reports given by Tweed and Francis. They give the impression they would have been willing to join the world Pentecostal grouping and saw little danger

---

[33] *The Pattern* 10.13 (July 1949), p. 3.
[34] *The Pattern* 10.13 (July 1949), p. 5.
[35] *The Pattern* 10.16 (mid-Aug 1949), pp. 6, 7.

in belonging. Jeffreys, with his insistent aversion, would have none of it. Those who worked with him were finding he brooked no opposition.

In the first five years after the ending of the war Jeffreys continued his mass evangelism. *The Pattern* becomes very largely a news sheet designed to advertise and celebrate his ministry. There are frequent photographs of large attentive crowds in an assortment of buildings and never a hint of failure or public criticism. He speaks of 'no less than 150 souls' who decided for Christ at a campaign in Copenhagen in 1949[36] or over 1,000 conversions in a trip to France and Switzerland[37] and 300 conversions in Stockwell, London, in the autumn of 1950[38] as well as big annual tent meetings in the beauty of the Lake District with the Bible-Pattern faithful. A summary of his campaigns abroad shows he crossed to the Continent in 1933, 1934, 1935, 1936, and then 1946, 1947, 1948.[39] In 1947 in Switzerland 574 conversions are recorded in eight days and in 1948 in Switzerland and France 1,100 decisions.[40] He was interviewed on Lausanne radio, mainly about healing, in 1948[41] though, when he went to campaign in Cardiff, he felt it necessary to explain publicly why he had resigned from Elim in comments that could not but have hurt the existing Elim church in the city.[42] In short, his evangelism continued after the war as steadily as it had done in the late 1930s.

By 1950, when the Bible-Pattern fellowship had been established for about 10 years, there are indications of subterranean instability. The Constitution was revised to give 'every qualified member of each church, a vote in the government of the church'.[43] Jeffreys wants to institute the Swedish system of allowing the church meeting a greater role in directing the spirituality of the congregation. Public discipline of backsliders can occur in this way. But the revision allows 'any member of the church at any time ... to put in

---

[36] *The Pattern* 10.20 (mid-Oct 1949), p. 5.
[37] *The Pattern* 11.11 (June 1950), p. 5.
[38] *The Pattern* 11.20 (mid Oct 1950), front cover.
[39] *The Pattern* 9.14 (mid-July 1948), p. 8.
[40] *The Pattern* 9.14 (mid-July 1948), p. 8.
[41] *The Pattern* 9.14 (mid-July 1948), pp. 6, 7.
[42] *The Pattern* 10.1 (Jan 1949), p. 5.
[43] *The Pattern* 11.14 (mid-July 1950), p. 3.

writing a proposal of non-confidence in the pastor' with the result that 'the vote on the change of minister which is taken at the church meeting every three years should be abolished'.[44] It is easy to imagine the consternation that such a change would have aroused in the hearts of the pastors. Their job security dropped dramatically since any malcontent within the congregation could legitimately try to get rid of them over and over again. It is hard to believe such a constitutional change would have been initiated by the pastors themselves or to imagine a widespread call by the laity for it. Jeffreys simply extrapolated the principle of extreme congregationalism and imposed it on the Bible-Pattern churches regardless of the consequences.

Another instability occurred with the training college Jeffreys was attempting to set up. Early in 1950 he advertised a Free Churches Bible College in Clapham Park, London SW4, and put Noel Brooks into the college as the Director of Studies, and *The Pattern* magazine describes him as such.[45] Yet, by December the plan was abandoned and the reason given for this is 'the sudden outbreak of war in the Far East and the growing uncertainty [of] world conditions' which 'have compelled us to reconsider our Free Churches Bible College'.[46] He wished now to have a college in every assembly rather than one college to which all students might be sent. The reason for closing the college was the outbreak of the Korean War, even though it took place on the other side of the world. Eschatological fear clouded Jeffreys' world-view and weakened his capacity to hold consistently to a course of action. When closure was announced, Brooks was upset and disillusioned. Within a short time he escaped from Jeffreys by accepting the pastorate of a Baptist congregation and later wrote:

> I became deeply involved for several years in a 'reforming' movement within a Pentecostal denomination which aimed at changing the mode of government and putting right what were thought to be 'injustices'. My idealism, in the end, was rudely shaken. Through a hard and bitter way, I learned two things: (a)

---

[44] *The Pattern* 11.14 (mid-July 1950), p. 4.
[45] *The Pattern* 11.3 (Feb 1950), p. 11.
[46] *The Pattern* 11.23-24 (Dec, mid-Dec 1950), p. 17.

that many things to which 'reformers' and 'preservers' fight and often suffer are frequently no more than an ecclesiastical scaffolding rather than a real building of God. (b) that the outward principles and policies for which men of all parties claim to be struggling ... are often a cover-up for their real motivations which may be personal and egotistic rather than spiritual and altruistic.[47]

1951–1955: Jeffreys Refuses to Mellow

Jeffreys continued his circuit of British preaching using buildings or, in the summer, a marquee. The gaps between preaching dates widened so that in the early part of the year he took a week off between engagements and his longest bookings would only run for about 10 days except in the summer when the effort was more sustained. Given that his 60th birthday fell in 1949 this slowing down was normal and his foreign tours stopped.

He ran into difficulties with *The Pattern* magazine and, in June 1951, split the publication into two with *The Revival Messenger* on alternate months. A single subscription covered both journals with the idea that *The Revival Messenger* would be suitable for the unconverted whilst *The Pattern* would contain slightly controversial articles suitable for a Christian readership. This arrangement did not last long and in November 1951 Jeffreys wrote to subscribers explaining 'we have had to face difficulties in the publication of our periodical, *The Pattern*, even having to find new printers at short notice owing to our printers changing hands'. And he went on to say a new arrangement would be put in place with the Bible Speaks to Britain organisation and its periodical which was run by James McWhirter. In effect the two magazines merged.[48]

Although it was still called *The Pattern* readers would now see articles by the journalist Hugh Redwood, the clergyman D.R. Davies, and the occasional Anglican bishop and with advertisements for hearing aids or food or Ovaltine as well as highlights of Jeffreys and

[47] Marilyn A. Hudson, *Noel Brooks: A Life Shining and Burning* (Whorl Books with CreateSpace, 2011), pp. 61, 62. The quotation comes from Brooks' papers and is undated.
[48] *The Pattern* 12.21 (Nov 1951), p. 1.

his ministry. The new combined journal felt much more modern with its short informative pieces, even if a monarchist emphasis was unmistakable. There were pictures of the Royal family and their children in most issues, and in this respect, it resembled much tabloid journalism of the time.

Reference to the Bible-Pattern churches and their conferences and ministers disappeared entirely from view. The Bible-Pattern pastors who had written in *The Pattern* and the reports given of decisions by the Pattern's Coordinating Council were no longer communicated to the readership. Instead of being a denominational magazine, *The Pattern* had now become a mixture between an instrument for holding the ministry of Jeffreys before the public and a journal for drumming up interest in McWhirter's showcase exhibition about the Bible as a central feature of British history.

The relationship between Jeffreys and McWhirter, or *The Pattern* and BSB, continued for about two years and the collaboration benefited both parties. At the Queen's Coronation in 1953 the article Jeffreys had written on the 1937 coronation was reprinted with suitable amendments. Jeffreys had hinted at the identity of the Royal family with the house of David and it is reasonable to assume this mystical evocation confirmed the mystique with which readers of the BSB wished to cloak the monarchy. Yet there must have been tensions when one of the staple contributors to the magazine, D.R. Davies, wrote a piece that advanced an almost Barthian view of Scripture: the words were less important than the divine truth contained in them. Play was made on the 'Word of God' as text and Jesus as the Word declared at the beginning of the Gospel of John.[49] Commander Macmillan, who was president of the Bible-Pattern churches, wrote a rebuttal with a headline on 'what the Bible *really* is' (original italics).[50]

1954 welcomed Billy Graham to Britain for one of his first major crusades. *The Pattern* had already been preparing for the event by showing photographs of huge arenas in the United States where Graham preached and now added cover photographs of Graham and his wife with plenty more pictures inside.[51] Anybody reading

---

[49] *The Pattern* 14.9 (May 1953), p. 2.
[50] *The Pattern* 14.10 (mid-May 1953), p. 2.
[51] *The Pattern* 15.5 (Mar 1954), front cover.

the magazine would conclude Billy Graham was a bigger evangelist than George Jeffreys; whereas Graham filled arenas, Jeffreys filled churches. When Graham counted his converts in thousands, Jeffreys in hundreds at the most. Putting the two evangelists side-by-side, the young Baptist Billy Graham was in an altogether higher league than the old Pentecostal.

We can assume that Jeffreys disliked the implied comparison so that, in the middle of 1954, a notice appeared saying *The Pattern* would now leave the BSB and launch out on its own again.[52] It made reference to memorable campaigns by Jeffreys in Birmingham even though a double page spread and photo of the Harringay crowd only served to demonstrate the superiority of Graham's reach. Jeffreys in *The Pattern*, now on its own, wrote at length about 'a revival such as they had in Bible days', which reads as an implied corrective to the big Billy Graham meetings.[53] Whereas Jeffreys expected to see miracles of healing, Graham, as a Southern Baptist, preached an unvarnished gospel focusing on justification by faith and avoiding any Pentecostal overtones.

Although the year of the coronation was also the year when Mount Everest was scaled for the first time and 1954 saw the running of the first sub-four-minute mile, neither of these events, which were widely believed to illustrate returning confidence among British people, were mentioned in *The Pattern*. Jeffreys began to sound and look old-fashioned. There are photographs of him preaching at Westminster Central Hall in 1955 and he wears a morning suit with grey striped trousers and a conservatively cut jacket.[54] His curly black hair is now silver and thinner and he looks more like the grand old man that he had become. But his eschatology had, if anything, darkened. The steps up to war at the end of the 1930s led, so it seemed, directly to the battlefield of Armageddon; but, in the 1950s, his fear was of a pan-religious organisation that would pander to the Antichrist. He was asked to provide a message for a Swedish newspaper and so sent these sombre words:

---

[52] *The Pattern* 15.7 (Apr 1954), p. iii.
[53] *The Pattern* 15.8 (mid-Apr 1954), pp. 6, 7.
[54] *The Pattern* 16.6 (mid-Mar 1955), p. 6.

In these closing days of the Age, the members of Christ's Body everywhere, especially in the Pentecostal fold, need each other's co-operation and support, for Satanic forces are descending upon the earth for the final attack upon the church, which is His Body.

The strategy of this final attack is revealed in the Word of God, so we need not be ignorant of the Enemy's devices. It is the official linking-up of the religious organisations and a super world-organisation under the pretext of Christian unity.

Thank God, the final plan for conquest over these forces of evil is also foretold in the Word of God. It is the going-forth of Divine power through the spiritual Body of Christ, against which the gates of Hell shall not prevail.

Let us, as Pentecostal people, take warnings of the Enemy's devices and move on in accordance with the Divine plan of conquest.[55]

How exactly he deduced a 'super world-organisation' would be brought into existence is unknown; presumably his mind was haunted by the harlot church in the book of Revelation. These fears, when other Pentecostals were delighted by the end of the war and the opportunities now open to them for worldwide evangelism, made Jeffreys a reactionary figure.

He engaged in a running battle with the organisation of the World Pentecostal Conference that was brought to London in 1952 and to Stockholm in 1955. In both instances Jeffreys used his journal to cast doubts on what was being attempted. He wanted the 'official British Pentecostal Fellowship' to stop being a fellowship of organisations and become a fellowship of individuals. A photograph of Pethrus and Jeffreys together in 1952 was printed, presumably to show there is no breach between them. But, if anything, Jeffreys was taking a harder line than Pethrus so that, despite attempted clarifications by Pethrus before the Stockholm conference, Jeffreys restated his doubts by asking whether the conference would 'perpetuate a world organisation'.[56] Refusing to leave the topic alone

---

[55] *The Pattern* 13.11 (June 1952), p. iv.
[56] *The Pattern* 16.3 (Feb 1955), p. 6.

he wrote another article maintaining the only way to prevent a permanent organisation was to 'openly constitute the 1955 Conference on an individual status and to call it by its right name'.[57] The Advisory Committee would have to be disbanded and the quarterly publication, *Pentecost*, edited by Donald Gee would also have to go. Not unnaturally Gee, and others who found the magazine extremely informative about Pentecostalism all over the world, rejected the calls made by Jeffreys. When the conference spoke about Christian unity as a 'fire burning on the altar of our hearts' Jeffreys ignored the reply and engaged in an argument with Gee over comparisons between the size of the Pentecostal movements in Britain and Sweden. The number of Swedish Pentecostals in relation to the Swedish population was about 20 times higher than in Britain and Jeffreys put this down to the method of church government employed in Sweden. Gee dismissed this suggestion by pointing out that huge Pentecostal church movements existed in other parts of the world, like Latin America, with various forms a government and that nothing could hang on church government alone; other factors were determinative.[58] Jeffreys would have none of this and pointed to his one-factor explanation.[59]

Reflection

The post-war decade took Jeffreys to the brink of old age. His zeal and energy had been devoted in the wartime years to building up the Bible-Pattern fellowship but even after Hitler was defeated and normal social and economic conditions began to reassert themselves, Jeffreys remained fixated upon church government, and his fixation apparently blinded him to humanitarian needs in post-war Europe. Having quarrelled with Elim, he made his demands for local church autonomy the condition of collaboration with British Pentecostals in Europe and overseas. He attempted to introduce the Swedish mode of church government to Britain even though a system very close to what Pethrus had established in Stockholm was already exemplified by British Assemblies of God. Although Jef-

[57] *The Pattern* 16.4 (mid-Feb 1955), p. 9.
[58] *The Pattern* 16.11 (June 1955), pp. 6, 7.
[59] *The Pattern* 16.11 (June 1955), pp. 7, 8.

freys nurtured the Bible-Pattern group, his dropping of any reference to their conferences or concerns during the period when his magazine was combined with McWhirter's BSB organisation – as well as his dropping of Brooks from Bible Pattern college – indicate he was willing to jettison the Bible-Pattern ministers and their people when it suited him. He did not, it is true, ever separate himself from them but his own World Revival Crusade organisation and the Revival Party as well as *The Pattern* magazine were at the core of his activities and given priority.

The criticisms made of him by Brooks, although they do not name him directly, are stinging. What looked like altruism was egotism and the reforming methods and principles were merely scaffolding that hardly touched the building of the church inside. The criticism of Brooks is that Jeffreys lost sight of the heart of Christian communities by so single-mindedly gazing at them through the filter of church government and then, in respect of the national and international Pentecostal conferences, finding himself driven by fear of eschatological events like the erection of a super-church and the final atomic conflagration when divine judgement would fall upon the earth.[60] While others delighted in the outpouring of the Spirit and the joyful optimism this brought, Jeffreys allowed his hopes to be clouded by a vision of impending doom.

In the 1920s and 1930s he frequently spoke about the Foursquare Gospel and this appeared in his writings and preaching. In the post-war period he spoke about the Bible as providing a pattern for church life and this became as important to him as the Foursquare Gospel had been earlier. His character shows obsessional traits as well as unbending adherence to selected principles and concepts. An evangelist, who consistently preaches the gospel to thousands of people in an attempt to convert them, must be utterly sure of his own rightness, particularly if he is to retain his evangelical zeal all his life. With Jeffreys, this obstinacy and passion had, in the first part of his ministry, been devoted to a Pentecostal proclamation of the gospel whereas, in the second part of his ministry, church government filled his mind. He never lost his evangelistic gifts, though had he mellowed and reached out to those whose

---

[60] *The Pattern* 16.9 (May 1955), p. 5.

opinions he could not quite accept, he would have become an elder statesman to Pentecostalism in Europe and perhaps the English-speaking world.

21

FINAL YEARS

Pleasure-Seeking Britain and Its Disappearing Empire

Princess Margaret, the Queen's sister, fell in love with Group Captain Peter Townsend who proposed to her. Townsend was a divorcee whose wife had left him in 1952. Shortly afterwards, the Princess asked the Queen for permission to marry and, following a consultation with the Archbishop of Canterbury, decided not to proceed. The only way she could marry a divorcee would be to surrender her royal status, as had happened during the abdication of her uncle in 1936. There followed an outpouring of popular sympathy for the Princess and a swell of criticism of the church for standing in the way of true love.[1]

Britain was changing and its place in the world was in flux. Churchill, very much a man for empire and monarchy, had become prime minister again in 1951 and saw the big picture of the international situation as a cold war between the democratic free world on one side of the 'iron curtain' and the Soviet bloc on the other. By trade and good management Britain gradually shrugged off postwar rationing and misery without retaining its global empire. Two prolonged world wars had broken its power. The vast sprawling

---

[1] David Kynaston, *Family Britain: 1951–57* (London, Bloomsbury, 2009), p. 533. Surveys of the time show approximately 15% of the population attended church on Sundays and, although 60% of non-churchgoers say that they 'used to attend', the headline figure for a survey in 1954 found 63% either never attended or only went once or twice a year.

subcontinent of India, after years of agitation, became independent of Britain's imperial rule in 1947 and was quickly followed by others: the Sudan in 1956, the Gold Coast (Ghana) in 1957, Malaysia the same year, and other African states shortly afterwards.

While the dismantling of British rule across the world was for the most part orderly and dignified and with all the ceremonial of a democratic hand-over, Colonel Nasser in Egypt acted militarily without consultation and in breach of previous undertakings.[2] In October 1956 he nationalised the Suez Canal. This was run jointly by the French and British, who had paid for its building. An international conference was called and the United Nations was brought in to mediate. Nasser insisted the canal could not be used by Israel which meant that Britain, France, and Israel were the three key players most threatened and affronted by Nasser's action – even if the rest of the world would also find their access to the canal restricted or more expensive. Secretly Britain, France, and Israel conceived of a plan whereby Israel would advance into Egypt and British and French forces would, in a police action, restrain Israel and seize control of the canal to restore it fully to the international community. Militarily, this plan was carried out like clockwork but the political and economic aspects collapsed. The United States refused point-blank to support British action and this made an immediate impact on sterling.[3] The British and French withdrew their ground troops and alternative international arrangements were made to re-open the canal. For those in London, and especially for those in the British government who thought they were acting properly to resist a 1930s-style dictator, the American rebuff was shocking. More than this, the rebuff indicated before the watching world the powerlessness of Britain in international affairs. As one cartoonist depicted events, the British lion had its tail pulled off by the Egyptian sphinx. As we shall see, men close to Jeffreys added their strident voices of dismay.

---

[2] Roberts, *History*, p. 426.

[3] Roberts, *History*, p. 429. The effect of the perceived American threat to sterling was said to have been exaggerated by Harold Macmillan as a way of bringing down Eden. Eisenhower, in an election year, did not want to risk a backlash from voters by supporting a foreign war.

These international realignments mattered little to the ordinary working man or woman in Britain who, having suffered, scrimped, and saved through the 1940s, now found material prosperity and labour-saving devices coming to their aid. Domestic appliances like washing machines and televisions spread through the population. Small cars gradually came within the reach of a family budget. Television branched out into the second channel that could challenge the BBC's middle class accents and self-righteous tone. ITV came on stream in the mid-fifties and brought with it advertising, which only further fuelled the desire for consumer goods, as well as gameshows, American comedies, and popular soaps that broadened popular culture and paved the way for the rise of the global music industry. Back at home *Dixon of Dock Green* (1955) featured an avuncular local policeman who helped the wheels of the community run smoothly. Ignoring their parents' small black and white TVs in the corner of the living room the younger generation were out on the dance floor jiving to Bill Haley and His Comets or swooning to Elvis; less compliant and less innocent, the Teddy Boys with their quiffs, suede shoes, and flick-knives formed gangs, identified with early rock music and fought each other mindlessly. The older generation shook their heads and through the films of the day, *The Cruel Sea* (1953), *The Dam Busters* (1955), and *Reach For The Sky* (1956), focused on the heroism of the wartime era and could be accused of living in the past or, equally, of celebrating the military triumphs of their era. For the younger intellectuals seething with discontent, John Osborne's *Look Back In Anger* (1956) caught the mood of the time. 'There aren't any good, brave causes left' rails the anti-hero. While for others, Samuel Beckett's *Waiting for Godot* (1953), a conversation between two tramps waiting for … what exactly? summarised the cynical stoicism of the *avant garde* view that human existence was an incomprehensible joke.

Finishing Well

Although there is scant reference to Jeffreys' health in *The Pattern* magazine, his preaching schedule was noticeably reducing as he approached 70. He sold his big canvas tent in 1955 and thereafter no longer carried out summer campaigns.[4] There is a retrospective and nostalgic tinge to the magazine's pages when Jeffreys writes. He casts his mind back to early days in Elim and marvels at God's blessing 'in spite of our blindness', meaning in spite of the system of church government he installed.[5] He writes another retrospective article in April 1956 and reaches out to Elim for unity between the Bible-Pattern and Elim congregations. His insistence on a model trust deed giving local church autonomy is narrowed to the four big congregations over which there has been most discussion. Whether he envisaged the Bible-Pattern churches as being a separate section within Elim or running autonomously alongside is unclear.

He makes a series of offers through the pages of the magazine, a type of megaphone diplomacy unsuited to delicate negotiation. In September 1956 he writes about the Elim congregation in Clapham, London, to ensure that his own pioneering work in 1922 is not air-brushed out of history.[6] The church's official souvenir programme announces the opening service of a new building in 1956 and he again makes the plea that various assemblies be granted a trust deed that will assure the registered members 'a voice and vote', and even accepts that they should pay a percentage of their regular income to the Elim Headquarters – though quite how he squared this payment with his denunciations of Babylonish religion is impossible to say. Yet his entreaties fail to move anyone even when he outlines a new threefold offer to join the Bible-Pattern congregation in Clapham to the Elim congregation nearby and place them under one roof in a new building to which the Bible-Pattern will contribute half the cost. All this would hinge on the Elim governing body's willingness to grant the new United Assembly a trust deed protecting the rights of registered members. Again the offer is rejected. Elim is un-moved. In a letter signed by E.J. Phillips in the summer of 1958, Elim respond to the earlier approach:

> I was asked to point out that it is within the power of the pre-sent trustees of the Churches to which you refer at Glasgow, Brighton, Kensington and Blackpool to grant local government

---

[4] Edsor, *'Set Your House in Order'*, p. 195.
[5] *The Pattern* 17.1 (Jan 1956), p. 3.
[6] *The Pattern* 17.9 (Sept 1956), p. 6.

to the trustees during the life-time of the beneficiaries. We understand that there has been no legal document to give effect to this.[7]

The point made by Elim is that Jeffreys has not handed over the reins of control to new local trustees of these four congregations when it is within his power to do so although, as a condition of his help, he insists that Elim should do so. Jeffreys demands democratisation from Elim while refusing to surrender his own trusteeship. This looks self-contradictory. Had these overtures been made ten years before, they might have been accepted; but, after the fusillade of words in the 1940s, Elim has learnt to live without their charismatic leader.

In February 1958 he wrote an open letter to Elim containing a generous offer: 'I'm ready to serve in the movement in making another appeal for an Elim Debt Clearance fund in an endeavour to pay off the present debts on all Elim church buildings in the British Isles' just so long as each church is given a new model Trust Deed allowing members to conduct their own affairs.[8] Again, he accepts that an agreed percentage of church income should be sent to support the Elim Headquarters administration. No reply to this offer is published and no further correspondence between Jeffreys and Elim takes place. He had spent much of 1958 confined to London and attending to 'prolonged legal business' and this is now concluded.[9] There will be no official, public, or symbolic reconciliation between Jeffreys and Elim – though five weeks before his death Jeffreys met Phillips and stated, 'I have nothing in my heart against you'.[10]

Post-war shortwave radio was becoming an evangelistic tool. It was already commandeered by the Great Powers to disseminate Marxist and Capitalist propaganda. Radio sets had dropped in price and were sold readily in developing countries with the result that strategically placed high-powered transmitters could reach huge populations without government censorship. The Swedish had established IBRA Radio and accepted prime-time Pentecostal preach-

[7] *The Pattern* 19.7 (July 1958), p. 7.
[8] *The Pattern* 19.5 (May 1958), p. 9.
[9] *The Pattern* 19.12 (Dec 1958), pp. 6, 7.
[10] Edsor, *'Set Your House in Order'*, p. 202. Edsor was present at the meeting.

ers. This suited George Jeffreys down to the ground. He did not
have to travel and his still commanding and melodious voice could
convey short gospel and teaching messages with great effect. He
broadcast three times in 1956[11] and again in February and August
1957; and, to add emphasis, his scripts were printed in *The Pattern*.

While Jeffreys was adapting to the new medium of communication, Britain was struggling to adapt to the new era. The loudest and
most strident voice in Bible-Pattern circles was its president, Commander Macmillan. A forceful article in 1956 headed, 'Blow the
trumpet in Zion! Sound an alarm!' spoke apocalyptically of the
darkening of the sun and 'the moon glowing red' because human
beings dared to trifle with the powers locked up in the atom.[12]

In Britain itself the Suez crisis horrified Commander Macmillan.
The 'main artery of Empire' was menaced by Colonel Nasser of
Egypt and 'the Russian Soviet and Asia stand ready to join in the
jackal chorus as they prepare to feast on the dead British Lion'.
Here was a lacerated cry of outrage and pain from the most senior
person in the Bible-Pattern movement who was also, not coincidentally, an official with the British-Israel World Federation. For
Macmillan, the humiliation of Britain was entirely a consequence of
moral and spiritual decline and 'the many insults to His Word, His
Day, His precious blood and His sacred law' perpetrated by the
godless populace. Indeed Macmillan watched the post-Suez Parliamentary debate from the public gallery and noted 'the dignified
bearing of our prime minister in contrast to the unprecedented volume of vulgar, and sometimes profane, abuse to which he was subjected in scenes of rowdy uproar'.[13]

We can assume Jeffreys shared Macmillan's sentiments but rather
than taking aim against British people or politics Jeffreys continued
to direct his concerns to the World Pentecostal Conference. Following his previous complaints about the basis for the conferences in
Zurich, Paris, and London, he wrote to the chairman of its Advisory Committee in Toronto saying the conference should be convened for individuals not churches: 'the World Conference of Pentecostal Churches is a misnomer as there is no proper basis for rep-

[11] *The Pattern* 17.2 (July 1956), pp. 6, 7.
[12] *The Pattern* 17.1 (Jan 1956), p. 6.
[13] *The Pattern* 18.1 (Jan 1957), pp. 6, 7.

resentation from the churches'.[14] Jeffreys reiterated his anxieties in September 1957 to the Bible-Pattern Church Fellowship's annual meeting which passed a resolution endorsing his apprehensions. This, perhaps, added weight to the complaining letters he sent out; but, when the replies eventually came in, they gave him no satisfaction. From Toronto R.E. McAlister wrote:

> I didn't name the World Conference; but I find no fault with the name that has been used up to the present ... I am very sure I would not set up the Advisory Committee in the way that it was done at Stockholm; but I am not finding fault with it, for it is functioning quite satisfactorily; so why should I be critical?'[15]

This was to miss the point of Jeffreys' complaint: it was not the technical arrangements that worried him but their permanence and what they might turn into. So, whether in his dealings with Elim or the World Pentecostal Conference, Jeffreys was not being listened to.

In England, by contrast, he continued to dominate the Bible-Pattern Fellowship. Its annual meeting was faithfully reported in *The Pattern* magazine. Jeffreys was always unanimously elected chairman and convened the meetings. Discussion was held and resolutions were passed and these were in line with the wishes Jeffreys expressed in his articles. In 1957 the Bible-Pattern reached 25 years of age and rejoiced in the Jubilee clearance of debts on church buildings, and it is reasonable to assume that much of the heavy-lifting in fund-raising was done by Jeffreys.[16]

Jeffreys celebrated his 70th birthday on 28 February 1959 and received telegrams and congratulations from many parts of the world. He gathered for a special lunch with close friends including the two remaining members of the Revival Party, Albert Edsor and Robert Darragh, who lived in the same house with him along with a housekeeper and, on this occasion, two visitors. At the end of the birthday Darragh went up to his bedroom but was clearly unwell and must have called his friends because they came in to pray with

---

[14] *The Pattern* 18.7 (July 1957), p. 4.
[15] *The Pattern* 19.6 (June 1958), p. 9.
[16] *The Pattern* 18.8 (Aug 1958), p. 6.

him before he died at 11pm.[17] Darragh had been with Jeffreys since
the very earliest days of the Evangelistic Band in Ulster and had
accompanied him on all his great crusades. He was the irrepressible
song leader whose charm and humour, as well as his fine singing
voice, inspired congregations to heights of worship. With his passing the fellowship forged during World War I in Ulster truly began
to disband. Darragh was irreplaceable.

Tributes to Darragh were plentiful and came by letters from
across the world where crusade meetings had been held. Among
those who had been acquainted with him longest was John Carter
of Assemblies of God who had known Darragh and Jeffreys since
1912 and witnessed their partnership over nearly 50 years. It was
imbued with deep affection:

> The fellowship that existed between these two unmarried and
> consecrated servants of God was like that of Jonathan and Da-
> vid. Mourning his death, David could say: 'I am distressed for
> thee my brother Jonathan: very pleasant hast thou been unto me:
> thy love to me was wonderful, passing the love of women'.[18]

Jeffreys fulfilled his obligation to preach on Easter Monday at
Westminster Central Hall; but, in the double page photographs of
the event, for the first time, rows of empty balcony seats are visible.
Jeffreys preached with exceptional clarity on salvation and healing
and saw over 90 conversions and many healings. The afternoon
gathering took the form of a memorial service and many tears were
shed for Darragh although there was 'a striking note of victory and
triumph' in the Easter hymns ('Up from the grave he arose') and a
further gospel appeal.[19] The shared sorrow of bereavement was
palpable – for many people loved Darragh – as well as a capacity to
rise collectively above it.

In the summer of that year Jeffreys was delighted to open The
People's Church at Clapham Common with a trust deed giving
power to the congregation to run its own affairs.[20] This was a won-

---

[17] *The Pattern* 20.5 (May 1959), p. 3.
[18] *The Pattern* 20.5 (May 1959), p. 11. He is quoting 2 Sam. 1.26. Original italics.
[19] *The Pattern* 20.5 (May 1959), p. 9.
[20] *The Pattern* 20.6 (June 1959), front cover, p. 66

derful demonstration of his undiminished capacity to establish congregations in their own buildings and he must have seen this as a
vindication of all he now stood for. There is, however, a sad footnote to this story since The People's Church was eventually converted into a block of apartments in what became an expensive area
of south London.[21] Here was one of the unforeseen pitfalls of local
autonomy: if the congregation dwindles to a few people, the last
remaining members can sell off the building and pocket the proceeds; there is a hidden incentive for a waning congregation to close
itself down.

The annual meeting of the Bible-Pattern Fellowship continued
to function as a support group for Jeffreys. It gave thanks for his
70th birthday and passed a resolution sympathising with his loss of
Darragh.[22] The summer edition of *The Pattern* celebrated the remarkable ministry of Jeffreys in Switzerland many years before but
in December there was no roundup of the year's preaching tour as
had been the custom. 1960 was quiet for Jeffreys and the space left
in the magazine by his reducing ministry is filled by British-Israel
material. The new pastor of Kensington Temple, Francis Thomas,
asserted, 'in no other race than the Celtic-Anglo-Saxon peoples are
the prophecies concerning Israel fulfilled',[23] and Macmillan, with his
over-realised eschatology, affirmed, 'The atomic threat is as the
sword of the cherubim in Eden guarding the way to the Tree of
life, lest man should seek to contaminate the heavens and universe'
and offered complex prophetic calculations of the sort seen before
and intended to show how close the end was.[24]

Almost certainly Jeffreys' concerns were behind a negative article
on the ecumenical movement written by Edsor. The article is unusual for its lengthy quotations from Hansard, the official record of
parliamentary debate in the House of Lords, showing how Geof-
frey Fisher, Archbishop of Canterbury, was willing to play with
words by claiming 'I am a Catholic' (presumably meaning he be-

---

[21] http://www.rightmove.co.uk/property-to-rent/property-39548017.html
(accessed 8 Aug 2016). It is true denominations can cash in the value of their
properties to pay the salaries of central staff but there are rules to prevent obvious personal gain.

[22] *The Pattern* 20.7 (June 1959), pp. 6, 7.

[23] *The Pattern* 20.1 (Jan 1960), p. 7.

[24] *The Pattern* 20.1 (Jan 1960), p. 10.

lieved in the universality of the church) even though he knew his
listeners would understand the word differently. Evangelical peers in
the House of Lords reminded Fisher of the Protestant heritage and
were unimpressed by his prevarications.[25]

Having expressed repeated forebodings about the World Pentecostal Conference, opposition was now turned against the growing
ecumenical movement as an offshoot of the World Council of
Churches. In this Edsor, presumably articulating the thoughts of
Jeffreys since they continued to live in the same house, is not alone.
Other preachers like Dr Martyn Lloyd-Jones were opposed to what
they believed to be a creeping drift towards Rome.[26] Rome itself, for
theological reasons, abstained from the ecumenical movement with
the result that the World Council of Churches found itself almost
entirely made up of liberal Protestant denominations with negligible
Pentecostal representation. Had the Pentecostals overcome their
fears and joined the WCC, it would have become a vehicle for conservative and Pentecostal churches across the world.[27]

Joining in the anti-WCC rhetoric Thomas Zimmerman, General
Superintendent of American Assemblies of God, criticised Donald
Gee of British AoG, who intended to go to the WCC's Delhi meeting.[28] Gee had already been recently attacked by Macmillan for a
refutation of BI teaching written in 1942.[29] Why Macmillan attacked
an article 20 years old is hard to say but Jeffreys must have sanc-
tioned the criticism. It is little wonder that Gee was uninterested in
a public exchange of views with Jeffreys on the World Pentecostal
Conference or any other topic.

[25] *The Pattern* 22.7 (July 1961), pp. 10-14.

[26] John Maiden, 'Lloyd-Jones and Roman Catholicism', in Andrew Atherstone
and David Ceri Jones (eds.), *Engaging with Martyn Lloyd-Jones* (Nottingham: Apollos,
2011), pp. 232-60. Lloyd-Jones and Jeffreys met in 1961 after the latter attended a
Sunday evening service at Westminster Chapel: see Edsor, *'Set Your House in Order'*, p. 161.

[27] Cecil M. Robeck, 'The Assemblies of God and Ecumenical Cooperation:
1920–1945', in Wonsuk Ma and Robert P. Menzies (eds.), *Pentecostalism in Context:
Essays in Honour of William W Menzies* (JPTSup 11; Sheffield: Sheffield Academic
Press, 1997), pp. 107-50.

[28] *The Pattern* 22.8 (Aug 1961), p. 15.

[29] *The Pattern* 20.9 (Sept 1960), p. 6.

In October 1961 Macmillan wrote a long review of *Sects and Society* by Bryan Wilson.[30] This book, the product of an intense academic study of Elim, characterised the clash between Jeffreys and E.J. Phillips as a classic battle between a charismatic leader and a bureaucrat. Wilson was a distinguished sociologist and his account continues to have value; but, in a criticism of it written later, Cartwright is scathing about its errors of fact.[31] At the time Wilson appeared to vindicate Jeffreys and show that his breach with Elim was justifiable, or at least, that is how Macmillan read it.

At the end of 1961, a young German student named Reinhard Bonnke studying at The Bible College of Wales in Swansea, was on his way home and, with a little money to spare, decided to take an unguided sightseeing tour of London. Eventually, he found himself near Clapham Common and decided to take a stroll through the neighbourhood without any plan in mind. As he walked, he came across a house with a nameplate on the front that said 'George Jeffreys' and wondered whether this could really be 'the great George Jeffreys who had founded the Elim Pentecostal churches in Ireland and England' and about whom he had read so much. He paused at the gate wondering whether he should introduce himself since he felt a link to the man who had 'ridden the tides of Pentecostal revival'.

I walked through the front garden gate and climbed the porch, pausing at the door. There I rang the bell. A lady opened the door.

'Pardon my intrusion, ma'am. Does the George Jeffreys live here who was that famous firebrand evangelist I have heard so much about?'

'Yes, he does'.

'May I see him?'

'No. Under no circumstances'.

She had hardly said no when I heard a deep voice from within the house say, 'Let the young man come in.'

---

[30] *The Pattern* 22.10 (Oct 1961), pp. 10-17.
[31] Cartwright, *Evangelists*, p. 138.

I squeezed past that lady in a heartbeat and into the house. As my eyes adjusted to the dim light, I saw him coming slowly down a staircase, holding it unsteadily as he made his way toward me. As he reached the landing, I stepped forward, took his hand, and introduced myself. I told him I had a call of God on my life to be an evangelist and to preach the gospel in Africa. That I had been to college in Swansea and was now returning to Germany.

What happened next was extraordinary. All of a sudden, he took me by the shoulders and fell to his knees, pulling me to the floor with him. He placed his hands on my head and began to bless me as a father blesses a son, as Abraham blessed Isaac, who blessed Jacob, and on and on. The room seemed to light up with the glory of God as he poured out his prayer over me. I do not remember the words with which he blessed me, but I do remember their effect. My body felt electrified, tingling with divine energy.

After about a half hour he finished. I stood up and helped him to his feet. He seemed very frail. We said goodbye. The lady came and escorted him away. He could hardly stand. Nor could I, for different reasons.[32]

Bonnke went on to become one of the most impressive Pentecostal evangelists of his generation and to hold gigantic crusades in Africa. When they met, Jeffreys was infirm, spiritually strong but hardly able to stand, and struggling to walk downstairs. This snapshot explains why Jeffreys was now preaching infrequently; his body had aged visibly; he only had a short time to live.[33]

Jeffreys spoke at Kensington Temple on Sunday evening, 14 January 1962, and followed what had become his usual custom by visiting homes to pray for those who were ill on Tuesday, 23 January. On Thursday the 25th Albert Edsor drove him and James MacLeod of Glasgow City Temple by car to Victoria Station in London to

[32] Reinhard Bonnke, *Living a Life of Fire: An Autobiography* (Elmhurst, IL: Harvester Services, Inc., Kindle edn, 2009), loc 2916.

[33] In another account of the same incident, Bonnke wrote, 'Thrilled, I entered, and there was George Jeffreys, looking to me like a man of 90, but then 72'. See Edsor, *'Set Your House in Order'*, p. 181, and taken from *Holy Ghost Evangelism* by Bonnke with George Canty.

collect posters announcing the Easter Monday rally at Westminster Central Hall. Robert Tweed and his wife were also with him on Thursday and he came to the door to bid them good night when they left.[34] On Friday morning Eric Marsh who had seen him at 8.00 am (presumably to give him his post or take in his breakfast) went back into the room an hour later and found Jeffreys had died. The death certificate records the cause of death as coronary thrombosis or, in layman's terms, a heart attack.[35] So he passed away peacefully without any long painful illness or undignified decline and in the house where he had lived with his housekeeper and friends for many years.

The first day of February, 1962, was bright and cloudless. A short service was held at the lecture room at 8 Clarence Avenue, Clapham, and prayer was offered by Cmdr Macmillan. The coffin was then moved to Kensington Temple and over 1,000 people came from all over the British Isles that afternoon. Albert Edsor, as he had done at the crusade meetings, played the piano, prayer was offered by Douglas Quy of IBRA radio representing Lewi Pethrus, and opening remarks were made by Robert Tweed recalling the early days in Ireland and other cherished memories of the Principal, 'especially the parting words on the night before his home-call, when he wished him and others "good night" but not "goodbye"'.[36] Eric Marsh, of the People's Church, Clapham, spoke of 'the great joy and pleasure Jeffreys' visits to the church always gave' and recalled how in his last meeting Jeffreys had brought the service to a close with a fervent appeal for salvation. Marsh referred to his own conversion 30 years previously in Sheffield when the whole city had been stirred and hundreds converted. 'He stated that the Principal's most earnest desire to the last was for the true unity of the Pentecostal bodies in the light of the Scriptures, and Christ's near return'.[37]

---

[34] Or perhaps they stayed overnight since the property was substantial. *The Pattern* 23.4 (Apr 1962), pp. 6, 12.

[35] The death certificate was signed on the 29 January 1962 after a post-mortem without an inquest.

[36] *The Pattern* 23.4 (Apr 1962), p. 16.

[37] *The Pattern* 23.4 (Apr 1962), p. 18.

Gwilym Francis recalled his own association with Jeffreys, and especially over the previous 21 years in the Bible-Pattern Church Fellowship. He summed up Jeffreys as a man who was faithful and fearless and always reaching out to bring others to Christ. He saw his prime achievement as being to bring the Pentecostal message from obscurity into great prominence through phenomenal campaigns and annual London meetings. Macmillan also paid tribute speaking of Jeffreys as 'God's gentleman, completely unspoiled to the end ... A Celtic man, with the restless creative soul of the Celt' and 'a gift of God to our bewildered generation'.[38] Pastor Hunziker had flown in from the Geneva church founded as a consequence of those revival meetings in Switzerland in 1935. He was impressed by the humble conclusion of Jeffreys' letters, 'a servant of Jesus Christ'.

The congregation was reminded that on Sunday 14 January, the last time he spoke publicly, Jeffreys had made an impassioned conversion appeal at the close of the evening service at Kensington Temple and had sung with G.I. Francis, in Welsh, the chorus:

Forgiveness, forgiveness, forgiveness is free;
No matter how sinful, how vile you may be.
O come to the saviour, O come to the savior
O come to him now and be saved.

The body was then moved slowly to the Streatham Cemetery and crowds thronged the pavements and many cars and taxis formed a procession. Extra police had been deputed to control the volume of traffic. They made their way in the bright sunshine to where Jeffreys was interred beside Darragh. At the graveside Tweed made a fervent gospel appeal and James MacLeod prayed. Representatives of Elim, Assemblies of God, and other Pentecostal bodies as well as other Christian Churches were present but the funeral service and all the arrangements of the day were entirely in the hands of men belonging to the Bible-Pattern Fellowship.

Jeffreys had made a will in 1959 and appointed Edsor and Tweed as his executors. The total value of Jeffreys' estate was surprisingly large at £20,641 but only reached the total it did in the last five

---

[38] *The Pattern* 23.4 (Apr 1962), p. 18.

years of his life through the legacies of good friends.[39] Jeffreys left £300 each to two of his sisters and £900 each to Darragh, Edsor, and Marsh with the residue of estate in its entirety going to the World Revival Crusade. Although only one paragraph long, Jeffreys explained why money was left to these three men:

> I do this because I feel it is my duty to make some provision for these three, for they have given me most faithful service in my work throughout the years, and the World Revival Crusade has not provided any superannuation for them as most religious bodies have done for their ministers.

The annual average wage of a manual worker in 1960 was £728[40] which means the two sisters' bequests that would have brought them comfort and additional financial security without making them wealthy. All three men recorded in the will lived at Clarence Avenue and under the same roof as Jeffreys. The sum each one received was substantial but only sufficient to purchase an annuity that would have yielded around £100 per year to supplement but not replace a standard old-age pension.[41] The rationale for these gifts was personal ('given me most faithful service') as well as practical (to provide superannuation). Tweed as the pastor of the Bible-Pattern congregation in Birmingham as well as the main trustee of another congregation would have been financially provided for and Marsh likewise would have been in possession of a salary from The People's Church in Clapham where he was pastor. Edsor, who was younger than the others, had faithfully served as pianist, chauffeur, and latterly as editor of *The Pattern*, and was ten years away from drawing his state pension.[42] He may have taken advantage of his inheritance to get married, which he did in 1963, and although he continued for the rest of his life to defend Jeffreys' achievements and reputation, he and his wife occupied an apartment in south London and, if anything, gave the impression of living in financially

---

[39] Edsor, *'Set Your House in Order'*, p. 177.

[40] See http://hansard.millbanksystems.com/written_answers/1960/nov/2-9/national-average-wages (accessed 11 Aug 2016).

[41] http://people.exeter.ac.uk/ipt201/research/Cannon%20and%20Tonks%-20FHR%20Final%20Version.pdf (accessed 11 Aug 2016).

[42] He was born in 1910. Edsor, *'Set Your House in Order'*, p. 19.

straitened circumstances.[43] The money from the bulk of the estate went to the Worldwide Revival Crusade but we have no details of expenditure because the Charity Commission no longer retains the relevant financial records. It is possible the apartment where Edsor and his wife lived was owned by the Crusade[44] and it is true that Edsor wrote and published a book in 1989 defending Jeffreys, and this is copyrighted to the World Revival Crusade which may have contributed to the cost of publication. According to Edsor the lion's share of the estate, amounting to £14,300, was paid towards Bible-Pattern congregations to assist in the purchase of their buildings.[45]

There is one odd feature of the will. It leaves a house in Hove, Sussex, to the World Revival Crusade if Darragh has predeceased Jeffreys.[46] The implication of this condition is that Darragh would have been sole possessor of the property had Jeffreys predeceased him or, to put this another way, the property was jointly owned. We do not know when Jeffreys bought this property or when he lived in it and what other arrangements he may have had with Darragh about its use. Jeffreys preached at Brighton at least annually and may have stayed in the house on those occasions; he had first preached at Brighton in June 1927 and so the property may have been purchased at any point after that time. Darragh was his most loyal and longest-serving colleague and their closeness was observable, as John Carter's earlier tribute indicates. A photograph taken at the Streatham Cemetery where Darragh was buried shows, on his gravestone, that the burial plot was shared with his cousin, Mrs A.

---

[43] This was the impression of Colonel Donald Underwood (conversation 27 Jan 2016).

[44] Suggested by Colonel Don Underwood (27 Jan 2016). If the estate totalled £20,641, this value presumably included the house in Hove. If we subtract £900 for Marsh and Edsor and £300 for the surviving sister, that would leave £18,541. Edsor records a figure of £14,300, which leaves a gap of over £4,000, enough to buy an apartment in Clapham, where Edsor lived. He and Tweed were executors of Jeffreys' will and it is reasonable to suppose that they were also trustees of the World Revival Crusade, especially as Edsor quotes a precise figure for the amount given by the Crusade to the Bible-Pattern Fellowship.

[45] Edsor, *'Set Your House in Order'*, p. 178.

[46] 20 Denmark Villas, Hove.

H. McCormick. It also shows Jeffreys was buried in the same plot although with a separate and larger headstone.[47]

Reflection

In the period from 1940, when Jeffreys finally left Elim, until 1955 when he sold his big tent, he worked as hard as he had ever done and with genuine success even if he never hit the high point of the early 1930s. Then his crusades resulted in the formation of new congregations; from 1940 onwards this was rare. He continued his summer revival tours in Switzerland and France until 1950 and must have called a halt at this point either because prolonged travel became too physically demanding or perhaps because his criticism of the World Pentecostal Conference in Zurich disturbed his relationships with the Swiss churches. Whatever the reason, he did not cease overseas travel because of a failure to draw crowds.

During the post-war period, his relationship with the Scandinavian churches strengthened. In his desire to universalise the Scandinavian model of church government, he found an ally in Lewi Pethrus, but Pethrus himself (born in 1884) was reaching retirement age. By the late 1950s, it was evident Assemblies of God and Elim, the largest two Pentecostal bodies in Britain, were quite unwilling to change their methods of church government just because Jeffreys wanted them to do so. The Assemblies of God was, in any case, already strong in its defence of local church autonomy and Elim had already made adjustments to its own system of government with the intention of becoming more inclusive or democratic. Jeffreys in the period before and during 1958, when he spent much of the year in legal work, made genuine offers to Elim in the hope of effecting a rapprochement. All these offers required Elim to recognise the ownership of buildings by local congregations; but, surprisingly, he accepted the principle of a fixed percentage of funds payable to Elim headquarters. Given his identification of central government with Babylonish religion, this was an extraordinary about-turn. The war with Elim was over and replaced by hopes for

---

[47] Albert Edsor, *George Jeffreys, Man of God: The Story of a Phenomenal Ministry* (London: Ludgate Press, 1964), facing page 135.

fresh fellowship. Nevertheless, the very principle of local autonomy Jeffreys had championed complicated any merger even if the Bible-Pattern's Advisory Committee was influential and might be persuaded to adjust its stance. Meanwhile Elim, recovering well after 1945, had found in Percy Brewster (1908–1980) a leader who, without reaching quite the level attained by Jeffreys, was restoring confidence at headquarters and out in the churches. It was now obvious, as it had not been in 1940, that Elim could prosper perfectly well without the charismatic celebrity of Jeffreys.

Twenty-one years after Jeffreys' death the Advisory Committee of the Bible-Pattern Fellowship issued a declaration in *The Pattern* magazine that an agreement had been reached to work with Elim 'ever more closely at local, regional, national and international levels' and called on members of both denominations to pray for a step-by-step fulfilment of God's will.[48] A year later, in March 1984, a dialogue with Elim was announced to 'remove the bitterness and malice of bygone days as we seek a righteous solution and reconciliation'.[49] These steps led two former members of the Advisory Committee to become ministers within the broader Elim Alliance and seven members of the Advisory Committee to join Elim Incorporated; of the seven, two were veteran supporters of Jeffreys, Robert Tweed and G.I. Francis. The Nottingham Bible-Pattern church, which had been central to the turbulence of the 1940 schism, affiliated itself to Elim and inducted an Elim pastor after 1986. The result of these moves 'committed the Bible-Pattern Church Fellowship [to] support the World Pentecostal Conference', thus reversing the separatist position Jeffreys had taken.[50] This turn of events could be interpreted as the happy fulfilment of the conciliatory offers made in the last years of Jeffreys' life. Yet, almost alone, Edsor, faithful disciple to the last, deplored what he took to be a needless surrender to Elim and withdrew his own Bible-Pattern congregation from the Fellowship and became entirely independent.[51]

---

[48] Edsor, *'Set Your House in Order'*, p. 118.
[49] Edsor, *'Set Your House in Order'*, p. 119.
[50] Edsor, *'Set Your House in Order'*, p. 120.
[51] Edsor, *'Set Your House in Order'*, p. 121.

If there was one enduring attitude within Jeffreys' life, it was his respect for the monarchy. In 1955 Commander Macmillan, President of the Bible-Pattern Fellowship and a full-time employee of the Southampton Harbour Board, was awarded an MBE which was conferred upon him at Buckingham Palace by the Queen. Macmillan received, as was customary, two or three tickets for the event and chose Jeffreys to accompany him. Jeffreys, presumably much to his delight, had an opportunity to enter the precincts of the Queen's Palace, and observe her at close quarters.[52] The following year, he sent his traditional telegram to the Queen on Easter Monday assuring her of the Bible-Pattern church's prayers as she carried the 'onerous duties of state'. Usually the Royal secretary replied but on this occasion the message appears to have come from the Queen herself. It read, 'I thank you and all those with you in sending your kind and loyal message which I sincerely appreciate. Elizabeth R'.[53]

Jeffreys maintained his belief in British-Israel and continued to argue that this position was an acceptable variant of prophetic interpretation of Scripture. He never insisted that BI doctrine should be propagated in Bible-Pattern churches and it was never a compulsory tenet of its ministers. The respect Jeffreys showed to the British monarchy may have stemmed from his British-Israel beliefs as his article on the Coronation suggested. Equally, he may have admired the monarchy like many thousands of others as an expression of idealised family life and a humanised symbol of the British state. While Jeffreys was speaking to Elim about church government and to the World Pentecostal Conference about its basis for membership and warning others of the Ecumenical Movement, Macmillan pulled no punches over British-Israel. His beliefs created a Protestant religious nationalism that was deeply pained by post-war moral laxity and the dismemberment of the British Empire. It was as much a matter of visceral patriotic conviction as of doctrine; and, given the sway Jeffreys held over the whole Bible-Pattern movement, it is inconceivable that Macmillan's views were voiced without Jeffreys' consent. So, although the Bible-Pattern Fellowship was, as it insisted, not a British-Israel denomination, it is also true to

---

[52] Edsor, *'Set Your House in Order'*, p. 148.
[53] Edsor, *'Set Your House in Order'*, p. 163.

say, as others claimed, that BI was integral to the way its leaders understood the world.

Albert Edsor was able to show that, beyond the official engagements and public persona, Jeffreys brought men and women to Christ and prayed for their healing. He remembers,

> during a passing visit we made to John Wycliffe's Church at Lutterworth in Leicestershire, when I was taken up with reading inscriptions about our great reformer of the 14th century, George Jeffreys was seated with the grave-digger in a pew showing him the plan of Salvation from the Scriptures.[54]

Jeffreys on the platform and Jeffreys in person were one and the same. Even in the last week of his life he visited sick people in their homes to pray for them and would do so unaffectedly and graciously.

Although the topic was never discussed in print in Jeffreys' lifetime, there have been subsequent questions about his sexuality.[55] He was buried in the same grave plot as Darragh and jointly owned a property with Darragh. Yet, beyond these two pieces of historical information, there is no evidence of homosexuality in Jeffreys' recorded behaviour. The Revival Party travelled together, lived together in a caravan during early crusades, and later shared the large property in Clarence Avenue, and at least two of its members, McWhirter and Edsor, married. The Revival Party functioned as a quasi-family giving Jeffreys emotional support and protecting him from the outer world. There were few occasions when he was alone and no occasions when he lived either alone or with only one other individual. He seems to have been a father figure to Edsor and there is no evidence in anything Edsor wrote which points to sexual activity. When the topic was raised with Jeffreys, he failed to understand what was being said and reacted as a complete innocent.[56] Edsor, who for the rest of his life, defended the reputation of Jeffreys eloquently and aggressively, would never have put information into the

---

[54] Edsor, *'Set Your House in Order'*, p. 148.
[55] E.g. Andrew Walker, *Exploring the Kingdom* (Guildford: Eagle, 4th edn, 1998), p. 259.
[56] Letter from Des Cartwright to Albert Edsor, 30 July 1986, and kept in the Cartwright Centre.

public domain that tarnished the great man. Writing of Jeffreys' death, he says, 'I had been with him as usual sharing the same room through the night hours and talked with him the next morning before 8 o'clock'.[57] It seems that Jeffreys needed someone to share his room, perhaps in case of diabetic coma. Similarly, it was Edsor who printed a photograph showing the joint grave plot. All these men, and certainly Jeffreys and Darragh, firmly believed in the resurrection of the body and accepted the biblical teaching that they would be raised in glory together at the return of Christ. Like those buried on the Mount of Olives in a prime position for the new Jerusalem, they wanted to find themselves in the company of friends on the Resurrection Morning when they welcomed Jesus.

---

[57] Edsor, *'Set Your House in Order'*, p. 179.

22

EPILOGUE

In the years immediately following Jeffrey's death the Bible-Pattern churches continued to function; and, as far as one can tell from their magazine, Jeffreys remained the figurehead of the Fellowship. *The Pattern* habitually reprinted old articles by Jeffreys or photographs of him or his campaigns to the extent that the Fellowship appeared to be living in the past.[1] When, in the 1980s, discussions took place between senior members of Elim and the Bible-Pattern Fellowship, the Bible-Pattern ministers were surprised to discover that, in the Elim boardroom where they met, there was a large photograph of Jeffreys on the wall in a prominent place.[2] They had been given to understand that Elim had entirely repudiated Jeffreys but this was not the case. Once the Bible-Pattern men saw that Elim did not disown its past, they were ready to talk and their churches, because they were autonomous, could decide where they wanted to affiliate. One group migrated into Elim, others to Assemblies of God, and yet others remained entirely independent. Elim, after hanging on through a downswing of demoralisation in the early 1940s – and the number of ministers attending the annual conference was extremely low in the first years after Jeffreys left –

---

[1] This was certainly the case up to 1966. There is a photo of Jeffreys on page 3 of the January 1966 issue of *The Pattern*, Jeffreys is recorded as the founder of the Bible-Pattern on the back cover and a book by Edsor on Jeffreys is advertised inside the front cover. The books of Jeffreys are advertised on the back cover. Articles by Jeffreys follow in later issues.

[2] Information given to me by John Glass.

picked up and recovered until today it is the largest classical Pentecostal denomination in the British Isles and probably the best funded.

So the Bible-Pattern Fellowship has all but disappeared while Elim has recovered its old strength. Insofar as one can argue from historical precedent, the implication must be that a responsive form of denominational central government, and particularly one that redistributes resources where they are needed, is more likely to prosper than a set of independent-minded congregations lacking a strong positive message or overarching identity. British-Israel doctrine became increasingly incredible in the 1960s as the British Empire faded away; and, consequently, Bible-Pattern churches had nothing distinctive to offer beyond what was preached in Elim or Assemblies of God. My memory of attending a meeting of the Bible-Pattern church around 1970 was of old hymns and little evidence of Pentecostal phenomena. The service may even have ended with the singing of the national anthem.

***

The background to the story of Jeffreys' life is found in the shock Britain sustained after World War I when its imperial status was severely challenged by the grey economic aftermath of the war and later, after 1945, destroyed by the loss of its colonies and dominions. The world of Jeffreys' childhood in the 1890s was far removed from the bleak 1950s with their Cold War threats and post-war rationing. The interweaving of British-Israel doctrine and British Empire sentiment helped to compose the character of Jeffreys that underlay his assumptions and attitudes. Beyond this foundational level of his personality one can see the impact of Welsh eloquence on him and through him. He grew up listening to sermons in a Welsh chapel and from a young age wanted to be a minister himself. He understood the dignity of the pulpit and its power and by all accounts his preaching was exceptional both for clarity and force. He was not histrionic or overtly emotional and had none of the showmanship of Aimee Semple McPherson. The description of him unobtrusively slipping onto the stage at the Royal Albert Hall is telling.[3] Equally, the descriptions of the way he prayed for those

---

[3] Landau, *God is My Adventure*, p. 153.

who were sick is touching: he knew that in himself he had no power to heal and was simply exercising such gifts as he believed the Holy Spirit imparted. He demonstrated humility and grace as he came down from the platform to mingle with the crowd and lay hands on the hundreds who needed healing.[4] The eloquence of Jeffreys bears comparison with the eloquence of the Welsh Prime Minister, Lloyd George, although the two exercised their gifts for very different purposes. Both, however, reached the summit of their powers about 20 years before they died and both found themselves somewhat sidelined in their latter years even if, when they wished to summon it, the extraordinary mesmeric quality of their oratory had not deserted them.

Despite his public profile, this is the first full-scale biography of Jeffreys to be written. Des Cartwright, an Elim Pastor and once its official historian, wrote *The Great Evangelists* in 1986 and essentially researched the lives of George and his brother Stephen up to about 1943 when Stephen died. The word limit imposed by his publisher prevented him writing at length about what Jeffreys accomplished after leaving Elim. This immediately provoked a vigorous (not to say angry) response from Albert Edsor who published a short pamphlet and then a longer biography, *'Set your House in Order'* (1989), that contained much reprinting of previous articles and crusade reports that had previously appeared in the *Elim Evangel* or *The Pattern*. Edsor was keen to rebut any notion that Jeffreys was mistaken in leaving Elim and so made high claims for the post-Elim period of ministry. He was also keen to deny that BI lay at the root of Jeffreys' departure from Elim and, in so doing, merely to echo what Jeffreys himself started to say in the 1940s.

There was correspondence between Edsor and Des Cartwright (though only one letter has survived) and a meeting between the two when a lengthy run of *The Pattern* in Edsor's possession was donated to Cartwright. Edsor had written a much earlier book on Jeffreys, *George Jeffreys: Man of God* (1964), which again focused on the public profile, evangelistic success, press reports, radio broadcasts, and testimonies of healing. It did not provide information about Jeffreys as a man or attempt to understand his private life or

---

[4] Landau, *God is My Adventure*, p. 157.

childhood. Nor does it give information on the material circumstances of Jeffrey's life except in passing. We do not know what Jeffreys liked to eat, how often he saw his family back in Wales, how he came to be reconciled with Stephen, how he prepared for his sermons, how he decided where to preach, what he thought privately about E.J. Phillips, whether, despite his public statements, he had any private regrets over the rupture with Elim, or what medical treatment he received. Nor are we given background details of the relationship between Leech and Jeffreys, and the influence of one on the other, or later, between Macmillan and Jeffreys although, had he thought to do so, Edsor might have provided this information. What we do know is that Edsor parted company with the Bible-Pattern Fellowship in late old age; and, from the tenor of his writings, he remained vigorous in his criticism of them and of Elim.[5]

Thousands of people heard Jeffreys preach and there are recordings of his voice made in a studio and available on YouTube though they lack the vitality generated in an address to an actual congregation. Rom Landau's *God is My Adventure* gives us the best description of one of the big meetings at the Royal Albert Hall and the Crystal Palace and contains an account of a short interview with Jeffreys. We have a tape recording of Jeffreys preaching live at Westminster Central Hall in 1955. Newspaper reports in the 1930s are factual and only occasionally do journalists animate the scenes they describe by direct quotation or interview. The greatest cache of information is to be found in the Cartwright Centre at Regents Theological College, the Elim complex in Malvern, and the most vivid insights are often in the letters written by Jeffreys to Phillips, sometimes on the back of a scrap of paper torn from an exercise book, and in the heat of a campaign. These letters were never seen by Bryan Wilson[6] with the result that his judgment of the relationship between Jeffreys and Phillips is deficient. These letters were collated by Cartwright who also collected and preserved many of the pamphlets that passed between Jeffreys and Elim in the 1940s. Moreover, Cartwright regularly went to hear Jeffreys preach at the Easter Monday meetings at Westminster Central Hall in the 1950s. Without

---

[5] See the previous chapter.
[6] Author of *Sects and Society*, see previous chapter. Commander Macmillan would not have seen these letters either.

the assiduous work done by Cartwright it would have been impossible for any later writer to have made a proper attempt to recreate or assess Jeffreys' remarkable ministry.

Bibliography

Allen, David, 'Signs and Wonders: the origins, growth, development and significance of Assemblies of God in Great Britain and Ireland, 1900-1980' (PhD, London University, 1990).

Anderson, R.A., *Vision of the Disinherited: The Making of American Pentecostalism* (Oxford: Oxford University Press, 1979).

Atherstone, Andrew and David Ceri Jones (eds.), *Engaging with Martyn Lloyd-Jones* (Nottingham: Apollos, 2011).

Bartleman, F., *Azusa Street* (Plainfield, NJ: Bridge Publishing, 1980).

Beevor, Anthony, *Stalingrad* (Harmondsworth: Penguin, 1999).

Blumhofer, E.L., *Aimee Semple McPherson: Everybody's Sister* (Grand Rapids, MI: Eerdmans, 2003).

Bonnke, Reinhard, *Living a Life of Fire: An Autobiography* (Kindle edn; Orlando, FL: E-R Productions, LLC, 2009).

Boulton, E.C.W., *George Jeffreys: A Ministry of the Miraculous* (London: Elim Publishing Office, 1928).

Brooks, Noel, *Fight for Faith and Freedom* (Southampton, UK: Revival Library; Kindle edn, 2014.

Brown, R.L., *The Welsh Evangelicals* (Cardiff Tongwynlais: Tair Eglwys Press, 1986).

Cain, P.J., 'Railways 1870-1914: The Maturity of the Private System', in M.J. Freeman and D.H. Aldcroft (eds.), *Transport in Victorian Britain* (Manchester: Manchester University Press, 1988).

Calder, Angus, *The People's War: Britain 1939-1945* (London: Jonathan Cape, 1969).

Canty, George, *Unpublished Manuscript* (Cheltenham: Typeset by Grenehurst Press, 1983).

Carter, John, *A Full Life* (Nottingham: Assemblies of God, 1979).

Cartwright, Desmond, *The Great Evangelists* (Basingstoke: Marshall Pickering, 1986).

—*The Real Wigglesworth* (Tonbridge: Sovereign World, 2000).

Cartwright C., J. and D. Holdaway (eds.), *Defining Moments: 100 Years of the Elim Pentecostal Church* (Elim Pentecostal Church, 2015).

Coogan, Tim Pat, *Ireland in the Twentieth Century* (London: Arrow, 2003).

Counsell, William, *Fire Beneath the Clock* (Nottingham: New Life Publishing, 2003).

Darragh, R.E., *In Defence of his Word* (London: Elim Publishing Company, 1932).

Davies, Kath, 'Cleaning up the Coal-face and Doing out the Kitchen: The Interpretation of Work and Workers in Wales', in Gaynor Kavanagh (ed.), *Making Histories in Museums* (London: Leicester University Press, 1996), pp. 105-15.

Davies, John, *A History of Wales* (Harmondsworth: Penguin, 1993).

Edsor, Albert W., *George Jeffreys, Man of God: The Story of a Phenomenal Ministry* (London: Ludgate Press, 1964).

— *'Set Your House in Order': God's Call to George Jeffreys as the Founder of the Elim Pentecostal Movement* (Chichester: New Wine, 1989).

Eliot, T.S. in 'A Cooking Egg' from *Poems* (New York: A.A. Knopf, 1920).

Elwyn Jones, Gareth, *The Education of a Nation* (Cardiff: University of Wales Press, 1997).

Evans, Eifion, *The Welsh Revival of 1904* (Bridgend: Bryntirion Press, 1987).

Farrar, F.W., *Darkness and Dawn or Scenes in the Days of Nero* (New York: Longmans, Green & Co, 1897).

Gardiner, Juliet, *Wartime Britain 1939-1945* (London: Headline Book Publishing, 2004).

Garrard, David, 'William FP Burton and the Birth of Congolese Pentecostalism', in Martin Lindhardt (ed.), *Pentecostalism in Africa* (Leiden: Brill, 2015), pp. 129-38.

Garrard, David, 'Burton's Early Years of Ministry and Doctrine under the Auspices of the PMU', *Journal of the European Pentecostal Theological Association* 32.1 (2012), pp. 3-14.

Gee, Donald, *Bonnington Toll: The Story of a First Pastorate* (London: Victory Press 1943).

—*These Men I Knew* (Nottingham: Assemblies of God Publishing House, 1980).

—*Wind and Flame* (Croydon: Assemblies of God Publishing House, 1967).

Graham, Billy, *Just as I am* (London: HarperCollins, 1998).

Harvey, John, 'The Agony in the Garden: Visions of the 1904 Revival', in D.W. Roberts (ed.), *Revival, Renewal and the Holy Spirit* (Carlisle: Paternoster, 2009), pp.

Hastings, Max, *Catastrophe: Europe goes to war in 1914* (London: Collins, 2013, Kindle edn, loc 501).

Hastings, Adrian, *A History of English Christianity 1920-1985* (London: Collins, 1986).

Hathaway, Malcolm, 'The Role of William Oliver Hutchinson and the Apostolic Faith Church in the Formation of British Pentecostal

Churches', *Journal of the European Pentecostal Theological Association* 16 (1996), pp. 40-57.

—'The Elim Pentecostal Church: Origins, Development and Distinctives', in K. Warrington (ed), *Pentecostal Perspectives* (Carlisle: Paternoster, 1998), pp. 1-39.

Hudson, Marilyn A., *Noel Brooks: A Life Shining and Burning* (Whorl Books with CreateSpace, 2011).

Hudson, Neil, 'A Schism and its Aftermath: an historical analysis of denominational discerption in the Elim Pentecostal Church, 1939-1940' (PhD, King's College, London, 1999).

Hywel-Davies, Jack, *The Kensington Temple Story* (Crowborough: Monarch, 1998).

Inge, W.R., *Lay Thoughts of a Dean* (London: Puttenham's Sons, 1926).

Iremonger, F.A., *William Temple: Archbishop of Canterbury, his Life and Letters* (London: OUP, 1948).

Jeffrey, Keith, *Ireland and the Great War* (Cambridge: Cambridge University Press, 2000).

Jeffreys, Edward, *Stephen Jeffreys: The Beloved Evangelist* (Luton: Redemption Tidings Bookroom, 1946).

Jeffreys, George, *Healing Rays* (London: Elim Publishing Company, 1932).

—*Healing Rays* (London: Elim, 1932).

—*The Miraculous Foursquare Gospel: Supernatural* (vol 2) (Clapham, London: Elim Publishing Company, 1930).

—*Pentecostal Rays: The Baptism and Gifts of the Holy Spirit* (Clapham, London: Elim Publishing Company, 1933).

Jenkins, Roy, *The Chancellors* (Basingstoke: Macmillan, 1998).

Jones, Brynmor Pierce, *An Instrument of Revival: The Complete Life of Evan Roberts 1878-1951* (South Plainfield, NJ: Bridge Publishing, 1995).

Jones, E.J.P. Maldwyn, 'An Analysis of the Role of E. J. Phillips and an Assessment of his Leadership in the Establishment of the Elim Movement as a Coherent Christian Denomination' (MA, Bangor University, 2011).

Kay, P.K., 'The Four-Fold Gospel in the Formation, Policy and Practice of the P.M.U.' (MA, University of Gloucester, 1995).

Kay, W.K., 'Marital Happiness and Children's Attitude to Religion', *British Journal of Religious Education* 3 (1981), pp. 102-105.

—Why did the Welsh Revival Stop?, in D.F. Roberts (ed.), *Revival, Renewal and the Holy Spirit* (Milton Keynes: Paternoster, 2009), pp. 169-84.

—'Sunderland's Legacy in New Denominations', *Journal of the European Pentecostal Theological Association* 28.2 (2008), pp. 183-99.

—'A History of British Assemblies of God' (PhD, University of Nottingham, 1989).

Kipling, Rudyard, *The Irish Guards in the Great War: The Second Batalion* (Staplehurst: Spellmount, 1997).

Kynaston, David, *Austerity Britain 1945-51* (London: Bloomsbury, 2007).

—*Family Britain: 1951-57* (London, Bloomsbury, 2009).

Landau, Rom, *God Is My Adventure: A Book on Modern Mystics, Masters, and Teachers* (London: Ivor Nicholson and Watson, 1935).

Leech, John, *Israel in Britain,* a point-by-point rebuttal of W.F.P. Burton's pamphlet *Why I Do not Believe the British-Israel Theory.*

Maiden, John, 'Lloyd-Jones and Roman Catholicism', in Andrew Atherstone and David Ceri Jones (eds.), *Engaging with Martyn Lloyd-Jones* (Nottingham: Apollos, 2011), pp. 232-60.

Manchester, William, *The Last Lion: Winston Spencer Churchill: Alone, 1932-1940* (Boston: Little, Brown and Company, 1982).

Massey, R., *Another Springtime: Donald Gee, Pentecostal Pioneer* (Guildford: Highland, 1992).

McWhirter, James, *Britain and Palestine in Prophecy* (London: Methuen & Co, 1937).

—*Every Barrier Swept Away* (Cardiff: Megiddo Press, 1983).

Missen, Alfred E., *The Sound of a Going* (Nottingham: Assemblies of God Publishing House, 1973).

Morgan, Densil, *The Span of the Cross* (Cardiff, University of Wales Press, 1999),

Muggeridge, Malcolm, *The Thirties: 1930-1940 in Great Britain* (London: Weidenfeld and Nicholson, 1940).

O'Brien, John, *Discrimination in Northern Ireland: Myth or Reality?* (Newcastle: Cambridge Scholars Publishing, 2010).

Orr, J. Edwin, *The Second Evangelical Awakening in Britain* (London: Marshall, Morgan & Scott, 1949).

Orwell, George, *The Road to Wigan Pier* (London: Victor Gollancz, Google Scholar edn, 1936).

—*Down and Out in Paris and London* (Harmondsworth: Penguin, 1933).

Overy, Richard, *The Morbid Age: Britain between the Wars* (London: Allen Lane, 2009).

Parr, J.N., *Divine Healing* (Springfield, MO: Gospel Publishing House, 1955).

Priestley, J.B., *English Journey* (London: Heron Books, 1933).

Pugh, Benjamin, '"There is power in the blood": The Role of the Blood of Jesus in the Spirituality of early British Pentecostalism', *Journal of the European Pentecostal Theological Association* 25 (2005), pp. 54-66.

Putnam, Robert D., *Bowling Alone* (London: Simon & Schuster, 2000).

Reisenauer, Eric M., 'British-Israel: Racial Identity in Imperial Britain, 1870-1920' (Loyola University Chicago, PhD, 1987).

Robeck, Cecil M., 'The Assemblies of God and Ecumenical Cooperation: 1920-1945', in Wonsuk Ma and Robert P. Menzies (eds.), *Pentecostalism in Context: essays in honour of William W Menzies* (JPTSup 11; Sheffield: Sheffield Academic Press, 1997), pp. 107-150.

Roberts, Andrew, *A History of the English-Speaking Peoples Since 1900* (London: Weidenfeld & Nicholson, 2006).

Robinson, J., *Pentecostal Origins: Early Pentecostalism in Ireland in the Context of the British Isles* (Carlisle: Paternoster, 2005).

Russell, Bertrand, *Has Man a Future?* (Harmondsworth: Penguin 1961).

Self, Robert, *Neville Chamberlain: a Biography* (Aldershot: Ashgate, 2006).

Stevenson, John, *British Society 1914-45* (Harmondsworth: Penguin, 1984).

Strachey, Lytton, *Eminent Victorians* (London: Chatto & Windus, 1918).

Sutton, M.A., *Aimee Semple McPherson and the Resurrection of Christian America* (Cambridge, MA: Harvard, 2007).

Taylor, A.J.P., *English History 1914-1945* (Harmondsworth: Penguin, 1975).

Thompson, Flora, *Lark Rise to Candleford* (Oxford: Oxford University Press, 1939),

Thompson, David, *England in the Twentieth Century* (Harmondsworth: Penguin, 1985).

Tudor Jones, R., *Faith and the Crisis of a Nation: Wales 1890-1914* (Cardiff: University of Wales Press, 2004).

Usher, John, 'The significance of Cecil H. Polhill for the development of early Pentecostalism', *Journal of the European Pentecostal Theological Association* 29.2 (2009), pp. 37-60.

Walker, Andrew, *Exploring the Kingdom* (fourth edn; Guildford: Eagle, 1998).

Warfield, Benjamin B., *Counterfeit Miracles* (Edinburgh: Banner of Truth, 1972).

Weeks, Gordon, *Chapter Thirty Two – Part of: a History of the Apostolic Church 1900-2000* (Barnsley, Yorks: Prontaprint, 2003).

White, Kent, *The Word of God Coming Again* (Bournemouth: AFC, 1919).

Williams, D.P., *Prophecy in Practice or Prophetical Ministry in the Church* (Penygroes: Apostolic Church, 1931).

Wilson, A.N., *After the Victorians: The World our Parents Knew* (New York: Farrar, Straus and Giroux: Kindle edn, 2005).

Wilson, John, 'The Relation between Ideology and Organization in a Small Religious Group: The British Israelites, *Review of Religious Research* 10 (1968), pp. 51-60.

Wilson, B.R., *Sects and Society: a Sociological Study of Three Religious Groups in Britain* (London: Heinemann, 1961).

Worsfold, James E., *The Origins of the Apostolic Church in Great Britain* (Wellington, New Zealand: Julian Literature Trust, 1991).

Index of Biblical (and other ancient) References

Index of Names and Subjects

15852468R00253

Printed in Great Britain
by Amazon